CITIES AFTER SOCIALISM

Studies in Urban and Social Change

Published by Blackwell in association with the *International Journal of Urban and Regional Research*. Series editors: Chris Pickvance, Margit Mayer and John Walton

Published

The City Builders
Susan S. Fainstein

Divided Cities
Susan S. Fainstein, Ian Gordon, and Michael Harloe (eds)

Fragmented Societies
Enzo Mingione

Free Markets and Food Riots
John Walton and David Seddon

The Resources of Poverty
Mercedes González de la Rocha

Post-Fordism
Ash Amin (ed.)

The People's Home?
Social Rented Housing in Europe and America
Michael Harloe

Cities after Socialism
Urban and Regional Change and Conflict in Post-Socialist Societies
Gregory Andrusz, Michael Harloe and Ivan Szelenyi (eds)

Forthcoming

Urban Social Movements and the State
Margit Mayer

Urban Poverty and the Underclass: A Reader
Enzo Mingione

CITIES AFTER SOCIALISM

URBAN AND REGIONAL CHANGE AND
CONFLICT IN POST-SOCIALIST SOCIETIES

Edited by Gregory Andrusz, Michael Harloe
and Ivan Szelenyi

BLACKWELL
Publishers

Editorial matter and organization copyright © Gregory Andrusz, Michael Harloe and
Ivan Szelenyi 1996

Copyright for all chapters rests with Urban Research Publications Ltd, with the exception
of Chapter 3, which is reproduced by kind permission of Cambridge University Press.

First published 1996

2 4 6 8 10 9 7 5 3 1

Blackwell Publishers Ltd
108 Cowley Road
Oxford OX4 1JF
UK

Blackwell Publishers Inc
238 Main Street
Cambridge, Massachusetts 02142
USA

British Library Cataloging in Publication Data

A CIP catalogue record for this book is available from the British Library.

Library of Congress Cataloging-in-Publication Data

Cities after socialism: urban and regional change and conflict in post-socialist societies
/ edited by Gregory Andrusz, Michael Harloe, Ivan Szelenyi.
    p.   cm.
Studies in urban and social change
Includes bibliographical references and index.
ISBN 1-55786-164-1. – ISBN 1-55786-165-X (pbk.)
1. Cities and towns – Communist countries. 2. Post-communism. I. Andrusz,
Gregory D. II. Harloe, Michael. III. Szelenyi, Ivan.
    HT119.C564   1996
    307.76'0947 – dc20   95-51981
                                                                             CIP

Typeset in Baskerville & Helvetica on 10½/12 pt
by Best-set Typesetter Ltd., Hong Kong

To our friends and colleagues in former Yugoslavia.
May they have cities to live in and peaceful lives to
live there.

Contents

Contributors

Gregory Andrusz
Faculty of Social Sciences, Middlesex University, Queensway, Enfield, Middlesex EN3 4SF

György Enyedi
Centre for Regional Studies, Hungarian Academy of Sciences, PO Box 527, Budapest H-1538, Hungary

Michael Harloe
Office of Research and European Liaison, University of Essex, Colchester CO4 3SQ

Hartmut Häussermann
Humboldt-Universität, Fachbereich Sozialwissenschaften, Unter den Linden 6, 10099 Berlin

Peter Marcuse
Graduate School of Architecture and Planning, Avery Hall, Columbia University, NY 10027

Chris Pickvance
Urban and Regional Studies Unit, Darwin College, University of Kent, Canterbury, Kent CT2 7NY

David M. Smith
Department of Geography, Queen Mary and Westfield College, Mile End Road, London E1 4NS

Raymond J. Struyk
The Urban Institute/USAID Shelter Cooperation Program, 19, Prospect Mira, Moscow 129090

Ivan Szelenyi
Department of Sociology, UCLA, Los Angeles, CA 90024-1551

Klaus von Beyme
Philosophisch-Historische Fakultät, Universität Heidelberg, Hauptstrasse 120, 69117 Heidelberg, Germany

Preface

From its inception in 1977, the *International Journal of Urban and Regional Research* had a particular interest in publishing analyses of urbanization in the state socialist countries. In the late 1980s, given the relative paucity of readily available literature on this topic, I thought that an edited collection of the best of these papers, together with some new material, would be a useful project. Greg Andrusz and Ivan Szelenyi agreed to become my co-editors in what we then thought would be a relatively easy and speedy task.

However, no sooner had we begun our book on 'socialist cities' than the objects of our attention began to slip, with ever accelerating speed, into history. In the late 1980s and early 1990s, as communism collapsed and as the new social, economic and political orders in the former state socialist countries began to take shape, the plans for this book, and the list of contributors, had to be revised several times. In fact, editing *Cities after Socialism* has been like trying to run down an up escalator (or vice versa – depending on one's ideological orientation). Readers should bear in mind that most of this book was written between 1993 and the early months of 1995.

I must thank all those who have kept their patience during the years that it has taken to bring this work to a conclusion, especially my co-editors, the contributors and our publisher. Thanks are also due to our friends and colleagues in the countries of Eastern Europe who have helped us in many different ways, during times that have been difficult and sometimes dangerous for them.

Michael Harloe
Colchester

1

Cities in the Transition

Michael Harloe

Writing about the February Revolution in Russia, precursor to the October Revolution that swept the Bolsheviks to power, Trotsky (1967/1932–3: 141–5) highlighted the leadership role played by the Petrograd workers and the crucial importance of political developments in the capital city. He writes '[i]t would be no exaggeration to say that Petrograd achieved the February revolution. The rest of the country adhered to it. There was no struggle anywhere except in Petrograd.' He adds, '[i]f the capital plays as dominating a role in the revolution as though it concentrated in itself the will of the nation, that is simply because the capital expresses most clearly and thoroughly the fundamental tendencies of the new society.' More prosaically, he points out that in Russia as elsewhere, the ruling class and those who sought to overthrow them naturally concentrated in the capital city, so, not to paraphrase Trotsky, this was where the action (mainly) was.

The Soviet system was born, therefore, as an immediate consequence of an urban-based struggle for dominance. Between 1989 and 1991 it died in similar locations. Much of the drama of these years was played out in the capital (and other major) cities of the Soviet Union and the state socialist countries of East and Central Europe. Inevitably those of us who observed as amazed and stunned onlookers from the West remember the television images of the struggle in the cities – the destruction of the Berlin Wall, the Velvet

Revolution in the streets of Prague, the resistance in the streets of Moscow to the 1991 coup that marked the final spasm of the Soviet system.

However, the role of cities and urbanization in the formation of capitalism and socialism, and the two transitions between them that we have witnessed in the East in this century, go far beyond the immediacies of the street politics of revolution. Behind the phenomenon of the Petrograd proletariat lay capitalist industrialization and its consequences, urbanization and the creation of a new class structure, together with a system of political domination that was essentially city based, in terms of its ruling elites and the state apparatus. Likewise, state socialism, with its emphasis on industrialization under the control of a centralized one-party state, created cities and ruled from them. Therefore, the cities of capitalism and socialism both shape and are shaped by their respective forms of economic organization, class formation and political structures. The socio-spatial organization of cities, their politics and administration, their housing and property markets, their patterns of social interaction are directly linked to the major features of the socialist and capitalist orders.

This book is concerned to identify and analyse some of these links and how they are changing in the process of transformation now occurring in Eastern Europe and the territories of the former Soviet Union (FSU). As will immediately become evident to the reader, this is no easy task, as it involves drawing conclusions about phenomena and processes that are still evolving at a rapid rate and, frequently, under chaotic circumstances. However, there are two reasons why periods of such tumultuous social and urban change pose a challenge to social science which ought not to be ignored. The first concerns the contribution that social science can make to policy debate and prescription. In the current case, as several of the following chapters demonstrate, a new urban society is evolving that is deeply but mistakenly influenced by drastically over-simplified and even dangerous attempts to reject and/or ignore the significance of persisting legacies from the socialist period. Similar dangers also lie in the over-eager adoption of presumed characteristics of capitalist economies and urban systems. The doctrines of neo-liberal economics, tried and found wanting in the West during the 1980s, are having a rerun a decade later in the East. One purpose, then, of this book is to substitute analysis for ideology in the task of understanding the urban transition that is now under way, and thus contribute to counteracting the belief that a new social order can be produced according to the neo-liberal (or any other) rule book.

A second aim links to the first but is more ambitious. It is to understand more about the distinctive nature of cities and urbanization in differing social formations, namely in the now abolished state socialist societies, in Western capitalist societies and, crucially in the context of this book, in the emergent forms of capitalist urbanization now occurring in the East. What were socialist cities, and what is succeeding them? What are the dynamics of this transition? Are these remade cities similar in most respects to those in the 'advanced' capitalist world? Or might they be more like the peripheral capitalist cities of the Third World, or some hybrid or new form? What, if anything, is the legacy of the old socialist urbanization for the emergent one? Is urbanization best understood as a functional consequence of advanced industrial societies, with technologically derived uniformities that far outweigh in importance the impact of capitalist and socialist modes of domination?

In this book some of these questions receive clearer answers than others, understandably, given the historical conjuncture in which it has been written. Some of the questions have only come on the agenda for urban social theory and research since the collapse of state socialism, others have been pursued by urban analysis since the early days of (what was) the 'new urban sociology' of the 1960s and 1970s. Discussing the debate on the nature of socialist urbanization some fifteen years ago, the current author suggested that it was at times of crisis that the nature of urban regimes might most clearly be revealed, hence their value in a research context (Harloe, 1981: 190–1). Subsequent work on the evolution of social housing in Western Europe and America has also shown the crucial significance of periods of societal crisis and restructuring in the longer-run determination of aspects of urban development (Harloe 1995). The crises associated with the transformation in the societies and cities of former state socialism, therefore, offer an opportunity to gain fresh insights into the nature of socialist urbanization and to lay the foundations to an understanding of the nature of its successor. And, in so far as the new bears some marks of the old upon it, a study of the transition period is, of course, essential.

THE NATURE OF THE TRANSITION AND THE SIGNIFICANCE OF CITIES IN IT

This last point leads naturally to an issue which is of much wider relevance than simply its significance for understanding the emergent patterns of urbanization. This concerns the theory of transition itself, what is involved in transition, how it proceeds and how it relates to the previous histories of the societies in which it takes place – does it involve a simple negation of the previous social order or a more complex mixture of rejection and adaption? Given the central place occupied by cities and urbanization in both state socialism and capitalism, sketched out above, it may readily be seen that these questions are just as applicable to the urban sphere as they are to society more generally.

In this introduction to a study of cities in transition, it would not be appropriate to provide an in-depth review of the rapidly burgeoning literature which is exploring the nature of the transition and the questions outlined in the last paragraph. Only some brief indications of key issues and perspectives can be attempted here. A useful starting point is to outline the three principal features of state socialism, the blueprint, as it were, for the system that developed in Russia after 1917, was more or less forcibly imposed on Eastern Europe after 1945, and was variably achieved in practice. These features were, first, state monopoly ownership of the means of production and of most of the means of collective consumption as well, together with the substitution of centralized planning for market-led distribution of investment, incomes and consumption goods and services. Second, there was the political domination of the Communist Party, acting through a centralized state apparatus, which sought to control and order every aspect of social, economic and political life. Finally, there was the development of a distinctive class structure or socialist rank order, with the elimination of the bourgeoisie as a distinctive social category, the creation of a modestly differentiated broad 'middle mass' of the population, a politico-military, industrial and intellectual elite, and an equally limited stratum or 'underclass' of those who were excluded from the mainstream of society.[1]

In a few short years at the end of the 1980s the centrally planned economies of state socialism disintegrated, although this was of course merely the culmination of a longer-term crisis in their functioning. At the same time, the Communist parties lost their grip on the state and soon ceased to exist at all (although some spawned successor parties). Finally, although this takes longer, transformations are under way in the class structure.

With some nuances this description of the nature of the ancien regime and its fate would be accepted by most of those seeking to explain the nature of the transition. But at this point a broad division occurs between what is probably the majority of social scientists (including those economists who have a serious track record of research in the former state socialist countries) and a wide range of public opinion (in both East and West), many of the international agencies now involved in the East, such as the World Bank and the IMF, the plethora of Western consultants and advisors who desire to act as the midwives of the new order, many in government and the public administration whom they advise, and so on.

What the latter group, more powerful by far than the former, has insisted upon, especially in the early years of neo-liberal economic 'reform' and privatization, is the notion, even the necessity for political and economic reasons, of the fastest possible abandonment of all aspects of state socialism and its replacement by (neo-)liberal democracy, with the least possible role for the state (and as decentralized an administration as possible) compatible with free markets and the private ownership and exploitation of capital. In short, as mentioned above, it insists upon the substitution for state socialism of capitalism wrought in the image of Reagan and Thatcher, Hayek and Friedmann.

From the start many social scientists were as sceptical about the viability of this destination for the societies of Eastern Europe and the FSU as they had been for its viability in the West in the previous decade. More importantly, as processes of economic, political and social restructuring unfolded, the empirical validity of the 'big bang' theory of the transition was soon called into question. Among the most valuable of the empirical studies of recent years have been those into the nature and effects of privatization. In a series of seminal contributions Stark (for example, 1990, 1992b) and his colleagues have drawn on earlier theories of institutional change in the context of enterprise privatization in a number of Eastern European countries, to point to the 'path-dependent' nature of the economic transition now occurring.[2] In his remarkable book on regional government reform in Italy, Robert Putnam (1993) has also pointed to its varied, hence path-dependent nature – as he says, path-dependence is just another way of saying 'where you get to depends on where you're coming from' (ibid.: 79). This is no less true when we enquire into the varied processes of economic reform after state socialism. It means that we cannot turn our backs on the legacy of the past if we want to understand the present. Nor can we accept, as some do, that 'state socialism' was a cross-nationally identical phenomenon, or that a similarly uniform description and analysis can be provided of the transition. Equally important is the remainder of the quotation from Putnam started above, 'and some destinations you simply cannot get to from here'. In other words, while it may be true but almost trivial to note that the transition is from state socialism to capitalism, what *sort* of capitalism it will turn out to be is an open question to which there are likely to be some varied answers.

This insistence on the value of recognizing the path-dependent nature of the transition, and therefore of paying heed to the impact of the past on the present and likely future, is one that informs the approach taken in this book. Socialist cities had their own physical and social structures; they do not just change overnight into capitalist cities, as unlike their predecessors as apples are to oranges. So the early part of our book reviews what were socialist cities, and many later contributors return to these matters as an essential component in their analyses of aspects of the urban transition.

Putnam's work is also thought-provoking when we come to consider the nature of political and class restructuring in the transition. His argument is that effective democracy requires strong, community-based networks of civic engagement which serve to engender societal trust and co-operation, and that this trust, the norms on which it is based and the networks in which social action based on trust is embedded, amount to a form of 'social capital'.[3] He writes:

> [s]tocks of social capital, such as trust, norms and networks, tend to be self-reinforcing and culminative. Virtuous circles result in social equilibrium with high levels of cooperation, trust, reciprocity, civic engagement, and collective well-being. These traits define the civic community. Conversely, the absence of these traits in the *un*civic community is also self-reinforcing. Defection, distrust, shirking, exploitation, isolation, disorder, and stagnation intensify one another in a suffocating miasma of vicious circles. (*Putnam, 1993: 177*)

Putnam suggests that societies may evolve towards the former or the latter of these situations. He adds that societies which are characterized by dense networks of interpersonal communication that are 'horizontal', that is joining agents of equivalent status and power, have the facility for developing the social capital that is the basis for democracy. However, societies that are dominated by 'vertical' networks, 'linking unequal agents in asymmetric relations of hierarchy and dependence' (ibid.: 173), are likely to demonstrate the traits of the uncivic community as noted above.

The relevance of this to the former state socialist countries is evident, for they were dominated by the vertical networks imposed by the one-party state. As several of the chapters in this book demonstrate, this was certainly the case with respect to urban development and urban life generally. For example, social organizations were controlled and manipulated by the regime, and most of the members of these bodies had little influence over their operations and objectives. A great deal of urban social provision, including much housing, was controlled by the managers of the economic enterprises, who were embedded in a vertical system of control and direction, at the head of which were the ministries in Moscow or other state socialist capitals.

As Putnam shows, in this situation there are various forms of resistance to domination, based on particularistic networks constructed, for example, around ethnicity or kinship groups that people feel they can trust. These networks and what they imply are in fact forms of social capital, but not the communitarian variety which Putnam sees as a precondition for effective democracy. In the former state socialist countries the development of the second or black economy, endemic favouritism and corruption neatly parallel the conditions which Putnam and others have found in southern Italy and in other vertically integrated polities and societies. In a passage which explicitly makes the comparison, he writes:

> [w]here norms and networks of civic engagement are lacking, the outlook for collective action appears bleak. The fate of the Mezzogiorno is an object lesson for the Third World today and the former Communist lands of Eurasia tomorrow, moving uncertainly towards self-government . . . For political stability, for government effectiveness, and even for economic progress social capital may be even more important than physical or human capital. Many of the former Communist societies had weak civic traditions before the advent of Communism, and totalitarian rule abused even that limited stock of social capital. Without norms of reciprocity and networks of civic engagement, the Hobbesian outcome of the Mezzogiorno – amoral familism, clientilism, lawlessness, ineffective government, and economic stagnation – seems likelier than successful democratisation and economic development. Palermo may represent the future of Moscow. (*Putnam, 1993: 183*)

Such considerations are of equal significance when we consider the emergent class structure of these societies in transition. Here, the outcomes of the mass privatizations of formerly state-owned assets, including in the context of this book housing and land, are of central importance. The actual terms of the conversion and redistribution of these assets differs greatly from the idealized models of most Western advocates of this process. In many cases it is those who have access to various forms of social capital, networks, connections and information, who are able to benefit at the expense of those whose stock of social capital is limited. Ex-members of the nomenclatura, the managers of (former) state enterprises, and those who were successful in the second or black economies of the former socialist societies (and frequently there were close links between all three groups) are likely to be among the beneficiaries, while others who lack their opportunities and connections lose out. Stark's (1990) study of the early progress of enterprise privatization in Hungary, subtitled 'From plan to market or from plan to clan?', illustrates just this process, showing for example how the managers of the former state enterprises were able to manipulate the situation to transfer the ownership of these assets to themselves – as he states, 'a process by which political capital is converted into economic capital' (ibid.: 366) – aided by contradictory legislation and conflicts between the various agencies which sought to control privatization.

Stark's conclusion is that privatization will not necessarily lead to the establishment of a Western-style free market economy in these countries. This is because of the ability of powerful social groups and their networks to impede marketization and capture the assets released by privatization for themselves. Hence the suggestion that the transition may be from plan to clan rather than to market. Other studies also show how privatization does not necessarily result in the establishment of Western-style economies. For example, Burawoy and Krotov's (1992) detailed research into a Russian furniture factory led them to conclude that a form of 'mechantile capitalism' was developing, founded on particularistic networks linking enterprises based on barter and not on the market. This involved the conversion of the former state bodies controlling industry into 'parastatal' centres of economic power and a system founded on trade, speculation and extortion, rather than any form of 'rational' modern capitalism.[4] And Sik's (1994) study of the former 'second economy' in Hungary, an economic system based on the same types of economic transaction found by Burawoy and Krotov, shows how it 'lubricated' the first economy under state socialism and how it now shapes the institutional conditions and the behaviour of those entering the new supposedly market economy. The networks, skills and behavioural patterns learnt in the second economy are a form of social capital used to gain position in the new economy and class structure. Detailed empirical work has shown just how significant this social capital can be. Thus Benácek's (1994) work on the structure and origins of Czech private entrepreneurs showed that 'there is a very strong link between the incidence of having been a communist bureaucrat in a top or middle rank managerial position and membership in an emerging class of private capitalist entrepreneurs' (ibid.: 162).

As already noted, this complex and cross-nationally (even regionally and locally)[5] varied redistribution of capital and power lies at the heart of the transformation of the class structure. In this process, access to capital and to social capital (and the successful conversion of the latter into the former) is central. Cities can be seen as stocks of physical assets whose privatization forms a large part of the capital involved in new class formation. But equally the dense networks of relationships which linked powerful actors in the state socialist cities, whether they were politicians, managers and bureaucrats with positions in the first economy, or families, ethnic groupings and other 'clans' in the second economy, are a form of social capital which can potentially be converted into actual capital. Of course, such capital is not confined to the urban population but, given the central role of the city in the economy and polity of state socialist societies, it may reasonably be asserted that much social capital is concentrated there.

In a recent paper which also draws on the concept of social capital to explore the process of class restructuring, Kolankiewicz (1995: 2) points to the need to 'examine how market, work and to a lesser extent status situation are being constructed through a combination of macro-policy and micro-practice as actors seek to adapt to the emerging market regime with the resources available to them and which they have taken from the redistributive system of state socialism'. Among the key changes highlighted by Kolankiewicz are the reduction of the relationship between the worker and his or her firm to one which is based on labour in exchange for wages, from the situation under state socialism in which, as several chapters in this book demonstrate, the enterprise was also responsible for the provision of many other collective and individual items of welfare – housing, medical services, child care, leisure provision and so on. So, as we shall see, privatization has immediate impacts on many aspects of urbanization and urban services. As Kolankiewicz also notes, this entails a new role for local government in (trying) to provide such services, a shift 'from place of work to place of residence and the local community as the focus of individual's lives' (ibid.: 3), and the simultaneous depoliticization of the workplace and politicization of local government. Echoing other themes noted by the contributors to this book, he adds that with the explosion of consumerism and the provision of leisure, recreation and cultural consumption by the market, new values are placed on activities previously subsidized by the state. Access to these goods will, of course, be on the basis of ability to pay and, as he states, 'style of life based on social separation will gradually overcome the social heterogeneity of socialist urban life and social-spatial segregation will reflect the emerging class order' (ibid.: 3–4).

Therefore, a process is occurring by which some goods and services that workers received under state socialism, determined partly through wages but also substantially through access to cheap housing, urban and other services and so on, and under direction of the one-party state according to its priorities, are being dismantled and a new redistributive order is emerging. As Kolankiewicz (ibid.: 5) comments, 'this hierarchy of redistribution did incorporate employees around a structure of rights and privileges and their dismantlement through market forces is . . . a politically and socially contentious process.'[6] Nowhere is this contention more evident, as we shall see, than in the struggle over the privatization of the physical assets of the city – land, housing and other real estate. But more generally the search for a new basis for citizenship in the urban context is evident, in the pressures on local authorities, for example, and in the growth and role of urban social movements. At the regional level the rise of nationalistic and ethnic populism is also linked to the search for forms of citizenship (and for forms of exclusion).

An obvious consequence of the new economic order, of considerable significance in cities, is the growth of mass unemployment and poverty, together with the process of exclusion and segregation, physical and social, that accompanies this development.

Turning from the situation of the losers in the transformation process to that of the winners, Kolankiewicz (1995: 7) focuses on the process of conversion of social capital to economic advantage and, in the longer run, to place in the class structure, pointing out 'that the manner in which political or organizational position can be exchanged for financial or entrepreneurial opportunity within the market order is not a given but is the object of intense conflict . . . between the political authors of legislation as much as those such as managers and directors who stand to gain from one or other policy option adopted'. He cites the example of conflict over property restitution in Poland as one instance of this. As a later chapter in this book shows, such conflicts surround housing and land privatization in every ex-state socialist nation.

To summarize, the transformation now taking place in the former state socialist nations is path-dependent, that is it is shaped by cross-nationally (and sub-nationally) variant historical legacies and current conjunctures. Rather than some simplistic and immediate process of abolition of the economic, political and social structures of state socialism and their replacement by those of an idealized Western capitalism, we see a conflictual and contradictory complex of social actions in which differing groups deploy what resources they have available to secure their position in the new order. In many cases a key asset is the social capital which was accrued in the previous regime. In addition, privatization provides some with valuable financial, property and other assets, while others lose out.

The urban transition now occurring shares many of these characteristics. But it is not, of course, a separate transition from the more general process of change that we have been discussing. The former socialist cities may, from this perspective, be viewed as a major source of both the economic assets (land, housing and other property) which are now being redistributed and of social capital, via the networks in which their populations are more or less embedded. There are other such connections as well. For example, the changing socio-spatial structure of the cities both expresses and helps to form the new class and status orders in these societies, as does the growth of various forms of urban marginality and poverty. The effects of changes in the role of economic enterprises and of the central state in the transition are reflected in the new roles of sub-national urban and regional governments, and struggles between different contenders for control of assets translate here into conflict between different levels and organs of government. The growth of urban social movements can be seen, in its most positive aspects at least, as a part of the development of horizontally rather than vertically integrated societies. Less positively, the growth of ethnic and other nationalist conflicts over cities and regions is evidence in the political sphere of a move towards 'clan'-based rather than democratic societies. Finally, we return to path-dependency in the urban context. Clearly the transition is *from* socialist cities, but what to is much less certain. With these considerations in mind, we now review and comment on the subsequent chapters.

SOCIALIST URBANIZATION AND THE TRANSITION IN CONTEXT

In chapter 2 Greg Andrusz sets the socialist cities and their successors in a broad historical, economic and socio-political context which, in stressing the cross-national variations in many of these matters, highlights the path-dependent nature of the urban transition. He outlines the main aspects of the state socialist system and its slow disintegration from the 1960s, together with the limited effects of economic reform from the 1970s onwards. Turning to the contemporary scene, the influence of the Western agencies' 'shock therapy' to 'transfuse the spirit of capitalism' into the former socialist economies is described, with the growth of various symptoms of economic pathology

– mass unemployment, rampant inflation, the growth of black econo-mies and organized economic crime.

Turning to the politics of the transition, Andrusz refers to the growth of ethnic and national conflict and territorial disintegration, together with the endemic conflict between various governmental agencies and levels of government over the control of budgets. He remarks on the growth of populist politics, based on the idea of unique communities with their own (more or less invented) histo-ries, and on the way in which there is a more general search for symbols or beliefs around which to mobilize and integrate, now communism no longer performs that role.

As far as the emergent class structure is concerned, there is, on the one hand, the reduction or abolition of many of the benefits that the socialist system distributed to the broad mass of the population and, on the other hand, the creation of a new middle class as a deliberate part of the marketization strategy. This new middle class comes from, for example, the managers of former state enterprises and other members of the nomenclatura, those who have accumulated wealth in the second economy, and genuinely new, small-scale entrepre-neurs. Popular attitudes to privatization are influenced by the per-sistence of earlier commitments to socialist values, and opposition is frequently based on the observation that it benefits the former nomenclatura and economic criminals. Andrusz notes that the strug-gle to appropriate real estate often plays a key role in class formation, and suggests that a new rentier class is being formed, dependent on landed property. In other cases, property is used as security for capital to be employed in new entrepreneurial activities elsewhere in the economy. Homelessness and rising crime related to property are some of the most dramatic consequences of the struggles over real estate.

Finally, Andrusz notes the change from community based on workplace to community based on residence and to the tendency for firms to rid themselves of their social assets and services. Other changes in the cities include the conversion of the urban landscape of socialism, its squares and monumental places, to commercialism, both of the more organized Western variety and also in forms that are more reminiscent of the bazaar economies of Third World cities (and forms of clan and mafia economic organization, rather than impersonal, capitalist, rational-legal forms). Outside the central places the process of ecological restructuring is well under way, with the creation of middle-class suburbs, on the one hand, and 'sink estates' of state housing, from which the middle class have fled, occupied by a new urban 'underclass', on the other hand.[7]

STATE SOCIALIST CITIES AND REGIONS

Chapters 3 and 4, by Smith and Enyedi, describe and analyse the principal characteristics of state socialist cities and urban policies and state socialist regions and regional policies respectively. Smith outlines the ideal-typical model of the socialist city, a combination, it was supposed, of economic efficiency, social justice in terms of access to urban goods and services, and a high quality of life for the urban populations. The reality was, of course, somewhat different. For example, the socialist city was more completely achieved in new towns than in those which had an inherited urban legacy, large facilities could not be distributed in urban space equitably, and there was differentiation in the quality of housing and in access by various social groups to it. Housing, in particular, was a part of the reward structure for elites and other favoured groups, and there were distinct areas of the city which had higher-status occupants, better housing, less crime and deviance, and so on. However, this socio-economic segregation was far more limited than in comparable capitalist cities, as was the incidence of ethnic segregation. This unequal access to urban goods and services, which Smith describes, is now being altered in the transition, but the benefits that state socialist redistribution provided for some, and the disadvantages it generated for others, may now aid them, or hinder them, in the struggle for advantage in the new system.

Enyedi's chapter has a descriptive purpose, to outline the main contours of regional development under state socialism, but also a theoretical one, to suggest that state socialist urbanization was merely a special variant of a more general 'stages' model of global urban development. This variation was caused by less fundamental factors, products of the late economic and urban modernization of Eastern Europe and the socialist political system. Viewed from this perspective, it seems, the period of socialist urbanization was just a detour, now concluded, away from a universal and broadly similar process of industrially based urbanization. While Enyedi develops his thesis with far greater subtlety and attention to the empirical facts of urbanization and regional development than many Western 'oilers' of the transition, his suggestion that there are common rules which determine modern urbanization and that the transition involves a return to such rules is not too distant from the analysis adopted by those who, for example, now seek to persuade East European governments that the institution of Western-style urban market processes and policies is essential. Many other contributors to this volume take a different view, but Szelenyi takes up the issue most directly in his concluding chapter, insisting upon the distinctive nature of state socialist cities and urbanization.

Many of these differences of analysis – though not all – are based on the interpretation of empirical evidence. Thus Enyedi notes the role of the second economy and of other mechanisms for defending group interests and promoting urban social processes (such as segregation) in opposition to official policies. But he sees this as evidence of Western-style market processes at work, albeit of a rather spontaneous nature, while others regard it as a very different form of capitalist or proto-capitalist activity. Enyedi, like others, also notes the significance of the pre-socialist urban and regional history of Eastern Europe to its later development, but his main conclusion is that this has resulted in delays in entering successive stages of the generalized process of urbanization.

Enyedi documents many of the principal facets of socialist urbanization that we have already remarked upon and which other chapters also describe. One key observation is that state socialist policies were biased in favour of the cities.[8] As he notes, the new socialist power in the region was urban based, and aimed to control the cities and to govern the country from them (one consequence was a lack of investment elsewhere, and a lack of policies for rural settlements until the 1970s). The various rigidities, contradictions and failures of socialist urbanization are described, as is the role that the lack of urban development that was not tied to an increasingly obsolescent form of industrialization played in accelerating economic stagnation from the 1960s. Urban and regional planning – like other state socialist policies – was the preserve of politicians, bureaucrats and experts, involving dialogues from which the general public were excluded. The key contradiction was between policies which aimed at equality of outcome and those which, their authors presumed, engendered efficiency (which meant agglomeration and large-scale projects with unequal accessibility by urban and rural populations). This conflict was most often resolved in favour of the latter priority, and thus in favour of the larger cities and their populations.

Other key features of socialist urbanization mentioned by Enyedi and many other analysts include the phenomenon of 'under-urbanization' – the failure of investment in urban housing and services to keep pace with the creation of urban jobs, thus resulting in large sections of the blue-collar working class living in rural settlements and commuting to work – as well as the role of the enterprise in providing housing and services, the lack of horizontal networks (for example, economic networks at the local or regional levels), and the dominance of workplace-based rather than residential communities in the cities.

CITIES IN THE TRANSITION: HOUSING AND LAND PRIVATIZATION

Chapters 5 and 6 focus on privatization. First, Marcuse provides a detailed analysis of housing and land privatization. He takes issue with the view, frequently held by proponents of the free market solution for the former state socialist societies, that privatization involves a simple transfer of the rights of ownership from the state to private individuals and enterprises. Ownership, he notes, is not a simple concept, as such perspectives assume; rather it refers to a bundle of rights which were divided between the state and individuals under state socialism as they are under capitalism. The privatization process, therefore, involves frequently conflictual repartitioning of these rights.

In order to establish his thesis, Marcuse first examines the nature of property rights under state socialism. Despite the image of state monopoly ownership, much land and housing remained in private hands in these societies, although the right to profit from such ownership was generally abolished and other matters, notably rents, were strictly controlled (and set at very low levels). This account also illustrates just how varied were the specific circumstances of individual countries, and how they changed over time. In rental housing, tenants enjoyed many of the rights which in the West accompany ownership – lifetime security of tenure and rights to pass this on to family members, for example. These and other property rights were guaranteed by the state, as such rights are in the West. Another significant feature of land and property under state socialism was the limited role played by the law in protecting rights and setting a planning framework. In the Soviet system these functions were performed by the state, through its centralized planning and administrative systems. This lack of a legal, regulatory and planning framework is now having to be made good in the post-socialist situation.

As we have noted, the process of transition involves a complex struggle between contending groups for economic advantage, political power and social position. The privatization of former state assets is a key part of all this. Marcuse's chapter provides an in-depth study of the nature of the contending interests with respect to land and property privatization and the consequences of their struggle. Generally, there are distinctive attitudes and interests involved in privatization, but in the case of housing and land there are some particular conflicts. Examples are those between the current occupants of property and their former owners, who frequently have rights of restitution; and between state and enterprise housing tenants, who wish to maintain their strong security of tenure and low rents, and the local authorities and other landlords, who wish to raise rents and reduce security. In the few years since the first laws enacting housing and land privatization were passed, there has been a movement away from blanket changes in rights affecting large and varied categories of property and circumstance, to more and more differentiated sets of rules, reflecting the impact of the contending interest groups on the policy-makers and legislators. Frequently, given especially the conflicts between levels of government over competencies in these matters, and the struggle for the control of local budgets, there has been endemic conflict and contradiction between the laws, policies and actions of public bodies.

The path-dependent nature of housing and land privatization is illustrated by Marcuse's discussion of developments in Russia and other countries. Broadly speaking, the most radical and complete conversion to private real-estate ownership has, of course, occurred in East Germany, where the West German system of property law and rights was simply imposed (although not without some peculiar difficulties due especially to the significance of restitution). Other countries, which, as we have noted, lacked such a ready-made system of legal regulation of private property rights, and where there was no dominant force to impose a solution on the struggle between contending interests, have felt their way towards the establishment of private property rights in complex, varied and often contradictory ways.

Despite these variations, Marcuse is able to draw some general conclusions about the obstacles to privatization and the conflicts that have arisen. The first is that private property rights continued to exist under state socialism, and are not simply something that is being (re)introduced now. One obvious implication is that those who had such rights under state socialism will seek to defend them and to gain advantage from them in the transition process, both in the conflicts over privatization and more generally. Quite what the previous distribution of rights was and how it enters into the transition process varies cross-nationally. Second, the initial destatification consisted of measures to sell state property, to decentralize decision making, and to provide for the management of property for the time being remaining under state control. In the case of housing, this decentralization was mainly to the local authorities, and it has resulted in endemic conflicts between central and local governments over matters such as the control of foreign private ownership, tenant security and so on. A key motivation for decentralization was the desire to remove the housing burden from central government budgets, although local authorities have resisted acceptance of financial burdens which they cannot meet.

A third complication lies in the problems caused by restitution, which involve, for example, the claims of long-term residents against absentee owners, and the conflict which arises when land on which there are restitution claims could be disposed of by the financially starved local authorities to large-scale commercial developers.

As we have mentioned, around these conflicts of interest there is growing an ever more complex web of legislation and policy, including the development of detailed property laws and procedures which were largely absent in the socialist state, with its central planning and politico-administrative direction. The lack of a stable legal framework, together with the lack of a system of planning regulation, means that there are many opportunities for interest groups to manipulate the situation, to gain advantages for themselves, and to benefit from the conversion of the advantages that they possessed under socialism into private property ownership in the new regime. At the same time, there are various sources of resistance to the spread of private ownership rights that are inherited from state socialism. These sources include tenants who wish to defend their strong rights to lifetime security and the ability to pass on tenancies to members of their family, as well as judges and administrators, who still adhere to the values inherent in socialist urbanization, and so on. Some of these attitudes derive from the pre-socialist periods, for example a desire to prevent the build-up of large-scale land holdings and to ban foreign land ownership. Such attitudes hinder the entry of large-scale capital into urban development and constitute a further source of political and legislative conflict. They also result, as Marcuse notes, in there frequently being a gap between what the law provides for and what actually occurs.

Marcuse concludes that systems of property rights are reflections of social relations between individuals and groups, but that much of the discussion in both the East and the West assumes that legal changes in property rights are not just a necessary but a sufficient condition for an actual change in these rights. This is not so, and such assertions obscure the fact that an intense struggle is taking place over property rights redistribution, which, as we have seen, is of direct relevance to wider processes of economic, political and class restructuring.

Marcuse, therefore, presents a radical critique of 'conventional wisdom' about the privatization of land and housing in the transition. By contrast, Struyk's chapter, focused more narrowly on housing privatization, contains an analysis which is much closer to that advocated by agencies such as the World Bank regarding the primacy of the rapid establishment of a real-estate market. However, Struyk also highlights some of the negative consequences of such policies. The symbolic importance of housing privatization as signifying the end of social ownership is noted, as is its value in terms of the reduction of budgetary burdens, the greater responsibility for management and maintenance that it was hoped would be transferred to residents, and its political popularity (at least in the initial stages). But the central reason for the advocacy of housing privatization by economic reformers has been the desire establish, as rapidly as possible, a market system with respect to housing and other real estate, as elsewhere in the economy. Only privatization could achieve this, given the time it would take to create a private market *de novo*.

From the economic reformers' perspective there would be various benefits flowing from the marketization of real estate. Mobility would be enhanced and the establishment of price signals would indicate to private developers where the optimum locations for their projects were. In short, capitalist urban development was predicated on privatization. At the same time, Struyk is aware of the obstacles to privatization and its inequitable consequences. As he notes, housing privatization involves a profound shift in housing consumers' attitudes, from those associated with property rights under socialism – linked to considerations of security of tenure and the ability to pass tenancies on to family members – to those associated with capitalism, in which housing is seen as a commodity with value in the market and a source of income and wealth. He also touches on the resistance of local officials to giving up sources of power and privilege in the transition, and on the adverse effect of housing privatization on low-income households and new entrants to the housing market.

Reviewing the progress of housing privatization in nine states in Eastern Europe and the FSU, Struyk, like Marcuse, shows just how varied the distribution of housing ownership was under state socialism. He also examines the changing relations between central and local government and the conflicts that have arisen over decentralization, which, as in the West, is being promoted as a way of improving consumer choice and as being more sensitive to local variations, but in practice is primarily motivated by budgetary concerns. In addition, Struyk's detailed evidence underlines some of the significant factors which have impeded the progress of privatization; for example, the strong rights which existing tenants of state housing have, their low rents and their exemption from property taxes. By contrast, owners, even if they pay little or nothing for the units, face major cost increases for management, maintenance and repairs, and tax payments. Various policies have been evolved which aim to remove such obstacles. But there are other problems as well, among them the difficulties created for the management of blocks of apartments in mixed state–private ownership, and the fact that uncertainties over the ultimate division between those units which are privatized and those which remain state property are inhibiting private-sector investment.

Such obstacles lead Struyk to suggest that in some countries up to half the units may never be privatized. Moreover, as studies of council-housing privatization in the UK have demonstrated (Forrest and Murie, 1988), privatization is selective: it is the better units, in the more desirable areas, inhabited by the more prosperous tenants that tend to be privatized. Here, paralleling other developments in the post-socialist society, it is noticeable that those who had privilege in the former society have tended to gain the most from housing privatization, and this adds to resentment among the rest of the population. As Struyk admits, privatization is not a socially just or equitable process. Some gain and others lose out, and many of the former are in this position by virtue of their ability to convert advantages gained in the old system to ones enjoyed in the new system. Such inequities, Struyk suggests, can only be justified by the imperative to remove all vestiges of the state socialist system of property rights and rapidly establish a Western-style market. He does believe, however, that steps will need to be taken to subsidize and support a social housing sector and, more generally, to provide access to affordable housing for those on low incomes and other disadvantaged groups. In this sense, it could be suggested, Struyk is arguing for the Western European version of the private housing market, rather than the US model which has been espoused by many economic reformers and international agencies.

THE EMERGENT CAPITALIST CITY: A GERMAN CASE STUDY

Nowhere was the contrast between state socialist and capitalist urbanization more clearly and starkly to be seen than in Berlin, the subject (with other former GDR cities) of chapter 7 by Hartmut Häussermann. Of course the fact that Berlin was a city divided between the two systems was the basic reason for this. However, the wartime destruction of both parts of the city and the doctrinal ortho-doxy of the East German Communist Party, plus the symbolic role that the city played with respect to contending economies and ideo-logies, added to the sharpness of this contrast. Since the fall of communism, Berlin has continued to be a key city for urban research due to the assimilation of East Germany into a mature, capitalist Western democracy. If Berlin was a particularly notable example of the ideal-typical state socialist city, it is now rapidly converting into what many would see as an ideal-typical version of an advanced capitalist city. This means that a closer look at Berlin in the transition may be a particularly illuminating exercise.

Häussermann outlines many of the features of socialist urbaniza-tion noted by other contributors to this book, but he has a particular focus on urban design and planning. He refers to the monumental, symbolic aspects of state socialist central places, and the way in which these physical forms reflected and sustained the city-based rule of the Communist Party and the state that Enyedi also noted. He explains that the lack of a land market gave planners and architects licence to use space in ways that are normally impossible in capitalist cities. More generally, urban policies were set by politicians and planners, the majority of the population having no significant say in the pro-cess. As in other Eastern European capitals, what remained of the historic sections of the city were ignored and allowed to deteriorate. They were viewed as capitalist relics; moreover, much of the building remained privately owned, so state socialism had no interest in sus-taining them. Above all, the drive for supposed economies of scale meant that large-scale projects on greenfield or razed sites were seen as the way to develop the cities of socialism – not perhaps so different from the way in which many professionals and politicians wanted to develop the cities of capitalism in the 1950s and 1960s, although they had to contend with more opposition – but, interestingly, by the latter years of the state socialist regime in Berlin there was rising resistance to such drastic urban renewal by the populations resident in the older areas of the city.

With regard to socio-spatial segregation, Häussermann confirms the picture set out by Smith. There were enclaves of housing for the privileged, who also enjoyed privileged access to other urban ser-vices. There was also a small sector of housing for those at the bottom of the social system, including dissidents, concentrated in the decay-ing historical districts. But most people lived in relatively unsegre-gated conditions in the new state housing areas. Häussermann too notes the key role played by enterprises rather than by community-based organisations and local government in urban development and service provision. As he states, in the GDR the company became the focal point for organizing 'the socialist way of life', a functional equivalent to the family or the feudal lord in other types of society. Echoing some of the points made earlier in this introductory chapter, he refers to the integration of decision making into a vertical structure guided by the central planning commissions and the lack of locally controlled resources, local decision-making power and an urban bourgeoisie – which class had historically been the mainstay of local government in Germany, as elsewhere.

With the collapse of the communist regime the system of vertically integrated urbanization was destroyed. However, actual urban change takes longer to occur and is unevenly developed. It is occurring first in the most economically dynamic, that is potentially profitable, regions, cities and city districts in East Germany (notably Berlin), and can be measured by the growth in property and land prices and the levels of speculative activity. In this process some cities become driven by speculation, while other stagnate. Overall, however, real-estate capitalism leads the marketization process in the East German territories, while the privatization of industrial assets has resulted in much less new investment and massive unemployment. Popular resentment at these changes and the persistence of some of the core socialist values, such as regard for social justice, for security of tenure and so on, place significant political and other obstacles in the way of marketization.

Häussermann provides a particularly clear insight into some of the consequences of the system shift for planning and local administration. As we have noted, under state socialism the planners and administrators were dominant forces in urban development. Now such development involves a much wider range of social actors, notably the private-sector owners and developers. Those East Germans who have survived in or have been elected to local government find themselves having to deal with a far more complex situation, with more conflicting interests than hitherto. As in the West, urban planning has become a form of urban management of private-sector-led development, and many East Germans have been ill equipped to cope with this change. In many cases they have been outflanked by newcomers who have seized opportunities to fulfil their own political or economic agendas – for example, the West German political nominees who were drafted into East German urban government, and a plethora of investors and speculators from the West. The destruction of the middle class in the years of state socialism left, according to Häussermann, a serious lack of the key stratum from which local politicians and administrators could be drawn.

Physically, the effects of these changes are already apparent. For

example, in city centres the institution of a private market in land
and rising land prices leads to a new pattern of land usage. Many
public institutions and ex-state socialist retail establishments are
forced to move out, unable to pay rising rents, while Western-style
office, leisure and other commercial developments take their place.
On the periphery, the lack of any effective framework for regulative
planning has led to speculative exploitation of greenfield sites for
shopping malls, car dealerships and so on. The rapid growth of car
ownership in the former GDR has enhanced the economic viability
of such developments. This also has relevance for the growth of
suburban housing developments for the better off.

Meanwhile, unsold social housing has been transferred to municipalities and co-operatives, with the lifting of rent restrictions and
security rights after a short transitional period. This will create an
acute crisis in the sector, as many tenants will not be able to pay
higher rents. As in Britain, such changes simply encourage all those
who can afford to do so to move out, creating a residualizing, deteriorating social-housing sector which its landlords cannot afford to
maintain or improve properly. Overall, therefore, there is a significant growth of socio-spatial segregation occurring, especially in the
more economically dynamic cities such as Berlin. And while relatively
little has yet changed in the older, pre-socialist, inner-city residential
areas (there are easier profits to be made in the central business
distinct and at the periphery), in many cases they are ultimately likely
to experience a gentrification and displacement of low-income
populations similar to those which have occurred elsewhere.

Such changes in patterns of urban land use are clearly reminiscent
of those in many US cities rather than in the cities of Western
Europe. Indeed, Häussermann suggests that one of the consequences of reunification may be the growth of this distinctive style of
urban development over the whole German territory, with the
squeezing out of the small-scale property owners and developers that
have played a key role historically in the cities of West Germany.

THE NEW POLITICS: URBAN SOCIAL
MOVEMENTS AND NATIONALISM

As we have seen, most contributors to this book are explicitly or
implicitly critical of the proposition that the shift from socialist to
post-socialist cities involves the collapse of one system and the rapid
installation of a new one, which contains no legacy from the past, to
fill the vacuum thus created. Chris Pickvance's chapter (chapter 8),

which examines the nature and role of urban social movements before and during the transition, is no exception. Referring to Stark's work on path-dependency, he argues that urban activism began to grow in the last years of the socialist regimes and that these have provided certain resources (forms of social capital in fact) which are deployed in the new situation. He also refers to a problem which is evident in several other chapters, namely the difficulty of interpreting similar empirical evidence of change (see, for example, the comments made above on Enyedi's chapter, or the contrasting interpretations of housing privatization and the emergent types of private real-estate market foreseen by Marcuse and Struyk respectively).

Pickvance first reviews the development of urban social movements under state socialism. Here there was a growing gap between ideology and the official system on the one hand, and actual practice on the other. Given the nature of the organization of urban life through a vertically integrated system, which excluded most citizens from any role in decision making, there was no 'space' envisaged for autonomous social movements to develop. However, control could never be that total and, as economic and political liberalization occurred in the face of the growing regime crisis, a range of community-based associations and pressure groups with limited autonomy did begin to emerge. The scope for such developments varied cross-nationally, depending on the detailed nature of the regime and the specific conjuncture, as well as the nature of the issues at stake. Pickvance's case studies of social movement formation in Budapest and Moscow, and in relation to housing and environmental issues, provide much evidence for these conclusions.

The second half of Pickvance's analysis describes developments since the collapse of communism in 1989/90. Overall, there has, unsurprisingly, been a major growth in various forms of grass-roots urban movements. In some cases in Moscow, these organizations grew out of self-management groups established in the last moments of communism, as devices to maintain control of the urban population. Some then developed independence and, when communist funding was cut off, obtained resources in other ways, such as the appropriation of property which was then rented out or sold. To a significant extent, the leadership of these organizations was composed of individuals with strong backgrounds of participation in communist organizations, who converted this social capital into political or economic advantage in the emergent urban system, using their leadership of grass-roots bodies as a stepping stone. Another example of 'asset conversion' via urban social movements is provided by the operations of housing partnerships in Moscow, that is, groups of residents that wanted to take advantage of the privatization laws by taking over not just their blocks of flats but also the valuable commercial space in these buildings. This brought such groups into conflict with city authorities, which wished to exploit commercial property to relieve their own budgets. Pickvance notes that housing partnerships were mainly formed by the highly educated inhabitants of potentially valuable blocks; another example of the attempt by those privileged under state socialism to carry their advantages over into the new, marketized city.

More generally, Pickvance highlights the significance of the endemic conflict between elected councillors and officials, and between differing levels of government, over who was to control and profit from the ownership of urban assets. Sometimes the grass-roots organizations have been able to exploit these conflicts to gain control of assets and achieve other objectives; sometimes they have lost out. He also examines, especially in relation to the fate of several Budapest movements, the tendency of such organizations to be co-opted by government or to have their demands deflected, outcomes that are frequently found to occur in Western cities as well.

Pickvance concludes that urban social movements before and during the transition have conformed with a four-stage model of development, very similar to that found in studies of other urban systems in transition out of authoritarian rule. While the authoritarian system prevails, there is little space for any autonomous movements to develop; as the regime's grip begins to slacken, such movements mushroom; only to decline in intensity, numbers and significance, as a 'normal' political system is established, to a continuing level of more moderate activity. However, he stresses the significance of persisting national variations in this passage. This is partly the product of the specific contemporary circumstances in each case, but may also be a consequence of much longer-term, persisting differences in the relationship between government and the citizenry, dating from even before the socialist period.

In conclusion, Pickvance suggests that the concept of the 'post-socialist' city does not refer to a homogeneous reality. His comparisons of Moscow and Budapest demonstrate that there were great variations between them, due to the different variants of state socialism which they had experienced and because the transition processes also varied.

As Andrusz notes in chapter 2, one of the most important consequences of the break-up of the Soviet system has been the growth of territorial conflict based on nationality and ethnicity. The wars in the territories of the former Yugoslavia, the destruction of the population of major and historic cities such as Sarajevo and Dubrovnik, and of many smaller settlements, are merely the largest-scale examples of such conflicts. Indeed, as Andrusz records, on the day the Soviet Union finally expired, 26 December 1991, there where no fewer than 164 recognized ethnic conflicts in progress in its territory. Klaus von Beyme's chapter (chapter 9) reviews the nature and development of these conflicts in the former state socialist nations.

He points out that many of the current divisions between nationalities and ethnic groups predated communism and were only suppressed, not eradicated, during the lifetime of state socialism. Such divisions, however, did not play a key role in bringing about the break-up of the system; this was mainly a product of its economic crisis. Instead, he suggests that they have subsequently provided an ideological basis for integration and mobilization, filling the vacuum left by the demise of communism, and that appeals by the intelligentsia for the construction of a 'civil society' were ineffective. Here he is describing another aspect of the dissolution of a vertically integrated society, in this case with respect to the political system, and the development of a new basis for societal organization. There are some interesting parallels with the economic transition, remembering Stark's characterization of the shift from plan to clan rather than to market. What von Beyme describes might be seen as a shift from autocracy to clan rather than to democracy, and to citizenship (and exclusion) based on concepts of nationality or ethnicity. There are also parallels between this situation and that found by Putnam in the Mezzogiorno, where instead of the development of a 'civic community' and functioning democratic institutions, there has persisted a politics based on mutual suspicion and lawlessness. The similarities between the Mezzogiorno's 'amoral familism' and mafia organization and what might be described as the amoral nationalism of the contemporary Balkans (and elsewhere in the former state socialist nations) are striking, at least with respect to their consequences for the development of civil society, citizenship and a democratic politics.

In fact, von Beyme himself makes a link between the growth of marketization and that of nationalism, referring to the relentless competition for housing, jobs and life-chances in the new society and to the resort to nationalism and ethnic mobilization in this situation. He suggests that conflict between ethnic and national groupings is particularly likely to occur in the cities and economically dynamic regions, in part because such areas attract economic migrants. Once again, however, the pattern varies cross-nationally, and according to the previous geo-political history of the territories in question. The borders of many of these nations have been frequently altered in this century, cutting across ethnic and other national groupings and giving rise to many long-suppressed demands for their readjustment. The political resort to a politics of nationalism and ethnicity, as a means of mobilizing political support, has brought such demands to the surface again. In many cases, this seems likely to play a major role in shaping the emergent post-socialist cities and regions.

CITIES AFTER SOCIALISM

In the final chapter of this book, Ivan Szelenyi draws on the detailed evidence regarding the nature of socialist cities and the urban transition, much of which has been included in the earlier chapters, to come to some general conclusions about the nature of socialist urbanization and how its key characteristics are being transformed.

In sharp contrast to Enyedi, and to Western analysts who have tended to see socialist urbanization as merely a variant of a more general model of global urban development, Szelenyi insists on the qualitatively different nature of socialist and capitalist cities. Moreover, he argues, there can be no certainty that the 'post-socialist' city is evolving towards the forms of capitalist city current in the core nations of the world system. Instead, some at least may be evolving forms of peripheral urbanization typical of the cities of the capitalist Third World, or some other variant or hybrid form.

The first part of his chapter marshals a variety of evidence to show that there were three distinctive features of socialist cities, in comparison with their capitalist counterparts. First, they achieved industrialization with less urban population growth and less spatial concentration for the population than in capitalist cities at similar stages of growth. In short, as he argued first many years ago (Szelenyi, 1983), they were 'under-urbanized'. Second, there was less urbanism, that is less diversity; less economizing with space, thus lower inner-city densities, and less urban marginality. Finally, these cities had a distinctive ecological structure. Earlier chapters in this book provide considerable evidence to support Szelenyi's contention that these were significant differences and that they were directly linked to key features of state socialism.

These chapters also provide a strong basis for the validity of Szelenyi's argument that all three aspects of socialist urbanization are now in dissolution. He refers, for example, to the growth of mass rural unemployment that is likely in time to result in mass urban migration and, although he does not put it in these terms, a possible transition from under-urbanization to the 'over-urbanization' characteristic of many Third World cities. The rapid growth of urban diversity and marginality is already evident, with the marketization of many formerly state-provided goods and services and the breakdown of forms of social control, the creation of bazaar and criminal economies (although these existed to a lesser extent before the collapse of communism), and various forms of deviancy, homelessness and so on. The changes in the physical form and functions of the inner cities noted by Häussermann and by Andrusz are all a part of the growing diversity as well. Finally, there are the changes in the ecological structure of the cities, also noted by Häussermann and others, with the development of suburbs and shopping malls, on the one hand, and residualizing areas of social housing, occupied by the economically marginal and other excluded groups, on the other hand.

Szelenyi sets out the background to this transition, the dismantling of state monopoly ownership and mass privatization, the end of one-party rule and the change from a socialist rank order to an emergent class-based stratification. He emphasizes, as we have in this introductory chapter, the path-dependent nature of the transition and of the transformation of property rights that lies at its heart. The current formations are unstable and it is far from certain that these societies, and their urban systems, are evolving towards the Western capitalist model. As he states, it is not clear where the former state socialist societies will be inserted in the world capitalist system, how close they will get to the core or how near to the periphery. In any event, no single destination is likely for the many and varied post-socialist cities and societies. To misquote Putnam, if Palermo may represent the future of Moscow, London or Paris may represent the future of Prague.

NOTES

1   Obviously, this is an account of the class structure which omits details of the rural class structure: agricultural workers were officially a part of the 'middle mass' but their status and life-chances differed from those of urban workers.

2   The concept of 'path-dependency' was developed by economic historians, studying the development of technology. But it has been taken up more widely by sociologists and political scientists who study institutional and organizational change (Powell, 1991: 193–4; North, 1990: 93–4).

3   The origins of this concept, according to Coleman (1990: 300–21), lie in work by Loury on the development of human capital and refer to 'the

set of resources that inhere in family relations and in community social organization and that are useful for the cognitive and social development of a child or young person' (ibid.: 300). However, Bourdieu has developed a more general conception of social capital, alongside his typology of others forms of capital, notably cultural. He defines social capital as 'the sum of the resources, actual or virtual, that accrue to an individual or group by virtue of possessing a durable network of more or less institutionalized relationships of mutual acquaintance and recognition' (Bourdieu and Wacquant, 1992: 119).

4   Burawoy and Krotov argue that the systemic features of an economy can be studied and conclusions arrived at on the basis of their single (excellent) case study. However, if we are to take the concept of path-dependency seriously, it seems more likely that 'merchantile capitalism' is but one variant of the several capitalisms that may emerge in Eastern Europe and the FSU.

5   Stark (1990: 392) suggests an interesting research agenda on locally based economic networks: '[r]esearch on small-scale producers would shift attention from *individuals'* aspirations for entrepreneurship to the features of *localities* that inhibit or encourage marketization. In such an ecological model, entrepreneurship is less a function of individual motivation than of social relations in a particular field. How, for example, do localities differ in linkages among small-scale producers along lines of credit, marketing, supply etc.? Will competition among political parties at the local level and the fact that local governments will face constraints in self-financing yield new patterns with some diversity across regions?' Of course, there has already been exploration of these local economic linkages in Western societies, famously in the 'Third Italy' (see, for example, Bagnasco, 1977).

6   It should be noted that the 'rights and privileges' accorded to workers under state socialism hardly amounted, as some have suggested, to a form of 'welfare state'. Ironically, it was in the state socialist countries that the welfare state as a tool for the reproduction of labour power and for legitimation – which is the classic Marxist explanation of the capitalist welfare state – appears to have been most clearly achieved. But as many studies have shown, access to *high-quality* housing, health care, education and so on was wholly or partially monopolized by the political and economic elites. Such a view is not inconsistent with Kolankiewicz's claim that the *loss* of access to, for example, cheap if frequently poor-quality housing and the uncertainties about the redistribution now occurring under 'post-socialism' are contentious.

7   The term 'underclass' is used in very different ways in different societies, and by different sociologists. In so far as it refers to a group which is cut off in significant respects from 'mainstream' society, this may apply to some of the 'new poor' in the former state socialist countries, such as gypsies, but not to the majority of this broad grouping.

8   In commenting on a draft of this chapter, Ivan Szelenyi noted that 'socialism was anti-infrastructure and this caused damage both to cities

and to the countryside, though, ironically, the countryside could cope with the problem somewhat more efficiently'. Nevertheless, the focus on cities in much state socialist land-use planning and resource allocation was clear.

2

Structural Change and Boundary Instability

Gregory Andrusz

Modern wars and revolutions (whether violent or peaceful) have more than once transformed European political boundaries and structures. These events have had cataclysmic effects on people's lives, disrupting families and communities, compelling migration, often in search of work, sometimes to avoid persecution. The Great War of 1914–18, the October Revolution of 1917, the triumph of Hitler in 1933 and Stalin's purges, World War II (1939–45), the coups in Central Europe in 1946–8 and the revolutions in East and Central Europe and the former Soviet Union in 1989–91 are major watersheds. We should not, however, be impetuous in our judgement on whether we are today witnessing the continued long march of economic and political liberalism. Today, given the fragility of the structures being established, the legacy of past boundary disputes in the post-communist region could cause these 'new democracies' to convert into military or right-wing authoritarian regimes, some (again) possibly monarchical in flavour.

The countries in the region under study have contiguous boundaries and eight of them are ethnically Slav.[1] Until 1918, with the exception of Bulgaria and Romania, which received full independence in 1878 after 500 years as parts of the Ottoman Empire, all these states were constituent parts of the Russian, German and Austro-Hungarian empires. The political regimes in the countries of East and Central Europe, which today are experiencing such vast upheavals, had been in power for about 40 years. As modern nation states they have only existed for 70 years. The changes which are discussed in this book have to be seen within this time span.

The geographical space of the former Russian Empire and its successor, the former Soviet Union (FSU), covers seven time zones and embraces totally different climatic conditions ranging from arctic to desert and sub-tropical, which heavily influences the types of agriculture, social relations and cultures found there. Natural resource endowments vary enormously. In the so-called European part of the FSU, republics on the Baltic Sea are quite different from those bordering the Black and Caspian Seas. Europe blends into Eurasia – the name of a territory occupied by peoples and states some of whom claim a socio-cultural and sometimes 'racial' link to Europe although their cultural and geographical ties are with Islamic Asia.

This chapter begins with an overview of the emergence of nation states in East and Central Europe in the aftermath of World War I. This is followed by a summary of the essential features of the Soviet-type system, which were adopted throughout the region after World War II. This leads to an examination of attempts to reform the system in the 1960s and its final rejection in the 1980s. The chapter then looks at the steps that are being taken to reintegrate these societies into the global market and the impediments to countries in the region becoming members of the European Union. Following discussion of the economic dimension of the transformation in East-Central Europe and the Commonwealth of Independent States (CIS), attention is turned to political and geographical boundary changes which have occurred. Reference is made here to ethnic strife (including Chechnya) in the context of the dissolution of the Soviet Union. Economic and political restructuring have had social consequences which are here discussed in terms of the emergence of new social classes, especially those associated with urban real estate, which is becoming an important source of competition and friction between groups in these societies. The final section considers the impact which these changes are having on urban space.

EAST-CENTRAL EUROPE IN THE CENTURY TO 1945

For centuries, the borders of the countries of Europe have been remarkably unstable. A degree of stability came from the agreed need to contain any state that sought to grow too large. Germany's consolidation under Bismarck made the country in 1880 the most populous in Europe (45.2 million) with the exception of Russia (97.7 million).[2] The unification of Germany and its political ascendancy paved the way for the two world wars of the twentieth century. Indeed, the political and economic division of European space over the past century has been the outcome of a Wagnerian duet (or zero-sum game) between these two states. The military defeat of the former in 1945 stemmed its ascent. The postponement of its climb to pre-eminence within the European theatre enabled Russia to extend its influence westward, a process sent into reverse with the almost total collapse of the Soviet Russian empire beginning in 1989 (Baranovsky and Spanger, 1992). Notwithstanding the considerable strains of financing German unification, the Deutschmark remains the key currency in Europe, and Germany retains its hegemonic economic position in Europe (Verheyen and Soe, 1993). German unification coincides with the disintegration of the Soviet empire and the slow (possibly temporary) dissolution of Russia itself.

During the nineteenth century the Austro-Hungarian Empire presented itself as another major actor in Eastern and Central Europe. It too faced Russia as a rival, in this case over the dismemberment of the Ottoman Empire with an eye to liberating Catholic and Orthodox Christians from the 'yoke' of Islam. Towards the end of its existence the dual monarchy of Austria and Hungary found itself in a position akin to that of the USSR towards the end of its existence a century later. The dominant ethnic groups, Germans and Magyars, in the one case, and Great Russians, in the other, formed less than half of the population of their respective empires. In both instances, national minorities were to play a part in the empire-disintegrating process, interjecting their needs just when the heads of state were of necessity introducing reform. In 1914, not long before his assassination by a Serbian student, the Archduke Ferdinand was on the point of reforming the empire by raising the status of some Slavs to that preserved for Austro-Germans and Hungarians. However, it was too late for palliatives.

The countries comprising much of Eastern Europe had for centuries been subject to Ottoman rule. Their response to alien government was to discover through their intelligentsia a pride in their culture, folklore and language and a sense of nationhood. Whilst this nurtured a sense of self-identity, they still needed the assistance of the major powers, which vied with one another to be 'the chivalrous champion'. Bulgaria, whose people were ethnically Slav and Orthodox in religion, was thus a legitimate client for Russia. This it duly became when, after a rising by the Bulgarians against the Turks was savagely quashed, the latter were defeated by the Russians in 1878.

The peace imposed saw the creation of a large Bulgarian state which encompassed much of what was to become southern Serbia and Greek Macedonia. Such was Great Power rivalry that the other powers demanded that Bulgaria be divided into two. In 1908 unification was permitted by Austria when it simultaneously took bites out of the Ottoman Empire in the form of Bosnia and Herzegovina, which, among other things, aggravated feelings between the Serbs and the Bulgarians. Macedonia was a major pawn in the tripartite tussle between Greece, Bulgaria and Serbia. In 1995 that contest once again sits malevolently on the horizon. Neither have the Bulgarians altogether forgotten or forgiven their domination by Turkey. The ambivalent attitude of the state and society towards ethnic Turks, who constitute 10 per cent of the population, makes their coexistence precarious.

Besides wanting to help 'fellow Slavs', the Russians had two other goals: first, to replace the Turks as the power in the region, and second, to block the extension of Austro-Hungarian power. This second objective brought the Germans into the conflict over the Ottoman heritage; for their pains they succeeded the Austro-Hungarians as Russia's main adversary. They were not, of course, passive victims; their engagement expressed their expansionist and frustrated imperialist design. By 1919 Russia had indeed superseded Turkey as the power in the region. In the aftermath of World War II, the former Ottoman lands fell into the political fiefdom of the Soviet Union.

In Russia at the turn of the century, the liberals – a small capitalist class and large sections of the intelligentsia – were desperate to throw off the yoke of their oppressors, the autocracy. But they were frightened by the prospect of revolution from below. Survival dictated the mutual dependency of the tsarist government and the liberals. Then, when in February 1917 the liberals were forced to abolish the monarchy, they found themselves in a vacuum with no solid foundation. The liberal Provisional Government finally collapsed inwards after the failed coup of the military under General Kornilov in July 1917. Although his venture failed, it made the upper classes, including the liberals, realize that a dictatorship would be the only way to govern. While they countenanced a dictatorship of the right, history presented the people with one from the left.

In the 1920s, the new, post-Versailles states of East and Central Europe created and grasped the dignifying symbols of independence such as flag, anthem and national bank. The self-respect conferred by nationhood gave rise to nationalism, which justified conflict between and even within countries. People lost their jobs because they had the 'wrong' nationality. The population of Poland was twice that of Czechoslovakia, which was twice as large as that of Hungary. The populations of these new states were far from being ethnically homogeneous: there were Slovaks, Croats, Slovenes and Serbs in Hungary, Czechs in Poland, Poles and Hungarians in Czechoslovakia. All three countries had substantial German and Jewish minorities. At the same time, the patchwork quilt stitched together at Versailles left industries and agriculture everywhere cut off from their sources of supply and their markets. New administrative and legal barriers hindered the flow of goods, capital and labour. Waterways, railways and telephone services were cut up into smaller segments that were less efficient and more expensive.

In November 1918, Poland reappeared on the map as a nation state for the first time since 1789, just when its principal enemies, Germany and Russia, had been seriously weakened by war and revolution and the third partitioner, Austria-Hungary, had totally disappeared. It immediately sought to regain its earlier, seventeenth-century glory, when its territory extended from the Baltic to the Black Sea. In 1920 it embarked upon its own 'Drang nach Osten' by annexing parts of the Ukraine, Byelorussia (Belarus) and Lithuania (including Vilnius). In the south and west it 'reclaimed' land from Austria and Germany (including Poznan and parts of Upper Silesia).

Czechoslovakia was vulnerable from the very beginning of its creation and faced the threat of losing Slovakia to Hungary. During the inter-war period Slovakia drifted towards the political right and showed itself disposed towards an accord with Hungary and Austria. While Poland expanded and Czechoslovakia struggled to survive as a separate entity, Hungary stood vanquished, its territory reduced by two-thirds. In 1920 it lost Transylvania, which it had for centuries 'owned' and in which Hungarian landlords ruled over a Romanian peasantry. It regained this in 1940, but in 1947 again ceded it to Romania. From the Romanian point of view, in 1940, one-third of the country's land surface and population were lost to Hungary and the USSR.

A number of treaties in the aftermath of World War I witnessed major movements of populations. These were pacific forms of what is today dubbed 'ethnic cleansing'. Of all the outcomes of that war in south-east Europe, the most important was probably the creation in 1921 of Yugoslavia. In the eyes of Serbs, although they only accounted for one-third of the population and occupied half the territory, this new state was Serbia writ large. Their claim rested on their early challenge to Turkey: a national uprising in 1804 won them autonomy under a hereditary Serbian prince. By the beginning of the twentieth century, geography placed Serbia at the interface between the Austro-Hungarian and Ottoman empires. At the same time, its nationalist ambitions focused on expanding its borders at the expense of any other group living on lands regarded as Serbian.

The boundaries set by the Treaty of Versailles were not universally acceptable. The outcome was a number of plebiscites and more conflicts. In 1920 all but two of Europe's 28 states could be described as democracies, and yet by the end of 1939, 16 of these had succumbed to dictatorships. In fact, between 1922 and 1942 the rise of fascism and other authoritarian, including monarchical, regimes forced the disappearance of the institutions of liberal democracy from almost all European states.

During the nineteenth century, Central Europe began a slow process of urbanization, and with it came the emergence of commercial and professional classes oriented towards a political and economic liberalism underpinned by a romantic form of nationalism. The slow rise of these classes to greater prominence paralleled the decline of the dominant landowning upper class, which accompanied the collapse of Austria-Hungary into Czechoslovakia, Hungary, Poland and Romania.

All the countries in the region were predominantly agrarian. In the early 1920s, peasants predominated in Bulgaria (80 per cent), Romania (78 per cent), Yugoslavia (75 per cent), Poland (63 per cent) and Hungary (55 per cent). Industrial development was in its initial stages and dependent on foreign capital. During the inter-war period foreigners owned 60 per cent of the capital in Poland and 50 per cent in Hungary. In the Balkans 50–70 per cent of the economy was foreign financed (Swain and Swain, 1993: 2). This made them prone to over-indebtedness, a pitfall which reappeared in the decades after World War II.

Urbanization and industrial development were sluggish in the 1920s and stagnant in the 1930s. In Romania, for instance, in 1912 only Bucharest had a population of over 100,000. Most of the country's urban inhabitants (16 per cent of the total) lived in settlements of under 20,000 people. Urbanization proceeded slowly, reaching just 21 per cent in 1948. Investment by indigenous and foreign capital throughout the region was attracted to the capital cities (Budapest, Warsaw, Sofia, Bucharest and Ploesti) and larger agglomerations.

At first the economies did make some progress, but they were then struck down by the Depression. Their under-capitalized agricultures suffered from the slump in world prices and their entry into the markets of the prosperous European states was frequently blocked. The promises made in 1919 to implement land reform never materialized, except in Czechoslovakia. Elsewhere right-wing dictatorships effected counter-revolutions and a *volte face* on the question of reform. The gold standard, which had 'managed' economic relations and sustained free trade within a system of essentially stable exchange rates, collapsed in the inter-war period. The economic vulnerability of the new sovereign states exposed their inability to defend their independence.

They responded to these economic circumstances by raising the levels of mutual distrust and by introducing regimes which were increasingly dictatorial or inept and impotent. Under threat, economically and 'psychologically', many of them resorted to the grace provided by 'the past' – a golden history to which governments paralysed by incompetence could turn. In doing so, the history which they wrote for themselves was transformed from being an academic subject into an instrument of populist and chauvinistic mobilization. In this the nationalists predated, in an attenuated form, the single element in the theory of totalitarianism that was wholly effective – the 'total' manufacture, manipulation and distortion of 'truth'. The same thing happened following the 'conversion' to communism in the 1940s and is repeating itself in the aftermath of its retreat.

THE ADOPTION OF THE SOVIET-TYPE ECONOMIC MODEL

A number of European states experienced severe destruction, population loss and political upheaval as a consequence of World War II. One outcome of the defeat of fascism was the impetus which it gave to working-class demands for greater democracy and for society to be rebuilt on a more egalitarian basis. People's lives should no longer be left to the 'anarchy' of the market. The state would in future intervene to control the 'commanding heights' of industry and to decide on investment policies.

The countries of East-Central Europe followed a trajectory similar to that of Russia and for similar reasons. Unlike Soviet Russia, which was able quickly to undo the ignominy of the Brest-Litovsk Treaty forced upon it in 1918, these countries were the passive recipients of the Treaty of Yalta, which for 45 years divided Europe into 'Western' and 'Soviet' zones of influence. By 1949 the seven countries were 'socialist' republics (describing themselves tautologically as 'people's democracies'). With the exception of Yugoslavia, which managed to break away from the Soviet yoke to become a member of the non-aligned nations, all had administrative-command economies whose key features were economic and political monopolies supported by a repressive state and a potent 'ideological state apparatus'.

The governments of the new republics were faced with rebuilding war-devastated economies which, even prior to the war, had – with the exception of eastern Germany (from 1949 to 1990, the German Democratic Republic) and the Czech lands – weakly developed industrial bases. Their pre-war social structures had persistent feudal features such as a politically powerful landed aristocracy, a large and impoverished peasantry, and a weak indigenous capitalist class. This similarity with pre-revolutionary Russia suggests that the Soviet model might have been historically appropriate for their economic transformation. In the event they adopted the political economy of Marxism, thus setting the region apart from most of its Western neighbours, which had opted for a Keynesian economic solution.

Both Keynes and Marx regarded unemployment as a feature of capitalist societies. State intervention, albeit under altogether different conditions, was posited as the solution to this problem. Their theories became orthodoxies which marched in time in the post-war period. However, the manner in which their goals of full employment and low inflation were to be achieved differed. Whereas the mixed economy was adopted by the Keynesian variant, in the East it was a wholly state-directed economy.

The administrative-command economy that was in existence from the late 1920s (in the USSR) to the early 1990s (in the USSR and Eastern Europe) operated according to its own logic and was in many ways consistent in itself. It was based on a central planning system in which financial institutions played a very secondary role. The model adopted in the Soviet Union and then later imposed in Eastern Europe characteristically had the following elements:

- industrialization and urbanization were to be based on state ownership of the means of production and the centrally planned determination of the use and allocation of resources;
- priority was given to investment and heavy industry;
- economic planning took precedence over physical (spatial) planning;
- investment-production plans and locational choices were to be based not on market or profit criteria but on planners' preferences, which took into consideration local, regional and national needs;
- land was to be nationalized; however, the systems of agriculture have varied between countries, with each state evolving its own combination of private, collective and state farming;

- the governments maintained monopoly control over foreign trade;
- the state provided cheap, highly subsidized public welfare goods and services, including food;
- light industry, consumer good production and the service sector were neglected.

The system had three other important features. First, it had a low level of inflation: in the Soviet Union, for example, during the period 1960–80 it stood at 0.14 per cent according to official data, and even Western estimates placed it below 1 per cent annually (Aage, 1989: 5). Second, there was no unemployment. Third, it was characterized by high female participation rates in the formal economy. This and other factors resulted in very low population growth rates. (In 1988, the population growth rates in percentages were: Bulgaria: 0.1; Czechoslovakia: 0.2; GDR: −0.2; Hungary: −0.1; Poland: 0.8; Romania: 0.4; Russia: 0.7.) These positive qualities of the system have been lost or abandoned, and today it stands roundly condemned. The spectre of which Marx wrote in the *Communist Manifesto* – 'A spectre is haunting Europe – the spectre of Communism. All the Powers of old Europe have entered into a holy alliance to exorcise this spectre' – did come to haunt Europe (and 'threaten' the world) and has had to be exorcised. The fact that the centrally planned economy challenged hegemonic liberalism required that all the principles for which it stood have been submerged in a torrent of bombastic criticism.

FROM REFORM TO REJECTION OF THE ADMINISTRATIVE-COMMAND ECONOMY

After a brief experiment with moderate economic reform between 1965 and 1968, the USSR turned its back on the idea.[3] Elsewhere in the region, in order to deal with the general crisis of the economic system, Hungary in the 1960s and Czechoslovakia in the 1970s experimented with replacing the command-administrative economy by a 'regulated market'. The introduction in 1968 of a 'new economic mechanism', and with it a much more liberal economy, distinguished Hungary from all the other East European countries. But even here state ownership remained untouched. Furthermore, although much was said about exporting to the West, Hungary maintained strong economic ties with the other East European countries because it was more profitable to sell on the markets of members of the Council for Mutual Economic Assistance (Comecon or CMEA). (This organization had been set up in 1949 in Moscow to facilitate trade between the USSR and East European countries.) In some instances, governments flirted with co-operatives, another form of social ownership. But, overall, fear, an anathematizing prohibition of the concept of private property, and, in the case of Czechoslovakia, direct military intervention by the Warsaw Pact (the Soviet Union) prevented not just the emergence of a market-oriented society, but also that of any non-state form of ownership (Chavance, 1994).

The Brezhnev years (1964–82) saw a decline in the rate of economic growth in the Soviet Union. By the end of the 1970s the economy was stagnating. As elsewhere in the region – for example, in Poland, the GDR and Czechoslovakia – economic growth was achieved, but at a very high ecological price. The rising living standards of the 1970s, which in the USSR were paid for by its export of oil, gas and other raw materials, brought both social and political stability. At the same time the leaderships in all the countries became totally cynical and corrupt, and the conviction about the ultimate goals of the system, which still existed in Khrushchev's regnum (1953–64), had all but vanished. It was into this moral void that Andropov came for a short time (November 1982–February 1984) to try to reinstall order and firmer government, which he did by dismissing some of Brezhnev's most dishonest and degenerate associates. His heir apparent, Mikhail Gorbachev, had to await the death of another septuagenarian, Chernenko, before becoming the General Secretary of the Communist Party of the Soviet Union (CPSU) in 1985. The defects in the administrative-planned economy, themselves part of a broader systemic crisis, had become ever more evident and urgently in need of change.

First, Soviet Marxist systems lacked the Schumpeterian advantage of capitalism, namely its ability to stimulate innovation through the competitive drive for profit. Although incentive systems did exist, the nature of Soviet-type economies meant that initiative was rarely rewarded. The outcome of the stultifying effect of bureaucratic inertia was declining growth rates, low productivity and misallocation of resources.

Second, neither the Soviet Union nor the larger economic bloc of Comecon (dissolved in June 1991, two days before the dissolution of the Warsaw Pact on 1 July) could insulate the socialist countries from the global economy and prevent the undermining of the Soviet Union's autarkic premise of economic development. The mass media, international travel and telecommunications ensured that the populations on the socialist campsite were aware that disparities in the standards of living between themselves and their Western neighbours were growing rather than declining. Moreover, people were now better educated and better informed than they were in the 1930s; their awareness of their social status and rights was also incomparably greater (Zaslavskaya, 1983; Yanowitch, 1989: 162).

Third, its declining growth rates meant that it could no longer run in the arms race and thus had to surrender its position on the pedestal preserved for superpowers. Essentially, the Soviet Union's commitments were too great for its economic capacity. This was because, as Zaslavskaya described the situation in the Soviet Union in 1983: 'The structure of the national economy long ago crossed the threshold of complexity when it was still possible to regulate it effectively from one single centre.'

Finally, mismanagement of the economy was coupled with widespread corruption and misappropriation, a characteristic which continues to typify the majority (if not all) the republics of the FSU and to a lesser extent of Eastern Europe (W.A. Clark, 1993). The importance of this factor should not be underestimated.

During his first four years, Gorbachev showed considerable political skill and perspicacity in maintaining the political initiative of radical change. From spring 1989 until the attempted coup in August 1991 by his senior colleagues – the prime minister, chairman of the KGB, the minister of defence and the minister of internal affairs – and his eventual forced resignation in December 1991, he basically responded to vested structures and conjunctural events which were beyond his control.

In 1987–8 the Soviet Union caught a fever of reform which quickly spread to its satraps in Europe and later to its own colonial republics, where it was met as a mixed blessing by the local leadership. The first step was the Law on State Enterprise passed in June 1987, granting industrial enterprises freedom from administrative tutelage and allowing them to use their profits to pay higher wages and expand their capacity. A new catchphrase was frequently repeated: 'Where ownership is by the whole people, property is owned by no one and therefore no one has any responsibility for it. The consequence is misuse, mismanagement and neglect.' This was recognition that there could be forms of property ownership other than that by the state.

Gorbachev's choice of model for economic reform was initially dictated by his need to behave in an ideologically correct manner and to demonstrate that he was a good Leninist. This he did by rediscovering the 'co-operative' property form, which was the subject (and title) of the last pamphlet written by Lenin before his death in 1924. Lenin's aphorism that 'socialism is a society of civilized cooperators' was often cited. Co-operative property was doctrinally acceptable, since, in the canons of Marxism, only private property meant exploitation (see Marcuse, chapter 5 in this volume). In May 1988, after a wide-ranging national debate, the Law on Co-operatives was passed. Co-operatives were encouraged in manufacturing, services, construction and in housing. A 'third way' between capitalism and statist socialism had been placed on the historical agenda. It soon passed into legislative history, as co-operatives became the battleground chosen by the 'old guard' (communists) on which to stake their position and to defend the Soviet system and its empire.

By 1990 the crisis in the Soviet economy had deepened, with the ruble depreciating further and increased shortages and disruptions in regional, sectoral and inter-republican trade. In August 1990, Gorbachev co-operated with Yeltsin and, together with a group of market-oriented economists, devised the so-called 'Shatalin Plan', which involved rapid marketization, privatization and devolution of economic power to the republics. Under pressure from the Council of Ministers, the military-industrial complex and other political elites, the deadlines written into the Shatalin Plan were lost, and so was the political momentum. The 'winter of discontent', 1990–1, led Gorbachev to make significant concessions to conservatives – a tactic which possibly delayed a coup for 18 months.

Economies in turmoil

In 1986 Gorbachev made it clear to East European leaders that the Soviet Union would not rescue them from domestic crises. The following year he rejected the existence of a single 'correct' model for socialism and then went on to declare that each state had the right to decide its own path. He applauded Polish and Hungarian leaders for the reforms which they were introducing and gave cautious encouragement to the more conservative leaderships of Bulgaria, Czechoslovakia, the GDR and Romania to move along the same path towards reform. In October 1989, the bicentenary year of the French revolution, Gorbachev officially acknowledged that member states of the Warsaw Pact were free to leave the alliance.

The breaching of the Berlin Wall and the collapse and mutation of regimes throughout the region in 1989 saw the defeat of the old guard in most countries (or just their bashing and bruising in most of the countries comprising the CIS). It also saw the virtual termination of the 'third way'. German unification led the market-piper's march to privatization. In 1990 the German government created a trustee agency, Treuhandanstalt, to privatize the East German economy. By the last day of 1994, when the agency went out of existence, it had disposed of about 14,000 companies. The Treuhand 'became the symbol of the brute force of capitalism': between the date of unification and the end of 1994 production in the east fell by more than a half, with 2.5 million jobs lost in manufacturing industry (Eisenhammer, 1995: 7).

Legislation introduced in a number of countries on the privatization of former state assets has required the creation of mechanisms for the equitable disposal of the nation's assets among the population. The policy of issuing vouchers or coupons conferring ownership rights, though laudable in principle, is fraught with dangers and difficulties, which are too complex to discuss in the present context. Suffice it to say that in June 1991 the Czechoslovak government began an estimated $6-billion privatization programme, involving the sale of six entire industries (including building materials, chemicals, engineering and electrical equipment). The move to introduce a market-driven economy was at the time one of the boldest and most co-ordinated initiatives in Eastern Europe. The programme marked the second phase of the massive privatization plan, which began in 1990 with the sale to a Belgian company of a controlling stake in Sklo Union, the country's biggest glass maker.

Then, at the end of 1992, in the Russian Federation, the State Property Committee distributed vouchers to all Russians born before September 1992. By the end of June 1994, of the 148 million allocated, 136 million had been used, and 14,000 medium-sized and large enterprises (70 per cent of all industrial enterprises) had been privatized into the hands of about 600 investment funds. As a result of this policy 40 million Russians now own shares in privatized enterprises and over 70 per cent of the industrial labour force is employed in private firms (*Argumenty i fakti*, 1994; *Economist*, 1994a, 1994b).

This decision by the Russian president to embrace the market economy wholeheartedly, by liberalizing prices, privatizing state assets and removing barriers to economic transformation, has not arrested the continuing fall in national output, exports and consumption.

Many of the countries in the region, on the advice of or under pressure from international agencies, embarked upon a policy of shock therapy, which included withdrawal of state subsidies, privatization of state assets, opening their economies to foreign competition, introducing a legal framework to facilitate the establishment of a free enterprise economy, the establishment virtually *ab initio* of a financial and banking sector, and a general institutional reform concerning taxation, accounting rules, business contracts and property rights. It also required price liberalization, which, according to some, is a *sine qua non* if political and economic liberalism and a civil society are to be established (Gellner, 1994). In meeting this desideratum, as table 2.1 shows, inflation, the evil which neo-liberal economics was intended to solve, has emerged with a vengeance. Price inflation in Russia rose from an average of 5.7 per cent in 1981–5 to 10 per cent in 1990 (Lane, 1992: 49). Retail prices rose by 144 per cent in 1991, then escalated to 2,318 per cent in 1992 before falling to 841 per cent in 1993. In some other republics of the FSU the situation has been even worse. Then in June 1995 Russia reached a monthly rate of inflation of 6.7 per cent, thereby recording the highest rate in the CIS.

In May 1994 the Russian prime minister stressed that every member of the Russian government had to understand that a strong ruble 'is the indispensable condition for the revival of the Russian economy' (Chernomyrdin, 1994). Then, in a seven-week period between 1 September and 10 October 1994, the ruble fell 29 per cent against the US dollar; it fell a further 22 per cent on 11 October to rest at R3,926 to the dollar. For much of 1994 the money supply was expanding by 13 per cent each month. These disastrous statistics are causally related to the fact that imports currently supply almost one half of Russia's consumer demand (*Economist*, 1994d: 44). In the eyes of foreign advisors and reformers, rescue is at hand, if only governments are bold enough to grasp it – unemployment, that Keynesian evil which lurks behind the curtain awaiting its call to save them from the greater evil of inflation.

The high degree of economic integration meant that, when Moscow introduced a tight money policy in early 1992, the economies of the other republics were immediately affected. Little was gained by those that tried to protect themselves by leaving the ruble zone. Trade dependency created by the central planning system meant that production failures in one of the new states caused a breakdown in supplies and cutbacks in production in another (OMRI, 1995).

Too often the formidable task set by (and for) governments has caused fiascos and created a fertile ground for fraudsters who, as 'biznesmen', have come to form the nouveau riche. Overall, as table 2.1 again illustrates, the result has been an enormous drop in GNP, comparable to that of the 1930s, a decline in living standards, high inflation and rising unemployment.

In those countries which were the first to embrace reform and which had more developed economies – such as the Czech Republic, Hungary, Poland and Slovenia, where GNP was predicted to rise by around 3 per cent in 1994 and 1995 – the level of inflation remains high and unemployment continues to rise. At the same time Russia's economy will decline a further 9 per cent; this is, however, an im-

Table 2.1 Key economic indicators for Central and Eastern Europe, 1990–5

	Growth in GNP (%)				
	1990–2	1992	1993	1994 (est.)	1995 (est.)
Bulgaria	−23.0	−7.1	−4.0	0.0	0.0
Czech Republic	−23.5	−6.6	−0.3	2.0	5.0
Hungary	−18.3	−5.0	−1.0	1.0	2.0
Poland	−17.0	2.6	4.0	4.0	3.0
Romania	−19.3	−15.4	1.0	0.0	1.0
Russia	n/a	−19.0	−12.0	−10.0	−2.0
Slovak Republic	n/a	−7.0	−4.1	0.0	2.0

	Rate of inflation (%)			
	1992	1993	1994 (est.)	1995 (est.)
Bulgaria	80	64	75	40
Czech Republic	11	21	11	10
Hungary	23	22	19	17
Poland	43	37	30	25
Romania	210	295	170	80
Russia	1,500	900	450	150
Slovak Republic	10	23	16	15

	Unemployment (%)			
	1992	1993	1994 (est.)	1995 (est.)
Bulgaria	15.2	16.3	17.0	17.0
Czech Republic	2.6	3.5	5.0	7.0
Hungary	12.3	12.2	11.0	11.0
Poland	13.6	15.7	16.0	15.0
Romania	8.4	10.2	13.0	15.0
Russia	1.3	1.4	n/a	n/a
Slovak Republic	10.4	14.4	16.0	16.0

Source: OECD Economic Report (quoted in *Gazeta Wyborcza*, 2–3 July 1994: 21)

provement on the declines of 12 and 17 per cent in 1993 and 1992 (*Moscow Times*, 1994). But even where positive changes in economic growth are registered, attention still has to be paid to the ways in which these gains are distributed (see below).

Another of the great systemic problems of this period of transformation is the decline in state revenues as a result of declining production, bankrupt public organizations, large-scale tax evasion by individuals and enterprises, and the expansion of the illegal tax haven provided by the 'second' (hidden, black) economy. The scale of the latter is formidable and its association with organized crime ('mafia') is politically and economically destabilizing. It has been estimated that organized crime accounts for 40 per cent of Russia's GNP.

Summary

The new states and governments are now experiencing an economic defeat in peacetime similar to that experienced by Germany in the aftermath of its wartime defeats: large public deficits, partly brought on by the inability of governments to increase taxes, forcing them to seek external funding from the political and economic victors, much of which is predestined to flow into subterranean channels; a contraction in the domestic economy; and high manufacturing costs, relative to Western Europe. Since most of the new governments have adhered to the pressure of the International Monetary Fund, the World Bank and other international financial institutions to maintain a strict monetary policy and restrict the size of the state budgetary deficit, given the falling state revenues mentioned earlier, annual cuts in public spending are now the norm. There are, however, signs that governments are wavering in their commitment to implement the shock treatment being urged upon them. This reflects changing attitudes among electorates, large sections of which – sometimes majorities – are looking more carefully at the criticisms levelled at the old system and more cynically at the benefits which economic liberalism allegedly brings.

REINTEGRATION INTO THE GLOBAL MARKET

The situation in which real existing socialist societies found themselves was, according to one Western theory of the 1960s, part of the

social evolutionary process of industrial societies. Although seemingly very different, the two economic systems, socialist and capitalist,
were said to be converging (Tinbergen, 1961). In one formulation of
the convergence theory, each system was learning from experience
and trying to overcome some of its own weaknesses and, in doing so,
was beginning to become more and more like the other. While
Tinbergen and others, such as J.K. Galbraith, considered that convergence meant that each system was adopting features of the other,
there were other writers who predicted that convergence was a one-
way movement, by which Soviet-type societies would evolve in the
direction of liberal democracies. 'Technological imperatives' and
'evolutionary universals' were invoked to explain why the economic
and political structures of capitalism would eventually be adopted in
Eastern Europe.

However, neither the theory nor the reality of convergence was
new, for European societies have been experiencing a continuing convergence as they have been penetrated by and have absorbed
the globalizing values of a hegemonic capitalism. As Marx noted in
1848:

> The bourgeoisie, by the rapid improvement of all instruments of
> production, by the immensely facilitated means of communication,
> draws all, even the most barbarian nations into civilisation. The cheap
> prices of its commodities are the heavy artillery with which it batters
> down all Chinese Walls, with which it forces the barbarians' intensely
> obstinate hatred of foreigners to capitulate. It compels all nations, on
> pain of extinction, to adopt the bourgeois mode of production; it
> compels them to introduce what it calls civilisation into their
> midst . . . In one word, it creates a world after its own image. (*Marx,
> 1848/1962: 38*)[4]

Today, 'Berlin Wall' could legitimately be substituted for 'Chinese
Wall', the former having a very similar, but in some ways greater,
symbolic significance. By the late 1960s Western businesses and multinational companies were making holes in the Wall and beginning
to fulfil Marx's prediction in regard to the 'barbarian nations' of the
'east' – although Marx had never regarded Germany (or Europe) as
'the East'.

So, although the penetration of Western capital into the region is
not a new phenomenon, only since the end of the 1980s have Western investors begun more seriously to investigate the region's potential. Between January 1990 and December 1993, the most important
destinations for 'invested or committed' Western capital – figures for
actual investment are considerably lower – were the Czech Republic

($11.8 billion), eastern Germany ($11.6 billion), Poland ($10 billion) and Hungary ($9.7 billion). Slovakia received less than $1 billion, Romania $700 million, Bulgaria $420 million. The essential point is the preference shown by Western investors for Mitteleuropa. In the first quarter of 1994, Russia attracted only $180 million of foreign investment (*Central European Economic Review*, 1994; *Moscow Times*, 1994).

The United States regards its bases in the region as another entry point into the European Union (EU) market. In its purchase of the Hungarian lighting company Tungsram, not only did the multinational General Electric restructure operations and reduce the workforce by 10,000 people, it also 'immediately acquired 7 per cent of the West European market'. Following their example, 'other American firms are hoping to use the cheap labour in Eastern Europe to export to Western Europe' (Embassy of the USA, 1993). The United States is the largest investor in the region ($18 billion), followed by Germany ($13 billion), France ($8 billion), the UK and Italy ($7.5 billion) (data from the Eastern European Investment Magazine database, cited in *Central European Economic Review*, 1994: 6). (Clearly, if the EU is treated as a political entity, then it is investing more than twice as much as the USA in the region.) These investments, a very high proportion of which have been in the service sector, have helped a little to alleviate the problem faced by firms in East and Central Europe in the wake of the dramatic fall in the Soviet market for exports.

While Brussels has hesitated in lowering trade barriers, which would enable East European countries to increase their exports to the EU, bits and pieces of these economies and their societies are gradually being incorporated into the EU as they become internationalized by Western companies, which are either buying into privatized state enterprises as joint venture partners or purchasing them outright.

Overall, fewer Western firms have been satisfied than dissatisfied by their excursions into these countries. A number of the world's largest corporations and consultancies – law firms, chartered accountants and auditors – have decided to take a small (barely cost-covering and even loss-making) stake in one or more of them. In light of the justifiable caution shown by small and medium-sized companies faced with the risk of investing east of the Oder, governments and international agencies, such as the EU's PHARE and TACIS programmes,[5] the US AID and British Know How Fund, are providing substantial grants in the form of technical assistance.

The underlying philosophy of these projects is that a transfusion of the spirit of capitalism is required; and nowhere is that ethos more likely to be cultivated than in the sector of small and medium-sized enterprises. The setting up of business centres, incubators and business study courses on how to construct a 'business plan' – all with the aim of assisting small-scale entrepreneurs – has become adopted as policy by the EU, the World Bank, the European Bank for Reconstruction and Development (EBRD) and even the Conference on Security and Co-operation in Europe (CSCE). Small firms are seen as the engine of growth, so although providing loans to them is a high risk, they are viewed as having the potential to exert a greater impact on the economic fabric of society than large credits to a few major enterprises. The notion that the catalyst for transforming administrative-command economies into private entrepreneur-based economies should be small, private businesses has been elevated by the collective genius of Brussels into a subsidizable principle.

There is little doubt that the privatization of state assets alone will not resolve the economic crises, which are still critical, especially in the CIS, Bulgaria and Romania. The establishment of a material and ideological infrastructure to support a flourishing small-business sector which introduces the population to an entrepreneurial culture need not in itself be negative, as long as it is recognized that not everyone in the population has the ability to become an Abraham Darby. For those entrepreneurs who earn an average living or who exist on the margin of solvency and who have imbibed the small world of Samuel Smiles, it means a tentative incorporation into the tax- and lawyer-paying economy. The successful and marginal alike become bait and then sustenance for the pernicious 'insurance companies' of organized criminals.

The region's integration into a Greater European economy is a different matter from being politically integrated into the EU. Yet Article 237 of the Treaty of Rome clearly states that any European state may apply for membership of the EC (EU), for the whole idea behind the Treaty was 'to lay the foundation of an ever closer union among the populations of Europe'. In 1992 the population of the EC was 344 million, compared with 256 million in the USA and 125 million in Japan, 97 million in East-Central Europe (Bulgaria, Czechoslovakia, Hungary, Poland and Romania) and 147 million in Russia. (The other regional blocs in the FSU include the Baltic States of Estonia, Latvia and Lithuania (8 million); Central Asia and Kazakhstan (49 million); the Caucasus (16 million); and the Slav republics of Belarus and the Ukraine (62 million).)

Central to the notion of political integration are the related issues of citizenship, labour mobility and immigration. As far as the EU is concerned, further regulations are being introduced restricting the entry of would-be in-migrants from the Maghreb and from Eastern Europe and the FSU. Thus, donations of aid in the form of loans and the transfer of technical know-how are accompanied by stricter enforcements of visa controls and the application of stringent criteria before allowing individuals to qualify for political asylum. In 1992, over a quarter of a million people had been granted refugee status in Europe; in 1972, the figure was a mere 13,000 (Joly et al., 1993). A rigorous policy of repatriating illegal immigrants is being pursued. Such deportations and restrictions on visas and work permits are unlikely to be relaxed in the near future. (Symptomatic of the change was the law passed in Germany restricting the constitutional right of 'ethnic Germans' living in the CIS to exercise their right to migrate to Germany. In 1980, 6,954 ethnic Germans emigrated from the FSU. Emigration reached its nadir in 1985, when 460 left. It peaked at 195,576 in 1992.)

Despite the expense, the EU policy will attempt to strengthen the economies of regions of out-migration in order to halt the 'Drang nach Westen'. High unemployment – unemployment in the EU stood at 17 million in June 1993, was forecast to rise to 20 million by the end of 1994, and will account for 12 per cent of the labour force in 1995 – compels politicians for electoral and economic reasons strictly to control population flows from Eastern Europe (*Economist*, 1993: 19). The problems created for Germany by its reunification may be seen as a paradigm in microcosm of the outcome of admitting the countries of Eastern Europe and the CIS into the EU.

Allowing (or preventing) access to the EU's labour markets is linked to one of the most important long-term problems facing western governments, namely, the serious moral and actuarial issues concerning entitlements to the public benefits conferred by citizenship and the ability of treasuries to pay them. This profoundly pragmatic reason for excluding people from Eastern Europe from becoming members of the labour force in Western Europe (with some claims to public benefits) or becoming citizens of a 'Greater Europe' (with much fuller citizenship entitlements) is underpinned by an historical and cultural prejudice. For some people (scholars, politicians and diplomats), 'central and eastern Europe are, as they have been from time immemorial, profoundly different from western Europe, economically much inferior and politically attuned to a national sovereignty which is fast losing ground in the west' (Calvocoressi, 1991: 255). While this notion of the contrast between the Eastern and Western countries is contestable, it reflects a pessimism which concludes that the 'European Community will not become pan-European, since it is inconceivable that its stronger western members will allow it to be overrun by weaker newcomers' (ibid.). This pessimism apart, by 1994 a number of East European countries already had 'Association Agreements' with the EU and have now been accepted in principle for admission to it. In April 1994 Hungary and Poland applied for membership, which they hope to achieve before the year 2000.

POLITICAL CHANGE AND TERRITORIAL FRAGMENTATION

The defeat of European fascism also saw a number of essentially minor readjustments to the frontiers laid down in 1919. These included the reincorporation into Belorussia of its western territories, annexed by Poland following the Russo-Polish War of 1920, and the westward shift of the Polish frontier to the Rivers Oder and Neisse (the Oder–Neisse Line). This led to the resettlement of large numbers of ethnic Poles from the eastern territories and to their spontaneous migration from the central provinces to the western, former German territories, which had as its concomitant the resettlement of Germans onto a reduced territory.

The eastern border between Poland and the former Soviet Union is still not altogether stable. Belarus borders Poland, where an Orthodox Christian enclave is claiming 'ethnic' recognition. The Ukraine also borders on Poland, as well as on Romania, Slovakia and Hungary. Even if the frontiers remain stable, the minorities within them may heed a patriotic, nationalist call to migrate or demand that their national enclave be incorporated into the adjoining state. Non-Romanians comprise 12 per cent of the population in Romania, with Hungarians, Germans and Gypsies forming the largest minorities (8 per cent, 1.6 per cent and 1.1 per cent respectively).

By 1987 Gorbachev had acknowledged that the political system itself was in need of overhaul, and quickly discovered the extent to which the population considered the political system illegitimate. That sense of illegitimacy was doubly felt in the satellite states and in the republics of the Union whose peoples expressed disdain for their humiliating subordination to the Soviet Union. Thus Gorbachev inadvertently called into question the authority of the Communist Party not just in the Soviet Union but throughout Moscow's empire and zone of influence. At first the national leaders engaged in bouts of self-flagellation of varying degres of authenticity. They decided to reform themselves in order to make themselves more 'respectable' and acceptable to a mass electorate at the hustings. Some of these ruling parties even decided to change their names from 'Communist' to 'Social Democrat'. In turning their backs on Marx and the *Communist Manifesto*, they professed to rejoin the political trajectory of Marx's proper historical adversary, J.S. Mill.

In little over 12 months, the three Baltic states had achieved full independence. They now face the choice of joining East-Central Europe or Scandinavia, with which they have closer linguistic and cultural ties. And, while Moldova is anxious to rejoin Romania, there is a movement in Belarus for closer integration with Russia. Fears of ethnic conflict in the FSU, at least as bad as that occurring in Yugoslavia, are well founded. Moldova is in the midst of civil war, violent ethnic clashes have occurred in Uzbekistan and, in the Caucasus, Georgia is torn by civil strife. Armenia, which is Orthodox Christian, sees its interests as lying in alliances with nominally Christian republics to the north, in the hope that it will be defended against the Islamic republic of Azerbaijan, which has cultural and religious ties with Azeris in Turkey and Iran, and which in January 1990 launched a pogrom directed against Armenians living in Azerbaijan.

The outcome of these conflicts, most visibly in the FSU, Yugoslavia and, to a much lesser degree, the former Czechoslovakia has been a process of 'territorial disintegration'. Previous 'autonomous regions' within the Russian Federation, defined as such by their ethnic (national) composition, declare themselves to be sovereign states; for instance, the formation of Tatarstan, Chechnya and Yakutiya. Lower-level administrative structures are also engaged in the same sort of amoebic subdivision, with ethnically identifiable districts claiming independence from higher-level jurisdictions. Third, new national territorial entities are being formed; witness the demand for autonomy by Russian Germans, the reconstitution of the Cossacks as a 'nation', and the latter's claim to territories in North Kazakhstan and northern Chechnya among others. Fourth, integral administrative entities, such as the Ekaterinburg oblast (formerly Sverdlovsk, which had been Yeltsin's Party-fiefdom), have claimed autonomy from Moscow. (This is akin to a French *département* or English county or German *Land* demanding sovereign status.)

The fragmentation of states and administrative sub-divisions has been accompanied by the blurring of boundaries between the legislative and executive bodies at the regional and city levels, and between the different levels over the issue of who controls the budget and its allocation. The matter of financial allocations is made even more difficult by the fact that powerful enterprises in the majority of republics in the Russian Federation can, with or without the help and/or connivance of their ministerial superiors, continue to allocate funds for projects which it decides to support. In 1993, one-quarter of Russia's economic space was still operating under special economic and legally imposed conditions, following successful actions by local bodies forcing concessions from the central government in the form of taxes, export quotas and import licences (Kirkov, 1993).

The 'new political thinking' which Gorbachev introduced contained as its central terms 'perestroika' (reconstruction), 'glasnost' (openness), 'uskorenie' (acceleration) and 'democratisation' (Gorbachev, 1987). The idea of 'glasnost', which Gorbachev had been advocating as early as December 1984, came to occupy a central place in the emerging political discourse. After a relapse into censorship over the Chernobyl nuclear disaster in April 1986, by 1990 not only were Stalin and the Stalinist system subjected to ferocious denunciations but even Lenin and Gorbachev were being criticized in print.

The 19th Party Congress, held in summer 1988, approved a wide range of political reforms, the most important of which was the creation of a new legislature, the Congress of People's Deputies, which was to be elected through a competitive general election. The first one took place in March 1989 and proved to be a decisive point in the fate of the Soviet Union. It offered an opportunity for nationally minded candidates, especially in the Baltic republics, to be elected – which they were – and thus took a step towards the breakup of the USSR. Sensing weakness in the Kremlin, in 1990, Lithuania became the first Soviet republic to rebel against the centre and declare its independence from the Soviet Union. Estonia, Latvia and Azerbaijan also declared their sovereignty. But it was the decision in June 1990 by the Russian Republic to declare its sovereignty which, in placing the leadership of the Russian Soviet Federal Socialist Republic (RSFSR) on a collision course with the Union centre, posed the greatest threat to the future of the Soviet Union. The demands of Lithuanian nationalists had a similar effect to that of the Serbian student in 1914; they caused the glass of empire to shatter. Even so, the destruction of empires by an iconoclastic nationalism has probably caused more sorrow than happiness.

A referendum on the Union held in March 1991 (from which the Baltic States, Armenia, Moldova and Georgia abstained) found that 76 per cent of those who voted (in a turnout of 80 per cent) were for the continuation of the Union. But, following the attempted coup in August, a state which for 70 years had been known as the Union of Soviet Socialist Republics found itself in free fall. In October 1991, the leadership tried to retain the initials of the new political entity, by calling it the Union of Sovereign Socialist Republics. This did not last long, and by November the political space, composed of an already diminished number of constituent states, rebaptized itself the Union of Sovereign States (USS). A referendum on independence in the Ukraine on 1 December revealed 90 per cent now opting for independence.

Five days later, at a meeting in Brest, the presidents of Belarus, Russia and the Ukraine formed a Commonwealth of Independent States, declaring that the USSR was 'ceasing its existence as a subject of international law and geo-political reality'. A meeting held in Almaty, Kazakhstan, on 21 December increased the membership from the three Slav states to 11 – the other four of the former Soviet Union, Georgia and the Baltic States preferred to remain outside the Commonwealth. The prospects for this new arrangement, the CIS, do not seem particularly auspicious. (At a meeting with journalists in the White House, Washington, in June 1994, President Bill Clinton said that he could see no objection to the former Soviet Union reconstituting itself if all the member states were in accord and had a mandate from their electorates to do so.)

On 25 December 1991, Gorbachev signed a decree divesting himself of the presidency of the USSR and transferred his powers as commander-in-chief of the armed forces to Yeltsin. The following day the USSR Supreme Soviet abolished itself, announcing that 'the Soviet Union no longer exists'. On the date on which the USSR was officially proclaimed dead, 164 ethno-territorial conflicts were registered within the boundaries of the former Soviet Union (Kolossov, 1992: 3).

'Great events' in human history, such as the nailing up of the Papal bull excommunicating Martin Luther, the Russian Revolution in 1917, or the 'fall' of the Berlin Wall, are usually culminating acts of numerous, quite ordinary events. The turning point in Germany was not the triumphal marching of East Germans through the Wall at the formidable Brandenburg Gate. The challenge to state power was much more prosaic and occurred when Germans, staggering under the weight of their plastic bags, left their country through the back door and crossed into a friendly neighbour's garden. Neither the plans of politicians nor the analyses and predictions of intellectuals foresaw the spectacle that was enacted.

If the crowd in 1989 was, as the Parisian mob had been in 1789, the historical agent of change, it had to share the stage with the insistent pressure of representatives of a more effective economic system and with the Russian Hamlet, who, in initiating the restructuring of the

Soviet economy and political system, decided the question of whether the empire was to be or not to be.

Nevertheless, the communist parties (normally renamed) have remained powerful forces in many countries because of their well-established and experienced, nation-wide apparatuses and their facility to appropriate the language of reform and, to some degree, its policies. The success of the strategy may be judged from the electoral fortunes of former communist parties in Lithuania, Poland (where in September 1993 they gained over two-thirds of the seats in the parliament), Bulgaria, Hungary and the Ukraine. The people's choice may in some cases turn out to be those parties that uphold stability ('stagnation' to others) as a valued goal and that offer evolution instead of world-up-turning radicalism.

Gorbachev was the architect of the demolition of the empire which he had set out merely to restructure. In declaring 'openness', Gorbachev provoked, like Martin Luther, the Protestants within to come out of their Catholic communist closet. Many old-style bargainers, match-makers and pushers (*tolkachi*) have merged with a form of Hyde Park democracy; that is, a democracy consisting of a myriad soap-box speakers, unorganized and unpractised in orderly, adversarial debate. The pivotal image derives from Hieronimus Bosch: the essentially fragile shell of authoritarianism when broken lets loose millions of anarchic souls. In Russia itself and in some of the former republics, Mikhail Bakunin, the nineteenth-century Russian founder of modern anarchism, rides triumphant, visible in the indiscipline found in all aspects of daily life. Presidential decrees are annulled by parliament (if not by the president himself within days of their promulgation), and even the concept, let alone the reality, of the rule of law lies moribund. The euphoria which accompanied the collapsing pack of Communist Party cards across the region has now turned in many places into disillusionment and resentment. Some Western observers see the choice facing Russia as being between a new despotism, which would mean the reintroduction of heavy-handed censorship, and anarchy.

Central to George Simmel's essay 'The metropolis and mental life' (1964) was the psychological need by individuals in the metropolis to be 'recognized' or 'seen'. This they achieved through striking the most dramatic and extravagant poses, through making gestures and through self-display in order to make an immediate impact on others. The same is now true of territorial groups that see themselves as constituting 'unique' communities, with their own histories, traditions and folklore expressed in language and dialect. Populist leaders use people's dreams, create others and meld them into a collective 'imagined community'. Today, as before 1914, sections of the intelligentsia, for a variety of quite subjective reasons including anger at the lack of esteem and privilege accorded to them by the earlier 'workers' states, prefer to focus on the ardent notion of national identity rather than on the practical concerns of citizenship.

Forecasts of imminent civil disorder following price liberalization and the rapid deterioration in the economy have repeatedly failed to materialize. Yet, while pent-up anger and dire poverty have not provoked revolt and insurrection, these feelings are being expressed in an upsurge in crime and lawlessness, which at times gives a flavour of organized chaos. The shift towards a market economy has been accompanied by a quantum leap in the number of 'economic crimes'. Since these are the norm rather than the exception, the death penalty, which in the 1970s was reintroduced into Russia for the theft of state property, has again been repealed.

Overall, a naive acceptance of the 'immutability of the iron laws of political economy' (price liberalization, unemployment, privatization) has created a blindspot to understanding the support that exists for anti-capitalist sentiments and movements. It is difficult to assess how widespread and how deep is the commitment to the idea of individual freedom. But in the CIS, Bulgaria and Romania, for instance, attention should be paid to cautions expressed by reform-oriented academics to the effect that 'we still do not know whether our society is capable of developing into a liberal capitalist economy' (Zaslavskaya, 1993). The crises of structure to which these societies are vulnerable manifest themselves in the immanent conflicts between fluid social groups which are only slowly crystallizing into classes. In these conditions, the search for a set of symbols or beliefs capable of integrating the whole society continues. To date, in the majority of countries, these beliefs are nationalistic, egalitarian or populist (Gulbinsky, 1992: 14).

Summary

The Soviet Union in its final throes sought to transform itself from being an entity held together by a constitution to a loose federative structure bound by treaties. Many parts of this disintegrating whole have come to face the prospect of their own division. The same is true of the new states in East and Central Europe. Shifting boundaries and populations are accompanied by debates and conflicts over decentralization of government and decision making; revenue raising and budgetary control; new forms of spatial and resource management; and, at the national levels, the creation of new currencies, the issuing of passports (and visas for entrants), the hoisting of flags and the striking of medals.

The dual polarization, reflected in the revolt of the masses against the established order and the conflict between society and state which occurred in the decade leading up to the revolutions of 1917, began to repeat itself as the countries of East and Central Europe and the USSR moved from the 1980s into the 1990s. As Seton-Watson once pointed out, societies moving artificially into capitalism are held together by the bureaucracy: '[i]t holds the power, the privileges and the means of repression . . . It is outwardly impressive. It weighs heavily on the backs of people . . . But like cast iron . . . a strong blow can shatter it to pieces. When it is destroyed there is anarchy' (Seton-Watson, 1967). This accurate depiction of the transition from bureaucratic socialism to capitalism is unwelcomely perceived by Western investors.

CLASS RESTRUCTURING IN POST-COMMUNIST SOCIETIES

The economic realities facing the governments and people of these countries are stark and harsh. They recite the catechism of liberalism: competition and higher productivity through the closure of inefficient factories and cuts in government expenditure. This implies the reduction or removal of subsidies to manufacturers, allowing them to go bankrupt if necessary (Mizsei, 1993), and a decrease in the number of state employees, including those working in the social services, health care and education.

Subsidies are to be targeted on low-income and vulnerable groups. At the same time, a remedy for industrial stagnation and contraction is being sought in the creation of a middle class, also apocalyptically referred to as 'the saviour of a national bourgeoisie'. Members of higher-income and well-qualified groups have to be pushed (by the removal of subsidies) and pulled (by the lure of higher earnings) to become entrepreneurs or to move as employees into the private sector (Patterson, 1993). The middle class in waiting is drawn from three principal sources: the present managers of state firms; those who amassed considerable (illegal) fortunes in the second economy; and new, small-scale entrepreneurs. Wide sections of the population resent the fact that the first two categories are the visible beneficiaries of the shift towards capitalism. The economic and budgetary crises in most countries derive in part from their attempts to raise revenue from taxation to meet the needs of a rapidly growing impoverished population.

In Poland, for example, according to World Bank criteria, those earning less than the country's lowest retirement pension ($86) are categorized as living in poverty. In 1993–4, 5.5 million people (14.4 per cent of the population) found themselves in this situation. Yet only one-third of those falling beneath the poverty line are unemployed; 60 per cent of families are in low-income jobs. Over one-third of the unemployed population in Poland are under 24 and two-thirds are under 35 years of age ('Transforming . . .', 1994; Jung, 1994).

From the beginning of 'perestroika', reformers were confronted with widespread hostility, some of it rooted in tradition and reinforced by the dominant Marxist ideology: an egalitarian value system and the belief that property is theft; the strong attachment to job security promised by the state; social justice and equity as against large income differentials; and remuneration by contribution not by outcome.

Yet Soviet Marxist ideology never shrank from invoking Marx's *Critique of the Gotha Programme* and Lenin's announcement that, in the setting of wage rates for workers of different skills, 'all thought of egalitarianism should be rejected'. Stalin was firmly against wage levelling. The fact that these were (more than merely nominal) workers' states meant that workers in the heavy-industry sector were especially favoured. Wages policy was a brutally obvious instrument of political mobilization. Thus, in general, the average wages of the blue-collar working class were much higher than for white-collar workers.

Remuneration was equally a tool in the hands of Gorbachev, hence his strategy to raise the relative wage levels of white-collar workers, including doctors and teachers, and to increase wage differentials generally, which was to compensate for the decision to liberalize prices. Stable prices have disappeared, and with them the notion of equality as a cherished objective of social policy.

The social base of reform has been objectively made up of four main social groups. Gorbachev and then other leaders sought first to cultivate an embryonic middle class by legalizing non-state economic activity, which initially meant encouraging co-operatives. Second, they set out to court the intelligentsia, who were eager to usurp the privileges of the philistine nomenklatura. Third, in order to succeed, reforms have to rely on gaining the support of the 'progressive' manual working class, the most highly skilled of which were strong proponents of change.

Fourth, they wanted to foster (if not create from scratch) an independent peasantry, by introducing laws on property and on land, which could lead to the emergence of a vigorous agricultural interest (Van Atta, 1993). Land and urban real estate constitute a visible and lucrative locus for, on the one hand, large and long-term capitalist accumulation and, on the other, simple, short-term profit to be consumed. The idea of privatizing *agricultural* land has frequently proved difficult to get accepted, and especially so where a strong, independent peasantry has not existed for a long time (as in Russia), or has never existed because the land was in the hands of a small number of landlords (see Marcuse, chapter 5 in this volume).

The restructuring of society along its different dimensions, including the mindsets of its population, is part of an interplay between different group interests. If large sections of the population in the United Kingdom continue to preserve their pre-Thatcherite attitudes, it is prudent to inquire how much more likely it is that large sections of the population in the region, who will not be beneficiaries of the greater income differentiation and the institutionalization of private property, will wish to preserve the collectivist values of the pre-reform period. In fact, a public opinion poll undertaken by the Russian Academy of Sciences found that support among Russians for reform had fallen from 40 per cent in 1988 to 25 per cent at the end of 1993. A majority considered that privatization had been undertaken for the benefit of the nomenklatura and criminals (Lloyd, 1994).

A not untypical reaction to the privatization process and economic reform was that expressed at a meeting held in an instrument-making factory in the (Russia–Kazakhstan) border city of Ural'sk: '[u]nder cover of the slogan of privatization for the people and the creation of millions of owners, in fact there is the nomenklatura-corrupt variant of privatization' (*ABV*, 1994).

Although rich people existed under state socialism, they did not earn very high incomes. Officially, there were no private wealth holders. Unearned incomes from property were limited to rental charges on one or part of a single residence. Unofficially, wealth was beginning to be accumulated. Although it was generally known in the West that extremely privileged groups did exist, it is only since perestroika that the scale and nature of their elite lifestyles has begun to be properly documented (Vaksberg, 1991).

Specialists on income distribution under socialism have tended to hold one of two very different views. On the one hand, the distribution of income is seen to be significantly less unequal and earnings differentials smaller than in comparable market economies (Vinokur and Ofer, 1987). According to the other school of thought, inequality in East and Central Europe and the Soviet Union was no less than under capitalism (Atkinson and Micklewright, 1992). Certainly large numbers of people were poor. But whether a distinctive underclass was in the process of formation *prior* to the onset of 'the transition' remains to be determined. Between a small privileged elite and a large stratum of poor people wallows the mass of the population.

A principal aim of the transfer to a market economy is to increase the standard of living in the region. Rises in average income levels will serve as the success indicator. It has always been assumed that privatization and other macro-economic adjustments would benefit some people more than others. However, the distributional aspects of restructuring were a secondary consideration, although one influential report did note that the transfer to a market economy 'will impose substantial hardship on many groups of the population during the transition' (IMF et al., 1991: 331). More often, the socialist goal of economic justice has been dismissed as tantamount to being arrant and infantile nonsense – a view that is only moderated by admonitions on the need for policies to 'cushion the less well-off from excessive burdens' by establishing safety nets and social guarantees. Wide-scale tax evasion and, consequently, falling government revenues – in Russia down from one-third of GDP in the first quarter of 1993 to one-fifth for the same period in 1994 – ensures that this well-meaning goal will not be achieved. The diluted influence of ministries and departments concerned with social protection has meant temporarily unfilled government portfolios in this sector.

Criticism of perestroika and the very idea that there could be Soviet millionaires emerged early on in the reform process, even among reformers (Rogovin, 1986). Yet, by 1990 a club for 'young millionaires' had been established in Moscow. By 1994 the capital boasted 58 casinos. At the same time, homelessness had a firm place on the public agenda. Refuges for homeless children just opened in the southern Russian city of Novorossiisk are the first since the Civil War (*Komsomol'skaya Pravda*, 1994). Although capitalism seems to be the most effective way of organizing the production of wealth, it cannot profess a keen interest in its distribution.

Class restructuring in post-communist societies is a complex process which is propelled by forces within each individual country. The extent to which Western states and supra-national agencies (the World Bank, EU) influence policy development and structures depends upon each country's history, geographical location, population size and economic profile and potential. In view of the focus of this book and the limited space in which the subject of class can be examined, it seems fitting to highlight class structuration around real estate.

REAL ESTATE AS A SOURCE OF CONFLICT
AND ACCUMULATION

The privatization of public assets and the creation *ab initio* of a banking and financial sector in these countries is creating two main wealth-owning classes: those who are actively involved in new wealth generation, and those who have, essentially, 'inherited' their wealth as a result of their position – for instance, because they were managers of state property or held political appointments and consequently had access to information and contacts. Such people might choose to step back from day-to-day management and become rentiers, thereby separating ownership from control, as discussed decades ago in the literature on the 'managerial revolution' (Berle and Means, 1932; Burnham, 1941). Although competition and animosity between the two groups tends to be quelled in the interest of mutual survival, feuding does occur. The emergence of this rentier class, members of which are sending their progeny to private schools in the UK, constitutes an important feature of the new class structuration. An equally significant development in this regard is the appearance of a petite bourgeoisie and a rentier class dependent on landed property. While the boundaries between the two types of 'rentier', dependent on the origin of their investment, are frequently blurred as individuals shift to and fro across them, they represent conceptually distinctive groupings.

Residential and non-residential buildings, together with land, are now in the process of being transferred into private ownership. The owners (and controllers) of land, housing, offices – in a word, land-lords as a class – are set to play a key role in the transformation of these societies and in the capital accumulation process. For this reason both the larger rentiers (who will also soon be earning a dividend from the privatization of former state property) and the small landlords and petit bourgeois shopkeepers are likely to enter into the political arena as an identifiable interest grouping. The manner in which they use their rents and earnings will influence the behaviour of national and foreign companies trading and investing in the region.

The policy of privatizing accommodation and encouraging private construction allows individuals to capitalize on their valuable asset. While some use the capital value of their property as collateral in business ventures, others see the immediate advantage to be gained from leasing. The growth of a small petit bourgeois landlord class, engaging in hedonistic consumerism, is accompanied by the emergence of a grand rentier class which is both politically and economically aggrandizing. Small-scale landlordism is acting as a modest stimulus to the embryonic private building sector. Some landlords are using their income to acquire larger properties, which they also let. The use, in some cases, of residential property as collateral for loans for commercial ventures (such as the importation of foreign commodities for sale) is hazardous and can literally be life-threatening where loans borrowed at high interest rates cannot be repaid.

In January 1993, the Russian parliament enacted a law transferring state housing to tenants free of charge, irrespective of its size and level of comfort. The privileged (for whatever reason), who enjoyed a use value of better-quality accommodation for a very minor charge, now benefit from the full fruits of its exchange value. But this gift to the better off was in part necessitated by the resistance which large numbers of people were expressing towards the idea of having to pay *anything* for the state property in which they were living and which the state wanted to privatize. However, this was not the case throughout the region (see Struyk, chapter 6 in this volume).

As soon as housing was converted into a commodity and became the subject of legal commercial transactions, its real market value rose to dizzy heights. The almost inevitable consequence was that this sphere of economic activity became an object of criminal interest. There is accumulating evidence, especially in the former Soviet Union, of housing transactions in which the vendors receive nothing at all, lose their apartments, and thereby swell the ranks of the homeless, or turn up as 'unidentified bodies'. According to data from the capital's directorate for criminal investigation, 115 owners of privatized flats in Moscow are currently listed as missing. In 1993, 17 murders in Moscow were found to be connected with property deals; for the first half of 1994, this number was 50. According to information from the police department, at least 500 people were made homeless between January and July 1994 as a result of housing fraud or criminal activity. (A useful research study could be conducted to examine the factors affecting the rate of crime and corruption associated with residential property in different countries.)

Changes in legislation and constitutional amendments on the ownership of urban (residential) land have been partly driven by the need for the law and constitution to catch up with and legalize reality. Confusion and conflict at the highest levels of government – especially in the FSU but also in other countries – have been almost an irrelevance, or at best an impediment, to processes on the ground.

Laws passed by the central state carry less weight and are even coun-
termanded by 'orders' (*prikaz*) emanating from local political chiefs
and by prevaricating local officials. Inattention to the law at the top
is matched by lawless behaviour at the bottom. So, for instance, even
before market transactions in land and real estate were legalized, one
Moscow 'estate agent' finalized the exchange of a private house with
a garden outside the capital's ring road for a flat in the city itself.
Although the house was worthless, because of its dilapidated condition, the fact that a house existed meant that there was no problem
in selling the plot (Orbant and Sinochkin, 1992). The desirability of
a site and the price paid for it reflect its location. Some residential
districts, because of lower levels of air and noise pollution, have
always been preferred to others (Derbinova et al., 1983).

In autumn 1992, when private house prices were only just beginning to rise, real-estate agents and property speculators rushed to
buy privately owned accommodation coming onto the market
(*Kommersant*, 1992). In the central districts of Prague and Budapest
the process began earlier. Hyperinflation in Russia and other republics in the CIS, high inflation elsewhere, and falling production
and exchange rates have combined to create a flight into property.
Besides its being a hedge against inflation, investment advisors
recommend commercial firms to purchase cheaper flats in less desirable (non-metropolitan) locations as a way of offsetting tax on
profits. So, while at the beginning of 1992 it was somewhat novel
to read articles entitled 'Businessmen prefer to invest their money
in real estate', by late 1993 the real-estate market was a flourishing business, and in 1994 construction was declared to be one
of the most profitable spheres of business activity in Moscow
(Tolokonnikov et al., 1994).

Legalized market transactions in property and land have necessitated the creation of an institutional infrastructure to bring order
into property dealings. Laws on mortgaging, designed to create the
legal parameters within which the private housing sector can be
financed, have passed the drafting stage in a number of countries.
Into the emerging coterie of inexperienced, indigenous estate agents
and building and property developers have come the experienced,
for instance, the (British) Royal Institute of Chartered Surveyors
(RICS). The preamble to the report on a seminar, co-organized by
the RICS and the Petersburg Committee for Property Management,
noted that 'despite political instability and legal muddle, real estate is
the most inflation-proof commodity and begins to acquire an attractiveness for both foreign and native investors'.

Governments are aware of the effect of these new changes on

lower-income groups. In most cases, subsistence minima have been defined so that poor families will be able to claim housing benefits. The widely advertised subsidies evoke bitter smiles at their size and provoke the question of whether the new benefits will be anything more than symbolic.

Land reform and its return to private ownership is, not unexpectedly, an important source of interest-group conflict. By mid-1994 the Russian Land Code had passed through the Cabinet committees and, despite continuing 'routine internecine disputes between ministries', the document was placed before parliament (Duma). The greatest impediment to the edict, which was issued by the Russian president in 1993, allowing entitled Russian citizens to be allocated a parcel of land, are the 'very large feudal latifundists who, in the Soviet form of omnipotent bureaucrats [*chinovniki*], are trying to use the privatization process to capitalize into their own hands the most valuable and income-generating commodity of all – land' (Savvateeva, 1994) (see Marcuse, chapter 5 in this volume).

For an increasing number of people who have acquired private property rights more or less legally, the route to wealth is to become a player at the real-estate roulette wheel. They comprise an important faction in the present robber-baron phase of societal transformation and could play a crucial role in the accumulation of capital. Those who stay the course and are successful will form the core of a rentier class. A proportion of their number will become founding members of an industrial bourgeoisie, and there are already hints of their impact on urban space and regional development.

URBAN SPACE

As recently as the early 1980s, writers were still claiming that the urban crisis under capitalism 'only aggravates the class contradictions which are manifested in the socio-spatial stratification of cities, the formation of ghettos and the creation of suburbs as residential areas for the privileged classes'. They prophesied doom for all attempts by Western governments to regulate, through new-town and model-city projects, the 'cancerous effects of agglomerations because of private enterprise and private property'. In socialist societies, by contrast, cities 'develop on the basis of the public ownership of the means of production within a planned economy which makes it possible to find rational solutions to the economic, social, demographic, ecological, spatial and other problems of urban development'. To this catalogue of success stories was added the successful solution of the housing problem. Hence 'a wholly new type of urbanization is developing in socialist society which is similar to urbanization in capitalist societies purely in certain external effects' (Kutsev, 1982: 11–15) (see the Smith, chapter 3; Haussermann, chapter 7; Enyedi, chapter 4; all in this volume).

Such tracts contained irritating truths; for example, that the external appearance of urbanization was similar in capitalist and socialist societies: the concentration of the population in large cities which were not overgrown villages but the epitome of assembly-line modernity created by the ubiquitous use of steel, concrete and cement. On the other hand, there was much to distinguish socialist and capitalist cities in their content. Today, the adoption of market relations is changing the content of the brick-and-mortar form of cities. This refers not only to proliferating criminality – for crime rates against the person and property have exploded. The social worlds within the pyramids of factories, offices and institutions are being transformed wholesale.

Under Soviet Marxism, responsibility for the principal decisions on education, health, housing and recreation were assumed not by individuals or families but by paternalistic state employers. Enterprises were required, in most cases by law, to allocate a percentage of their wage fund or profits to a social fund. Enterprise activity was guided by a social as well as an economic rationality.

The 'community', therefore, was more associated with where people worked than with where they lived. It almost seemed as if the designers of social policy were as much influenced by the writings of Durkheim, especially his book *The division of labour in society*, as by Marx. The reconstitution of 'occupational associations' was Durkheim's prescription for 'moral regeneration'. For him, the occupational association was the only one 'which is close enough to the individual for him to be able to rely directly upon it' (Durkheim, 1921: 18). In East and Central Europe, people's lives revolved around the workplace, which met their cradle-to-grave needs. The company or organization lay as an intermediary between the individual and the state: '[a] nation can be maintained only if, between the state and the individual, there is intercalated a whole series of secondary groups near enough to individuals to attract them strongly in their sphere of action and drag them into the general torrent of social life. We have just shown how occupational groups are suited to fill this role' (Durkheim, 1893/1964: 28).

While the state was the distant 'father', the direct exerter of influence and direction was an avuncular employer. Now that nexus between caring employer and employee is being ruptured. Thus, the political and economic changes which are accompanying reform are leaving the population bereft not just of a paternalistic 'state' but also of 'extended family' support. Case studies reveal that the impact of enterprise restructuring on the local (residential) community, and specifically on its discharge of its social functions, depends on 'the social and institutional embeddedness of the enterprise in the local community' (E. Clark and Soulsby, 1994). Such a micro-sociology also shows, however, that the general trend is towards a disposal of recreational, sporting, training and health-care facilities and canteens by selling them off, franchising them to private contractors or donating them to the local authority.

The change in content and function applies equally to those squares and boulevards which catered for the 'mass spectacle'. The monumentalism of the space and the rituals conducted in them were designed to create feelings of security, permanence and pride among the people and their rulers. Today those spaces, such as Red Square in Moscow and Wencelas Square in Prague, become decorated with the truly ephemeral – the inflatable Disneyland castle and, once again, the trader's stall. The 'great men' who guided the destiny of their states from the top of plinths and mausolea overlooking the squares have been replaced by 'small men' feeding the population from their private kebab stands (see Häussermann, chapter 7; Szelenyi, chapter 10; both in this volume).

The literal and metaphorical demolition of the Berlin Wall has been accompanied by the transmogrification of social theory into business studies. Pieces of concrete are sold as souvenirs and the Wall becomes a 'text'. Budapest, Berlin, Warsaw, Vienna and Moscow become the destinations of pilgrims whose shrine is the market place. A neologism has been created to describe this new phenomenon: the 'shoptur'. In many cities, travel agents exist solely on their earnings from voyagers embarking on the 'shoptur'; that is, a medley of people who carry with them to markets in other cities (sometimes located in other countries) as many goods as they can physically bear in order to sell them and buy with the proceeds from their sale goods to be sold at home. These they dispose of through family and social networks, standing on the street, through their own kiosk or through an intermediary who rents shelf space and a counter in a shop. The shop itself may be in the foyer of a former (or existing) ministry, academic institution or institute. Every state agency is now trying to earn a living by leasing out space. Halls, stairways, seminar and committee rooms, basements – all become trading places. In virtually every case, certainly in the CIS, a rent is paid to the owner and an insurance fee to organized crime.

Buildings become, in terms of the wide variety of people passing through them, microcosms of the city. Here in the foyer of a ministry

is a meeting place of international consultants and civil servants, of
ministers and their impoverished staff, of petit bourgeois merchants,
many of them women and unemployed, of 'shopturists' and the
clients of all of them. Missing are only the members of the new elites.
The appropriation, use and design of space are a reaction to the
austerity and uniformity of high modernism, and are both a gleeful
and a malicious statement about the preciousness of commerce and
commodities. The assertion of the autonomous individual is eulo-
gized in the eclectic and pastiche. Grand designs are rejected or
neglected and political responsibility for those on low incomes, large
and lone-mother families, invalids and pensioners is assigned to the
forum of repetitious rhetoric. This growing mass of people, communities of the poor, constitute a vast reserve of labour power that
survives by begging and peddling.

The mono-functional building has been replaced by a kaleido-
scopic arrangement of space. The transactions which take place –
whether between dealers of imported cars, trading at the interface of
multinational corporations and indigenous elites, or between the
poor themselves – cannot, for reasons mentioned earlier, be described as 'market relations', except in the western provinces of the
region (the Czech Republic and Hungary). Although for the
populations of the region, the idea of a market has seemed easy to
understand, in effect their notion corresponds far more closely to
that of a 'bazaar' or (medieval) fair than to the market which, in
Western culture, has its origins in the philosophy of possessive individualism of Hobbes and Locke (Macpherson, 1962). Moreover, the
'shoptur', the bazaar, street trading and informal networking – even
when the commodities being traded are minerals, hydrocarbons
and hi-tech weaponry – are more compatible with clan and mafia
structures than with transactions which take place on the impersonal,
'rational-legal' (capitalist) market. For those with access to resources, including those in parliament, the warning given by the
president of the Ukraine in October 1994 that, unless industrial
subsidies were cut, mass privatization introduced and farm land sold
off, the republic could 'turn into a raw materials colony on the
outskirts of the world economy' (*Economist*, 1994c: 44), falls on deaf
ears. Many of them would selfishly consider this outcome to be not a
'bad thing'.

Certainties and visions, planning on a large scale and the selection
of the technologically rational are being replaced by a post-modernist conception. Paradoxically, the post-modernist view that regional
architecture should stand as part of the resistance movement to the
homogenizing forces of global capitalism (Frampton, 1985) is being

rejected by the architects, politicians and clients of post-communist societies. The future is seen to lie with capitalism, its social relations, architectural designs and forms – a system which finds it easy to incorporate symbols and embellishments of the local culture. But a state cannot simply decree that its citizens build a society founded on the social relations of a triumphant individualism. This abstract idea, like nation, has to be given a real form in new buildings which are symbols of social integration. In countries which are Islamic or have titular Islamic populations, such a building is the mosque. In other countries the refurbished cathedral or monastery becomes a symbol of cultural and national identity.

CONCLUSION

Societies east of the Oder–Neisse Line, extending into Eurasia, are in a state of dramatic flux. The Treaty of Versailles created the majority of the states of East and Central Europe. The Yalta Agreement allocated them to a power, the Soviet Union, which imposed its ideology upon them. The inherent weaknesses of administrative-command economies led in the years 1988–92 to their collapse; the former foundations on which these societies were organized – almost total state control over property and the total monopoly of power vested with one political party – have been largely rejected. The experiment in finding an alternative to capitalism, which began with the Russian Revolution of 1917, had not worked.

However, the initiation rite ('shock therapy') through which they are required to pass in order to become members of a union organized by their western neighbours is proving painful. Recondite explanations offered by economists (fresh from business schools) are being rebuffed in favour of placebos prescribed by nationalists. If 'patriotic' Basques and Bretons, Corsicans and Catalans can beat the nationalist drum, then it is only to be expected that the same drumroll will be heard in East and Central Europe and in the republics of the FSU. In other words, the boundaries of some nation states are still disputed. Intolerance is in the air, and 'ethnic cleansing' as practised in the former Yugoslavia could be imitated by others. The reshaping of regional and urban space to 'accommodate' minorities is on the political agenda. New elites and national bourgeoisies (including rentiers), in pursuit of their own objectives – political power, status, material wealth – could establish loose and fragile alliances under a nationalist banner.

In order to avert mutant forms of national socialism taking root,

Western governments and supra-national agencies are likely to divert more attention to searching for ways to provide households with a detached (not necessarily privately owned) house. At the same time, the Western car manufacturers (with the Koreans usurping the role played by the Italians in the 1960s), followed by the massive 'automotive support industry', will seek to meet the demand for private car ownership. The detached single house and the private car have come to be seen as the quintessential representative symbols of the social system which is being emulated. Members of the *nouveau riche* and older elites, who are now able openly to deploy their illegally accumulated wealth, are already the clients for houses on new residential estates, each with its sauna and swimming pool and communal tennis court (Sitinkov, 1992), to which they drive in expensive cars and which they enter through electronically controlled gates.

The scene is set: the slow colonization of land behind the latest range of tower blocks and the rebuilding of summer shacks ('dachas') by those who accumulate sufficient savings. Some housing estates in cities already have bad reputations and have even acquired the soubriquet of 'sink'. They will be joined by others and deteriorate still further to become the refuges of a post-communist underclass, including petty criminals and serious recidivists, alcoholics and other drug addicts, refugees and ethnic minorities.

This hypothetical description of the ecological development of large cities in the region is compatible with the laissez-faire model of society used to describe Chicago in the 1920s. Such a 'natural area' with its own rules and way of life could be contained and policed. However, it is possible that a political leader like Vladimir Zhirinovskii, the nationalistic leader of the largest party in the Russian Duma, would not adopt a tolerant 'live and let live' policy towards such estates and their inhabitants. He and other leaders like him would be more likely to choose someone such as Mussolini or Franco as a role model. The events in Yugoslavia, Moldova and Chechnya can leave no doubt about the willingness of governments to use extreme violence to achieve their objectives.

While the scene might generally be set, a deviation from the path is conceivable. The repudiation of state socialism may not mean a rejection of other collectivist solutions. The issue is too large to embark on in this chapter, but it may be posed. The legacy which the population has inherited, combined with the experiences of the younger generation, could lead them to seek a communitarian approach to the construction of their societies, the rationale for which has been firmly set on the critical agenda (Avineri, 1992). But even if this were to occur, it would be within the more general movement from an 'administrative-planned' to an 'administrative-market' economy. The newly created joint-stock companies have a high percentage of state ownership. The state is able to influence the private sector through banks, many of which are, for a variety of reasons, forging closer relations with the state. Therefore, while banks and industry receive their legitimation from the state, the latter is legitimized by being seen to support the existence of private finance and a private industrial sector.

NOTES

1 Bulgaria, Belarus, Czech Republic, Poland, Russia, Slovakia, Ukraine, Yugoslavia.
2 In 1881 Britain's population stood at 29.7 million.
3 In retrospect, we can see just how strong was the parallel between, on the one hand, the recognition by Tsar Nicholas I in 1842 that, although serfdom was an evil, it could not be reformed because of the threat which reform would create for public order (Field, 1976) and, on the other, the threat to public order which could be caused by the second 'de-serfment' of the Russian population occasioned by perestroika. (The process of re-enserfment began in the 1930s when the 'peasantry, liberated by the 1917 revolution, reverted to a position close to the worse examples of servile dependency' (Edel'man, 1989: 24).)
4 In this particular regard, Marx would have disagreed little with Francis Fukuyama's (1990, see also 1989) much-publicized view: 'In the past generation there have been two developments of world historical significance. The first is the emergence of liberal democracy as the only global ideology and the second is the victory of market principles. These two revolutions are closely connected and represent a larger, secular pattern of evolution.'
5 By the end of 1994 TACIS had spent ECU 1,870 million on over 2,000 projects.

3

The Socialist City

David M. Smith

[W]e have yet to create the socialist city.

(B.S. Khorev, 1975)

[C]ities in Eastern Europe are 'socialist' not in the sense that they are necessarily better or worse than they used to be, or better or worse than comparable cities in capitalist countries. They are socialist in that they are different.

(I. Szelenyi, 1983)

Is there (or was there) a distinctively socialist city? This question is of practical as well as academic interest, for cities of the future will to some extent reflect those of the past – the more so if rigidities of pre-existing forms impede the process of change. If socialism in Eastern Europe and the Soviet Union created such resilient urban structures as not to be easily altered by post-socialist society, the kinds of city inherited from the old regimes will survive, at least in part, well into the next century. And, in so far as urban life must adapt to the existing built environment, the socialist city will act as a constraint on the development of new social formations.

Some commentators deny the existence of a 'socialist city'. To the extent that the cities created or substantially modified under socialism may have failed to reflect distinctively socialist principles, such a view could be sustained. For example, if communal rather than family living represents the socialist way of life, then arrangements of this kind characterize only a small minority of existing accommodation in most cities, and even then their origin and preservation is likely to have been a case more of practical necessity than of ideological preference. If equality in housing conditions, local environmental quality and access to services is a distinctive aspiration of socialism, then the urban landscape of the planned urban unit (or *mikroraion*) might more persuasively be described as socialist. However, the concept of the neighbourhood unit with integral service facilities is by no means exclusive to Eastern Europe and the former USSR; indeed, it might be regarded as emblematic of the urban development of modernism. A broader view of urban spatial structure, with carefully planned functional zones tied together with cheap public transport, might suggest a more calculated order than in the typical capitalist city. But this scale is no more likely to yield anything really distinctive, which could be derived from socialist principles, than the level of the locality.

Thus, we are faced with the more realistic possibility that, if there is a socialist city, it is simply that regimes committed in principle (if not always in practice) to some form of socialism produced cities which are different from those in other kinds of society. The difference may simply be in the extent to which such features as neighbourhood units, land-use planning and public transport predominated, rather than in a fundamental alternative to the capitalist city. The focus of this chapter is on features of the Eastern European and former Soviet city which appear to differentiate them from the cities of the advanced capitalist world in this sense. Given the wide scope of the topic, the emphasis is on some (but by no means all) features of spatial structure which actually invite comparison of the supposedly 'socialist' city with those of Western Europe and North America: general physical organization, socio-economic differentiation and ethnic segregation. A summary of the empirical evidence, highlighted by reference to case studies, leads to some more interpretative observations on inequality in the socialist city.

PHYSICAL ORGANIZATION

The question of whether there might be a distinctive socialist city was the focus of a seminal work by French and Hamilton (1979). They drew attention to the neglect of the cities of the socialist world, compared with the voluminous literature on urban structure in North America and Western Europe and also in the developing world. Writing on urbanization, planning and housing in Eastern Europe and the Soviet Union subsequently expanded (see, for example, Bater, 1980; Andrusz, 1984; Morton and Stuart, 1984), but as French (1987: 310) pointed out later, the internal geography of the city still received only restricted attention.

Socialism certainly gave rise to the expectation of a different kind of city from those of the Anglo-American textbooks. Urban living has a particular significance in Marxism, as a progressive force encouraging collective rather than individual identity, and city planning was viewed as an important means of achieving political purposes (Andrusz, 1987). Central planning along with state ownership of land meant that urban development could be subjected to much greater control than under capitalism. The internal structure of the socialist city was supposed to be planned to facilitate the delivery of a wide range of social services as means of collective consumption, in addition to facilitating the planned development of the productive forces in the interests of the efficient operation of the economy. Cheap public transport was a high priority, to ensure convenient access to work, leisure and other sources of need satisfaction. The public provision of housing was one of the most important means by which the state sought to ensure satisfactory and relatively egalitarian living standards for all, and it was the apartment blocks which came to predominate which give such a special character to the urban landscape.

A description of how the ideal socialist city might be organized is provided by Demko and Regulska (1987: 290):

> The abolition of private property, removal of privileged classes, and application of equity principles espoused by Marxist/socialist leaders should radically alter urban patterns. In the housing arena, the expectation would be one of non-discriminatory, non-spatially differentiated housing in general. No social or occupational group would have better or more favourably located residential sites so that one would find a randomly distributed housing pattern. Similarly, public services of all kinds, including transportation, should be of equal quality, availability and accessibility, Commuting to work . . . would be minimised and no group would be more dependent on or penalised by such travel than others. Such amenities as high quality physical environment, including recreational environment, would be equally accessible to all. All such urban conditions would be similarly equitably arranged and available.

Of the various reasons why reality might depart from such an ideal, history is probably the most important. Socialism could not be built overnight, and nor could its cities. In one of the first textbooks to give serious treatment to the socialist city, Rugg (1972: 252–6) made a distinction between 'partially-changed cities' and 'new cities'. Those which have been partially changed by socialism originated in an earlier era, like the large and long-established national capitals of Moscow, Budapest, Prague and Warsaw. But even within this group there were differences in the extent to which socialist planning has replaced the pre-existing urban fabric, depending on the extent of the war damage and the resources devoted to construction, for example. The new cities were usually created for some specific function associated with industrial production or mineral extraction, their form representing the purest version of the planned socialist city with its stark functionality. Another contribution of the historical dimension is the time taken to construct the new city, or to impose it on the past, with different periods, planning styles and building standards generating diversity in the urban landscape.

As was suggested at the outset, there is a view that the cities of Eastern Europe and the Soviet Union are not fundamentally different from those of the advanced capitalist world, especially Western Europe. They share much of the same historical and physical legacy, and are subject to the same forces of modern industrial society. Friedrichs (1988: 128) claims that: '[e]xcept for a short period in the early 1920s . . . there are no specific socialist types of land use, distribution of new housing, internal organisation of residential blocks, or location of companies. Even the principal goal of socialist city planning – to locate new residential areas close to working areas – has been pursued in Western planning too.' However, while it may be hard to find evidence of highly distinctive urban and residential forms, to argue that modern industrial cities are all very much the same is to overlook some special features of those in socialist countries, not least with respect to their general spatial structure.

A simple model of the growth of the Eastern European city, devised by Ian Hamilton, is illustrated in figure 3.1. The city comprises several distinct zones, which he described as follows (French and Hamilton, 1979: 227):

(1) the historic medieval or renaissance core; (2) inner commercial, housing, and industrial areas from the capitalist period; (3) a zone of socialist transition or renewal, where modern construction is partially and progressively replacing inherited urban or relict-village areas; (4) socialist housing of the 1950s; (5) integrated socialist neighbourhoods and residential districts of the 1960s and 1970s [and 1980s]; (6) open or planted 'isolation belts'; (7) industrial or related zones; and (8) open countryside, forests, or hills, including tourist complexes. Broadly speaking, outward expansion of the city areas yields a concentric-zonal pattern, successive stages of building being readily recognisable in architectural styles and skylines. This pattern tends to 'overlay' a more sectoral or 'wedge-like' distribution of functional zones associated with particular site qualities, historic traditions, and major transport arteries. Fundamentally distinct, however, are the pre-socialist inner and socialist outer urban areas.

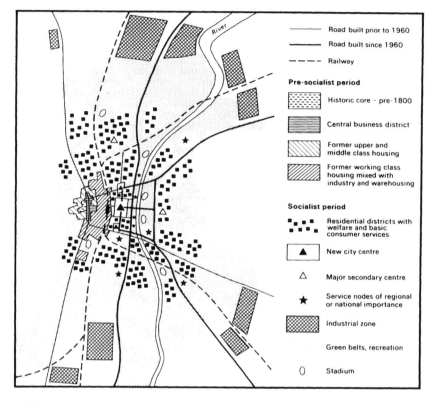

Figure 3.1   Model of the growth of an Eastern European socialist city
Source: French and Hamilton (1979: 228, figure 9.3)

The inherited inner area will be subject to more differentiation than the socialist outer area with its planned uniformity. The historic core and its preservation may have necessitated construction of a new city centre, as in figure 3.1.

This model indicates some similarity with the advanced capitalist city, at least to the extent of finding broad zones of differentiation in the forms of sectors and wedges. But how far is this pattern indicative of socio-economic differences, of the kind which we have come to associate with the spatial form of the capitalist city? This is a question to be addressed in the major part of this chapter. But before leaving the physical organization of the socialist city, something needs to be said about the built environment at a more local scale.

Following the Russian Revolution in 1917, one of the first pragmatic steps taken to create a more equal society was the confiscation and reallocation of large houses of wealthy families in inner parts of the city. But the need for comprehensive urban planning was quickly recognized and, to facilitate this, land was nationalized and much of the economy and infrastructure was also taken over by the state or municipal authorities. However, industrialization had immediate priority, and it was 1935 before a general plan was approved for Moscow. And it was well after World War II before substantial impact was made on the city's enormous housing problem, when Khrushchev initiated a major programme of housing development in the late 1950s.

It was at about this time that the *mikroraion* (micro-region or district) became the basic building block of the Soviet city. This comprised a neighbourhood unit of living spaces in the form of blocks of flats, along with associated services, for perhaps 5,000 to 15,000 people. Pedestrian precincts linked restaurants, nurseries, kindergartens, club rooms, libraries and sports facilities, as well as educational, health, retail and cultural services. The level of provision was supposed to be on a per capita basis, involving specific norms for the number of restaurant seats, square metres of shopping space, and number of health-service personnel, for example. Thus, people were all to have a wide range of day-to-day needs satisfied within their immediate locality, often within a short walk of where they lived. This, together with per capita norms within similar or identical blocks of flats, suggests something approaching equality in living standards as the likely and, of course, desired outcome (see French, 1994, for further discussion).

At a broader spatial scale, each *mikroraion* was supposed to form part of a nested hierarchy of service provision. Thus, several micro-districts may have been aggregated to form a larger residential complex of perhaps 30,000 to 50,000 population, for the provision of a wider range of services within a radius of 1,000 to 1,200 metres, compared with 150 to 200 metres for the *mikroraion* (French and Hamilton, 1979: 102); one variant of this type of structure is illustrated in Bater (1980: 102). Residential districts were aggregated up into urban districts of 100,000 to 300,000 inhabitants, which themselves formed part of urban zones with perhaps a million people in a major sector of the city. In health care, for example, the polyclinic providing basic outpatient services might cater for the 20,000 to 50,000 population of three micro-districts, with general hospitals serving a wider area of perhaps 300,000, and major specialist hospitals in each of the larger zones.

The concept of the *mikroraion* was quickly adopted in other socialist countries. It proved to be well suited to the needs of rapid post-war reconstruction and renewed urban expansion, particularly in the

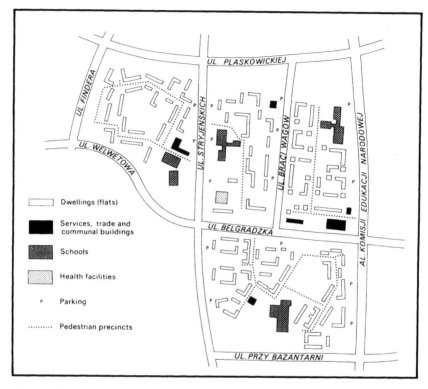

Figure 3.2   Layout of housing estate of the late 1970s at Wyzyny in the
Ursynow-Natolin district on the southern edge of Warsaw
Source: redrawn from the plan on public display

1960s when mass prefabricated techniques came to predominate in
urban housing construction. Figure 3.2 illustrates the kind of estate
which was being built in the outer areas of Warsaw in the late 1970s,
revealing more diversity and imagination of layout than in the earlier
phase of the Soviet *mikroraion* (as illustrated in Rugg, 1972: 51).

How far a city as a whole could be described as socialist in its
physical organization was largely a matter of the extent to which it
was dominated by the *mikroraion*. In some cities, like the rapidly
renewed Moscow and the almost completely rebuilt Warsaw, the
mikroraion became virtually ubiquitous, albeit with variations in details of layout and height of apartment blocks as styles changed with
the times. In other cities, such as Prague, most of the pre-socialist
urban fabric survived the war, and much of it also avoided subsequent redevelopment by virtue of its continuing capacity to function.

Elsewhere, cities with single-family dwellings of relatively poor quality would have the *mikroraion* imposed more rapidly than those with more substantial pre-socialist housing stock, depending on the priority given to a particular city's needs within some broader strategy of resource allocation. In any event, the uneven adoption of modern urban construction, both among and between cities, created considerable variety in the physical organization and appearance of the Eastern European and Soviet city.

SOCIO-ECONOMIC DIFFERENTIATION IN THE SOVIET CITY

The special significance of socio-economic differentiation in the socialist city is obvious. Socialist society was supposed to be relatively egalitarian, particularly in comparison with capitalist society. And the physical organization of the city, and of urban life in general, was supposed to promote collectivist sentiments, as well as giving practical material expression to egalitarian ideals. In so far as socio-economic differentiation could be detected in the socialist city, there was a contradiction with the strict egalitarianism of communism implicit in the dictum 'to each according to need'. Material advantage might be effectively hidden behind the walls of externally homogeneous apartment blocks, but if socio-economic differentiation achieved a more conspicuous expression, in the urban landscape or as discernible patterns of segregation, then the contradiction was all the more potent as a possible threat to the legitimacy of the prevailing political order. This section reviews evidence of socio-economic differentiation in the Soviet city, exemplified by Moscow, followed by references to some other cities.

While the individual *mikroraion* could be expected to deliver something like equal access to all elements of the urban infrastructure built into it, this was not the case with the broader intra-city structure of service provision. The need to locate at least some facilities centrally in relation to large populations, in the interests of efficiency, operated against the more even distribution required to approach equal accessibility. Another source of inequality in the planned spatial distribution of services was the time lag between construction of the housing blocks and the related services, as part of the general problem of uneven attainment of the norms which were supposed to ensure local parity of services. Quality of services could also vary among districts, with the superior facilities provided for workers at particular enterprises not open to other people living nearby.

Some parts of a city like Moscow would therefore have better access to services than others. The inner districts would be at a particular advantage, for it was here that the more specialized facilities tended to be concentrated (often as a legacy of history), and from here that accessibility to other parts of the city would be best because of the (historical) focus of transport lines. The central part of the city was therefore 'distinguished by the presence of theatres, a built-up area in keeping with Moscow's prominence as the nation's capital, a well-rounded urban environment and a high density of retail outlets selling manufactured goods' (Barbash and Gutnov, 1980: 567–8; Smith, 1987: 77–82). There were outliers of such facilities at major transport nodes further out.

Housing space was allocated according to a per capita entitlement, the minimum having been set at 9 square metres in 1922. While this had been achieved as an average standard in Moscow by 1970, large numbers of families had much less while others enjoyed well above the average (Bater, 1986: 96; see also Hamilton, 1993). Inequality in living space was exacerbated by variations in quality of accommodation.

Housing quality varied on two main dimensions: type of tenure, and period of construction. Housing tenure in the former USSR divided roughly into three-quarters 'socialized' and one quarter privately owner-occupied. Private housing was often of poor quality by conventional (state) standards; it was confined largely to the fringes of cities, to small towns and to the countryside, with very little in Moscow. The socialized sector was further subdivided into government, industrial or departmental, and co-operative housing. In 1989 almost three-quarters of Moscow housing was owned by the city government, and 16 per cent by industrial and other ministries which had built for their own workers. While some enterprises may have provided good housing as well as services at the place of work, period of construction seems to have been a more important source of differentiation in housing stock than the particular institution responsible for it.

As a general rule, the later the construction the better the quality of state housing, but this is not always the case. For example, in the 1930s under Stalin a number of large apartment blocks were built in ornate style and to relatively high standards, for members of the Party and other privileged groups. However, those constructed during the early period of large-scale residential development initiated by Khrushchev were often badly built; they are now deteriorating and are widely regarded as slums (French, 1987, 1994). More recently constructed accommodation in micro-districts on the edge of the city is generally of a higher standard.

The third element of socialized housing, the co-operative, was an important source of qualitative differentiation under socialism. Co-operative housing was constructed on behalf of groups of individuals, usually based on a workplace association (such as a particular enterprise or ministry), who thereby acquired collective ownership of their complex or block. Membership required an initial monetary deposit, and monthly payments higher than rent for a state apartment. Co-operative housing was concentrated in the largest cities; it accounted for about 10 per cent of all housing in Moscow in the 1980s. While not conspicuously different from the best state housing in external appearance, co-operative housing was usually built to higher standards.

The relationship between socio-economic status and housing at the end of the socialist era has been examined by Ellen Hamilton (1993), at the scale of the 33 regions into which Moscow is divided. She measured social status by people with higher education, car ownership, residents convicted of crime, and proportion of juveniles in the population. The first two are fairly conventional affluence indicators often used in Western research, while the other two would be expected to reveal relatively low family incomes. These four conditions were found to have similar degrees of inequality among Moscow regions, as measured by the coefficient of variation, and are also highly correlated one with another (see table 3.1). When compared with per capita living space there is a clear spatial correspondence:

Table 3.1 Indicators of social status of the population of Moscow by region, 1989

Indicator	Coefficient of variation	Correlation coefficient r with other indicators		
		2	3	4
1 People with higher education per 1,000 population aged 15 and over	24.1	0.80	−0.76	−0.75
2 Cars per 1,000 population	14.8		−0.66	−0.68
3 Residents convicted of crime per 1,000 population aged 15 and over	15.8			−0.60
4 Juveniles aged under 15 per 1,000 population	10.6			

Source: Hamilton (1993: 200, 201, tables 3 and 4)

the higher-status population and the more spacious accommodation is concentrated in the inner parts of the city and the western regions. There is also evidence that these patterns are closely reflected in people's perceptions of the relative prestige of residential areas (Siderov, 1992).

Hamilton (1993) goes on to explore the role of the state housing allocation system in accounting for her observations. While housing had been considered a right of every citizen, with distribution according to need and not to ability to pay, it has also been treated as a privilege and reward for social categories of workers. The correspondence between high-status population and most spacious housing suggests that those whose labour was most valued by the state enjoyed a double advantage. Low rents implied a state housing subsidy, the greater the more space people had. As high status would also be rewarded by relatively high incomes, those most able to pay for housing received the largest state subsidies. While this might be perfectly consistent with the socialist dictum of 'to each according to quantity and quality of labour contribution', particular groups may have been able to ensure for themselves superior housing, along with other benefits, merely by virtue of their capacity to influence the allocation system.

Soviet socialist society had a distinct elite, comprising the upper levels in political, administrative, managerial, military, academic and artistic life. As the capital city of a country with a high degree of central control, Moscow had a disproportionately high share of such people. As well as having relatively high salaries, they were rewarded by access to special facilities providing health care or goods not generally available, for example. An additional allocation of housing space may also have been provided, often in special buildings. Evidence from a variety of sources suggests some spatial concentration of the elite (French, 1994, ch. 6). For example, Matthews (1979: 107–8) pointed to the old Arbat district in central Moscow as being a favourite location for blocks of prestige flats belonging to the Central Committee of the Communist Party and the KGB, and to villas built on the Lenin Hills near Moscow State University as well as new blocks in central locations; French (1987: 313–14) reported a wedge of inner Moscow with a high proportion of apartment blocks inhabited by the elite. There were also areas of fine *dachas* outside the city.

Thus, despite a planning process driven by egalitarian ideals, inequality in living standards was evident in socialist Moscow. Some of this could be attributed to the hierarchical structure of service provision and to the process of physical development over time as well as space. But there is also evidence of some spatial sorting of the population by occupational group. The spatial form of socio-economic differentiation suggested by the available evidence may be summarized as follows (Smith, 1987: 86). The inner areas presented a variety of environments and social groups, with some good housing which combined with access to cultural facilities to generate what may to most people have been the best of all worlds in Moscow, other than that of the discreet enclaves of the elite. In contrast, there were the remains of the poor inner-city housing areas, less substantial than in other Soviet cities, occupied by people of markedly lower social status than the intelligentsia and professional groups that tended to predominate in the inner city. The outer areas were differentiated by wedges of varying environmental quality and socio-economic status, with the better sectors having relatively high proportions of co-operative housing and the occupations that tend to go with it, the inhabitants trading off higher levels of access to cultural facilities, shopping and other services in the city centre for new housing of good quality and proximity to open space on the edge of the city. In the outer sectors where state housing predominates, environmental quality was better than in those old, inner areas occupied by people of lower occupational status, except for their favourable access to services.

This description suggests elements of both the concentric zone and wedge models of urban spatial structure. The question of which of these two forms predominates in Moscow has exercised the curiosity of a number of observers. S.I. Kabakova, who attempted to estimate land values in the Soviet city, came up with almost perfect concentric zones (Bater, 1980: 127, figure 5). French suggests that at first glance the Burgess model could have some relevance for Moscow, given the street pattern of concentric rings and radials and the concentration of central area functions, but also finds some evidence for the Hoyt sectors in the location of industry, in the tendency of particular social groups to move outwards in the same sector, and in the planned green wedges (French and Hamilton, 1979: 90–2; French, 1987: 311, 313). The most thorough analysis of the applicability of the two descriptive models to Moscow, by Barbash (1982), confirms that one is not obviously more convincing than the other and that it depends on which element of environment, economy or society is considered.

Evidence from other Soviet cities to substantiate particular patterns is rare. An early exception is found in a study of the city of Ufa by L.N. Fenin, who explored the link between social groups and their location (summarized in Matthews, 1979: 112–13). Information was compiled on the inhabitants of three types of district: the old centre, the newly constructed areas, and the outer areas characterized by a high proportion of privately owned dwellings with garden plots. Although no district was socially exclusive, the intelligentsia more frequently lived in the centre, while the outer districts had a larger share of artisans. The newly built districts generally came in between. Fenin also suggested a gradation of income corresponding with the three types, with the central district leading.

The areas of private housing on the edge of cities like Ufa reflected the pace of urbanization, and the failure of the city authorities to keep up with housing demand by state construction. Private housing might lack such amenities as running water, but to the migrant from the countryside these fringe areas provided a first foothold in the city, with the ability to supplement uncertain official supplies of food from their own plot. And some apartment dwellers may have envied the freedom which private housing offered. Thus, qualitative differences between inner and outer areas were very much matters of perception, depending on individual or family attitudes and values.

At the risk of some simplification, the following broad typology of socio-economic and environmental differentiation in the larger Soviet city may be suggested:

1   inner, high-status areas of good housing, occupied largely by professional groups; some congestion and pollution, but good access to central services (added to which were special places and privileges of the elite);

2   inner, low-status areas of old and deteriorating property; environment affected by industrial or commercial development, but good access to facilities of the city centre;

3   outer areas of relatively high status (more or less distant from the centre, depending on the size and growth pattern of the city), with relatively high proportions of co-operative flats; employment predominantly white-collar; service provision and/or transport to the city centre fairly good;

4   outer areas of lower status, with a predominance of state housing, and a relatively high proportion of in-migrants; mainly manual employment; industry with a detrimental environmental impact; access to services low, and exacerbated by time lags in construction of infrastructure;

5   peri-urban areas and suburban enclaves of private housing of very poor quality, much of it occupied by recent migrants from the countryside; low or non-existent service provision.

To these may be added, for the sake of completeness:

6   quarters occupied by distinctive ethnic groups, possibly but not neces-
    sarily in lower-status occupations; probably comprising socially cohesive
    communities; housing possibly reflecting cultural preferences; service
    provision depending on position within the general spatial structure of
    the city.

The situation of such ethnic groups will be taken up later in this
chapter.

While housing, occupation and access to the service infrastructure
predominate in this typology, there are strong indications that it is
reflected in some other social conditions. In health, for example,
there is the evidence from Moscow suggesting an association between
child health and occupational status (Barbash, 1983, summarized in
Smith, 1987: 84–5). Quality of education is also likely to have been
associated with local population characteristics. Social pathologies
such as crime, alcoholism and what the Soviets called 'hooliganism'
were also connected with particular parts of the city; these tended to
be the old and deteriorating neighbourhoods, usually in the central
area, along with some of the new, lower-status residential complexes
in the outer districts, with a predominance of single rural migrants
no longer subject to traditional controls of family and community
(Morton and Stuart, 1984: 122–3; Andrusz, 1984: 218; French 1987:
312).

A further element in the social geography of the Soviet city was
the tendency for family size to be negatively associated with socio-
economic status. The peripheral zones customarily accommodated a
younger population with larger average family size (Bater, 1986: 94).
Spatial sorting may have been a response to the differential attraction
of particular parts of the city in relation to stage in the family life
cycle, but there may also have been a less voluntary element in
population shifts as people were displaced by inner-city renewal
bringing in those of higher status (Andrusz, 1984: 218).

How far did such zones comprise extensive areas of the city with
relatively homogeneous character, as opposed to more of a mosaic or
patchwork of internal diversity? In Soviet urban planning, any tendency towards social separation and associated bourgeois class attitudes should have been prevented by residential mixing, at least by
neighbourhood and preferably by residential block. Firm evidence
on the extent to which such mixing was achieved is rare, but it was
probably less than the socialist ideal. Nevertheless, Andrusz (1984:
220) asserts that, '[g]enerally speaking however, and with singular
exceptions, blocks of flats in the Soviet Union are characterised by
social class heterogeneity – certainly by Anglo-American standards.'

French and Hamilton (1979: 98) stated that social segregation tended to be by building, rather than by street or area. However, this may have been true more of the inner than the outer residential areas. Bater (1986: 94) suggested that, in the new micro-districts and in suburban tracts of individual houses engulfed in the process of urban expansion, 'the social-class composition of particular neighbourhoods is not always as varied as Soviet planning policy suggests it ought to be.' Areas of housing built by industrial enterprises almost inevitably had a working-class character, and tracts of private housing had a similar composition. Higher-status people had other choices, with better housing and environment.

There was certainly some clustering of accommodation for higher-status groups and the elite, as was observed above with respect to Moscow. Bater (1980: 101) suggests that this led to a degree of residential segregation as early as the Stalin era. Concentrations of co-operatives may also have existed in certain parts of the city but French (1987: 314–15) points out that sites for such housing were controlled by the local authority, which had the power to prevent spatial clustering of those who could afford such accommodation. For members of the elite allocated good state housing, apartment size and furnishings may have mattered more than location (Bater, 1984: 149). And there was always the chance factor, which may have enabled an enterprising or fortunate individual to take advantage of that uncertain flexibility and inefficiency which characterized the Soviet bureaucracy.

In view of the imprecision and ambivalence of some of the evidence, the most appropriate conclusion, following Andrusz (1984: 220) is that, '[i]t is impossible in Soviet cities to identify ghettos, whether rich or poor: there are only tendencies towards the congregation of social groups.' But, as he emphasized throughout his study of the Soviet urban scene, there was an association between housing quality, tenure, social group and spatial location; this, along with differentiation of the urban infrastructure, generated a distinctive kind of city with its own emergent patterns of inequality. How far this generalization holds for other Eastern European countries, where there is more direct evidence of both the processes involved and their outcomes, will be examined in the section which follows.

Other evidence of socio-economic differentiation

Some of the most thorough investigations of socio-economic differentiation within cities outside the former Soviet Union cover the

cities of Warsaw, Prague and Budapest. In the first two cases, historical comparisons can be made, to reveal something of the impact of
socialism on the pre-socialist city. The evidence is summarized here,
followed by a study of the two regional centres of Pecs and Szeged in
Hungary.

Warsaw has a special place in the creation of the socialist city. Its
population had reached almost 1.3 million in 1939, but five years of
wartime devastation left barely 162,000 people in 1945. The new
society therefore had almost complete freedom to reconstruct a
major city according to new ideals. Two important principles were
'the right to adequate living conditions in cities – by the proper
location of service centres for education, culture, etc.' and 'the principle of social equality – by applying uniform criteria with respect to
every social group and area' (Regulska, 1987: 326). By 1949 sufficient
progress had been made for President Bierut (quoted in Regulska,
1987: 327) to proclaim:

> New Warsaw cannot be a reproduction of the old one, it cannot be
> only an improved repetition of pre-war concentration of private capi-
> talist interests of the society, it cannot be a reflection of contradictions
> dividing this society, it cannot be a scene and base for exploitation of
> people and expansion of the privileges of the owners' class . . . New
> Warsaw should become a socialist capital. The fight for the ideological
> image of our city must be carried out with full consciousness and with
> all the required energy directed towards this goal. New Warsaw
> through the development of industry will become the centre of pro-
> duction, the city of workers.

In 1949 all existing housing was 'communalized' or taken into
state control, except for small, one-family dwellings. Then the state
(or city of Warsaw) took the major role in new housing construction.
But pressure on resources led to the encouragement of large-scale
co-operative development from the late 1950s, tapping people's savings in return for a shorter waiting time, and to a decline in city-
financed construction, which was discontinued in 1973. Initially,
co-operatives paid much more attention than municipal authorities
to the appearance of housing estates and the supply of services, but
as co-operatives came to dominate the scene such concerns seem to
have become less important (Ciechocinska, 1987: 11). Modern estates on the fringe of the city often lacked good transport as well as
services, though quality of accommodation may have been some
compensation. Thus urban environmental attributes as well as the
dwellings themselves came to vary with the location, date of construction and housing tenure.

Something of the impact of socialist reconstruction has been revealed by Weclawowicz (1979). He analysed variables measuring population characteristics, occupation and housing by enumeration districts in 1931, and derived an index of 'economic-class position' describing the principal component of differentiation which could be extracted from the data. There was a clear decline in socio-economic status, from the compact central zone, through a transitional zone, and out into a peripheral zone. The reversal of the usual generalization concerning the capitalist city could be explained by the fact that the process of outward movement of wealthier people had begun from Warsaw only after 1981, generating few high-status areas on the periphery.

The population of Warsaw in 1970, at 1,315,000, was not much greater than in 1931. But the physical structure of the city had been very largely renewed. Weclawowicz (1979) chose variables which coincided as far as possible with those used for 1931, and derived an index reflecting educational and occupational characteristics along with form of housing tenure as the principal component of differentiation. This captured what he termed 'socio-occupational position', rather than economic-class status as in 1931, because it was less concerned with income differentials which predominated under capitalism than with the broader social evaluation of labour in particular occupations. The highest index values tended to be in the central part of the city, reflecting the concentration of writers, journalists and artists along with others occupying crucial (and privileged) positions and working in nearby offices, educational institutions and so on. This was the outcome of a selective housing policy which enabled these groups to settle in central locations which had been rebuilt soon after the war. The lowest values identified areas dominated by housing construction of the 1960s.

Weclawowicz concluded that there had been great changes in spatial structure between 1931 and 1970. In the inter-war period Warsaw had an urban form strongly differentiated by class, whereas the pattern in 1970 was more a reflection of socio-occupational position, a selective housing policy, and stages of settling the post-war city. The classic models of the capitalist city, with their wedges, concentric zones and multiple nuclei, were too simplistic to describe Warsaw's spatial structure in 1970, which was more of a mosaic differentiated in local detail. Later research at the broader scale of the Warsaw urban region reveals a 'substantial increase of spatial disparities' between 1978 and 1988 (Weclawowicz, 1991: 29; 1992), reflecting the prevailing social and political transformation and in particular the increasing shortage of housing.

Another interpretation of socio-spatial disparities in Warsaw, at the end of the 1970s, is offered by Dangschat and Blasius (1987; see also Dangschat, 1987). They identified distinct clusters of districts, defined mainly by age and type of housing. Education appeared to be an important means by which access to a differentiated housing stock was determined. These authors claim that disparities in Warsaw were not fundamentally different from those in their Western European counterparts. An alternative position is advanced by Ciechocinska (1987: 22–4), who is closer to Weclawowicz (1979) in asserting: '[t]he pattern of sociospatial differences in Warsaw differs considerably from the text-book examples of social inequalities which occur in many developed and third world countries.' She saw the basic source of inequality as the shortage of housing, which generated a distinctive process of differential access. The shortage could mean a wait of many years for a housing co-operative unit, but especially valuable employees in managerial or leadership positions had a better chance of obtaining such flats. Only families with incomes well below the average could obtain city-owned flats, and their concentration usually in older parts of the city led to strong socio-spatial differentiation. Constraints on the exchange of flats, along with the housing shortage, meant that most people were tied to their accommodation virtually for life. Such stability was conducive to a perpetuation of the existing differences in the socio-spatial structure.

Prague has a population of about 1.2 million in the city, 1.6 million in the wider metropolis. The special interest of this city is that, unlike Moscow or Warsaw, Prague has seen the formation of socialist society largely on a pre-existing physical structure typical of the European city of industrial capitalism. Prague was the first major Eastern European city to be the subject of thorough investigation of internal differentiation after the advent of socialism (Musil, 1968). This was followed up by a comparison of the city in 1930 and 1970 (Mateju et al., 1979), similar to that of Weclawowicz in Warsaw. The pattern for 1930 revealed five types of area, differentiated according to such conditions as proportion of working class in the economically active population, dwellings with a bathroom, and density of occupation. As Mateju et al. (1979: 190) saw it: '[t]he urban fringes were becoming proletarian, while wealthy strata tended to retreat from the centre of the city and from the industrial areas of the intermediate zone into newly built residential quarters. The city's centre was inhabited by the petty bourgeoisie, clerks and working-class aristocracy.'

It was onto this pattern that a new order was imposed. The early years of the socialist period, up to the latter part of the 1950s, were characterized largely by the redistribution of existing housing stock. Geographical differences were evened out, with the proportion of manual workers in the inner zones increasing to about 40 per cent in 1961 compared with a little over a quarter in 1930 (Musil, 1987: 31). The 1960s saw the beginning of a phase of accelerated housing construction, which continued through the 1970s. Large estates were built on the fringe of the city, to relieve congestion in the centre and facilitate reconstruction of the inner areas as well as to accommodate the growing workforce. The social ecology identified in 1970, reflecting the first part of this phase, revealed types of area similar to those of 1930, but with significant changes in the character of various parts of the city. Differences among the areas identified had become smaller than in 1930, as reflected in decreases in the ratio of maximum to minimum values from 1.18 to 1.14 for proportion of the population that was working class, 3.39 to 1.69 for dwellings with a bathroom, and 1.62 to 1.14 in the number of persons per room.

The socio-economic (or class) structure had become much less important in the spatial differentiation of Prague. More significant in 1970 was the material quality of the urban environment, with a distinction between the old, obsolescent parts of the city and the newly developed areas, along with family and age structure (Mateju et al., 1979: 192–3; Musil, 1987: 32–3). A process of homogenization of urban space had been set in motion, but there was still spatial differentiation arising from the inherited built environment, its variability, and how it compared with new construction. And there was a social dimension to this differentiation: some areas still had a relatively high-status population, while old people were more likely to be in poor and overcrowded housing. The greatest social homogeneity was found in the new outer suburbs, where housing was allocated to families with similar characteristics on the basis of need.

The 1980s appear to have been characterized by a growing differentiation within both the old and new parts of Prague. The better-quality housing became dispersed, unlike that of the pre-socialist period. And in the new housing estates, state, enterprise and co-operative blocks of flats were mixed. Thus, Musil (1987: 35) saw 'an increase of heterogeneity in macrostructure', accompanied by 'a certain homogenisation which contributes to the emergence of problem areas', occupied by old people and less-qualified workers, in the inner districts and some older industrial parts of the city.

The inherited built form of the capitalist city clearly had an important bearing on the changing social geography of Prague during the socialist period. To quote Musil (1987: 32):

even an extensive house building programme carried out in the sixties
– and, it may be added, even in the seventies – combined with many
other deep social changes, were not able to completely transform the
inherited features of Prague's social ecology. The inner parts of the
city did not essentially change and the traditional attraction of certain
districts for certain social groups remained rather strong. Also the
inherited location of industrial as well as non-industrial workplaces
undoubtedly played an important role in shaping the ecological pattern of the city.

The socialist period expanded the city and created new residential
areas of relatively uniform quality, at least with respect to state housing. But districts of poor housing and low environmental quality
remained. Access to housing of varied quality, along with the freedom of those with the means and ability to build or acquire private
housing or join a co-operative, provided scope for people to differentiate themselves, in terms of their accommodation and the local
environment which goes with it.

Budapest has a population of about 2.1 million people. The city
suffered considerable damage during World War II, and the rest of
the 1940s was preoccupied with repair or reconstruction. Some subdivision of housing took place, and redistribution was accelerated
when the Communist Party took over in 1948–9 (Hegedus and
Tosics, 1983: 475–6). There were attempts to restrict the growth of
Budapest in the 1950s, which exacerbated a housing shortage com-
pounded by poor quality and lack of amenities within the existing
stock.

At the end of the 1950s, plans were drawn up to build 250,000 new
dwellings in the city, 80 per cent of them from public funds. However, the economy could not support this level of activity; official
prejudice against the private sector was relaxed, so that, in the 1960s
and 1970s, 30–40 per cent of construction came from private building by those who could afford it. The public housing programme,
with its high-rise estates, required relatively open areas, and these
were found mainly between the densely built city centre and suburban settlements annexed to the city in 1950. These new dwellings
were the subject of allocation criteria favouring large families, predominantly of the working class. The very best housing remained the
high-quality single-family and multi-family blocks of the traditional
residential districts. The most obsolete and run-down area was between the inner city and the estates. A process of spatial sorting of the
population was thus taking place, associated with growing polarization of housing classes (Hegedus and Tosics, 1983: 483, 489).

While the 1970s had seen a reassertion of social need criteria in housing distribution, Hegedus and Tosics (1983: 491) claimed that this was not reflected in a moderation of segregation tendencies. However, this interpretation has been questioned by Sillince (1985: 146–7), who showed that variations in the ratio between 'physical' (manual) and 'non-physical' workers in each of the 22 districts of Budapest had gone down sequentially from 1960 to 1980. His interpretation is that social class segregation had progressively fallen over these 20 years. Some support is provided by Ladányi (1989: 560–1), who found the spatial segregation of five out of six socio-economic groups decreasing during the 1970s.

The geographical features displayed by Sillince's ratio of physical to non-physical workers shows a high degree of consistency from year to year. In other words, the pattern of social differentiation had not changed much over two decades, with the more working-class districts concentrated in the south and west and those with a higher proportion of non-physical workers in the central and western parts of the city. Further detail at a finer spatial scale is provided by Ladányi (1989). He concludes that the higher-status regions of the city are the most compact and segregated, while the lowest-status regions, although sharply separated from the high-status groups, are more dispersed and segregated on a smaller scale. This suggests a patchwork or mosaic of socio-economic differentiation, rather than broad homogeneous zones. Ladányi (1989: 565–6) summarizes the situation as follows:

> Workers, or more precisely, poor people . . . lived in the worst, furthermost parts of the city, without any conveniences, which were polluted and located next to industry, or they lived in deteriorated, or originally poor-quality apartment-houses, or in poor one-family houses near railroads or main streets, in the back apartments of the older apartment-houses without any conveniences, in concierge-flats, in subtenancy, as night-lodgers, in cellars or in attics etc. . . . The highest-status social groups symbolise their 'being different' by their spatial separation and, as they have enough power, they can develop their 'own' part of the city.

Pecs and Szeged, regional centres in Hungary with populations a little less than 200,000, are the subject of one of the most thorough investigations of housing inequality under socialism. In 1968, George Konrad and Ivan Szelenyi carried out a survey involving 2,300 families in the two cities. They were particularly concerned with how the unequal distribution of social privileges and disadvantages, arising from the differentiation of socialist society, was related to the spatial distribution and mobility of the social groups concerned. The account here is based on Szelenyi (1983).

The allocation of occupational groups among different kinds of housing revealed a striking distinction between relatively high proportions of bureaucrats, intellectuals, technicians and clerical workers in first-class state housing and lower proportions of skilled, semi-skilled and unskilled workers. The same distinction was shown for those with their own bank-financed or co-operative apartment. However, in private housing, usually of poor quality, the situation was reversed. So in general, the higher-status groups received better housing, with the highest state subsidies. Those who had been awarded state housing included 37 per cent of the high bureaucrats and almost 40 per cent of intellectuals, compared with figures of around 21 to 15 per cent for the skilled, semi-skilled and unskilled workers. Again, the situation was reversed for those who had built or bought their own houses, with only 26 per cent of bureaucrats and 21 per cent of intellectuals in this category compared with about 35 per cent of skilled and semi-skilled workers and 44 per cent of the unskilled.

Szelenyi (1983: 63) summarized the spatial sorting process as follows:

> the social groups with the highest incomes move steadily towards the highest housing classes in the state and market sectors, and come close to monopolising them. Below that, the highest class of housing available to most of those with lower incomes is the second market class, i.e. the range of family houses omitting the superior 'villa' category. The housing options and opportunities of these lower classes are limited more by state policies which allocate state housing and credit than by the people's capacity to pay. Public policy thus provides that, on average, the richer classes get better housing for less money and effort, while the poorer classes get worse housing at the cost of more money or effort, or both.

So, whereas under socialism housing is supposed to have a special significance as an equalizing element of state provision, received as a right and not as a reflection of income, in Pecs and Szeged it was found to be a source of inequality compounding other inequalities arising from occupational status.

Szelenyi went on to consider the spatial structure of the two cities, to see whether there was any correspondence between the physical and functional characteristics of areas, their housing, and their demographic and social composition. Relatively high proportions of intellectuals, other white-collar workers and skilled blue-collar workers lived in the new multi-storey housing estates, fitted with bathrooms, water, gas and electricity, and, to a lesser extent, in the city centre. Correspondingly lower proportions of the professionals lived in the more industrial areas and outer zones of private village-style dwellings. Unskilled workers made up more than half the households in these zones of poorer housing, with only 18 per cent in the new state housing areas. Szelenyi (1983: 117) concluded:

> the degree of segregation of our cities is measurable. It is also clear that all the measured social and spatial advantages tend to be superimposed on one another to increase the privilege of the privileged, while the corresponding disadvantages go together to worsen the situation of the disadvantaged. The higher social classes with the higher status and the better educational qualifications are situated in the better zones of the city; the lower social classes with lower status and less education tend to live in the poorer zones.

Furthermore, those with low incomes who got poor housing in poor districts typically paid more for it than the richer people did for better housing in better districts. State housing allocation favoured those of high status, the workers seeking new accommodation largely being forced out of the city to build for themselves. Thus, contrary to the expectations of socialist ideals, the housing allocation system was found to have a regressive redistributional impact: a finding confirmed by others elsewhere (for example, Hamilton, 1993, in Moscow – see above).

ETHNIC SEGREGATION

Socio-economic differentiation in the capitalist city often has an ethnic or racial dimension. The cities of Eastern Europe and the Soviet Union had distinct and often substantial ethnic quarters in the pre-socialist period, most notably the Jewish ghettos. The elimination of the ghettos by the Nazis represented one of the most dramatic changes in the internal structure of cities which came under socialist regimes after World War II. Warsaw and Lodz in Poland are obvious cases where large Jewish populations were exterminated, with their former residential areas, religious edifices and so on almost entirely destroyed. Only occasionally did the physical structures of the ghetto survive the holocaust, as in Prague and Krakow.

Evidence from Soviet cities points to some ethnic segregation continuing during the socialist period. For example, although the major cities of Soviet Central Asia are now predominately Slavic, many of the indigenous people still prefer to live in traditional quarters, Samarkand being a case in point (see French and Hamilton, 1979: 145–65, for a discussion of Islamic cities). However, detailed investigations, including mapping, are rare.

A notable exception is a study of Kazan, capital of what used to be the Tartar Autonomous Soviet Socialist Republic. Rukavishnikov (1978; see Bater, 1984: 152–6; 1986: 98–9, for summaries) produced detailed maps for 1974 based on a survey, and also reconstructed features of the city at the turn of the century so that the present (or recent past) could be compared with the pre-revolutionary patterns. Kazan was originally an ethnically homogeneous city populated by Tartars. Russians began to move in when the middle and upper Volga country was annexed by the Russian state *c.*1550. The proportion of Russians steadily increased, so that by around the end of the nineteenth century, when the total population was roughly 150,000, Tartars accounted for 15–20 per cent. A clear spatial separation of the two groups could then be identified: the better eastern part of the city was inhabited by predominantly Russians and the western part by Tartars. It was also possible to identify distinct areas occupied by merchants, at the intersection of the Tartar and Russian districts, and by the nobility, in the Russian district away from the city centre in the higher and more attractive parts of the city. Thus, according to Rukavishnikov (1978: 64):

> pre-Revolutionary Kazan confirms the well-known proposition that capitalist cities are characterised by settlement in socially and ecologically different parts of the city according to class affiliation. The contrasts of pre-Revolutionary Kazan were defined not so much by ethnic as social factors, for the conditions of life of the Russian and Tartar proletariat were virtually the same.

Since the Revolution the population of Kazan has greatly increased, to exceed one million. The proportion of Tartars has also increased, with migration from the surrounding territory; by the time of the 1974 survey it had reached 31.1 per cent, with 64.1 per cent of Russians, and the balance made up by other ethnic groups. Districts with relatively high proportions of Tartars could still be identified, roughly corresponding with those at the turn of the century. But nowhere did Tartars exceed 80 per cent of the total population; they were to be found living in all parts of the city, often side by side with Russians. Rukavishnikov (1978: 73) refers to the 'mosaic ethnic structure of socialist Kazan in the 1970s', compared with the more evident segregation of the capitalist city.

As to the social geography of Kazan in the 1970s, revealed by occupational structure, Rukavishnikov (1978: 68) claimed: '[n]o rigid relationship between an individual's status in society and his place of residence is to be found.' However, his maps do suggest a peripheral dominance of workers and a concentration of professionals in the central parts of the city. Some degree of social segregation must therefore be recognized, although the development of the city under socialism clearly generated more spatial diversity. While high social status and Russian origin were much less closely associated than before the Revolution, there must have been some relationship between ethnic group and living conditions in Kazan, because Tartars predominated in the original (and poorer) Tartar parts of the city as well as on the urban fringes. Rukavishnikov (1978: 72, 74–5) also found such a relationship in the industrial city of Al'met'evsk, with Tartars primarily in zones of old and modern private housing, which is usually of inferior quality. And, while no localization of social strata was said to exist here, highly qualified professionals, creative intellectuals and managers were found to live primarily in newly built areas, presumably in state flats, and in those adjacent to the city centre.

Two further cases may be presented briefly, to show the distribution of different national groups among broad subdivisions (regions) of two capitals of former Soviet republics. The first is Alma-Ata, capital of the Kazakh Republic. Russians comprised about 660,000 or 59.1 per cent of the total population of 1,117,000 in 1989, outnumbering the Kazakhs by almost three to one. However, this ratio is

Table 3.2 Distribution of Kazakh and Russian population in the city of Alma-Ata (percentage of total), by region, 1989

Region	Kazakh	Russian	Other
Alatayskiy	23.7	60.0	16.3
Ayezovskiy	17.8	61.5	20.7
Kalininskiy	25.9	56.3	17.8
Leninskiy	21.3	59.1	19.6
Moskovskiy	15.9	61.9	23.2
Oktyabr'skiy	14.5	64.8	20.7
Sovyetskiy	30.4	54.1	15.5
Fruntsenskiy	28.6	54.2	17.2
City	22.5	59.1	18.4

Source: Goskomstat Kazakhskoi SSR, Alma-Atinskoe gorodskoe uprav'lenie statistiki, Itogi vsesoyuznoi perepisi naselenyia 1989 goda (Alma-Ata, 1990)

smaller than it was in 1979, when the percentage of Russians was 65.9, compared with 16.7 Kazakhs. Table 3.2 shows variations in the proportions of the national groups among the eight regions into which the city is divided. The highest proportion of Kazakhs is in the central Sovyetskiy region, followed by Fruntsenskiy to the east. The lowest proportions are in the northern Moskovskiy and Octyabr'skiy regions, where there are the highest proportion of Russians. But despite the variations shown, and the broad geographical pattern, the picture is one of predominantly mixed populations rather than of strong spatial segregation: an impression reinforced by the personal observations of residents.

Smaller ethnic or national groups may be subject to greater spatial concentration, however. In Alma-Ata there is a distinctive area of Turkish and Chechen people (from the northern Caucasus), relocated by Stalin. Initially they were socially deprived, but today their level of living is reported to be relatively high due to their activity in the alternative or informal economy. However, they are still concentrated in a relatively poor part of the city in an ecological sense.

The second case is Tbilisi, capital of the Republic of Georgia. Here Georgians predominate, with 752,000 or 62.1 per cent of the total population of 1,211,000; the Russians (149,000) are actually exceeded by the Armenians (176,000). The figures in table 3.3 identify

Table 3.3 Distribution of national populations in the city of Tbilisi (percentages), by region, 1987

Region	Georgian	Russian	Armenian	Other
Leninskiy	66.9	12.0	8.6	12.5
Pervomansky	71.8	11.3	10.1	6.8
Oktyabr'skiy	62.4	8.8	18.1	10.7
Kalininskiy	71.9	8.4	11.2	8.5
Ordzonikidze	77.9	7.4	6.1	8.6
Kirovskiy	42.6	8.9	23.8	24.7
Im. 26 Komissarov	38.1	17.6	35.6	8.7
Zavodskiy	38.1	24.7	19.7	17.5
Gladinskiy	66.9	12.0	8.6	12.5
Saburtalinskiy	77.9	7.4	6.1	8.6
City	62.1	12.3	14.5	11.1

Source: *Goskomstat Gruzinskoy SSR, Tbilisskoe gorodskoe uprav'lenie gosudarstvennoy statistiki, Naselenyie, zdravookhranenie I sotsal'noe obespenenie v gorode Tbilisi* (Tbilisi, 1987)

two regions where Armenians comprise about a third and a quarter, respectively. Similarly, there is one region, covering the eastern extremity of the city, in which Russians make up a quarter of the total population. The impression is, then, of somewhat greater segregation than in Alma-Ata. The Georgian population exceeds three-quarters of the total in some regions, but falls to less than 40 per cent in others. The size of the Russian population here and, more particularly, in cities like Alma-Ata has important implications for future political and social stability, in the face of the reassertion of nationalism.

INEQUALITY IN THE SOCIALIST CITY

Discussion of the socio-economic or ethnic differentiation of the socialist city leads to the central issue of inequality with a spatial expression. Among both indigenous and Western students of the East European and Soviet city, there is almost universal agreement that the degree of social segregation and inequality under socialism was less than under capitalism. However, there are substantial differences in interpretation of both the spatial pattern of inequality and its extent. Some observers argue that urban inequalities were very greatly reduced under socialism, and that what did exist could best be described as a mosaic or patchwork, or in similar terms. This is essentially the conclusion arrived at by Weclawowicz (1979, 1981) in his studies of Warsaw and other Polish cities, and adopted by French and Hamilton (1979: 16–17). However, this view has been challenged by Dangschat (1987) in particular, who found 'surprisingly high' segregation of social groups by education, age and household size in Warsaw, contradicting what he described as the conventional wisdom of a low rate of social segregation in the socialist city. In place of the mosaic pattern, or segregation at the level of the apartment block, this alternative view claims the existence of relatively large and homogeneous areas in socialist cities. In a review of earlier experience and more recent research, Szelenyi (1987: 6) is sympathetic to this position:

> due to public ownership of most central urban land, due to the uniquely state socialist, exceptionally high degree of concentration of financing and of construction-firms, [an] unusually high proportion of new urban housing in socialist cities is being built in large estates, in a geographically concentrated way. Socialist city planning creates large geographic areas which are quite homogenous in terms of the nature

and quality of their housing stock and, as follows logically [from privileged, class-specific access to housing], they are also homogenous in terms of the occupational composition of their inhabitants.

There is evidence in the cases presented in this chapter to support both points of view. However, they seem as much if not more the outcome of the particular method used, and especially of the level of spatial disaggregation adopted, as of the reality they attempt to portray. The most sensible resolution would appear to be that some broad spatial differentiation of inequality in occupational status, education, housing, certain demographic characteristics, and (less conspicuously) income is very likely to be found in medium-sized and large cities, but punctuated by smaller distinctive areas differentiated by the survival of pre-revolutionary/pre-war housing, and by enclaves of superior or inferior state housing or co-operatives. Much depends on the history of the city in question, its pattern of (re)development, and the survival or otherwise of distinctive social areas, local communities or environments.

Turning to the process whereby socio-economic differentiation or inequality arises in the socialist city, this will clearly be different from what occurs under capitalism. However, residential segregation can be expected where there are socio-economic disparities within urban society, a variable housing stock, spatial concentrations of differing housing conditions, and competition for dwellings within the housing system. To these might be added differences in local levels of service provision and general environmental quality. And some residential sorting can also be expected to arise from the existence of distinctive ethnic or cultural groups, as well as from variations in family structure which lead to residential selectivity. All these conditions were in fact met, to a greater or lesser extent, under Eastern European and Soviet socialism. Some socio-economic segregation was the inevitable outcome. And once residential segregation has been established, the inequalities may be self-reinforcing.

The broad features of the process of intra-urban differentiation are sketched out in figure 3.3. On the right-hand side is the variable housing stock, service infrastructure and local environmental quality, patterned by pre-socialist forms as well as by new urban development. To the left is a suggestion of the means whereby differential access arises, from the productive and redistributive mechanisms and the role of individuals within them. While details may require modification in the light of how particular societies function nationally, this is general enough to capture the essence of the Eastern European socialist city as an inegalitarian system.

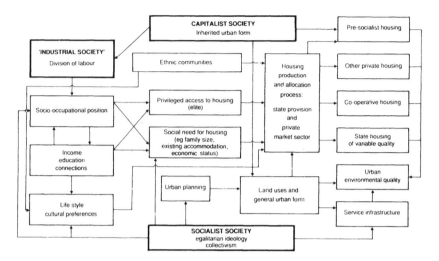

Figure 3.3   Elements of the process of inequality in the socialist city
Source: Smith (1989: 72, figure 8.2)

What we have observed, then, is the central paradox of the social-ism which actually existed: the continuation of inequality in a society built on supposedly egalitarian ideals. To quote Szelenyi (1987: 7), '[a]n ideologically egalitarian housing policy and urban planning produced an inegalitarian system of housing allocation, and pro-duced, and keeps reproducing, the residential segregation of occupational groups.' It is not that those who ran the societies con-cerned somehow deliberately subverted the system: '[t]hey create inegalitarian cities not because they wish to do so, but because they operate as key agents in a new social structure, which is shaped by new types of class antagonisms.' That such a society was ultimately self-destructive is, now, a matter of history. But the cities thus created, their people as well as the built environment, will continue an active role in the formation of post-socialist society and its cities, just as the socialist city and society could not completely transcend its own past.

NOTES

This chapter draws on work first published in Smith (1989), by permission of Cambridge University Press. The author is grateful for the assistance of the following colleagues in the cities in question: B. Domanski (Krakow), M. Ciechocinska and G. Weclawowicz (Warsaw), M. Tajin (Alma Ata), A.

Berozhkin, L. Smirnyagin and the late V.M. Gokhman (Moscow), N. Barbash (formerly in Moscow), and R. Gachechiladze and A. Rondeli (Tblisi). None bears responsibility for my findings. Some of the research on which this chapter is based has been supported by grants from the British Academy and British Council. Rachel Jagger provided valuable assistance with translation of some sources of data.

4

Urbanization under Socialism

György Enyedi

The aim of this chapter is to define and analyse the special features of East Central European urbanization in the socialist period, up to its termination in 1989. I outline some important characteristics of this urbanization, which were present across the region, and differed from typical aspects of Western urbanization. I then analyse the sources of these differences. Finally, I discuss the relationship between East Central European urbanization and the global urbanization process: was the former merely a product of the state socialist system, or was it a regional variant of global processes, with some special features rooted in a longer-term historical development and with some continuities with the pre-socialist period? Of course, one could ask whether this last question is still relevant, as the state socialist system has disappeared from Europe. However, it seems reasonable to assume that there may be important lessons to be learnt from the analysis of the last 45 or more years and that now is an appropriate time to draw some conclusions about socialist urbanization.

The first requirements are to define 'East Central Europe' and 'urbanization'. East Central Europe, as a political geographical unit, was created by the political division of Europe after 1945. It was composed of eight countries which referred to their political and social systems as 'socialist': Albania, Bulgaria, Czechoslovakia, the German Democratic Republic, Hungary, Poland, Romania and Yugoslavia. There is no generally accepted definition of urbanization. Since all definitions are teleological – designed for a purpose – there have been numerous definitions of this concept. For the purposes of this chapter, urbanization is a spatial process. It is the spatial reorganization of society by which, first, the geographical distribution of the population of a given country changes and (at least in the first stages of modern urbanization) gradually concentrates in cities and urban agglomerations; and, second, the urban life style, urban social structure and technology diffuse into the countryside, so that an urban/rural continuum (or a unified settlement system) replaces the earlier sharp urban/rural dichotomy.

In the first part of the chapter I discuss how socialist urbanization is to be interpreted; the second part examines the costs and consequences of delayed urbanization; the third part examines the principles of urban development strategy adopted in East Central Europe; finally, I summarize the special features of East Central European urbanization.

WAS THERE A SOCIALIST URBANIZATION?

In answering this question, our starting point is similar to that adopted by French and Hamilton (1979) in their important study of urbanization in socialist countries. Their answer is in the affirmative, and virtually all urban geographers in the East and the West have agreed that there were crucial differences between socialist and capitalist urbanization. These differences originated from the collective (mainly state) ownership of urban land and infrastructure, from the centrally planned allocation of development funds, and from the existence of comprehensive strategies for the development of the national settlement network in the socialist countries. By contrast, capitalist urbanization is led by market competition, private property, real-estate profitability, local decision-making, and physical planning on a city-by-city basis.

For East Central European Marxist urban sociologists and urban geographers, the assertion of the special nature of socialist urbanization was theoretically grounded. In addition, Western neo-Marxist urban sociologists and geographers linked Western urban problems to the contradictions of class-based societies and the capitalist mode of production (Castells, 1983; Harvey, 1973, 1985). The implicit suggestion was that socialist urbanization would provide solutions to such problems as excessive urban growth, urban residential segregation and so forth. But this assumption was not borne out by the empirical evidence. This in turn led neo-Weberian urban sociologists to argue that it was not the mode of production but rather its level that determined the nature of urbanization. Large-scale industrial technology had its own logic of location, which operated in all types of industrialized society, whatever their official ideologies. Thus urban problems in Western Europe only differed from those in Eastern Europe in so far as the latter were more developed (Pahl, 1977a).

My hypothesis is that socialist urbanization (more precisely, the urbanization of East Central European countries) was not a new model of modern urbanization. Rather, East Central European socialist countries replicated stages of a more generally applicable global process of urban development. However, these countries also exhibited special characteristics at each stage of urbanization. These had two sources: first, delayed economic and urban modernization and, second, the socialist political system. Thus I completely accept neither the neo-Weberian nor the neo-Marxist view: differences between East and West were neither solely the result of delayed development nor wholly systemic.

First, let us consider the stages of the global urbanization process. In the 1970s, urban geographers recognized that urban growth and the growing population concentration in metropolitan areas were not ever-continuing processes. Census data from the most developed Western countries showed signs of the ending of the period of population concentration and the start of population relocation towards non-metropolitan areas (Berry, 1981; Hansen, 1977; Van den Berg et al., 1982). Theories were formulated to explain these spatial changes. These distinguished between different stages of modern urbanization. The first stage is characterized by industrial take-off, by the rapid growth of industrial employment, by a strong rural-to-urban migration and by the spectacular growth of the cities. The second stage involves technical and structural changes in industry, which result in a decline in industrial employment and a rapid growth in the tertiary sector. Population continues to concentrate in urban areas, but in a relatively deconcentrated manner, in the form of suburbanization and the extension and selective growth of the small and medium city network. The third stage introduces an absolute deconcentration of the population, with population growth centred on non-metropolitan areas. The economy is characterized by the rapid growth of tertiary and especially quaternary sectors, by a new internal organization of the production system and by the introduction and propagation of high technology. Some authors refer to this stage as 'counterurbanization' (Berry, 1980). Whether this stage is followed by a fourth one, with a return to concentration or continued deconcentration, is not of importance for this discussion.

Empirical evidence has convinced me that the validity of this model is not restricted to the most developed Western countries, but that it is a globally applicable model (Enyedi, 1984). New stages were first developed in centres of economic and industrial innovation: the first and second stages in Western Europe, the third in North America. They were transmitted from these core areas to other parts of the world, with different countries embarking on different stages at different times. Each national pattern reproduced basic common features (that is, those criteria that define urbanization as a spatial process) of each stage, but not in the form of an exact copy of what had occurred in the originating centre of innovation. The reason why there were special features of a given stage in areas that urbanized later was due to the historical, nationally specific continuities in settlement development that persisted even in a changed environment.

So East Central European countries reproduced the basic features of the first stage of modern urbanization. Most of these countries then entered the second stage, reproducing its basic features. This shows that behind the facade of the differences and similarities of capitalist and socialist urbanization there was a common pattern of causality: the process of modern urbanization. This common process was more significant than the varying social structures that carried it; thus modern urbanization was able to develop in socialist and capitalist societies. Fundamental characteristics which were common to the urbanization processes of the two social systems include:

- rural-to-urban migration and the urban concentration of the population, a consequence of urbanization;
- the spatial separation of working zones and residences;
- suburban development;
- in the more developed northern half of East Central Europe, the decline in urban growth and relative increase in the importance of small and medium-sized centres in urban development;
- the growing importance of tertiary and quaternary employment, which changes the locational pattern of workplaces.

These phenomena were regulated by different mechanisms in the two social systems, but, I suggest, the basic processes producing these phenomena were closely similar or identical. Different mechanisms are simply different forms of expression of the process. For example, the role of market-level land values is one of the frequently quoted differences between socialist and capitalist urbanization. Although

Western cities have zoning and other land-use regulations and their governments have intervened directly in housing and infrastructural development, the development of functional zones within cities and the different types and forms of use of urban land have, nevertheless, been largely led by the micro-geography of land prices. More precisely, it was the locational value of urban land which lay behind the territorial regularities in its usage, that is its 'rational' usage (minimization of human efforts in terms of cost, travel time, etc., for performing the functions and/or maximizing the output of the function). In a market economy, the locational value is expressed in monetary terms. In a planned economy, the same basic ordering of locational values was expressed in detailed construction regulations, norms, comprehensive physical plans, resource allocations and so on. Locational patterns were similar in Western and Eastern European cities: government offices, shopping areas, residential and recreational zones have similar locational requirements for optimal functioning. Consequently, the locational map of an East Central European city did not differ substantially from a Western one of the same size, importance and functional type, even though governments had more formal power to shape the urban environment in the East than in the West.

So the importance of planning has been over-emphasized as the key feature of socialist urbanization. The complexities of the social system meant that in practice the urban system could not be planned and guided in a normative way. The role of planning, in fact, is to apply some 'corrections' to the spontaneous processes of urbanization. It is not possible to start anew with a planned system; at best (or rather worst) one can intervene in the normal process of urbanization by planning arbitrarily. We shall discuss below how the 'classical' goals of socialist urban policies had to be changed, because they were inappropriate in this context. In the 1920s, Western European and Soviet *avant garde* urbanists supposed that social processes could be changed by construction (Kopp, 1970). This proved erroneous. Built on a massive scale, standardized apartments did not make society more homogeneous; living at close quarters did not engender collectivism but rather social tension and neurosis.

Finally, there were two other factors which made the normal process of urbanization in the East and the West similar. First, the development of East Central Europe as a whole has lagged behind that of Western Europe for centuries, and it has tried again and again to close the gap. For this reason the countries of the region have imitated, or attempted to follow, Western patterns of political institutions, economic organization and urbanization. After 1945, the newly established socialist governments again tried to catch up with the West through radical social changes, rapid economic growth and accelerated urbanization. Marxist ideology refused to adopt the life style of the Western societies, but needed to achieve their levels of material wealth to establish the socialist (that is, egalitarian) well being of the population in the generally poor East Central European countries. Consequently, these societies followed Soviet patterns in formulating their policy goals and Western approaches to technological development in cities. However, technology is not neutral. In the West this technology was based on economic prosperity and designed to satisfy differentiated individual consumption. Its adoption in East Central Europe increased levels of social differentiation.

Second, planned urbanization, based on state housing and the central allocation of infrastructural investment, created only the built environment, not the social structures and relations accompanying urbanization. This built environment was occupied by people making their individual decisions in terms of choosing a settlement location, accepting a new job, searching for a new apartment and choosing education for their children. Individual goals were quite straightforward: they involved access to adequate housing; access to places of work, services and family members; and social status – living in a well-regarded neighbourhood (Kansky, 1976). My belief is that the average citizen set his or her goals in basically the same way whether living in Eastern or Western Europe. In fact, these choices expressed a certain perception of urban space which is a part of a shared European culture. The goals set by government were very different: these served the purposes of regional and social equalization, industrial location, or strategy. When governmental and individual goals conflicted, government had the power to constrain the expression of individual interests, but not to change the aspirations and ambitions that lay behind them.

In all societies, people's individual, informal response to public policies has feedback effects on the latter. But this was especially significant in East Central Europe. Here individuals devised hidden mechanisms for defending their interests and for promoting urban social processes in opposition to official policies, rejecting some of the values of 'socialist' urbanization in favour of a continuation of 'bourgeois' attitudes and ideology. For example, citizens did not accept the egalitarian goal with respect to residential location; they attempted to raise their social status by moving to better-regarded areas. In the cities, where the private housing market was all but abolished, the patterns of apartment occupancy were related in complex ways to the relative prestige of different areas. This sustained social segregation.

This individualistic approach to urbanization was largely based on the second economy. Services, goods and information related to housing circulated in this private network. The second economy was the locus of market relations, of consumer choice, of autonomous economic decisions – it was in fact a parallel society.

Thus, the similarities between Eastern and Western European urbanization were of fundamental significance. They derived from the common rules of modern urbanization and from continuities in the historical development of European urbanization.

LATE DEVELOPMENT

Late development is one of the most important and long-persisting sources of the peculiarities of East Central European urbanization. The region was located on the margins of the urbanization of the classical world. The Roman Empire established several cities on those parts of the territory which belonged to it in the last centuries of its existence (the first to the fifth centuries AD). But most of these cities were small military outposts, and they disappeared after the empire collapsed.

Medieval urbanization started later in East Central than in Western Europe, and Western-type cities only penetrated the northern half of the region. There is a controversy among urban historians about whether the Germanic cities built by German settlers were the only 'real' cities in medieval East Central Europe, or whether the Slavs, Romanians and Hungarians also built such cities. It appears as if the original Western type of medieval city originated in France, was adapted by the Germans in the tenth century, and was transferred, partly by German settlers and partly by French and Italian religious orders, to East Central Europe. Western types of city became widespread in Bohemia and Saxonia in the eleventh and twelfth centuries and reached Hungary and Poland in the thirteenth and fourteenth centuries. They never became important on the Hungarian and Romanian plains, where large market towns constituted the urban network for centuries. The urban innovation of the multi-functional medieval city with a regular street plan did not penetrate the Balkan peninsula at all, because this region was incorporated into the Ottoman Empire for 500 years (from the fourteenth to the nineteenth centuries). So European-style urban development was excluded from the southern part of East Central Europe until this latter century (Enyedi, 1978).

In the Middle Ages we can identify a single highly urbanized area where a dense urban network developed. This area included Saxonia, Thuringia, Bohemia, the central part of Moravia, and Silesia. This territory is still the urban-industrial core of East Central Europe. The urban network was poorly developed elsewhere, especially south from the Carpathian mountains. There were only a few great cities at that time: Buda, Prague, Brno, Danzig and Krakow. There was no town with more than 5,000 inhabitants on the Balkan peninsula (except Constantinople).

Modern urbanization started in the Czech-German region delineated above. Here, merchantile capitalism promoted a handicraft industry which then developed into a manufacturing industry. Industrial enterprises were small-scale, located near mineral resources or water power and on the large landed estates. This early industrialization created a dense urban network, in which small and medium-sized cities were dominant. The process of growth was slow and thus did not lead to massive migration and spectacular urban expansion. Even nineteenth- and twentieth-century urbanization did not disturb the balance of this urban network. In 1930, a third of Czech communes contained some manufacturing industry and three-quarters of the industrial settlements had fewer than 2,500 inhabitants. In this manner, however, by the beginning of the socialist era, the Czech region, Silesia, and the southern part of the GDR were already highly urbanized (Kansky, 1976; Musil, 1980).

Urban development in Hungary and Poland was delayed because both countries had lost their independence at an early stage. Hungary was divided into three parts in the sixteenth century. The central region was occupied by the Turks for 150 years, Transylvania became an independent principality, and the remaining area became a part of the Habsburg Empire. After the Ottoman occupation ended, Hungary and Transylvania became provinces of this empire too. By the end of the eighteenth century, Poland was divided between Prussia, Russia and the Habsburg Empire.

In fact, none of the present East Central European states was independent at the beginning of the nineteenth century (except what became the GDR, then part of Prussia), when the first stage of modern urbanization was already fully developed in Western Europe. The region was dominated by four powers: Russia, Prussia, and the Habsburg and Ottoman empires. The industrial-urban development of Bohemia was contained within the Habsburg Empire; when Czechoslovakia became independent in 1918, the new state contained 75 per cent of the industry of the former Austro-Hungarian Empire. With the exception of the core area, modern urbanization only began in the second half of the nineteenth century and did not then become general throughout the region. Isolated examples of mining and industrial development occurred, mostly by foreign capital. Industrial take-off, leading to modern urbanization, was limited to a handful of cities, which remained isolated within a predominantly pre-industrial urban network.

Between the two world wars, economic stagnation characterized the whole region (Ranki, 1983). As urban development was so strongly tied to industrialization, service functions remained poorly developed in local centres. Backward farming did not need much in the way of industrial goods and services, and the peasants' monetary income was limited. The process of industrialization was hampered in Germany (as a consequence of World War I) and in Czechoslovakia (as a consequence of the break-up of the large Austro-Hungarian market). It was interrupted and went into decline in Poland and Hungary; for instance, in 1938 Polish industrial output was still below the level that it had reached in 1913. Industry did advance in the Balkan countries from the 1920s, notably in Romania. However, it was confined to a few settlements, leaving these countries as still basically rural ones.

Thus industrialization and modern urbanization were late, slow and, in some countries, interrupted for a time. Moreover, the industries that did develop differed from those that the classical Industrial Revolution had produced a century earlier. For example, the food industry played a far more important part than in Western Europe, and this sector did not engender major urbanization. Foreign capital invested in large, concentrated enterprises, located in a limited number of settlements, usually in the largest cities. Urban development remained geographically strongly polarized.

The territorial consequences of World War I disturbed earlier urbanization processes. New boundaries imposed by the Paris peace treaties in 1920 cut off traditional linkages within the urban network. The Hungarian network was seriously cut down; all its secondary centres were incorporated into the surrounding countries, and Budapest, the capital city, remained the only sizeable urban centre in the new state. At the same time, the newly established countries had difficulties in integrating their inherited, fragmented urban networks into unified national settlement systems. In Romania and Czechoslovakia two, and in Yugoslavia at least three, strikingly different urban systems existed within the new boundaries. Aspects of this fragmentation are still evident; it takes a long time to form a new urban network (and recent events such as the civil war in former Yugoslavia will revive old divisions and promote a new pattern of fragmented urban network development). Uneven urban development plus these boundary changes have produced a unique situation where different stages of urban development have been contained within the settlement networks of small countries, which are, for example, no larger in area than Kentucky.

So in East Central Europe the first stage of modern urbanization penetrated the predominantly rural system slowly. As late as 1950, the region was overwhelmingly rural: the share of the rural population was over 80 per cent in Bulgaria and Yugoslavia, over 70 per cent in Romania and Poland, and 60 per cent in Hungary. Thus the theories and practices of socialist urbanization were introduced into a poorly urbanized, largely pre-industrial settlement network.

URBAN DEVELOPMENT STRATEGIES IN THE SOCIALIST ERA

Between 1945 and 1948, communist parties took over power throughout the region. Industrial, financial and commercial enterprises were nationalized, and attempts were made to collectivize agriculture. The building of a socialist society on the Soviet model was declared as the basic goal by the ruling parties and governments. The nationalizations represented the first step to achieving this goal, making collective ownership dominant.

The next task was to close the economic gap between the industrialized West and the peripheral East, hence the utmost importance was attached to rapid industrial growth. Industrialization, and consequently the development of the first stage of modern urbanization, speeded up remarkably after 1950. Agriculture and the rural population provided the resources for this, the former being heavily taxed and the latter confined to a low standard of living. The Soviet industrial pattern was followed: energy production, mining and heavy engineering were the leading sectors. All these were organized in large production units, in concentrated locations. So only some cities were transformed by this industrial take-off in the 1950s. These cities attracted many rural migrants and became 'strongholds of the working class', which entitled them to certain privileges at the expense of rural communes and the non-industrialized cities.

There were two basic principles of socialist urbanization: egalitarianism and planned urbanization. The former involved the equalization of living conditions within the settlement network and within individual settlements. Egalitarianism was a popular slogan in East Central Europe, where there were striking differences in living conditions between cities and regions, and where there were highly segregated areas and shanty towns within the large cities. Egalitarian principles were followed in the production of large state housing complexes, all of whose apartments had the same layouts and amenities. Each person had a right to the same amount of space, and the population of the new housing was socially mixed. The aim was that the basic public services were evenly distributed within the residential areas, applying general norms, such as the number of kindergarten places or the size of general-store shopfloor per 10,000 inhabitants. The shanty towns were torn down and replaced by government housing. It was, however, more difficult to follow the egalitarian rules in the older parts of cities, although the local authorities tried to do so by partitioning large apartments and villas and by multi-occupancy of large units. Therefore, egalitarian urbanism had its biggest opportunities in the newly established 'socialist' cities.

There was a generally accepted hypothesis that, with the advancement of socialism, society would become more and more homogeneous, so the egalitarian use of urban land would be in harmony with the social structure. It was believed that many of the persisting inequalities were inherited from the capitalist past and that they would disappear in the process of socialist development. Those currently disadvantaged – sub-tenants, residents of workers' hostels and so on – would all have their own apartments in five, ten or fifteen years.

In reality, as its economy matured, the socialist society became more and more stratified. While East Central European societies became more egalitarian in the sense that the class of the very rich disappeared and the share of those who were very poor diminished, there was much more differentiation within the working classes than hitherto. The size and importance of the white-collar professions grew remarkably. In consequence, the meaning of egalitarianism was repeatedly re-evaluated from the 1950s onwards.

From the late 1960s, the slogan of egalitarianism was combined with that of efficiency. Governments were unable to meet their promises in terms of the output of housing and public services. Shortages in infrastructure became permanent, as such investment was postponed time and time again. However, egalitarianism under conditions of shortage creates inequalities. If governments fail to supply everyone with public services, they have to choose whom they will supply. Privileged classes, social groups and individuals will have better access to scarce goods or services than those who are poorer, less powerful or less well informed. Hence the growing inequalities under 'egalitarian' central bureaucratic distribution first analysed by Szelényi and Konrád (1969).

The official belief was in fact that the dispersal of infrastructural investments and public services across the whole settlement network was inefficient, and equality had to be combined with efficiency. So infrastructural investments had to be concentrated in selected places only. This resulted in economies of scale being applied to the public services in an unjustified manner: economic efficiency is not a valid criterion to be applied to the location of a non-economic institution such as a school. Of course, Western European welfare states faced similar problems, and in the 1960s several research projects were carried out to define the optimal city size (Jacobs, 1964; Richardson, 1973). Despite their differing results there was a consensus on two matters; first, large metropolitan areas are less efficient (that is, more expensive) forms of urbanization than medium-sized cities; second, the rural population has to be clustered in larger settlements to provide an efficient size for modernization. However, East Central European urbanists were continually disconcerted by the existence of the rural settlements, because they could not apply the principles and tools of socialist urbanization to them, mainly because these settlements were excluded from state housing construction. Except for a few workers' colonies built by state farms, rural housing remained largely private and more differentiated than urban housing.

Planning in the socialist countries was much more comprehensive than in the West, and it also controlled the financial-economic basis of urbanization. In the classical Soviet model, planning embraced all aspects of urban development and was based on collective ownership and the strict government control of urban land and infrastructure. Central planning authorities decided the location of the various forms of infrastructural development, and the local authorities were simply expected to execute them.

However, despite this detailed planning, actual urban development had many 'spontaneous' elements. Central planning was essentially sectoral planning. In this system the individual elements of urban development – housing, public health, transport and communication, education, etc. – were planned separately by different ministries. City councils had the task of trying to co-ordinate this development, but they had no decision-making power. So poorly co-ordinated sectoral decisions frequently produced bottlenecks in infrastructural development.

The countries of East Central Europe interpreted and applied these socialist principles in widely varying ways. However, we can highlight a few general characteristics of the settlement development strategies that emerged. First, we can distinguish between the different periods of urban policy development in the socialist era. In the 1950s there was no explicit urban policy, and sectoral planning was dominant. Principles of socialist urbanization were applied sporadically, in certain sectors such as state housing and in certain settlements. Each country established a few 'socialist' cities, emulating the Soviet example. In the USSR over 1,000 new cities had been built since the October Revolution, in most cases located near natural resources. The economic development of Siberia and the Soviet Far East had opened up new territories, which therefore required new towns to be built. By contrast, in densely populated East Central Europe, the new towns served to demonstrate the rapid successes achieved by their communist governments and as locations for experiments in socialist urban planning. But after up to four decades of existence most of these cities had remained as company towns or had developed into industrial suburbs of neighbouring cities. Finally, during this first period a small amount of manufacturing industry was located in less well-developed rural areas, which promoted urban growth in these under-urbanized areas.

In the late 1950s and early 1960s, the first comprehensive regional and urban strategies were developed and applied, based on the principle of industrial decentralization. Modern industry was then located in some of the provincial cities, and this contributed to the development of a modern urban system, levelling out unemployment among different regions and reducing inter-regional migration. Cities were still regarded principally as sites for industry. In the first long-term Hungarian urban development strategy, published in 1962, cities were classified by planners according to their capacity for accommodating industry. Thus their development prospects were designated according to this criterion.

In the 1970s, an important change took place in views about the role of cities. They were no longer to be regarded simply as a sites for industrial production; now their central place functions were emphasized. The cross-regional and cross-city equalization of living conditions became the main theme of the new urban and regional policies. Thus the territorial organization and accessibility of public services became as important as industrial location, and the integration of the urban and rural settlement networks into a unified whole became the long-term goal.

A second general characteristic of settlement strategies in East Central Europe concerned the treatment of urban growth. On the one hand, in order to diminish regional inequalities, the decentralization of industry, and later tertiary and quaternary activities, was welcomed, and regulations attempted to limit the growth of those large cities where infrastructural shortages were most acute. On the other hand, centralization and concentration were highly valued in the socialist political and decision-making system. Politicians and government officials as well as state enterprise managers were convinced that 'big is beautiful' – large enterprises, hospitals, restaurants and so on were more efficient than small ones. Urban and regional strategies constantly sought to find compromise solutions to this conflict between equality and (supposed) efficiency. Suggested solutions included 'centralized decentralization' (that is, locating industry in under-developed regions but in a few large centres), and keeping provincial production units under the strict control of the large enterprise headquarters.

The alternative development strategies were discussed by experts and decision-makers, focusing on political, economic and strictly professional issues. Little if any attention was paid to the opinions of the population at large about these matters, despite the fact that they had a great impact on its life. Public participation was reduced to a largely symbolic involvement (such as voluntary work performed in free time to help provide a new facility such as a playground), or to exhibitions of city plans with the opportunity for the public to leave written comments. The power of the citizenry and of the local authorities in urban and regional planning remained very limited.

A third general issue concerned the role of rural development in the long-term strategies. The abolition of the social differences between the town and the countryside had been a cornerstone of Marxist theory. This objective had a special significance in East Central Europe, where rural poverty and backwardness affected a large proportion of the population. Sectoral plans made important provisions to modernize the countryside (electrification and road construction, for example). However, in theory and in practice Marxist governments were biased in favour of the cities. As has repeatedly been noted, Marx and Engels, in the *Communist Manifesto*, bemoaned the 'idiocy of rural life' and called for the 'gradual abolition of the distinction between the town and the country'. Lenin described the cities as the 'centres of the economic, political and spiritual life of the people and the major source of progress' (Demko and Regulska, 1987). And in fact the new socialist power in the region was urban-based. It aimed to control the cities and govern the countries from them; consequently the cities enjoyed advantages in the allocation of development funds by the central planners. Socialist governments were suspicious of the countryside, where the farming population, suffering from heavy taxes, compulsory deliveries of foodstuffs and collectivization, was reluctant to support ambitious programmes of industrialization. In addition, rural development offered no professional challenges for the physical planners, because there was little room for spectacular new projects. In fact, until the 1970s there was no valid strategy for the development of rural settlements.

A fourth issue was that, across the region, urban development strategies paid much attention to the development of an hierarchical urban network. As already noted, there was no well-developed urban network in pre-war East Central Europe, except in Bohemia and the (now former) GDR. Contrary to what had earlier occurred in Western Europe, the formation of a modern urban network was a process directed from above, in two respects. First, urban development was promoted and directed from the top governmental level by the allocation of development funds. Second, the first priority was to modernize the top of the urban hierarchy (the capital city and the large regional centres), then the medium-size cities were dealt with, and finally the process was completed by expanding and developing small cities, the base of the whole system. This 'reverse' urbanization is typical everywhere where modern economic development was delayed, including in the developing countries. As a consequence, there was a period when the settlement network was split into two parts: the modern cities and the traditional local centres, with an inability to maintain adequate linkages between the modern sector and the countryside.

Later on, as we have already noted, this urbanization from above did focus on integrating the urban and rural settlement networks. For this purpose it was assumed that it would be important to provide non-agricultural jobs for the rural population in the large villages. Basic public services also had to be made more accessible. But, because of the continuing shortage of infrastructural investment, it was thought necessary to speed up the process of concentration of the rural settlements for efficient modernization by running down the smallest villages. These 'non-viable' villages were selected by the planners arbitrarily, without taking into consideration the opinions of the people affected (Ronnas, 1984).

A final common characteristic was that urban planners regarded it as an important task to ensure the continuous increase in the urban share of the population. Having a high proportion of rural population became a symbol of the backward past; the gap between East Central and Western Europe in this respect also had to be narrowed. This accounts, for example, for the incorporation of many suburban areas into the administrative areas of the cities.

So the desire for rapid urban development was one aspect of the broader programme of 'catching up with the West'. However, the advocates of rapid urban growth miscalculated over two matters. First, the high proportion of the urban population in the West was the product of a centuries-old, organic development, originating 'from below'; while the post-war urbanization of East Central Europe occurred over a much shorter period and under different social conditions. Second, the size of the urban population per se does not have any wider significance with respect to economic and social development. There are high levels of urban population in several developing countries; for example, Latin America is as highly urbanized as Europe.

SPECIAL FEATURES OF URBAN DEVELOPMENT IN EAST CENTRAL EUROPE

East Central European urbanization had two basic but special features that I noted earlier: it was delayed, and it was centrally planned and managed for over 40 years. Scholarly literature has focused on these two characteristics. But here I want to mention four other elements.

First, there was the excessive role of industrialization in urbanization. Before World War II, industry was concentrated in small enclaves within the region. The post-war industrial take-off introduced industry to every part of the region. During socialist urbanization, tertiary functions and infrastructural investments were seriously neglected, as all efforts focused on industrialization. Infrastructural investment was classified as 'non-productive', a consumer of national income rather than a producer of it. However, the low efficiency of the industrial investments resulted in acute capital shortages. Only industrial investment forced the central authorities to allocate some money for infrastructural investments in transport, telecommunications and other facilities to meet the industrial needs; residential infrastructure developed as a spin-off from this. Moreover, infrastructural development was postponed in tertiary cities and rural areas. So, at least in the first phase of urbanization, industrial and urban development were identical. This situation was formally theorized by Soviet urban geography and was expressed in urban policies (Pokshishevsky and Lappo, 1976). Growth and decline in cities depended on their industrial functions. Urban attraction zones corresponded with industrial commuter zones, and the traditional central-place roles were degraded.

By the 1970s, industrial growth had slowed down and the take-off

phase was coming to an end in most East Central European countries. Now the state socialist system made it impossible for these
societies to move forward into the post-industrial era: there were no
resources for R & D or for expanding the service sector. The economies remained frozen at their late-1970s levels. Slow growth, then
stagnation and finally decline in the 1980s again widened the gap
with the West.

A second feature was the continuing importance of the rural
sector in the process of urbanization. The persistence of a relatively
large rural sector was the result of late development and of the short
period of industrial take-off, as well as the neglect of the tertiary
sector.

Rural development has had a contradictory character in East Central Europe. On the one hand, there were radical changes in the
social structure. On the other hand, there was still an urban/rural
dichotomy in living conditions. A marked sign of the social change
was the high proportion of industrial workers among the rural residents. Daily commuting was widespread in most countries. These
commuters were mainly blue-collar workers who lived in rural-type
suburbs. They were generally first-generation industrial workers who
did not settle in the cities, partly because of the urban housing
shortages but mainly because of the economic advantages of combin-
ing urban and rural work. In fact, in some countries the proportion
of industrial workers in the rural population became higher than
that in the urban population. The cities became strongholds of white-
collar employees.

Before World War II, rural areas were seriously under-developed
in most countries of the region. Despite the substantial improvement
in rural living conditions post-war, the rural population – whatever
their social status – continued to suffer from serious disadvantages.
The general neglect of infrastructural investment hit the rural areas
more seriously than it did the cities. Rural people found it very
difficult to gain access to a number of subsidized public services, and
rural incomes lagged behind urban ones. These settlement inequalities were a serious aspect of social discrimination in East Central
Europe.

However, urbanization remained imperfect in the cities too. In
fact, a section of the urban population retained some rural attributes.
These included the strong links that they kept up with their rural
areas of origin. Much of the urban population consisted of first-
generation rural immigrants. Former peasants poured into the cities
in such numbers that they modified traditional patterns of urban life:
they partly 'ruralized' the cities (Simic, 1973). In 1970, two-thirds of

the population of Belgrade, Yugoslavia's capital city, consisted of first-generation immigrants from the provinces. Rural populations helped their urban relatives in many ways (food, financial aid for housing and so on), making an indirect contribution to urban development from rural resources. New urban dwellers returned to their villages during their paid holidays, for example to help with the harvest. In countries where second homes are common, the land round these was intensively cultivated by urban families. In Hungary, for example, a quarter of urban households had auxiliary farms.

In addition, there were rural elements in suburbanization, unlike the situation in the blue-collar suburbs in Western Europe and the USA. In East Central Europe, suburban workers continued to maintain a rural life style by living in large, single-family homes, built, at least in part, by themselves, with large, intensively cultivated gardens with orchards, vineyards and some sort of livestock. Rural migrants were also able to relocate some of their other rural habits and traditions to the suburbs. For example, migrants from the same village often tried to live in the same streets or neighbourhoods in their new settlements.

A third commonality was that there was little cohesion within the urban networks. They were created by centrally guided urbanization 'from above'. The economic and service relations between the settlements were designated by the government. In state socialism all services were 'public'; they were organized and sited by the public administration. So the hierarchy of public administration provided the framework for almost every form of inter-urban relationship. There were no locally or regionally based economic networks; the state economy was commanded by the various centralized government agencies.

Finally, the structure and functioning of urban society differed greatly from that of Western cities. Even before the communist takeover, East Central European cities had special features: the middle class was extremely limited, the business elite was intermingled with the political and aristocratic elite, and social strata were partly organized on non-market principles, whether on the basis of position, authority, hierarchical rank or respect – a form of post-feudal, status-based system. In the socialist urban social systems a new elite was formed by the 'nomenklatura', which included the party leadership, the managers of the state economy, and the leaders of the public administration. There was also a massive proletarianization, in which most people became state employees. Local social systems disintegrated as grassroots social organizations and interest groups were abolished. Centrally controlled and organized professional, cultural and other associations were the only ones that were permissible. Many forms of social activity were related to the workplace, so this replaced the settlement and its urban community as the locus for political socialization. By the late 1980s, however, this important and contradictory chapter in the history of East Central European urbanization was at an end.

5

Privatization and its Discontents: Property Rights in Land and Housing in the Transition in Eastern Europe

Peter Marcuse

PRIVATIZATION AND ITS MEANINGS

Privatization

'Privatization' is the dominant theme in the contemporary reform of housing policy in Eastern Europe.[1] Property rights lie at the heart of that process. And property rights in residential land, on which this chapter focuses, are among the most controversial aspects of privatization.

Yet privatization is a surprisingly murky concept. 'Privatization = Divestment of government ownership' is not a sound conceptual formulation of the process; privatization is not the same thing as destatification. Ownership, to begin with, is a bundle of rights (see P. Marcuse, 1994a); they were divided between government and individuals under state socialism, and they are divided between government and individuals in Western capitalist countries. Rights to use and to limit use, rights to build and to limit building, rights to sell and to tax the proceeds of sale, rights to transfer on death and to determine survivors' claims, all are divided in varying ways in varying countries; nowhere are they absolute on either the private or the governmental side.

'Private' is itself a troublesome category. Divestment by government is only a negative formulation; it matters to whom property is divested. Speak to the average person in Eastern Europe, and private ownership of housing means the resident owns the place where he or she is living. That is hardly the definition in the West, where absentee landlord ownership is taken for granted as part of the housing market. Realtors in the West would not consider non-profit ownership private ownership, although it is certainly not government ownership; at best they would consider it a third form of ownership, between public and private. In the East, co-operative ownership was considered a form of social ownership; in the West, legally it is private.

Privatization is often considered the undoing of something unnaturally imposed by socialist regimes on a former 'natural' condition, that is, private ownership. But that conceptualization also is wrong. 'Private' ownership did not always precede 'governmental' ownership; indeed, anthropologically speaking, individual rights in property probably came after social rights, and were carved out of them. The forms of ownership under the tsars were very different from those established under Anglo-Saxon law or under the Napoleonic codes (Berman, 1950: 130ff; Sawicki, 1977: 20–7). Feudal land tenures, such as those that predominated in much of Eastern Europe through the nineteenth century, were private in a very different sense from the one in use today. Much of Prussian law and of the law of the Austro-Hungarian empire continued to be effective even in state socialist times in the countries previously subject to them.

The privatization process is further complicated by a confusion of subject-matter. The dominant concern has been with privatization of economic processes, introducing private ownership and profit motivation into the production of goods and services. Factories, shops, technological innovations are to be privatized to increase production, rationalize distribution, and accelerate growth of GNP. The logic in the realm of production, however – whatever its merits, a discussion of which is not the intent of this chapter – is quite different from the logic in the sphere of consumption: here the question of profit is subordinate to the question of use, the consumption of many items is better done collectively than individually (parks, transportation, urbanity), and issues of fairness, justice and social concern may play a larger role than questions of efficiency or growth (dealing with the handicapped, the homeless, children). The assumption that privatization is a uniform process, with property rights necessarily applying to all possible items of private ownership alike, conceals major cleavages of substance. Pre-existing distinctions between personal and state property in Soviet law recognized such a cleavage (discussed in more detail below); most discussions of privatization in Eastern Europe today do not.

If 'privatization' is equated more generally, as it often is, with 'property rights reform', then of course 'reform' requires definition. There are widely differing understandings of what property rights reform means. The dominant view runs somewhat as follows:

> A democratic society requires a private market. A private market requires a corresponding system of private property rights. Such a system has been extensively developed in advanced Western countries, but is missing in the countries of Eastern Europe.[2] The task for property rights reform in the East is now to establish such a set of rights where none existed before, a task which requires both legislation and the establishment of an institutional structure to implement that legislation. General principles, preferably written into constitutions, providing for the protection of private property and its disposition by its owners free of state control, are the logical first step in this double task. Uniformity of the application of such principles to all possible forms of property is eminently desirable.
>
> While the direction in which reform must go is clear, implementing it is hard. The forces of resistance are primarily the established nomenklatura of the state socialist system; they are abetted by the lack of understanding of most citizens as to what a system of laws and property rights is. Both a political and an educational campaign are necessary to convince citizens and their leaders as to the true direction property rights reform must take. Land is a particularly difficult area for such reform, because people have such deeply embedded but counter-productive traditional views about it.

A more historically oriented account of what is happening in Eastern Europe today might, however, run as follows:

> The state socialist systems had a well developed system of property rights, based on that established in the Soviet Union in its early period. That system had been heavily modified under Stalin to combine with its early ideological character pragmatic rules permitting everyday stability but subject to the interests of centralized power. While taking over the Soviet system as it stood at the end of World War II, most countries within the Soviet sphere at the same time preserved significant aspects of their own pre-existing legal systems, rules governing land ownership being prominent among them.
>
> The state socialist system of property rights had provided benefits for many persons for certain purposes, although it precluded other benefits. Its separate treatment of the means of production from objects of individual use and consumption played an important role in defining the stability of everyday life. This is particularly true as to residential land and housing, where individual protections were often stronger (although other economic benefits weaker) than in the West.

Reluctance to surrender real protections accounts for the wide-spread resistance to the mass importation of Western conceptions of property rights. The nomenklatura are divided on the issues; some can translate prior benefits easily into Western private property terms, others, particularly those with political rather than economic advantages, have less incentive to support Western-style reform. Economic pressures from the West, and their growing internal corollaries, are strong for reform. On the other hand, the more locally responsive the official, the more foot-dragging is likely to take place. Constitutional provisions are of little relevance, given the fluid institutional structure of legal reform.

This is the interpretation that underlies this chapter.

Property/ownership

Clearly established legal rights in property, and mechanisms for their enforcement, lie at the heart of modern Western legal systems. Many discussions of privatization assume that, in contrast, property rights did not exist in Soviet-style systems. But whether they did or not depends on the definition of property.

The most widely accepted definition of such rights in Western jurisprudence is that 'property' is a bundle of rights which are relations among persons and institutions with regard to a thing. Under that definition, socialist systems embodied conceptions of property rights as much as Western systems did, although they were different rights. This conception of property rights can be expressed in different ways, each making the same point. C.B. MacPherson (1978: 6), the leading contemporary theorist of property rights in the West, formulates it thus: '[Property is a set of] enforceable claims of persons to some use or benefit of something.' Thus it is conventional in Western law to speak of property ownership as 'a bundle of rights with respect to a thing', and to analyse the way the individual rights in that bundle are divided up and the terms of their exercise. It is therefore clear that, in the West, 'the law of ownership is not a set of rules fixing what I may or may not do to a thing but a set of rules fixing what other people may or may not prevent me from doing to the thing, and what I may or may not prevent them from doing to the thing' (J.W. Turner, 1941). The 'rights' in the bundle of rights that constitutes property thus consist of a set of relationships among people, relationships which can be, and have been, variously defined in various legal systems throughout history.[3] As MacPherson (1978: 2, 4, 5) says:

Property . . . is usually treated as identical with *private* property. [This] is a genuine misconception, which . . . can be traced historically to . . . the period of the rise of the capitalist market society . . . The definition of property . . . is often taken to rule out the idea of *common* property. . . . it does not . . . A right to use the common things, however limited, is a right of individuals . . . the state *creates* the rights, the individuals *have* the rights . . . [S]tate property . . . is . . . akin to private property . . . the state itself is taking and exercising the powers of a corporation: it is acting as an artificial person.

Such definitions of property, property rights and ownership are just as applicable to the analysis of relationships in the countries of real existing socialism as they are to private market economies. The distribution of the benefits and obligations of ownership, of the rights in the bundle, are indeed very different in the two systems; but property rights exist in both.[4]

SOVIET PROPERTY RIGHTS

But property rights do not exist in a vacuum. Both the theories on which they are based and their implementation in practice have evolved historically and changed over time. The Soviet history has a particularly complex relationship between theory and practice, with political and economic changes dictating shifts in theory, but with strongly held theory also influencing fundamental practices – not, indeed, so differently from the pattern in Western states in the area of law and jurisprudence.

'Soviet' is used throughout this section to refer to the Soviet Union, but deviations in other countries of Eastern Europe are referred to where relevant.

Soviet theory

The broad-sweep history of property rights in the twentieth century in Eastern Europe may be summarized as follows (the description is based on the history in Russia and applies only with significant variations to other countries of Eastern Europe). Pre-socialist rights in land had many elements of feudal relationships in them (Berman, 1950: 130ff). One typical Western observer comments, 'the very notion of landownership – that is, the right to possess, use and sell land – never really existed before [1917] in Russia' (ADEF: 1992).

The socialist period began with the goal of the 'abolition of private property', but precisely what that was to mean was unclear. Marxist theory, rapidly hardening into a legitimating ideology, played a significant role in the debate in the early days.[5] But as time went on, practice began to dictate theory rather than the reverse. By the time Stalin consolidated his power, theoretical debate was essentially irrelevant to the formulation of policy in the Soviet Union; only in the GDR could the argument be made that theory significantly influenced practice in the post-war years. The issue of ownership directly by the producers, in early theory held to be the purpose of nationalization, was removed from public discussion; the formality of nationalization was held by itself to create socialist cities, quite at variance with the discussions of the early period.[6]

The law continued to change after any reliance on theory came to an end, and simply varied according to the prosaic needs of the day. The handling of co-operatives is a typical example. Co-operatives were seen as a manifestation, at best, of non-revolutionary working-class struggle, unnecessary and, in Lenin's early view, perhaps even dangerous under socialism. Yet they were alternately encouraged and discouraged, by both legal and administrative measures, throughout the history of the Soviet Union, depending on the felt need to stimulate economic development and marshall private resources in periods of stagnation, or the pressure to centralize state control in periods of growth (Andrusz, 1992).

At the end of the socialist period in a few countries, the early Gorbachev Soviet Union and the Wende GDR in particular, some intellectually interesting but historically evanescent efforts were devoted to thinking through alternative non-capitalist, non-state forms of ownership and land control. Finally, the political collapse of the older socialist governmental structures and political parties and the invasion of Western capital, Western consultants and Western ideology led to the formal adoption of programmes of privatization, with, however, very different impacts. While the final results are not yet clear, one can quite clearly see the forces among which the tension will be decisive today. They are discussed later.

We start with a brief history of the socialist theory of property rights. We then turn to the concrete handling of land ownership over time in the Soviet Union, ending this section with an overview of the mature Soviet system as of the mid-1980s.

The history of Soviet theory

Consistent with the refusal of Marx and Engels to speculate about the details of a post-capitalist state, much was left unclear in their writings as to the form of property rights under socialism, the ownership of land, and in general the role of law. But two points were clear: first, the ownership of land should be nationalized; and, second, nationalization did *not* mean either state ownership with a rental arrangement with users, or control over land in the hands of the immediate users themselves.

Left unclear was how the use of land should in fact be allocated, how rights to use should be distributed, what decision-making mechanism nationalization implied. That which appeared clear was put into practice by the socialist states, if with varying degrees of thoroughness, but what was unclear in Marx and Engels was never satisfactorily worked out in any of the socialist countries. As Trotsky remarked ten years after the revolution, '[a] revolution in the forms of ownership does not solve the problem of socialism but only raises it!' (quoted in Berman, 1950: 52). Debates were intense in the 1920s in the Soviet Union about whether social ownership meant public ownership, that is, openness to use by all members of the public, or state ownership, which might then restrict public use; whether state ownership was simply a form of private ownership, the owner being the state, or whether it was a unique and, at least in the case of land, an exclusive form of ownership; whether 'the state' referred exclusively to the national state, or included the government of the republics, and/or governments at the local level; and whether land was simply a subcategory of 'the means of production', or stood in a category all its own – the latter being the widely accepted view, based indeed in some discussions in Marx.[7]

Beyond and underlying these questions, the whole role of law in a socialist society was under debate. Ownership arrangements were supposed to be embedded in a legal system that was fundamentally different from those in capitalist countries. Marx (1859/1968: 182–3) himself had seen law and property relations as intimately related to the economic structure of society; in one of his most famous formulations:[8]

> At a certain stage of their development, the material productive forces of society come into conflict with the existing relations of production, or – what is but a legal expression of the same thing – of the property relations within which they have been at work hitherto. From forms of development of the productive forces these relations turn into their fetters. Then begins an epoch of social revolution. With the change of the economic foundation the entire immense superstructure is more or less rapidly transformed.

The early Soviet interpretation of Marx's approach was that law was necessarily an expression of bourgeois relationships: that it was built on the concept of the contract as the foundation of relation-ships among atomistic individuals; and that it was therefore incom-patible with a socialist society. The withering away of the state would involve the withering away of law. During a transitional period, dur-ing the dictatorship of the proletariat, some forms of bourgeois law might be required to maintain proletarian rule, but that did not make it proletarian law; such a thing was a contradiction in terms, for the proletariat was committed to the abolition of the market and economic individualism, and thus to the abolition of the law, which was their expression (Berman, 1950: 200ff and fn. 7; Schlesinger, 1945; Gsovski, 1945: 166ff).

Landed property was particularly repugnant to socialist law, in this view. Not only was it a matter of the consumption/production dis-tinction in general, under which, as Marx had said, in socialism 'nothing can pass to the ownership of individuals except individual means of consumption' (Marx, 1875/1968: 324); landed property was also peculiarly symptomatic of the difference between capitalist and post-capitalist forms of law. According to Pashukanis (1927/ 1978: 126–7), the leading early theorist of law in the Soviet Union:

> the relationship of a person to the product of his labour (for example to the plot of land he cultivates himself) is elementary and accessible even to the most primitive turn of mind. It is for precisely this reason that the apologists of private property are particularly fond of appeal-ing to this primitive relation, for they know that its ideological force far outweighs its economic significance for modern society. [But] . . . there is no morphological connection between . . . private appropriation as the precondition for unlimited personal usage, and private appropriation as the condition for subsequent alienation in the act of exchange . . . Capitalist landed property . . . does not presup-pose any kind of organic bond between the land and its owner. On the contrary, it is only conceivable when land changes hands with complete freedom.

The meaning of nationalization was a core question in these dis-cussions. Theoretically, public property was to be directly under the control of the workers and peasants, the immediate producers. But the theoretical form such control should take remained elusive; in practice, nationalization became defined in essentially capitalist terms, that is, as the traditional rights of ownership simply trans-ferred from private persons to the state in its corporate aspect. Na-tionalization was then followed by an evolutionary refinement of the content of 'non-capitalist' ownership, with the development of other forms of ownership, less prominent in capitalist societies, featuring primarily forms of 'common ownership' in MacPherson's terms. Such new forms were explicitly debated and theoretically justified in some countries, simply allowed to emerge in practice in others, sometimes even in technical conflict with explicitly legal forms. Something akin to a 'right to squat' (an oxymoron in capitalist terms) based on need might even have been said to have developed.

But the mature Soviet system rejected such informal occupancy arrangements. The distribution of rights of ownership was regulated in detail by Soviet law. The debate over the societal meaning of 'socialist law' was closed. Pashukanis was forced to recant, and was executed in 1937. The official Soviet approach took an entirely different tack from his, claiming a higher type of legality than bourgeois law, rather than rejecting all law:

> Socialist law is law of a new, special, and higher historical type, first of all because of its economic base, of its class content. It is an instrument of class and policy, reflecting the governing will of the toilers led by the working class . . . a society based on social, socialist property. It is of an anti-exploitative nature . . . At the same time socialist law . . . conforms totally to the general concept of law. It is not only the heir to all of the wealth of legal cultures coming from the past, but also a social form which assures a leap forward in the development and enrichment of legal culture, a new higher level in legal progress.[9]

As we shall see, the evolution of Soviet law concerning property ownership and land did in fact have characteristics of an 'anti-exploitative nature', while at the same time remaining susceptible to analysis in very conventional Western jurisprudential terms (property as a bundle of rights).

The history of the practice

The second decree adopted by the All-Russian Congress of Workers', Soldiers', and Peasants' Soviets on the day after the revolution abolished 'the private ownership of land' (Andrusz, 1984: 13). Two months later all commercial operations with urban real estate were stopped. By August of 1918 the process of detailing nationalization, covering large buildings as well as land, had begun. What in fact initially happened was simply the physical occupation by peasants of the land they had been working, and the denial of the rights to ownership of urban land to those who had previously exercised them. How such rights were henceforth to be exercised, in what combinations and by whom was not decided in the early decrees, except negatively: in cities of over 10,000 population, for instance, private individuals were prohibited from building or developing land. Those provisions were somewhat liberalized, but their basic principles were kept during the period of the New Economic Policy. Legislation of August 1921, for instance, allowed private construction on urban land on lots allocated for that purpose by government. A cadastre system of registering land by location, use, and 'natural, economic and legal status' was prescribed, but never methodically implemented.

From the outset, peasant households' land ownership was put in a separate category, and, while land as such might be 'nationalized', the traditional rights of peasants to the land that they themselves worked for their own households was not tampered with. Those rights had been established since 1861 in the Emancipation Statutes ending serfdom. They were considered theoretically petit bourgeois by the leadership of the Communist Party, but nevertheless too important to interfere with; thus they were ultimately simply labelled 'peasant household property', termed a 'form of socialist ownership' different both from personal property and from socialized, state or collective, property. Rights to the use of land constituting garden plots, the key component of peasant household property, were decided by land agencies, not by courts (Berman, 1950: 187, 189; Sawicki, 1977).

In no other country in Eastern Europe was all land nationalized; in all others, substantial land and housing remained in private hands. Bulgaria is probably the extreme case, predominantly agricultural at the time of Soviet occupation; the GDR is more typical, in that there were several waves of nationalization of specific categories of land, including at various points that of war criminals, that of emigrants, that of large estates (over 100 hectares), and that of nationalized industries. The result was, for the GDR, that at the time of the collapse of the regime over half of all housing was still technically privately or personally owned.[10]

During the period of the New Economic Policy, beginning in 1921, many of the rights of ownership, in particular the long-term rights of use, were explicitly given (often simply in recognition of the factual situation) to the enterprises that occupied the property. With the forced collectivization of agriculture in the 1930s the situation changed. Full control of the disposition of land was put under the control of the state, and delegated to enterprises; in the case of agricultural lands, to collective and state farms and local soviets. Private property was recognized only as to consumer goods and collectibles, money, bank deposits and state bonds; small plots of land were made available to families for private farming operations, as part of peasant household property, but within severe limits.

The 'abolition of private property', celebrated in the early decrees of the revolutionary government in 1917 and 1918, was preserved as a concept in the 1936 Constitution, but with supplementation by the concept of 'personal ownership', functionally equivalent to conventional concepts of 'ownership' in the West less the right of disposition at a profit – without the right to derive 'non-labour income' from its ownership.[11] 'Personal property' comprised items (including one house, and land that the household could personally cultivate, in the agricultural case) of personal use only. Its formulation was permissive; '[t]he right of personal ownership of citizens . . . shall be permitted by law.' The 1977 Constitution went further in its language; '[personal property is] protected by the state.' The two major limitations were clearly grounded in theory: one, that property should not be 'used to the prejudice of the interests of society', language not so dissimilar from Western language, as noted above, and two, that property might not be used to derive 'non-labour' income, to make a 'profit', in ordinary Western terms, a prohibition directly at variance with capitalist conceptions (Hazard et al., 1984: 228).

The Soviet system in its mature phase

In the Soviet system (that existing in the Soviet Union – references to variations in other countries are made where important) in the last phase of its existence, there were thus two legally recognized forms of ownership of property.[12] First, there was *socialist ownership*, the way in which all land and all of the 'means of production' were held. It included three classes of owner: the state (as to whose property the Constitution adds: 'belonging to all the people'); 'public organizations', including state enterprises and collective farms; and co-operatives. Second, there was *personal ownership*, the way in which items of personal use, including dwellings (free-standing, or apartments in multi-unit buildings), plots of land assigned for use for private agricultural production, and items of household and purely personal use, including tools for handicraft production, could be held.[13]

The percentage distribution of ownership of housing in Russia by these categories in 1990 was as shown in table 5.1. By land area, state property occupied 67 per cent of the total land area, 79 per cent of urban land.

Land was *per se* owned by the state, and could be neither sold nor mortgaged (Osakwe, 1991: fn. 13). Decisions as to its use were del-

Table 5.1   Distribution of ownership of housing in Russia (percentages), 1990

	Total	Urban	Rural	New construction
State	67	79	37	78
Public and construction co-operatives	4	5	0	13
Personal	26	15	54	9
All owners	100	100	100	100

Source: Berezin et al. (1992: 8, 11)
Note: The authors give no explanation for the fact that the figures do not add up to 100 per cent

egated to municipal authorities, which were also entitled to collect rents for its use. In Western terms municipalities might be considered the 'owners' of such land. Users could be given the rights to use land, for specified purposes, for an indefinite period, but did not have the right to sell or lease it to others, as part of the general prohibition against 'non-labour income', and their use of it could be terminated substantially at will by the municipal government. Neither rent nor property taxes were payable.

Buildings were considered as immovable property, not as part of the land on which they were built. Enterprises or individuals could thus 'own' buildings, but their rights were hardly greater than those of the owners of land, except that limited rights to lease were allowed. The concept of 'operative management of property' was introduced in 1981, and gave enterprises the rights of 'possession, use, and disposition' of property, but only for the uses assigned to it by the state (Schneider, 1990: 453). Rents had to be within levels set for that type of house by each republic (Lowry, 1992: 3–4). In no case could property be pledged as security, however, because there was no right to levy against property pledged by a judgement creditor (Schneider, 1990: 452, 456).

In co-operative apartments, residents held joint ownership of the buildings, but individual residents could only sell their units through the co-operative, or lease them to others with the co-operative's consent (Andrusz, 1992; Lowry, 1992: 6). Single-family houses were considered personal property, unlike the land on which they were built, and could be disposed of like any other personal property.

Housing had a privileged position in land use. Not only was a general 'right to housing' incorporated in the Constitution, but the private ownership of housing was explicitly protected:

On the basis of Article 13 of the USSR Constitution, the personal ownership of citizens in a dwelling shall be protected by the state. Individual dwelling construction serves to satisfy a citizen's need for a place to live, and the state assists in every way in the individual construction of houses by means of allocating plots of land.[14]

Private house building was encouraged, the degree of encouragement generally varying with the periodic rising and falling of the level of construction of public housing.[15] In some countries, such private construction and ownership were major parts of the housing construction system, as in Poland, Hungary and Bulgaria; in others they were only minor, as in the GDR. The proportion of private construction roughly parallels the degree of urbanization; private construction is much more likely to occur in rural than in urban areas. In all cases, however, whether private owner-occupation and owner-occupant construction were encouraged or not, the development of a private commercial construction industry was discouraged or prohibited; only state enterprises or individuals for their own use were allowed to build. And of course the speculative private development of land in multiple lots was not possible.

Ownership was limited to one dwelling per citizen, but private rental of dwellings was legally permitted, either in unlimited number, as in countries in which there had not been complete nationalization and private landlord owners remained, or, even in the Soviet Union, where the leasing of the one dwelling a person might have was also permitted.[16] The clarification of the legality of sub-letting was the primary purpose of such provisions, but detailed arrangements for continued occupancy after the break-up of a family were also considered. While the right to rent existed as a matter of law, its value was limited by the existence of strong rent control: in the Soviet Union, by maximum rates established by each republic (Hazard et al., 1984: 238), generally limited to an amount equal to the landlord's costs (Alexeev, 1991: 5); in other countries by varying formulae. In the GDR, for instance, rents were held substantially to the levels existing at the time rent controls were first established under the Nazis, in 1937, and thus the right to rent was considered substantially valueless by many owners. They therefore 'abandoned' their property – particularly those that left for the West – and the state took it over and managed it, paying more or less attention to the formalities of title. The newly revived claims of these 'former owners' are now the cause of much controversy and litigation in Germany.

Ownership carried with it obligations, over and above the general one to 'use property in the interests of society'. The Russian Republic's Housing Code (during the Soviet era), for instance, provided; '[c]itizens who have a dwelling house in personal ownership shall be obligated to ensure the preservation thereof, to make current and capital repairs at their own expense, and to maintain the territory adjacent to the house in order' (cited in Hazard et al., 1984: 239). Again, there are analogies in Western law: in building and health codes, up to some minimum standard, and in the duty of a mortgagor to a mortgagee not to commit waste as to the mortgaged property; but the duties vary significantly in the extent of their obligation, and only in exceptional situations is there a bar to demolition, as the Russian provisions imply. Western law distinguishes sharply between duties to a private party and duties to the state. The duty to maintain a pavement in front of one's house, often provided for by law in the West, is analogous to the duty 'to maintain the territory adjacent to the house'; but the pavement is public property in the West, while the duty under the Russian code also applies to the personal property of the resident. Liability to third parties injured by an owner's failure to maintain makes the substance of the Russian provision not so dissimilar from the substance of Western counterparts. The bundle of rights and obligations analysis is applicable to both.

Nor was the role of law so different. Substantive social justice may have been the original objective of Soviet provisions, but procedural niceties were given scope even when they conflicted with social objectives. Take the case of a statute providing that land should be allocated by a settlement soviet first to those who lacked a dwelling, with a provision that anyone who sold a house would not be considered 'lacking a dwelling' for ten years after the sale. S. made a gift of her house to her daughter and the next day applied for an allocation of land from the soviet. The application was granted; but the daughter proceeded to sell the house she had been given. The allocation to the mother was nevertheless upheld, as complying with the letter of the law; the transfer to the daughter was a gift, not a sale, and what the daughter did with the gift after receipt was not relevant under the statute.

Underlying the details of property rights as formally stated in Soviet law, nevertheless, was the spirit of the Soviet Law on Property. which stated; '[t]he use of any form of property must preclude the alienation of the worker from the means of production and the exploitation of man by man' (cited in Stephan, 1991: fn. 85). One interpretation of the immediate motivation behind the inclusion of this language in legislation generally liberalizing the handling of property is that it was designed to prevent exorbitant speculative profits by intermediaries, co-operatives, etc., in the evolving private sector (Schneider, 1990: 458). The general sense of the language is not far from that of those earlier provisions which state that property may only be used consistently with the public good, or that its use must serve the public interest. But it is neither the wording of the law nor the frequency with which it has been applied through the courts that is important here. Rather, it expresses a fundamental assumption made by citizens of the Eastern European countries, certainly of the Soviet Union, that there was a definite set of property rights in existence, stable rights, rights on which they could rely and that the state would respect and implement, rights which included, as to land and housing, rights of occupancy and use for themselves and their families. It is precisely the prevalence of this assumption and its negation in the process of transition to privatization and its legal structures that has made that transition so difficult all over Eastern Europe.

To understand the dynamics of the transition, it is necessary to look closely at precisely what the fundamental differences are between the previously existing system and that being introduced, and at the same time to look at the similarities and the contradictions within each which the transition is not likely to affect. The failure to understand these differences and similarities explains much of the general public discontent with the process of privatization that has surfaced during its course thus far.

SOVIET AND WESTERN PROPERTY RIGHTS COMPARED

The differences between the mature phase of Soviet law regarding the 'ownership' of land and housing and conventional Western law may be summarized under seven broad headings.[17]

The seven key differences

The concept of social ownership, described in the preceding section, which may include state ownership and co-operative or not-profit or state enterprise ownership, does not exist in capitalist countries, and the concept of *personal ownership* has a quite different meaning. As a theoretical category it is difficult to translate into conventional Western juridical terms, but its components are not unfamiliar. The rules of ownership – the bundle of rights that go with ownership – are divided into two major categories under Soviet law. Following the mature Soviet definitions of ownership, they were generally consistent in all of the state socialist countries.

Personal ownership parallels ownership by individual natural persons in conventional Western law; the distribution of rights within the bundle of rights was quite different, but the identification of what the rights mean is readily translatable into accepted Western terms. That the rights were identifiable holds true for social ownership as well; with social ownership, however, the holder of the bulk of those rights, for example 'all the people', was at first sight not so readily translatable. The problem is nevertheless theoretical, rather than practical; in practice, the state exercised the bulk of the rights of ownership other than the rights of use, and in fact ultimately controlled rights of use also directly or indirectly. The theoretical problem is serious, however. It results not so much from a difficulty of translating concepts from one system to the other, but rather from the problem within socialist theory of making concrete what the Marxist conception of 'social ownership' actually is, as we have seen in tracing the history of the Soviet theory.

'Private' ownership was not a phrase used in its Western sense (non-state ownership) in Eastern Europe, but the bundle of rights most closely associated with private ownership in the West was associated with personal ownership in the East.

In capitalist systems, differentiating among different types of property (for instance, among land, buildings, tools, stocks and bonds, factories, stores, clothing) as to forms of permissible ownership *is the exception,*[18] and the striving is for uniformity; *in socialist systems, different objects were treated fundamentally differently* from each other legally (for instance, items of personal use, 'personal property', from land or from the means of production). Those things that might be individually 'owned' were restricted to the use of personal property, and quite different laws and rules applied to all other possible items of ownership (such as factories, intangible assets, things used in common).[19] Thus, individuals may 'own' cars, but not buses; single family houses, but not apartment houses; plots of land they can cultivate themselves, but not land tilled by tenant farmers; a hammer and saw, but not an assembly line; an individual workshop, but not a factory.

Land was a unique object of ownership, under capitalism as under socialism, as indeed it was in feudal times. It has a unique ideological baggage; transactions affecting it are formulated differently, recorded differently, subject to different rules of law and equity, susceptible to orders for specific performance, all as distinguished from other forms of property. In socialist law, land collectively or co-operatively farmed, or farmed by state enterprises, was treated as were the means of production: it could not be privately owned, it 'belonged to' the state. But land used personally by individuals was also treated differently from other items of personal property. It was subject to the constitutional requirement that it be used 'rationally'. The logic here was system-transcendent (Friedmann, 1972: 105–7).

In capitalist systems, *the right of use is derived from, and subordinated to, the rights of ownership; in socialist systems, the rights of use (for specific types of property, 'personal property') was accorded a higher position than the rights of ownership.* 'Ownership' in the Soviet Union included some, but not all, of that bundle of rights that is conventionally associated with the term in the West. Its closest analogy in Western law was probably the traditional German *Erbpacht*, granting rights of use and disposition, but not 'title'; in civil law jurisdictions, usufruct, the right of full use and enjoyment of another's property, but without the right to alter its substance, to consume it (a concept derived from Roman law), is somewhat comparable. In the Soviet Union it included the right to pass by inheritance, unrestricted as to legatee at least since 1961, but not the right to sell; or (for the specifics varied from country to country and time to time) the right to sell only to individuals designated by a public entity, and/or without profit; it did not include the right to rent out (except sometimes for limited times, at limited rents, and to limited individuals) or the right to mortgage; it included the right to build (subject of course to building and planning restrictions, as in the West) but not the right to obtain unlimited building supplies on the open market; it included the right to be compensated if the property was taken by the state so as to prevent its further use by its owner, but at an amount equal to what was paid for it plus the value of labour and materials added, not its 'market value' at the time of taking.[20]

Rights of use, on the other hand, even if referred to as 'tenancy', equalled or exceeded in many ways those conventionally associated with 'ownership', and certainly were far stronger than those associated with conventional tenancy in United States. As Bertrand Renaud (1990: 11) summarized, '[p]roperty rights for tenants in public housing are often stronger and more valuable than ownership because the occupancy rights to heavily subsidized units are permanent and can be transferred to relatives.' Protection against eviction, for instance, becoming today a hot political issue, is one of the bundle of rights to use housing; it was accorded recognition as an almost unlimited right in the past in Eastern Europe, but is generally subordinate to or balanced against the rights of non-user owners in Western law.

In capitalist systems, there is a largely unrestricted right to make a profit on disposition of that which is owned, including profits derived from the increase in price resulting from increases in land values, from scarcity, etc. (often called speculation). *Such a right to dispose for a profit did not exist in the socialist systems,* although the right to recapture the value of labour and materials invested in property did often exist. (The legal right of disposition in general existed in both systems and was limited in some ways in both.) The right to dispose of a house or personally used land to unrelated individuals of the 'owner's' choice, even if not at a profit, was also a right denied under Soviet law, even if no profit was involved. If no profit was made, however, and if the transferor was unrelated, the difference between having the state select from a list of its compiling, as opposed to having the owner select from among friends, may not have been vast.

The right of personal use (as opposed to the unlimited right of disposition) was sanctioned, indeed guaranteed state protection, in socialist law, as to specifically defined items of personal use (see above).[21] The theory behind the prohibition against disposition for a profit was the general principle that 'labour incomes shall comprise the basis of personal ownership.' Rent or speculative gains or interest were 'non-labour income', and hence not allowed. That part of the bundle of rights that is the right to dispose at a profit, or the right to speculate, did not exist in Soviet law (practice of course was something else). Sometimes the border-line between speculation and return for labour is thin indeed: if scarce goods are produced or grown, for instance oranges in Georgia and flown to market, the price at which they are sold will reflect a 'profit'; is that remuneration for the labour of growing them and bringing them to market, or a profit based on their scarcity value over and above the labour and costs invested? Yet while the border-line is fuzzy and the cautions about black markets and non-legal activities must be remembered, as to land and housing the principle of non-speculation generally held.

In capitalist systems, *the judicial system and the judges who make decisions in it are relied on as the primary enforcement mechanism for the protection of property rights; in socialist systems, the courts played a much lesser role,* while the 'executive' and 'legislative' (the two were not neatly divided) institutions and their personnel played a much larger one. The rights of the state in socialist systems were thus not effectively limited by constitutional provisions or legally binding tradition, nor was there a division of state powers in which the judiciary was expected to defend individual rights against the state. Rather, individual rights were seen as a component of an overall schema in which individual ownership should serve (or not be inconsistent with) the common good.

In capitalist systems, planning for the compatibility of land uses with one another, and planning for optimal efficiency and other social goals, is handled primarily by state regulation of private activity, and by private agreements. 'Proprietary' or 'entrepreneurial' functions of government are very limited. In socialist systems, what we would call proprietary functions of the state were vast, almost to the exclusion of private proprietorship, and the governmental and proprietary functions of the state were vested in the same public bodies. Both planning and initiative were state roles; the concept of state 'regulation' of private activities as the mode of planning urban development played a very limited role. No distinction was made between governmental and enterprise activities of the state; the large scale of its enterprise functions avoided many of the restrictions on governmental functions that plague the West, for example in urban land-use planning. If that distinction is not observed, the wholesale effort to reduce the role of the state now under way may lessen the state's ability to carry out its properly governmental functions in the process of reducing its enterprise role.

Under state socialism, the merger of governmental (including planning and public development) functions with enterprise functions had made 'planning law' as such unnecessary: there was no need for a separate body of law under which government could control its own developmental and land-use activities. But when those activities are privatized, rights of control, of decision-making as to social impacts, are also affected. By implication, if no rights for such control are retained by government, they are lodged in the new private owners. That is, in legal terms, what has happened.

Finally, the context for the exercise of rights must be distinguished. The real content of property rights depends on the societal situation in which they are exercised. The right to buy is not of much use without the money with which to buy; land ownership in a vast and agricultural country means something quite different from ownership in a small urban one; the tax system is an important influence on land use (although, when the state owns the land, payments of rent, or the remission of profits to a state-owned enterprise, may be analogized to the payments of taxes); when private economic power (wealth, income) is distributed relatively evenly, its political meaning is quite different from the situation in which there are wide disparities.

Thus there are major substantive differences between property rights in the Soviet and Western systems. But to see the difference simply as one in which the Soviet system was based on the primacy of 'public' rights while the Western gave primacy to the 'private' is a gross oversimplification, and not only conceals the real differences but also overlooks fundamental similarities between the two, both in jurisprudential theory and in practice.

Commonalities and parallel tensions

The parallels between the two systems run in two directions: 'public' ownership in the Soviet Union can be viewed as a variation of 'private' ownership, and 'private' ownership in the capitalist systems can be seen as subordinate to 'public' rights.

Using the 'bundle of rights' analysis developed in Western jurisprudence, state enterprises (as to the means of production) and users (as to items of consumption) had in effect all of the rights of ownership attendant on that legal form in the West, with two exceptions: the right to dispose of the property owned to a person or entity of the owner's choice, and the right to make a personal profit on the disposition. The lawsuits collected in various studies of the Soviet legal system suggest litigation between 'owners' that sounds, *mutatis mutandis*, just like actions for unlawful conversion, for trespass, for damages for breach of contract, even for nuisance (Hazard et al., 1984).

There ought, stepping back from the narrow legal analysis of forms, to be one decisive difference between capitalist and socialist handling of such 'private' controversies: under socialism, each of the 'private' parties was in fact 'owned' by the state (in theory, society) so that a single entity has been responsible for the actions of both of the parties. The point comes up even more strikingly where the actions of a third party are used to justify, say, the inability to perform a contract: the central planning agency did not provide scrubbers in smoke stacks to reduce air pollution, so a factory cannot be charged with violation of environmental laws. But the central planning agency controls both the polluting factory and the factory that produces scrubbers; it has simply planned badly, and it, rather than its subordinates, should be held accountable for violation of the environmental laws. But with that argument the central planning agency is likely to become the defendant in almost every 'private' suit between enterprises, and the courts become simply an oversight agency for central planning. On another level: the Supreme Soviet both approves the central plan and sets environmental standards. If a factory operating in conformity with the plan violates those standards, the Supreme Soviet itself is responsible both for the standards and for their violation. A few parallels might be found in a Western country with a strong separation of powers, but under the Soviet system it was the preponderant fact of life.

There were two possible legal responses to this dilemma. One was to seek to hold individuals, rather than juridical entities, responsible in either contract or criminal law for what they did or did not do *as individuals* in dealing with a given situation. But there was as much reluctance in Soviet law as there is in Western law to 'pierce the corporate veil' and create individual liability for corporate acts. The other is, in fact, to shift responsibility from the judicial to either the executive or the legislative branches. That did indeed happen; a small part of the bloated bureaucracies of Eastern Europe were explicable by the reduced role of the judiciary and the increased responsibilities for settling controversies placed in administrative hands within government.

If the Soviet system can be seen as paralleling the Western, but with 'public' bodies as 'private' owners, the Western system can be seen as founded on the primacy of the 'public'. For the extent to which private rights are protected in the West is entirely dependent on public decisions. In historical practice – and the point is of course critical – the state has enshrined key protections for private property in constitutions and rules of law which in fact seem to give a fundamental priority to private rights, but that is not a logically sustainable view of the underlying legal situation. What the state has given the state can take away, in the West as in the East.

The parallels between the socialist and the capitalist systems run not only in theory but also in practice, and are particularly noteworthy in the problems neither has solved. Each has grappled with certain inevitable tensions, conflicts and contradictions in the field of urban property ownership, and neither has resolved them successfully. To the extent that they make the transition from state socialist to Western capitalist law more difficult, the difficulties cannot be blamed on the previous system; no current system has resolved them successfully. The key tensions may be summarized as four-fold.

The first is the tension between publicly oriented and publicly determined urban development and the maximization of private property rights. The tension is particularly visible in practice, but barely recognized in theory or rhetoric, Western or Eastern, in the formerly state socialist countries of Eastern Europe. On the one hand, there is the drive to privatize ownership of all possible objects of ownership, including real estate, and the concomitant efforts at change of the system of property rights to permit the same range of use and disposition as private market capitalist countries are seen to enjoy. On the other hand, there remains the conviction that urban development should serve the interests of the citizenry in general and be firmly under public control.

Read, for instance, the following extract from the newly adopted Law of the Russian Federation on the Principles of Urban Development:[22]

> The law is aimed at the creation of a healthy and safe habitat for the population, *and* at the equal protection of the rights and interests protected by law of the subjects of urban development activity in questions of urban development . . . irrespective of the type of property and citizenship.
>
> Urban development in the Russian Federation . . . is performed proceeding from the interests of the citizens . . . national, ethnic, historical, and cultural characteristics; ecological, environmental . . . conditions; and with regard for societal opinion as expressed by municipal government agencies, citizen meetings, and through other territorial forms of direct democracy.
>
> . . . The subjects of urban development activity . . . are: citizens, their associations, public and other organizations, institutions, businesses, and other legal entities, which are the customers, investors, builders, developers of urban development . . . , contractors and users of the objects of investment and urban development activity regardless of the form of property, as well as countries, . . . foreign and legal entities and natural persons; . . . government agencies and the architectural and urban development agencies within their jurisdiction, as well as municipal government agencies which carry out urban development activity.

The tension between the two different aims embodied in this legislation are well known in the Western experience. The conflict between public control of land use and the rights of private property have given rise to a constant flow of cases to the United States Supreme Court, for instance, and engendered some of the most bitterly debated legal controversies in American judicial history. In the process, a compromise has been reached in the United States, and compromises along different lines in other private market economies, in which the aspiration to full public control has been whittled down by the protection given to certain private property rights, but other rights that might be attached to private property have been denied recognition by the courts. Every landowner, for instance, has the constitutional right to make *some* use of his, her or its property, but not necessarily the right to build on it, and certainly not the right to build to any height he, she or it wants.

This tension between the public interest and the maximization of individual private interests is reflected in two places in any system of law: laws defining public powers, and laws defining private property rights – the two ends of one spectrum. Under prior state socialist systems of law, public powers, in the form of the power of the state, took precedence over virtually all (but not all – certain rights of private use of personal property, for instance) individual private rights. The United States probably represents the extreme of a balance in the opposite direction; public action may not limit private rights without clear and affirmative constitutional justification. Public trust doctrine, based in part on feudal rights of 'ownership' in the sovereign, passed on to 'the people' with the abolition of monarchy, can be interpreted as one attempt to resolve the public/private tension within an overarching framework, but it remains one among several alternative proposals nowhere developed in full in the Anglo-Saxon system of law-making by judicial precedent.[23]

One of the key problems in changing the rules governing the use and disposition of property in the formerly state socialist countries lies in the failure to recognize this tension, or to realize that it is not unique to socialist systems.[24] The tension of course emerges in practice; the result is the development of transitional laws that provide a sweeping guarantee of private rights in real estate, permeated by exceptions and continuing postponements of implementation, with modifications by other simultaneously effective legislation concerning governmental powers, powers of municipalities being frequently invoked.

A second tension permeating any system of property rights is that between conflicting private interests: between landlords and tenants, buyers and sellers, mortgagors and mortgagees, creditors and debtors, and so forth. That tension, in private market economies, produces most of the civil legislation that comes before the courts, and is generally resolved by extremely complex rules and precedents whose interpretation guarantees the prosperity of an entire profession. In the state socialist economies, the tension had been largely resolved very simply: rights to individual use of personal property were protected, no other private rights were recognized.[25]

This tension among different private interests in property, and more specifically between different categories of owners and users of real estate, is in many cases avoided in current formerly state socialist countries, through pragmatic consideration of the rights of users against owners, tenants against landlords, former owners against present occupants. The result is pragmatic legislation, and even more pragmatic implementation, such as that of rights to buy state housing or to remain in private housing with various rental regulations, regulation of evictions, setting of rents in public housing. Shifting political situations will undoubtedly produce shifting results over the course of many years to come.

In other cases the tension remains to be resolved. The new Russian Constitution, for instance, guarantees the right to housing; the new mortgage law purports to give a right to foreclosure, and eviction on foreclosure. Many Russian officials believe the constitutional provision negates the possibility of foreclosure (S.B. Butler, 1992); that in turn negates much of the usefulness of mortgage arrangements. The problem is not one of logic, but of a conflict of interests between those who see themselves primarily as users of existing housing and those interested either in moving or in being active in the housing supply sector. It is a tension known in the West as well as the East.

The third tension which of necessity permeates any system of private property rights is that between some conception of distributive justice and the preservation of the status quo, the stability of an existing distribution. The tension expresses itself in contemporary Western-style democracies in the arguments about progressive taxation, taxing (thus invading) property rights differentially for the rich and for the poor, and in arguments about the welfare state, giving property rights to the poor in greater proportion than to the rich. Laws against price fixing, fair advertising laws, laws restricting unfair trade practices, and usury laws all reflect the same tension between state permission for unbridled private use of property rights and their limitation in some distributive interest. John Locke initially raised this problem for Western jurisprudence, in seeking an ethical grounding for certain forms of ownership and rejecting ownership lacking such an ethical basis. It remains, even philosophically, unresolved.

Fourth, a tension exists between the concentration of economic power and the democratization of political power. This tension, much more recognized in political theory than in legislative practice in the West – witness the difficulties of regulating campaign contributions in the United States, for instance – has not existed as a tension in the state socialist countries, for the simple reason that economic and political power were concentrated in the same hands. That coincidence of power is precisely one of the proclaimed targets of current reform efforts in Eastern Europe. The pre-socialist political power of large land owners and industrialists had been destroyed by nationalization of large estates and limitations on the extent of private ownership of land. Concern that similar political power may gather in undemocratic fashion colours resistance to the repeal of these state socialist laws, and contributes to the desire to impose restrictions on foreign ownership of land in almost all of the East European countries.

The distinctions and comparisons made in this section may seem very technical and abstruse, but they are tremendously important in practice. Current debates about privatization often blur them, and the blurring is not neutral. In a World Bank report on housing, for instance, the recommendation that 'governments should seek to transfer publicly-owned housing to residents, and should seek opportunities to involve the private sector in the administration and maintenance of public housing' comes under the heading of 'property rights development' (Mayo, 1991: 14; other World Bank reports contain similar statements). Such a recommendation, whether appropriate or not, is a question not of 'property rights development', but of the reallocation of already existing rights that have been lodged elsewhere in the past.[26] After a trenchant critique of past state socialist practices in housing, another report calls for a 'clarification of property rights'; but in fact the recommendations are for reallocation, with more rights to owners, less to tenants and less to government.[27] Reducing subsidies, similarly, may be a 'restructuring of property rights', but not in the sense of defining or clarifying or 'reforming' rights, but simply of ending a particular right (Renaud, 1991: 22, 59).

A senior Russian official is quoted (Andrusz, 1993: 26) as saying, 'public ownership means that there is "no owner", . . . as a consequence, no one, neither tenants nor state officials, has an interest in looking after it.' But public officials are charged with the responsibility of looking after public property, and do so, all over the world, and highways and fighter planes and space satellites are generally well maintained; and certainly tenants have an interest in looking after the dwellings in which they live, particularly if they expect to live in them for a long time. If under-resourced public employees are unable to maintain parks or public spaces to acceptable standards, that is more probably to do with the lack of resources than the form of ownership. Between public and private there is sometimes a no man's land, such as common spaces in residential buildings, where responsibility is unclear or divided, but that is true whether the common space is owned by a private landlord, a condominium association of owners, or the state. In any event, 'what belongs to all belongs to no one', a common popular formulation, is not an accurate statement of legal relations. It is at best a sociological statement (and certainly, thus broadly phrased, wrong sociologically; nationalism would be incomprehensible, co-operatives unworkable, and kinship economically irrelevant if it were true). In the transition from the Soviet system to its successors, changes in the law relating to ownership and property rights are not clarifications of neutral rights, but the substitution of one set of rights for another, with substantial and differential impacts on different groups in society. Those differential impacts are blurred by over-simplifications, by viewing the process of change as one which under socialism went from private to public and now needs to return to private again. Careful legal analysis can help avoid that blurring. Let us now turn to examine how that transition is developing in practice.

THE TRANSITION FROM SOVIET PROPERTY RIGHTS

The politics of privatization

A picture of the line-up of interests and the differing positions they have taken on privatization is essential to make sense of how that process has developed. 'Reformer' and 'hard-liner' are hardly adequate descriptions of the divisions around the issue; 'liberal' and 'conservative' are, if anything, even less helpful. Some of the leading reformers of the Gorbachev era are now among those urging restraint in privatization; other old-time Party bureaucrats are among those urging shock therapy. Liberals, in the American sense of the term, are concerned with the social costs of privatization, and frequently oppose 'liberal' policies in the European sense of maximum scope for the free market; conservatives often press for maintenance of a strong state role in the economy.

The conflicts about privatization cannot in any case be reduced to a simple 'for' or 'against'; the issues are much more complicated. Perhaps the most basic complication is the mixing of issues around ownership rights in business enterprises with issues about ownership rights in consumption goods (including housing). Politically, major interests, both domestic and international, are interested in the formulation of rights to the ownership of factories, office buildings, commercial enterprises, productively used land. Profit, and sometimes power, are the prizes here. For consumer goods, on the other hand, the quality of use is the concern of ownership. Here foreigners who are not local consumers are little concerned, and the impact on economic growth runs along quite different channels. Profit conflicts directly with personal use in this area.

The two – production and consumption – are of course not separate spheres, and particularly in the planning of cities and the production of housing services they are inseparable; yet they are different. The theoretical differences under Soviet law have already been touched on. The repercussions today are clear in looking at the nature of the interests at conflict in the debate over privatization. One set is concerned generally with ownership in the economic sphere; the other more narrowly with ownership affecting residential land and housing.[28]

We may distinguish at least four general positions on the question of property rights over productive resources (including land). The first advocates the widest possible protection by the state of private rights to property, and the narrowest possible regulation by the state of those rights. Those adapting this position, committed to the most rapid possible introduction of Western-style markets, and with them Western private-property systems, may be generally concerned to further economic growth and the accumulation of wealth: international agencies, foreign investors, the local managerial elite, many (probably most) political leaders, and many disillusioned citizens. Others espouse this position solely for their own private benefit. They include a significant part of the old nomenklatura, the old managerial elite, new speculators, either conventional entrepreneurs or the new mafia; their concern is private profit, their ideological position pragmatic. They would be accepted in the West as normal, producer, profit-oriented interests.

The opposite position, opposing privatization in principal and holding out for a retention of maximum state rights to control over property, is held by what is a small and will be, barring major political upheaval, a diminishing segment of the old nomenklatura. Here one may speak of entrenched hard-liners, those in positions of power and privilege under the old regimes of state socialism, desiring to retain politically based power and privilege, resisting the change to private economically based wealth and bending only enough to permit the old structures, centred on the old Communist Parties, to be preserved. Their position is not so much ideologically based 'hard-line' as it is simple defence of self-interest. Kolosi and Szelenyi (1993: 158) cite two Hungarian sociologists (E. Hankiss and E. Szalai) who have explored the divisions within the old nomenklatura on the issue of privatization and property rights. They suggest an 'old elite', the so-called hard-liners, hoping to retain their power based on old arrangements; an 'old new elite', a technocratic group already oriented towards transforming itself into a new 'propertied class' under the old system; and a 'new new elite', with much the same goals, but politically victorious over the 'old new elite' in the process of transformation. It is an analysis consistent with that suggested here.

An intermediate position, often formulated in terms of commitment to a 'social market', is found among some early reformers who considered themselves socialists. They hope to introduce fundamental changes which might fulfil the original promises of socialist theory (including public control over the 'means of production') while ridding it of bureaucratic forms. They are often persons who held some public position prior to the collapse of the old system. Mikhail Gorbachev would probably be in this grouping. They are often found within the ranks of the 'successor parties' to the old Communist Parties (most of whom are now in fact reluctant social democrats, not any longer socialists).

An agnostic position on the privatization of businesses is probably held by the majority of citizens in the East. They are concerned first and foremost about jobs, with tremendous ambivalence not about the desire for change, which was general, but about the speed and uncertainty of change. They are caught between the promise of the predominant rhetoric and the immediate negative changes visible in their everyday lives. They understand the importance of efficiency and growth, but have no clear perspective on how changes in this direction might be produced without severe infringement on their quality of life.

The privatization of housing brings into play a cross-cutting set of interests. They include direct producer and profit-oriented interests also, but a broader and more clearly articulated set of user or consumption interests. The division runs along a basic fault line separating producer/owner-type interests (generally profit-oriented) from resident interests (generally consumption-oriented, although consumption and profit are blended for some owner-occupants). Key groupings include, first, producer/owner-type interests, including landlords, the owners of rental property, legally not permitted in most state socialist countries, but continuing to exist in some legally and in others outside the law – as privatization continues, however, their number increases, as will their political weight.

A second group consists of former owners of property, in most Eastern European countries entitled either to restitution or to compensation, having direct interests in specific parcels of land, in some countries covering up to half the housing stock and virtually all of the pre-war stock, and in some countries involving major institutions such as the Catholic church in Poland;[29] investors/speculators, ranging from international development and construction firms to home-grown entrepreneurs, some legitimate, some mafia types or former party hacks on the shady side of the law, having in common a desire to protect investments in real estate entered into for profit.

Third, there are resident-type interests, including residents of property subject to restitution claims, and most immediately threatened with dispossession and eviction;[30] residents of publicly built and publicly (generally municipally) owned housing, whose occupancy of publicly subsidized housing is seen as a heavy drain on local budgets, but who are numerous enough to be an effective lobbying group; and residents of enterprise-owned housing, whose fate in theory rests with the fate of the enterprise, but who have frequently succeeded in gaining a separation of enterprise housing from enterprise production, and may then find themselves in a position similar to that of residents of public housing.

These groups have very different interests, often in conflict with each other, and many of these conflicts centre on questions of property rights. Landlords want enforceable rights to set and collect rents, with easy and quick rights to evict; tenants want stable rents and security of occupancy. Urban owner-occupants are concerned with zoning protections for their residential uses; agricultural owners may be happy to have their rights to change use unrestricted, if the value of their land for other uses goes up. Mortgage lenders want rights of quick foreclosure; owner-occupant mortgagees want protection against foreclosure if hardship strikes. Owners of existing buildings want protection against surrounding change; owners of developable sites want the right to develop freely.

The evolving history suggests that such differences will come ever more to the fore, and that blanket changes in rights will give way to much more complex and differentiated modifications. Practice seems likely to lead theory here. Add a final complicating issue, and a central one: the interests of governmental officials in reducing state deficits by reducing expenditures. Often outside pressures, from international lending agencies, for instance, compound the problem. Again, the matter is often over-simplified: continued state ownership of housing is assumed to constitute a financial burden involving subsidies that would not have to be paid if the same housing were in private ownership. As Berezin et al. (1992: 16, emphasis added) note, '[t]he initial conditions for privatization [of housing in the Russian Federation] *were developed with a single aim: to first eliminate from state responsibility* the oldest housing, which was also the cheapest in terms of price but at the same time the most expensive to maintain.'

The assumption is that if such housing were private, there would be less burden on the state. But, as most Western housing experts involved have frequently pointed out in discussions with their Eastern colleagues, if housing is to be privatized and social unrest prevented, some form of subsidy is necessary, some form of payments to cover the difference between affordable and actual housing costs.[31] Housing allowances are then generally recommended, but whether the net costs of such allowances will be more or less than the net costs of continuing state ownership at subsidized rents is an unknown. Distributional equity is likely to be greater with a system of income-based housing allowances; but the financial burden on the state could be either higher or lower, depending on the level of speculative increases in private housing prices, the extent of inefficiencies or corruption in public vs. private management, the state of landlord–tenant relations, the sought-after level of profits in private housing rental, and other hard-to-predict factors.

The legislative history of the transition: Russia

The history of privatization in Eastern Europe can be traced in the constitutional and legislative actions of the countries involved. Russia (the Soviet Union, initially) is the focus in this section, the former because its checkered path displays most clearly the complex tensions involved, the latter because, during its brief transitional period, it highlighted the ideological implications of the transition most clearly. The next section deals briefly with highlights of the developments in other Eastern European countries. Subsequently a generalized model of the transition is suggested, bringing in in note form the experiences of other East European countries.

The early attempts at reform of socialism

The beginnings of the transition from real existing socialism in most of the countries of Eastern Europe were led by those who saw themselves as reformers of socialism. Even in the heyday of real existing socialism, market forms found a place within the strongly centralized state-run systems of production and distribution, in some cases out of pragmatism, as with 'goulash communism' under Kadar in Hungary, in others out of a concern about failures in the centralized economy, as under Khrushchev in the Soviet Union (for the logic behind these developments see H. Marcuse, 1958; P. Marcuse, 1994b). But that tendency was little reflected either in changes in property relations or in their ideological underpinnings: no 'reform' of socialism was contemplated. With perestroika, it was different. Gorbachev (cited in Stephan, 1991: 35), for instance, saw his efforts as 'encroaching on socialism, but only the socialism that was built bureaucratically, under which the country veered off the path on which it had embarked in 1917'. At the beginning of the breakthrough by the dissidents in the GDR in the fall of 1989, many leaders of the reform movement had similar positions (see P. Marcuse, 1991: 13–24, 169–75). Similar developments can be found during the early period of Havel's presidency in Czechoslovakia, Solidarity's ascendancy in Poland, and the transition in Hungary, and in Bulgaria. A GDR writer in the reform wing of the Party there wrote in 1990, '[i]n all socialistic countries the qualitative development of the relations of ownership, the change in their content and the forms of implementation of socialist ownership, have moved into the centre of the societal strategies of the ruling Communist Parties.'[32] Whether those 'societal strategies' were aimed at preserving the power of an existing stratum of society, or at a fundamental reform of legal structures that had proved inequitable or unworkable, is an open question. The Soviet Union is probably at the conservative end of the spectrum, and its reforms appear as compromises between continued adherence to structures that had provided privileges and power in the past, on the one hand, and flexibility to open the door to different forms of economic activity and perhaps broader sharing in power and wealth, on the other. In the GDR, the reforms that were proposed appear to have been intended to go further, but what their outcome might have been we will never know.

In the Soviet Union under Gorbachev, few specific proposals for the reform of housing or land ownership were put forward, and Gorbachev himself remained committed to the principle of socialist, in the sense of collective and social if not governmental, ownership. That was in fact consistent with the formulations of the Soviet constitution. The wide range of ideas that were floated may, however, be seen by looking at some of the proposals (see also, Charley, 1992: 28–30):

Suppose the state established a 'social guarantee' of a minimum standard of housing for all, perhaps in terms of a minimum number of square meters per person, with a minimum list of amenities: heat, hot water, toilet facilities, cooking facilities, etc.[33] Suppose all rent were abolished up to that level for each household.[34] Over that level, an amount would be charged corresponding to real costs. Below that level, goes the radical proposal, the state would be required to pay the household the real cost of supplying what the household was not getting, or perhaps be given some amount of housing over and above the minimum standard when it was finally given that to which it was entitled, or, as it was subsequently called, a 'housing promissory note' (*Andrusz, 1993: 8*).

Low rent and low wages went in tandem when the state was both houser and employer. In a sense, therefore, cheap housing (including the promise of future cheap housing) was a compensation for work, a substitute for increased wages. How much should now be charged for housing, given that, in the future, houser and employer will be separated, should depend on how much of that housing has already been 'earned'. Thus length of time worked should be a factor in setting new rents.[35]

State property should be preserved, but made 'property of the whole people'. For that, 'it is not enough to write fine words in a constitution. What is needed is democratic social control over the means of production and the administration, with wide participation by the masses in the discussion and implementing of decisions' (*Kagarlitsky, 1989: 77*).

In the GDR similar proposals were worked out during the *Wende*, with the support of tenants' groups there (P. Marcuse and Staufenbiel, 1991; P. Marcuse, 1990):

Let a minimum guaranteed level of housing be established, but with rent for that minimal level fixed at the rates then prevailing for all housing, which was low but not nominal. Adjustments to that base rent would then be made according to income, so that the low income, elderly, disabled, unemployed, etc., would pay a lower rent; the well-to-do a higher rent, up to the actual cost. Those in units above the minimum would have to pay at a higher rate for the extra space or amenities; those in less than the minimum would pay at a lower rate even for what they had.

Implicit in these and other proposals was a retention of key aspects of socialist property rights: that 'ownership' would remain with the state; that rights to occupancy would continue to be guaranteed, with rights to pass on to family members on death, but not to sell or rent at a profit; that when the unit was no longer in the family, its occupancy would be determined by the state. Particularly important for housing was the retention of the distinction between 'personally used and co-operative property' and all other property, with 'personally used property' singled out for particular protection.[36]

A variety of other proposals, intermediate between socialist and capitalist in their handling of property rights, were floated in other countries in Eastern Europe. In Hungary, for instance, dividing 'ownership' rights between the state as current holder and the occupant, who would purchase some proportion of them, was suggested. So was the separation of the obligation to manage and repair from the obligations of ownership, so that, for instance, management firms, which might be established by the occupants of a development themselves, might be formed and compete for management contracts, either with or without state subsidies.

But these early public discussions did not, in any country, reflect the depth of the underlying crisis. While they found scattered political support, particularly at the municipal level (Andrusz, 1993: 20), they bore no practical political relationship to those forces pushing for full-scale implementation of private market relations, and with them the legal structures of private property ownership, as rapidly as possible. Here the other two of the four forces producing the current tensions came into play: those we have described as the 'free marketeers' and 'average citizens'. Among the former were businessmen (and a few women), managers, some professionals and officials, from within the countries themselves and from without, the latter being supported by many advisers from the World Bank, the International Monetary Fund, and Western academics and professionals, most of whom saw rapid privatization as a desirable combination of profit opportunity with the best long-term route to economic growth. Among the 'average citizens' were a mass of plain people, worried about their own jobs, their housing, the availability not only of desirable consumer goods not hitherto available but, as time went on, of staples as well, thoroughly disillusioned with the former system proclaiming itself socialist and seeing its diametric opposite, capitalism, as the salvation, but at the same time influenced by the hardships the transition seems to be bringing in its wake.

Would introducing a 'totally new set of property rights' fatally undermine the ideological foundation of Soviet Marxism's project? It depends on *which* property rights were introduced/abolished. In classic Marxist terms, private ownership of personal property, excepting only the right to sell at a profit, is not inconsistent with the definition of socialism; on the other hand, private ownership of the 'means of production', including the right to profit from other people's labour through that ownership, would indeed undermine socialism in any accepted sense of the word. The giving of judicially enforceable rights against arbitrary actions of the state might indeed be inconceivable under the conditions of real existing socialism; the priority of collective over individual rights is, however (although with quite varying definitions of terms), embedded in socialist theory. The line between those modifications of property rights found in real existing socialist societies consistent with Marxist theory and those modifications undermining that theory was one some attempted to draw at the beginning of the 'reform' periods in various countries; in none was the effort brought to fruition, and in none did it remain relevant for very long.

Chronology of the transition

A chronological narrative of events in the Soviet Union and in the Russian Federation presents a complex picture. Broadly, the period of perestroika under Gorbachev, ending with the dissolution of the Soviet Union in December 1991, was characterized at the Soviet level by a broadening of the forms of ownership and protections accorded to a more diversified set of possible rights in property and the 'demonopolization of the state economy', but within the framework of the existing socialist system and continuing protection for socialist forms. In the Russian Republic under Yeltsin (beginning even before its independence), parallel measures were intended to go much further, ideologically rejecting socialist forms and in principle fully accepting Western market definitions of what should be private property rights. The forces at play, and thus the real issues, were common to both periods, if in constantly shifting balance.

The pattern can be most easily followed by tracing separately the ideological formulations of property rights in general, the handling of land ownership, and the treatment of housing.

The interest of the Soviet government in obtaining foreign investment and the interest of foreigners in investing, given legal protections, provided the initial impetus for changes in Soviet property law. In the Joint Venture Decree of January 1987, provision was made for private ownership by such ventures of property as would normally have been socially owned – buildings, for instance (Schneider, 1990: 454ff) – but land was specifically excluded. In the first comprehensive effort to change property laws, namely the Draft Law on Property promulgated by Gorbachev as chairman of the Supreme Soviet in November 1989, the opening provisions still refer to the priority of 'socialist property', and provide that the 'state promotes the augmentation of socialist property and ensures equal conditions for the development of all its varieties and forms' (Schneider, 1990: 458). Gorbachev at the time stated he was attempting to 'dissociate himself from the campaigners for private property' (*New York Times*, 17 November 1989, p. A16).

The Congress of People's Deputies comprehensively revised the constitution as it affected property rights in the spring and summer of 1990.[37] The references in the draft law to 'socialist property' were dropped, but the term 'private property' was not introduced. 'Personal property' was changed to 'citizen's property', and the door was opened to profit not based on labour: profit was permitted from 'any economic activity not prohibited by law'. The concept of 'socialist property' was retained, including both 'state property' and 'collective property', but the definition of 'collective property' was expanded to include leaseholding enterprises and joint stock companies as well as co-operatives (Schneider, 1990: 449; Stephan, 1991: 58); playing with words, indeed, but of crucial actual importance. Subsequently, the Russian Law on Ownership (December 1991) provided for a four-part division of tenures: private (individuals and legal entities), social organizations, state entities, and joint ventures and foriegn entities. The separate treatment of foreign ownership was a characteristic of early reform measures. On 7 December 1992, Russia's Congress of People's Deputies approved the final version of a constitutional amendment specifically allowing landowners to mortgage their property and to sell it provided there was no change in use. A prohibition on selling land to foreigners was defeated. The language distinguished among different 'forms of ownership: . . . private, collective ("general joint, general shared"), state, municipal, and ownership of public associations'. The language establishing the limits of 'ownership' was not so different from earlier socialist concepts: 'property may not be used for purposes contrary to the interests of society or the rights and freedoms of other citizens.' The compromise nature of the provisions continued: rights of sale were limited: sales of land to local soviets or to natural persons for housing construction were permitted, but where ownership was obtained free of charge, plots of land could only be sold to natural persons for any other use after 10 years. Land was always handled differently from other property.[38] The private ownership of land was specially provided for in the 1990 Soviet provisions; inheritable life tenure was provided for, but not alienation by private persons.[39] 'Ownership' remained 'in the people inhabiting a given territory', thus the republics, so the subsequent dissolution of the Soviet Union into its constituent parts caused no additional legal turmoil on the land question.

But ideological conceptions mixed uneasily with practical ones. The provisions on joint ventures permitted the contribution to a joint venture of 'rights to use land', but did not permit transfers of title. Even under current Western concepts, what is 'title to land' other than some combination of rights to its use? But then there are restrictions on specific rights: a prohibition on 'purchase and sale, donations, pledging, and free exchanges of land', which are unenforceable if not approved by the councils of people's deputies. Further, rights of use of land may be revoked if the 'use' is changed. The new legal situation could in theory have permitted the leasing of land, even on long-term leases, and the transfer of practically all other rights of ownership from the state to private, profit-motivated (as well as 'use-motivated') individuals or firms. But then it did not provide explicitly for any mechanisms for such leasing. On the other hand, rights of use of land would explicitly pass with a transfer of ownership of the building situated on it, and compensation would have been paid if improvements made were rendered valueless by state action. The legal provisions were not contradictory; they simply did not put together the bundle of rights that Western business-oriented investors would expect.

Differentiating between different types of land use provided an opportunity to lessen the real contradiction between the ingrained (socialist and partially pre-socialist) objection to private speculation in land and the new desire to privatize. In April 1991, for instance, in the new Land Code of the Russian Federation, three types of land tenure were provided for: first, inheritable life tenure, for single-family homes and garden plots, providing indefinite rights of use and inheritance, but not rights to sell or lease; second, full ownership, but with detailed restrictions, and prohibitions on sale during the first 10 years of ownership or leases for more than five years; third, leasehold, for no longer than 50 years, and without the right to sublet. Continuing to distinguish land by its uses, the Russian Federation Law on Land Reform (as amended on 20 December 1992) permitted those legally entitled to use land for dachas, orchards, private subsidiary plots, and individual housing construction to choose among three forms of 'land relationships: ownership, lifetime inheritable possession, or use, including leasing'. Rights of ownership are limited to continuing existing permitted uses, however. And while the current users are permitted to choose among these 'land relationships' simply by registration, norms are established as to the amount of land that may be thus registered without payment; above the norm, payment has to be made to the local soviet at an agreed price.

Many of these concrete differentiations were, however, wiped out by a presidential decree in December 1993, apparently not so much to achieve substantive change as to restrict local powers implicit in the Land Code and move authority from local soviets to administrative bodies (Struyk and Kosareva, 1994: 32–3). The form of ownership defined as 'inheritable life tenure' was abolished by the decree, on the assumption that other private rights of ownership were adequate to achieve its purpose. The 1993 Russian Constitution consolidated much of this prior law: private ownership was protected, provided it did not 'violate the rights and legitimate interests of others', and use was to be on 'conditions and procedures' established by law, in theory continuing broad state rights over land (S.B. Butler and O'Leary, 1994b: 551–3). But, as to land, only individual citizens have clear rights of 'ownership'; land ownership by legal entities is not contemplated (Struyk and Kosareva, 1994: 34).

Property rights in housing were quite consistently differentiated from such rights in land, or in business property. However (un)enforceable, a 'right' to housing had been a part of the 1936 Constitution. The possible sticks in that bundle were both spelled out and limited in article 58 of the December 1992 amendments to the Russian Constitution: a 'right to housing' remained, but diluted to a more market-oriented formulation.[40] The new 1993 Russian Constitution swung back, and in article 40 imposed on the state the obligation of providing housing 'free or at affordable cost to low-income and other citizens indicated in the law'. Such provisions reflect shifting ideological compromises rather than changes in actual policy.

The Law on the Privatization of the Housing Stock in the Russian Soviet Federal Socialist Republic (RSFSR), adopted in June 1991, might be interpreted to give tenants in public and publicly owned enterprise housing a right to purchase the units they occupied, but the bundle of rights they were given was limited: a voucher for only a standard amount, only for one unit, only for a unit legally allocated to that household, only for standard units in standard buildings. In December 1992 the law was amended to repeal the duty to pay for a unit being privately acquired. But in both cases the crucial question (which determines the usefulness of the 'right of privatization' to a household) of payment for costs of maintenance and repairs or improvement was left largely to local discretion, the assumption being that the market will ultimately determine the amount. The earlier, although limited, right to affordable housing was thus implicitly repealed, and rent control over private housing was explicitly repealed; a general obligation on local governments to provide for housing allowances was added for social housing. For those living in buildings in poor condition, Struyk and Kosareva (1994: 65; and see

Struyk, chapter 6, this volume) formulate it thus: 'taking a unit is essentially receiving the right to pay for future rehabilitation.'

Both ownership and rental arrangements are covered in the Law of the Russian Federation on Basic Principles of Federal Housing Policy, 'the most progressive [sic] major reform law enacted in Eastern Europe by the end of 1992'; it was adopted shortly after the Law on Land Reform in December 1992 (Struyk and Kosareva, 1994: 20; S.B. Butler, 1992: 6). It provides for a range of private rights in housing, including rights to buy, sell and rent, without limitation as to number of units. Its primary difference from conventional Western forms is in two areas: the concept of *naym*, and the role of 'social norms'. Rights referred to as '*naym*' are the equivalent of a lease for life (there is no reference in the statute to inheritability), for premises in conformity with the social norm. Those norms are minimum size standards established by state government bodies within the Russian Federation. The law provides citizens with a right to housing commensurate with that social norm, 'under the terms of *naym*', either through direct provision or through subsidy; in *naym* contracts, the rent is set so as to cover maintenance and repair expenses and communal services, but not costs of construction. The law explicitly recognizes private ownership of rental housing, but provides certain protection for tenants; eviction for default in rental payment for six months is permitted under a rental agreement, but (at least in the governmental housing stock) the evicted tenant is to be 'provided with housing space meeting sanitary and technical requirements'; regulation of social rents is left to government bodies within the Russian Federation.

In summary: in some areas, the bundle of rights granted by 'ownership' in the United States is by now essentially provided, if in other forms, by 'rights of use' in Russia, to the point that in some key areas 'for most practical purposes the two forms of tenure are identical' (S.B. Butler and O'Leary, 1994b: 559). In other areas, economic realities and public debates about the socially tolerable have led to restrictions on rights of disposition and use that continue earlier non-economic market traditions. The net result of the complex legislative history is that the privatization of housing in Russia has not been a consistent movement in the direction of a Western model, but rather a shifting set of compromises between both conflicting interests and the conflicting views they engender. Putting the Russian experience together with those of other Eastern European countries, one finds a fairly consistent pattern that such compromises have taken. The next section summarizes key Eastern European experiences, and the following section generalizes from these.

The legislative history: Central and Southeastern Europe

Developments in other formerly 'socialist' countries in Eastern Europe follow generally along the same lines, although with major variations depending on their individual histories.[41]

East Germany

East Germany is the extreme model of transition from state socialism to private market capitalism. The legal system of West Germany was simply taken over *in toto*, including property rights and their enforcement; alone among the countries making the transition, there was no doubt or hesitation on where East Germany was going or what the details of the legal system would be. But of course the implementation of the change was not simply a matter of legislative decree; transfers and changes of rights had to be effectuated for specific pieces of property, from and to specific individuals and groups, and with specific histories.

The chosen instrument for the transition was the Treuhandanstalt (Treuhand for short), a public trusteeship established in June 1990, still before unification but after election results had made unification inevitable.[42] The last session of the Round Table, held 12 March 1990, devoted much of its time to questions of property ownership, and ended up recommending that a new office (a '*Kartellamt*') be set up to evaluate property in public ownership and arrange for its distribution to the individual residents of the GDR. What survived, after the elections, was the establishment of the Treuhand, whose assignment was the transfer of all state-owned property held as *Volkseigentum* (owned by the people) into private hands. Three very different purposes were seen by various interests for the Treuhand's privatization activities: the conversion of property rights in East Germany to the private forms recognized in the West, so that they could be dealt with in familiar terms in the private market; achieving justice in the handling of expropriated property, through either return to original owners or provision of compensation for it; and the capture for the state of the value of state-owned property being privatized, as a contribution to the national budget. The Treuhand was, over the objection of many East Germans, put under the jurisdiction of the ministry of finance rather than the ministry of economics; the idea that the Treuhand might be an active agent to modernize the economy of the GDR, although occasionally spoken about, was thus never high on its own agenda.

The Treuhand has been in charge of the disposition of some 8,000 enterprises, including 30,000–40,000 separate businesses. It is estimated to own or have owned 40 per cent of the total land in East Germany. It has 15 regional offices and 2,500 employees (indirectly, it is of course the employer of all of the employees of its subsidiaries; this means perhaps 3,000,000 persons!), and may be the largest holding company in the world.[43] Its operations, in fact, ratify the equation of public or social ownership with state ownership; the concept that 'ownership' should devolve from the state to the citizenry, discussed in the early days of the *Wende* and partially implemented in other East European countries, is not in play. The Treuhand is assuming all debts of the GDR government. Technically, if the proceeds of the sale of all of the assets entrusted to it exceeds those debts, the balance could be distributed to the citizenry; but no one considers that even a remote possibility. It is as if the state were a corporation and its assets being liquidated, with any surplus distributed to its stockholders. The distinction between governmental functions and governmental debts incurred in the exercise of those functions (such as infrastructure provision or defence) and state proprietary functions and their debts (such as running a manufacturing plant) is not considered.

But government is not a private corporation, and, while the Treuhand in theory is to operate so as to maximize the value of its assets,[44] at least two social considerations are superimposed on that principle. One relates to employment; where a new buyer is likely to increase employment in a way an original owner would not, the Treuhand may disregard the original owner's claim to restitution and instead convey the proper to the employment-maximizing new buyer, the original owner receiving compensation instead. Similarly, where the return of residential property would result in gross injustice to some intervening occupant or intervening builder, a sale to that intevenor is possible, again with compensation to the original owner. In both cases the Treuhand mixes traditional 'ownership' behaviour with guidelines developed for social policy reasons. Property rights issues do not get in the way; property ownership has, after all, been considered 'invested with a public interest' from the days of the Weimar constitution on. In operation, the Treuhand has encountered predictable difficulties. Land in agricultural areas was merged into co-operatives early in the evolution of the GDR; it is neither physically easy, not desired by most members of the co-operatives, to reverse that process. Lease arrangements between the co-operatives and the Treuhand, where a return to individual ownership is not feasible, have thus become common.

Other countries are experimenting with some type of conversion of enterprises from state to private ownership through the issuance of shares that are then sold or distributed in equal (and small) amounts to the citizenry at large. Where title to land has been recognized as 'owned by' the enterprise while under state ownership, that land will presumably go with the rest of its business into the hands of its new stockholders. We may assume such land will thereafter be dealt with as any land used for business purposes in the West, and it is not discussed further here.

Reprivatization has been a major problem in the GDR. German records as to ownership prior to the establishment of the Soviet-style socialist system are good. Some cases thus appear deceptively simple; where title was never changed by the GDR on the land records, for instance, but simply a notation of 'under state administration' was entered, the FRG will simply recognize the claims of the original owner of record, and has adopted legislation ending all state administration as of 31 December 1992. So no further action to restore 'ownership' to the prior owner of record is legally necessary. But the actual owner still needs to be found, since those named 40 or more years ago are almost all relocated or dead. And decisions as to changes made in the course of the 40 years need to be made: does the original owner get the benefit of improvements publicly made by tenants in the interim? Does he or she get compensation for neglect, assistance in rehabilitation where there has been inadequate maintenance, damages? Do residents who have invested in what they believed (in good faith and under then prevailing law) was theirs, to use and enjoy indefinitely, keep any rights as to either continued use or compensation?[45]

Even more complex are the situations where title was in fact transferred legally to the state, a situation covering most publicly owned downtown land and land on which new housing was constructed. Here, under the terms of the Treaty of Unification, there is to be reprivatization, and return takes precedence over compensation, but one or the other must take place. Finally, and unique to the GDR, there are the cases where claims for restitution antedate the founding of the GDR itself; that is, where property, predominantly but not exclusively that of Jews, was confiscated by the Nazis, and then reconfiscated in one form or another under GDR law. Claims for return or compensation in such cases had been recognized by the FRG as to properties in its territories, and the procedures there followed will now be applied to properties in the GDR. Understandably, where these complexities come together, full settlement of all claims may well last 10 years or more.

In the meantime, however, properties for which there is real demand are being converted to their desired uses.[46] Private real-estate brokers in the West are experienced at structuring deals with contingency clauses, making the amounts and timing of payments dependent on clarification of issues, providing options to buy in leases, separating out interests and controlling uses for various periods of time. Given the commitment of the Treuhand to return properties to their most economically beneficial use as quickly as possible, the recognition that ownership is a bundle of separable rights has paved the way for rapid changes of ownership and use where the market shows the potential for profit.[47]

Hungary

Hungary is at the opposite end of the spectrum from the countries of the former Soviet Union in its privatization policies. It and Poland had incorporated in their legal systems Western models most clearly even under socialism, and Hungary had substantial freedom for market forces (the so-called 'goulash communism', initiated under Kadar) even before the Gorbachev-era changes (for a general historical overview, see Szakadat, 1993). Its 1949 Soviet-model constitution established the 'social ownership of the means of production', a phrase broader than national or state ownership (Gray et al., 1992: 2). Pursuant to the New Economic Mechanism of 1968, the constitution was amended explicitly to provide for the protection of personal property, balanced with the protection of the public interest, a formulation consistent with most state socialist property rights conceptions. Foreign companies were allowed to establish joint ventures with Hungarian enterprises from 1974 (Frydman et al., 1993: 113).

The Hungarian Civil Code of 1959, although oddly enough modelled in part on the West German Civil Code, established the conventional state socialist distinctions among different types of property: social (state-owned, natural resources, means of production, etc.) ownership, which was owned 'by the entire people' and co-operative ownership (affecting 90 per cent of agricultural land), but also personal property. In the Gorbachev era, Hungary was the earliest to begin revising its system of property rights. Act I of 1987 on land permitted the acquisition of real estate by any Hungarian citizen without limitation. Foreigners may also own real property, requiring permission (readily granted) from the Hungarian ministry of finance for non-agricultural land, and requiring a different permission for agricultural land; but even foreign-owned Hungarian corporate entities may own real property 'related to the company's objectives', a limitation that has not imposed severe hindrances on foreign investment in land. Mortgages had also long been legally recognized, although restrictions on foreclosure and eviction (under Hungary's 1971 Housing Act; the legal forms and rights are recognized, simply more limited by law in Hungary than is customary in the West) hinder their use (Gray et al., 1992; Gray, 1992a: 6).

The revised Hungarian Constitution of 1989 raised the protection of private property, including the right to compensation on expropriation, to the constitutional level.[48] By introducing a separation of powers and establishment of an independent judiciary, it gave a more conventionally Western substance to such rights.[49] Compensation was to be measured by market value even under prior Hungarian law, but that provision was rarely followed closely, market value in any event being a dubious concept under state socialism, and exchanges of property were permissible in lieu of compensation. The only change thus far in the formal provisions of the law is to provide also for compensation for bans on construction exceeding three years.

While the constitution formally equalized the status of social ownership and private or personal ownership, in terms of protection of rights, Law XIV of 1991 purported to abolish all forms of socialist ownership (Gray, 1992a: 9). That of course is an ideological formulation; the real questions are in each case how the bundle of rights of ownership is divided and distributed. More significant, in practice, in relation to non-social ownership are provisions such as those removing the earlier 50-hectare limit on private land ownership, or removing the prohibition against owning more than one housing unit, and freeing rents on properties newly coming into rental use that might be owned (Baar, 1993). In relation to socially owned property, in 1990 the property of state enterprises was transferred to a state property agency charged with privatization. Most other state-owned land was transferred to local government, including buildings and residential units, and this, through various arrangements, is authorized in turn to sell that property (Gray, 1992a: 10–11).

Restitution has been handled differently, and similarly pragmatically, in Hungary. Under the Compensation Act, compensation coupons are given to any owner of property expropriated under post-1939 laws, with a ceiling of 5 million forints. The limitation (and a sliding scale of compensation up to it: 100 per cent up to 200,000 forints, then 50 per cent up to 300,000 forints, then 30 per cent up to 500,000 forints, then 10 per cent) reflects the continuing belief that real property should not be monopolized; the issuance of coupons, usable only to purchase state assets (theoretically including the land in compensation for whose taking they are issued), effectively ameliorates the drain on the state budget. The controversies in which lawyers and legislators are now involved having to do with property rights are not about clarity or concept, but about 'simple' issues of conflicts of interests (Gray, 1992a: 14ff). For instance, mortgages have been recognized since the days of the civil code. Should claims for wages have priority over mortgages in bankruptcy proceedings? The issue is no different in Hungary from that in the United States; it is not a question of property rights 'reform', but of making delicate decisions balancing competing interests. What rights should residents have against eviction when there is a foreclosure on the property in which they are living? Hungarian law has typically been protective of tenants; tenant advocates in the United States argue it should be more so there. The issue is as difficult in the US as in Hungary. What proportion of condominium residents (condominiums have been recognized since the 1920s) should have to approve before renovation of a building can take place? The decision can be a difficult one, but its incorporation into existing law is not.

Romania

In Romania, a new constitution was approved on 21 November 1991. It guarantees private property rights, but provides that 'the contents and limitations of [these rights] are established by law' (see Gray et al., 1992, and for the subsequent details). Foreigners are flatly denied the right to own land.[50] The supreme court may declare an Act of parliament unconstitutional, but parliament may over-rule such a decision by a two-thirds vote. Assets of enterprises may be sold separately by the enterprise; that includes land. But, under Law 58/1991, the right of the purchaser to sell, lease or transfer use is restricted for one year after the conclusion of the contract of sale. For agricultural land, if owned as co-operatives, strict restitution in kind is provided for; for land in state farms, the farms are converted to stock companies, and former owners given shares. There is a limit of 10 hectares that may be reprivatized per family (Frydman et al., 1993: 223), and a total limit of 100 hectares for land acquired by purchase. As in most other East European countries, there is a prohibition (with slight exceptions) on the conversion of agricultural land to other uses.

Urban land has been owned entirely by the state. An early decree permitted it to be leased by the state, but not sold. Under the subsequently enacted Land Law, the owner of a building was also given 'ownership' of the land on which the building was located; that provision also was intended to apply to state enterprises. Office build-ings are not covered by the Land Law, and are not thus far being privatized; housing is. State-owned housing was already permitted to be sold to its occupants in 1973, accompanied by the rights of use of the land on which it was located. Prices have been set at one-fifth to one-tenth of 'market value'. Where claims for restitution by prior owners are pending, no decision has yet been made as to the balance of rights sought. Something less than half of all state-owned apart-ments have been bought by their tenants under these provisions (Frydman et al., 1993: 257).

Czechoslovakia

In Czechoslovakia, the socialist Civil Code of 1964 had set forth a quite typical hierarchy of forms of property: state, co-operative, per-sonal and private, with severe limitations on what could be owned as private property (for these and subsequent details see Gray, 1992b).[51] The limitations on private property ownership were removed in January 1991, and the hierarchy of ownership forms abolished by amendments to the code at the beginning of 1992.[52] Most land had not been nationalized; even in agricultural co-operatives, landowners had been required to join the co-operatives and surrendered their rights of use and transfer to them, but had retained formal title to their lands.[53] The situation was different in urban areas, however, where most buildings and land were nationalized between 1955 and 1961 and may well remain different for some time. After the Velvet Revolution, privatization of both land and buildings was undertaken. Restrictions on foreign ownership were imposed, nevertheless: no foreign investor domiciled abroad was allowed to acquire land in Czechoslovakia. Surprisingly, though, even wholly foreign-owned business entities if domiciled in Czechoslovakia were allowed to pur-chase land without limitations (Frydman et al., 1993: 61).

In the 'small privatization programme' for small businesses (now terminated), 23,000 units were privatized, largely at the request of interested buyers, often at auction; but the sales in perhaps three-quarters of all cases did not include the real estate used by the business, which remained government-owned and leased to the en-terprise, generally for between three and five years at a fixed rent. Unlike those in other countries, such as Bulgaria, the proceeds of sales were put into a special fund to bolster the banking system, but not made available for budgetary uses.[54] Much of privatization under this act was of small business and retail establishments in urban areas; the leasing arrangement thus permits continued state planning controls, although the decision to lease rather than sell was made rather because of the possibility of competing claims to real estate from former owners. The 'large' privatization law, covering primarily enterprise property, paid careful attention to the formalities of prior socialist law. It covered property nationalized under the socialist government, after 1948; it thus excluded property nationalized immediately after the war, for example that of war criminals. It provided for compensation along the lines of the 1948 legislation, which had also provided for payments that were never made. It excluded properties taken from political parties and churches. Only resident citizens could claim restitution. Implicitly, thus, the law recognized a certain legitimacy to certain earlier actions. A third law provided for restitution of agricultural land to its former owners, if resident citizens; a fourth for restitution of land confiscated from ethnic Germans and Hungarians after the war, if the owners remained in the country and were citizens. It is too early to assess these laws' results.

The formal privatization of housing has proceeded very slowly. Current residents in the 25 per cent of all units government-owned are to have first option to buy, but in no event to be forced to move. Continuing subsidies are foreseen, while rents are being raised (in privately owned apartments, rent controls remain, but a 100 per cent rent increase was permitted on 1 July 1992). Free maintenance is still provided by the state in state-owned units, where rents lag behind price increases (Frydman et al., 1993: 90). Evictions may only take place if alternative equivalent housing is found. Formal 'ownership' of units by their occupants may not appear much of an advantage to them.

Slovenia

Slovenia's regulation of land and ownership rights took place against a background of Austro-Hungarian and Yugoslav post-war law. The basic principles of the Austro-Hungarian empire, as reflected in the Allgemeines Bürgerliches Gesetzbuch, very similar to that in Prussia, remained technically in place from 1811, and still are so. Registration of title to land continued technically to be required even during the socialist period of Yugoslav government, but was largely ignored in practice, contributing to the conflicts about restitution that plague most of the formerly socialist countries (for these and subsequent details see Gray and Stiblar, 1992). In the formalities of title and registration, the comprehensive Yugoslav law of 1980 retained much of the original Austro-Hungarian forms, and the socialist modifications were largely removed by amendments in 1990, leaving a formal structure close to what it had been in the previous century.

Socialist forms of ownership in Yugoslavia after the war differed in one significant aspect from that in most other socialist countries. Yugoslavia had, as did most others, three forms of property: 'social', 'co-operative', and 'private'. But 'social', which covered primarily business enterprises and properties, was subject to the system of worker self-management; the right to use (usufruct) was assigned by the state, but actual use was controlled by the enterprise and its workers. Co-operative ownership was not extensive, but private ownership, confined to personal ownership, was wide-spread; it was permitted for single-family houses or 2–3 apartments per person, not including vacation homes, and for small craft enterprises and small private farms up to 10 hectares (later increased to 30 hectares). Although land holdings over 25 hectares were nationalized in 1948, and holdings over 10 hectares in 1953, 85 per cent of all land was privately owned in Slovenia at the time of independence.

Slovenia adopted its first constitution as a republic on 23 December 1991, a year after the referendum for independence from Yugoslavia. The constitution in general terms established 'protection for private property', and listed it as essential to economic development, but forbade foreign ownership except where property was inherited. A 'right to housing' is established, and land, particularly agricultural land, is 'especially' protected. A special constitutional court, with power to annul legislation, is created. But mortgages and mortgage foreclosure proceedings posed a problem: if foreigners were allowed to hold mortgages on real property, wished for by many foreigners whose investments were much desired for economic development, then foreigners could, on default, become owners of real property by the back door, so to speak. The right of foreigners to hold mortgages was thus temporarily suspended in October 1991, till the issue could be resolved. Land ownership by foreigners was a sticking point in Yugoslav law, and remains one in Slovenia. The 1980 Yugoslav prohibition against real property ownership by foreigners has remained substantially in effect (although 5–30-year leases are possible). It had been modified by the Yugoslav legislation of 1990 on property relations to permit ownership of commercial property and 99-year leases, and was then incorporated in the 1991 Slovenian constitution.

Reprivatization of land nationalized under Yugoslav law has been decided upon under the Slovene Law on Denationalization of November 1991. Reprivatization affects all nationalized property, including property confiscated from Nazi collaborators, and is estimated to affect about 7 per cent of all property in Slovenia. Citizens of Yugoslavia as of the time of nationalization, or their heirs, are eligible to file claims; legal entities other than religious organizations are not. In-kind return takes precedence over compensation wherever possible. Reprivatization of social housing (which accounted for about 70 per cent of all apartments and houses in Slovenia before independence) involves sales more than restitution, because most of it was state-built. Current tenants have priority rights, prices and terms of sale are favourable, and sales are expected to go well. Where housing was not state-built and had been nationalized, previous owners' claims conflict with those of current tenants. Previous owners are given priority, and may choose return of the property or compensation. If they choose return, they may not evict current tenants; current tenants are entitled to 30 per cent of the value of the property plus a 'housing credit' in similar amount if they vacate within two years. One might thus consider the value of 'tenancy' in the Yugoslav socialist system, which included, as in other socialist systems, rights to life-time use, assignability to relatives, and below-cost rents, as equal to up to 60 per cent of the value of 'ownership' in the conventional Western sense.

Bulgaria

In Bulgaria, the constitution of 1947 provided for a conventional socialist classification of property: social ownership, co-operative and individual. The constitution of 1971 replaced 'individual' with the two categories 'social organization' and 'personal' (for these and subsequent details see Dandelova, personal communication, 1994; Gray and Ianachkov, 1992). Individual property could not include commercial property, but could include owner-occupied housing. Most residential property and all industrial property were nationalized in 1947 and 1948. Much of such residential property was, however, sold to tenants after nationalization (or, for new construction, after completion) at non-speculative prices in the 1950s and 1960s. Before the overthrow of real existing socialism, 83.8 per cent of all housing was privately owned, and rights to land accompanied that ownership; from the late 1970s on, individual and co-operative housing construction accounted for about half of what was built (Tsenkova, 1994).

Amendments to the Property Act in 1990 replaced the former categories of ownership with two: state and private. The new constitution of 1991 equalized the status of all forms of property, eliminated pre-existing restrictions on the number of properties an individual could own, and made land freely disposable, with restrictions on the prices charged for housing being gradually eliminated.

In fact, as far back as the first transitional government, dominated by the Bulgarian Socialist Party, the sale of state and municipally owned housing had been authorized largely as a revenue-raising device, and the law was implemented effectively. Both state-owned land and residential property have been largely privatized, mostly through restitution to prior owners; 18,717 claims have been filed for return of housing units to previous owners, of which 11,815 have been approved, and 96 per cent of all land eligible for restitution has been transferred or claimed by prior owners (Bogetic and Wilton, 1992: 6). On the other hand, former owners of commercial property used in the meantime by state enterprises are entitled only to a proportionate share of the ownership of those enterprises, when privatized (Frydman et al., 1993: 34). Only 9.5 per cent of all housing in Bulgaria remained governmentally owned by 1992 (Dandelova, personal communication, 1994).

Co-operative land ownership in the agricultural sector was at first protected for co-operatives that 're-registered'; then dissolution of co-operatives was encouraged; finally, the present Law on Co-operatives gave those that continued under new legislation prescribing democratic forms of management special tax and other concessions, reflecting the substantial real advantages that this 'social' form of ownership had provided (Frydman et al., 1993: 14).

Foreign ownership of assets, and specifically of land, continues severely restricted, however. Under the constitution, foreign citizens and legal entities may not acquire property in land except by inheritance, and even then it may only go to a former Bulgarian national (Frydman et al., 1993: 20). Restrictions are even tighter for agricultural land: no majority-foreign-owned firm may acquire ownership rights. For non-agricultural land, such firms may own buildings and 'usufructual rights' to the land on which they are located, but not 'title', and in special areas the permission of the council of ministers is required even for acquisition of such rights (Frydman et al., 1993: 20).

Poland

In Poland, the majority of urban land was owned by the state (for these and subsequent details see Gray et al., 1992); all land in Warsaw was publicly owned, and only 30 per cent in cities was estimated to be in private hands as of 1990.[55] Agricultural land, on the other hand, was overwhelmingly privately owned (Frydman et al., 1993: 174). While private ownership was legally possible, including private sales and purchases, state regulation went into the smallest detail, and essentially resulted in full state control over property rights. The first house owned was considered 'personal property'; additional units might be owned, but were considered 'private property', and regulated as to rents, assignment of tenants, etc. State controls are being reduced, but to Westerners still seems to impose many obstacles to free exchange.

The Polish Civil Code, adopted in 1964, was modelled on the French Napoleonic Code; in several commentators' view, 'after being recently purged of socialist rhetoric, the Code is suitable for a market economy' (Gray et al., 1992: 284). The 1952 constitution had established two categories of ownership, social ownership and personal property. In December 1989, an amendment to the constitution eliminated the category 'socialist property', and provided a 'guarantee [of] the complete protection of personal property'. Several months later, the distinction between personal and private property, discussed at the outset of this chapter, was abolished. Thus the distinctions among types of property, fundamental to socialist law, were eliminated. For formerly socialist property, conflicts between different governmental entities pose a major problem.

While the separation of powers introduced in Poland, as in Romania, gives the highest court the power to protect private property rights against state action, decisions of that court can be overturned by a two-thirds vote of parliament. Practice, rather than the legal structure or the formal definition of property rights, remains the problem, from the point of view of investors; there is wide discretion and 'general lack of experience and competence' of judges, and thus legal uncertainty about the handling of individual cases. In other cases, legislation has simply been consistently unused in earlier years, and there is resistance to its application today; that holds for eviction legislation, for instance, where the desirability of enforcement is not simply a matter of 'clarity' but one of real conflicts of interest between tenants on the one side and landlords and investors on the other. In the privatization process, foreign individuals and firms may acquire land only with a special permit from the Minister of Internal Affairs; permits are generally not difficult to obtain (Frydman et al., 1993: 168).

THE LEGISLATIVE HISTORY OF PRIVATIZATION: A GENERALIZED MODEL

The above details of the process of privatization in Eastern Europe are not a complete account, and will not be current when this is read;

the field is too fast-moving. It is based largely on secondary sources, so misunderstandings are inevitable. But in any event the mass of detail can overwhelm. I believe, however, that a general pattern emerges from all the detail, and that a generalized model can be described tracing the main threads of development that all Eastern European countries, more or less, have followed in the first half of the 1990s. Such a model can in any event be useful as a starting point for analysis.

The components that make up the model of legal/legislative changes include:

- pre-socialist legal forms;
- imposition of state socialism;
- reforms within state socialism;
- constitutional provisions of the transition;
- generalized legislation for destatification, including authorization for sales to private entities, decentralization of state ownership rights, and provisions for management of property continuing in state ownership;
- restitution to former owners;
- implementing legislation, including technical facilitation of market transfers, differentiation according to types of property, differentiation according to types of owner/ownership entity; judicial procedures for enforcement of ownership rights;
- regulatory land-use and planning controls;
- comprehensive housing policy formulation.

Pre-socialist legal forms

The countries of Eastern Europe had, before the advent of state socialism, a wide variety of different legal systems, and pre-socialist legal forms survived in the socialist period in many countries (see, for example, the cases of Poland and Hungary, noted above). Pre-capitalist legal traditions in many of the countries of the former Soviet Union continue to have influence, according to some commentators, if more in the role of the courts and the acceptance of arbitrary decision-making than in the actual terms of legislation. These historic variations have, however, had more influence on procedural than on substantive aspects of privatization.

Imposition of state socialism

Private property existed under state socialist regimes throughout their histories, if in very varying degrees; it was not 'introduced' onto a tabula rasa after the collapse of those regimes.[56] Focusing on land

and housing, the range ran from the Soviet Union, where all land and much housing was nationalized immediately after the revolution of 1917, to Poland, where land as such was never nationalized. At the centre of the spectrum was probably East Germany, where no general nationalization of land took place, but where a series of decrees nationalized the land of Nazis and war criminals, then holdings over 100 hectares and the land of those who left the country, and pressured collectivization created large co-operative holdings in the countryside (P. Marcuse and Schumann, 1992). In almost all countries of Eastern Europe, housing that was owner-occupied prior to the advent of state socialism could remain in that tenure, barring special circumstances. Even property owned by private landlords and rented out to tenants could remain privately 'owned' in most countries, although strong public regulation, affecting usually both the setting of rents and the selection of occupants, limited the benefits of that 'ownership' severely. In East Germany, 20 per cent of all dwelling units continued to be privately rented, for instance (P. Marcuse and Schumann, 1992: 84), and it continued to maintain during the entire state socialist period the official record books for the entry of transactions affecting land in the same form as they had been handled for the preceding decades. And in every country in Eastern Europe, private transactions affecting dachas, summer or second homes, were wide-spread, whether these were technically 'privately owned', as in Hungary or Poland, or 'publicly owned', as in the Soviet Union.

Reforms within state socialism

Rigid as may have been the imposition of Soviet forms on the states of Eastern Europe in the post-war period, there were significant modifications incorporated in many states thereafter. To some extent, the very nature of the Stalinist system demanded modification if it was to extend its existence.[57] The changes of the Khrushchev era in the Soviet Union, the ups and downs of liberalization after the Prague Spring in Czechoslovakia, Kadar's 'goulash communism', all included changes in the actual, if not the formal, handling of private property rights. The Gorbachev-era experiments with revision of arrangements for decision-making over the use of property may be seen as a continuation of this line of development as well as the beginning of the transition.

In general, those responsible for rewriting property laws after the end of the period of state socialism paid little attention either to these reforms or to the refinements of tenure arrangements during that period, and tried, on the one hand, to revert to legal relationships existing before the advent of state socialism (in the few cases, such as East Germany, in which fully developed market provisions had existed), and on the other hand, and more often, with outside help to write entire new codes of property rights and ownership. Thus four separate streams of legal thinking flowed into the new arrangements: (1) those existing prior to state socialism, well developed in the more central European countries but of little use in the countries of the Soviet Union except for the Baltics; (2) those created during state socialism, theoretically ignored in the rewriting of laws and constitutions, but nevertheless of major political importance in both shaping and administering them in detail; (3) those developed, in practice as well as in law, during the various reform periods in the periods of liberalization under state socialism; and (4) those newly brought into play through local free market advocates, ideologically committed but inexperienced in Western law, and through foreign consultants and advisers, inexperienced in local laws and practices.

Constitutional provisions of the transition

The legal story generally begins with constitutional changes – although in reality the exploration of joint ventures with foreign firms concerned about their legal protections was already under way substantially earlier. In a few countries, notably the Soviet Union under Gorbachev and East Germany under Modrow, there were efforts to find what might be described as either a reformed socialist or a third way alternative in a new formulation of property rights (for East Germany see P. Marcuse and Schumann, 1992: 127ff). The (abortive) draft of a new constitution in East Germany, arguably one of the most progressive in the world, has continued to have repercussions, if subdued ones, in the united Germany; apart from that, few results of the early reform period have left any trace.

The new constitutions typically contained three provisions on property rights as they affected housing and land; a provision doing away with the reference to 'socialist ownership', and permitting a large number of varied forms of 'private ownership'; a provision guaranteeing the 'rights of private property'; and a provision protecting the public interest in land and natural resources.[58] The last of these provisions was quite varied from country to country, and in general represented both a political compromise and an uncertainty about how far privatization should really go.

Generalized legislation for destatification

Constitutional provisions are not self-enforcing; they require legislation for their implementation. When it came to legislation, the
sweeping tenor of constitutional provisions was dropped, but with
very varying effectiveness. The first round of legislation, in almost
every country, consisted of three types of provision: those authorizing
sales of socialist, state-owned property; those for decentralization
of decision-making over the disposition of such property; and those
for the management of property remaining, currently, under state
control.

Authorization for sales to private entities

Initial legislation implementing constitutional provisions for privatization were by and large focused on the privatization of the ownership of businesses, with both land and housing being dealt with only
in very general fashion, and requiring implementation by further
governmental action to be effective. For formal purposes the most
important effect of this initial legislation was to specify, and in most
cases shift, the locus of decision-making over the privatization of land
and housing to a more local level (see below). Practically, there was
another result, not publicly anticipated: many members of the old
nomenklatura used their positions and the uncertainties of legislation to procure transfers of property to themselves, so that the very
first beneficiaries of the early waves of general legislation were the
more flexible and entrepreneurial of the old elite and the old new
elite, in Hankiss and Szalai's phrase. In the GDR, for instance, the
members of the central committee of the party and top government
leaders had individual houses assigned to them in a secured enclave
called Wandlitz. When individuals were initially given the opportunity to obtain title to housing they already occupied, some of the top
leadership were among the first to take advantage of the opportunity.
When their actions came to light in the press, a public furore caused
substantial revision of the process.

Decentralization of state ownership rights

The locus of 'ownership' within the state was under state socialism
not a matter of major concern, because of the strongly centralized
and hierarchical distribution of power. In one of the classic cases of
out-of-context use of legal concepts, 'ownership' was considered by
most Westerners (inappropriately) to be in the central state, and to

include all of the bundle of rights that might, but need not, attend it; since the central state did not always have all of those rights, many considered ownership 'indeterminate' (Gray et al., 1992: 288). That simply meant that all of those rights did not reside in one entity. The dispersion of certain rights amongst different levels of government may have caused some bureaucratic difficulties under state socialism, but ultimately the strongly centralized control of the party over all levels of government made the dispersion of little substantive importance.[59] In the transition, with the disappearance of this centralized political control, the attempt generally has been to bring all those rights together in one place within government, whether at the central state, regional, local or sub-local level.

At what level? With the end of state socialism, decentralization of ownership became very attractive even to centralized regimes: it not only fitted in well with the new atmosphere of democratization, but also removed a large headache from already overburdened new central governments – both deciding what to do and paying for the costs of doing it. Thus in almost every country in Eastern Europe, the rights and obligations of 'ownership' of 'state' housing was handed down from the central government, to municipal governments in most cases. Where local or regional housing bodies had previously had managerial responsibilities, they now became 'owners', assuming the financial burdens previously shouldered through subsidies from the central state. Decentralization is in substance a transfer of property rights and obligations from central government to local government, but it is rarely handled as such (that is, there are no deeds of conveyance, recorded transfers of title, etc.); rather, central legislation simply grants powers of control and disposition to local government. This was the pattern in almost all of Eastern Europe. In Hungary, 'ownership' was further handed down by the municipal government of Budapest to districts within the city. In East Germany, the vertical responsibilities of the municipal housing organizations were severed, and they were made independent agencies responsible to municipal government alone, and allowed legally to sell the units they owned. For property remaining in central state 'ownership' (property of centrally owned enterprises, for instance, often including land and sometimes housing), virtually every East European country set up a separate agency to handle privatization. That agency has also in many cases been the rule as to the restitution of formerly privately owned but nationalized property (see further below and, for a detailed discussion of each country, Frydman et al., 1993).

The results have often produced either conflict or confusion or both. Local governments have generally been delegated discretion in those areas that are the most troublesome for central government and involve existing subsidies or other drains on the central budget. Thus state-owned housing, for example, is a general subject for decentralization, seen primarily from the central side as a divestiture of financial responsibility. Central governments, on the other hand, have kept or tried to keep control where matters of political principle seem to be involved, controlling by national legislation, for instance, the rights of foreigners to buy, the ownership of land, or the eviction of tenants. Rent controls are sometimes seen as central government issues, maintenance of housing rarely.

Provisions for management of property continuing in state ownership

Finally, the early spate of legislative and administrative action dealing with property rights after the transition contained a variety of decisions intended to prepare the way for full privatization. From the legal point of view the most interesting of these is the issuance of vouchers entitling the holder to acquire ownership of previously state-held assets, at some valuation to be administratively fixed. Theoretically, these were a transfer of ownership to some share of a fixed body of assets, treated as fungible as they might be in a fully effective private market for assets traded in that market. In practice, since none of the formerly state socialist countries has such a market yet, their distribution and redemption may have some of the characteristics of a state lottery as well. (For provisions relating to state housing, see below.)

Restitution to former owners

The claims of former owners to restitution of their property have been recognized in every country of Eastern Europe except those of the pre-1939 Soviet Union.[60] The general principal of restitution once being established, implementing legislation has been very diverse. It involves decisions as to rights of current users against rights of prior owners; valuation for purposes of compensation, and allocation of value added after nationalization; and the relevance of the social desirability of current uses and proposed uses, with priority given to cases where employment will be generated. The treatment of property acquired for purposes such as highway construction, analogous to Western eminent domain, was subject to further compensation. As to some of these issues, there is general agreement:

- Restitution or compensation? The universal practice is restitution wherever possible, on the simple grounds that compensation is too expensive for the governmental budget, and private sources for compensation (proceeds, for instance, from unclaimed property, or from the sale of structures built by the state) are inadequate. In almost all countries the process of privatization has been turned over to some form of quasi-governmental body under some form of trust arrangement, in large part to avoid politicization of the process in both the bad and the good sense of that term – insulating it, it is hoped, both from corruption and from popular pressures. Where there has been new construction on nationalized property, compensation is the rule, unless the prior owners commit themselves to additional investment, in which case they may be given first rights to reacquire. When property is not restored to the prior owners, the trust frequently places it on the market so that it may be transferred to private ownership as soon as possible.
- The rights of those in occupancy vs. those of the old owners? Here the lines are most clearly drawn, and pressure-group organizations, if not indeed social movements, have begun to form on each side. Thus far, former owners are ahead in theory in most countries, actual residents in practice: legislation generally provides for a return of ownership to prior owners who can prove their title, but postpones giving them rights of occupancy for some fixed time, limiting their control and their rights to raise rents in the interim. But in all likelihood the postponement will be just that, and sooner or later full return to former owners will take place. It is possible that in a few countries fewer rights will be given to foreign owners than to current citizens or returning owners, but that is not likely to make much difference to current residents.

There are many anomalies surrounding restitution and this is not the place for an extended discussion of the complex legal issues involved, perhaps most visibly in East Germany, where restitution to owners not only of property taken by the GDR, but also of property confiscated by the Nazis, is being undertaken. While issues of restitution are only transitional, they will have a major impact on the distribution of ownership in Eastern Europe; estimates are that between 19 per cent and 60 per cent of all land will be involved by the time the process is over, the least in predominantly rural countries like Albania or Bulgaria where the title to property remained private (even if many rights attached to ownership did not) under state socialism.

Implementing legislation

All of the above actions – constitutional, legislative and administrative – were explicitly seen as changing property rights, and were debated and adopted as instruments of political and economic change. A whole series of subsequent measures has been undertaken in a different vein, purporting simply to implement policy decisions already taken. They include technical facilitation of market transfers, and formal differentiation in the application of the rules of privatization among types of property and types of owner.

Technical facilitation of market transfers

Provisions for the registration of title, for the execution and recording of mortgages, for judicial proceedings to enforce property rights, including the protection of financial interests secured by real property such as procedures for mortgage foreclosure and eviction, and revision of property tax arrangements have all been the subject of intensive activity in all Eastern European countries. The World Bank has been in the forefront of supporting such activities, and hosts of Western consultants have been involved in the process. At some point a detailed look at the distributional consequences of such activities might be interesting; their net impact is certainly to strengthen specific rights of ownership of property, and to weaken others, but the process is still too open and the evidence too anecdotal to permit any detailed conclusions.

Differentiation according to types of property

As implementation progressed, it became readily apparent that differentiation among the types of property to be privatized was necessary: partly on logical grounds (privatization of a truck factory was obviously different from privatization of a corner grocery shop) and partly on political grounds (entirely different interests were affected by privatization of factories and of single family houses). There were various major types of action.

With regard to *publicly built and owned housing,* measures moved in three not always consistent directions. First, there was a transfer of 'ownership' from the central state to some lower body, generally the municipality, in some cases districts or wards within the municipality. Ownership, in these cases, meant the responsibility for management and disposition, but with restricted discretion: the provisions governing both management and disposition in most cases continued to be governed by national legislation as to rents, rights of tenants to buy, etc., although often a range of discretion was allowed municipalities.

Second, there was an adjustment of rents and payment for utilities, maintenance and repairs, so that the heavily subsidized rents of the state socialist period would more nearly cover at least the operating costs of the housing, reducing (transferring to the state) part of the tenants' previous 'right' to a fixed low rent. The adjustments were generally made on a flat basis, that is, a percentage increase in existing rents, usually measured on a standard per-square-metre basis, rather than attempting to approach a market level which would take into account factors such as location, amenities and age. Because rents had previously been so low, every country undertook increases in a staged manner, aiming at an eventual rent that would cover the full economic cost of maintaining the housing, providing utilities, and in some cases amortizing the construction cost or the remaining indebtedness arising from construction. That indebtedness had previously been meaningful only on paper, since the state was on both sides of the debt; now it became real.

Finally, there was some formula for the transfer of 'ownership' to sitting tenants. Here the provisions vary widely from country to country. On paper, tenants in almost all countries have a right to buy, but in some it is at a fixed price per square metre, in others vouchers are issued which may be used only to purchase units, it stilll others again residents have the option of applying rent to a purchase price, and in others again ownership was given free up to a certain number of square metres per person. Once residents 'buy', they have unlimited rights to resell; limited equity arrangements are not common. The whole procedure is still highly problematic, however, because of an economic and a legal factor: economically, most residents now enjoy heavily subsidized rents, and have little incentive to increase their costs by 'buying'; legally, the sharing of ownership rights and obligations among many households in a multi-family building, particularly when the state or the municipality continues to own non-buying residents' units, is an undeveloped area of the law, with condominium-like arrangements only slowly coming into discussion. Surprisingly, no efforts have been made to move ownership into the hands of organizations of tenants or co-operatives, although the suggestions have been made.

In respect to *housing privately owned before socialism and nationalized,* virtually every country outside the Soviet Union has adopted some provision for restitution, giving priority to the interests of the former owners. The issues were discussed earlier. For *housing privately owned during socialism,* title in the private owner is universally recognized. Where houses were owned privately, but land was not, the situation is more complicated, and is discussed below. In the case of *privately owned housing,* controls on the private setting of rents were reduced, and many restrictions of the use of property were lifted without replacement by Western-style land-use controls; thus the ability of the owner of agricultural land to develop that land for a shopping centre, certainly a right of major value in a market system, was often newly transferred to such owners.

As to *land*, all countries have special provisions, but they are quite varied. Unlike other objects of ownership, land was originally exempted from sweeping provisions, including constitutional ones, governing privatization. Deviation from public ownership here came piece-meal and ad hoc. Land considered as a natural resource, such as forests, national parks and waterways, remains in public ownership in almost all countries. In many cases much of it had always been so, even before state socialism. Because public ownership of publicly used or publicly important land had been a feature of state socialism that had generally wide support, and because it is not in theory inconsistent with Western conceptions, it has been one of the areas in which old forms and practices have survived most strongly. The symbolic meaning of land is often reflected in such provisions.[61] Residential land under single-family or smaller multi-family houses partly owner-occupied, and either continuously privately owned or subject to restitution, was considered privately owned, although implementation of rights of ownership was subject to protection of current users and the unavailability of many of the institutional structures for exercising rights in land.

Whom land may be sold to has frequently been restricted, both to prevent an excess concentration of land in a few hands, and to prevent foreigners from becoming absentee owners. The connection between large land holdings and political power is a matter of long experience in most of Eastern Europe, and the identification of national sovereignty with ownership of land as a basic ingredient of nationhood is also deeply rooted.[62] The restrictions on foreign ownership are, however, slowly giving way to the need to connect foreign investment with title to land. Land connected with enterprises, both industrial and commercial in urban areas, has been treated differently from other types of land, generally under special legislation affecting property rights in the enterprises themselves. Foreign investors, in particular, have generally been concerned with title to the land on which the enterprise in which they invest is located. Thus in theory entitlement to that land goes with ownership of the enterprise. But the set of rights going to an owner of such land is often not spelled out to the satisfaction of investors, and does not approach Western patterns of property rights, with access to foreclosure procedures, eviction, etc. In many cases, the problem is resolved in practice not by sales but by long-term leases, in which the details of the distribution of rights can be clearly spelled out by contract. An intermediate form of ownership, 'private inheritable possession', analogous to *Erbpacht* in traditional German law, has been experimented with in a few cases. It is, in a sense, a survival of the popularly accepted concept of ownership for use but without rights of sale or profit. It does not seem likely to come into wide-spread use.

Agricultural land is generally treated separately from urban land, industrial land or land used for housing, and is not considered in detail here; in general provisions are for the breaking up of co-operatives and collective farms and a return to individual ownership, but limitations on the size of privatized farms are being considered in several countries. It remains a contentious issue.

Differentiation according to types of owner/ownership entity

In relation to the legal entities that may hold property rights, new provisions have been adopted in all countries, but are continually subject to refinement. Such legislation is generally (with the exception of the condominium and co-operative forms) developed without specific regard to housing or land. The institutional structures which are needed to make them effective, from recording to judicial enforcement, while they technically do not pose major problems in formulation, are often lacking, but are being slowly created. Foreign technical assistance plays a particularly important role here. The focus of legislative effort has, however, been on enabling business entities to operate, not on possible housing-sector entities.

Co-operatives present an interesting anomaly for the transition, an example of the lack of congruence between substance and legal form. Because co-operative ownership was considered a form of social ownership under socialism, there has been some tendency to consider taking property out of co-operative ownership as one aspect of privatization – even though under traditional Western conceptions co-operative ownership *is* private ownership. Further, unlike some other forms of social ownership, co-operatives, particularly in agriculture, had been economic successes even in market terms; often their members resisted ideologically driven privatization out of pure self-interest (as in Bulgaria). The result of the confusion has been legislation in a few countries forcing co-operatives to dissolve and distribute their assets to their members, or giving members an option to reacquire property they originally contributed to a co-operative (an option often not voluntarily exercised in the case of many agricultural co-operatives at least), or forcing the creation of smaller co-operatives out of larger ones (as in Slovakia). Very little attention has been paid to 'third-sector' ownership entities, or what are called in many West European countries socially tied ownership forms, such as mutual housing associations, limited equity co-operatives, or land trusts.

Judicial procedures for enforcement of ownership rights

None of these legislative provisions as to ownership and ownership rights will have, ultimately, any meaning unless it is enforceable, and the universal (although not inevitable) trend has been towards enforceability through a Western-style judicial system, including courts of law whose authority to make decisions about private rights will be recognized and enforced by the state. In designing judicial systems capable of implementing property rights in their new forms, part of the issue is technical, part political. Technically, the judicial structure is established or in process in all countries to enforce the distribution of rights which new property legislation has created. But 'technically' and 'practically' are two different things. Judges need to be sitting who are willing to act according to new laws and new priorities; the political priorities that dictated much judicial conduct in the past needs to be rejected by those accustomed to it for many years. Speedy action, regularized paperwork, sufficient personnel, and even appropriate physical quarters are often lacking. Remedying these problems is, however, only a matter of time in most places.

Politically, the role of the judiciary in the system may say much, in the long run, about what property rights reform will mean. In the United States-type judicial system, the ability of a high court to over-rule national legislation based on its reading of a written constitution has, over the years, been a solid foundation for the protection of private rights of profitable ownership.[63] Most Eastern Europe countries have rather opted for a British model, without judicial review of legislative acts, but not without substantial debates. In a politically stable situation, the difference may not be so great; in a period of instability, the absence of judicial review opens the door for greater legislative – whether democratic or not – control of private property rights.

Regulatory land-use controls and planning procedures

These have been problematic thus far. The issue is a new one for most governments; in the past, the state itself initiated: it planned and determined and implemented land uses itself. As it privatizes land, either new forms of control will be put in place, or the private market will determine land uses. Thus far movement has been more in the direction of market decision-making than of new planning controls.[64] On the one side, municipalities have been eager, since they must now divest themselves of ownership of city land and buildings, to do so at the highest price possible, since the new pressures on the local budget are everywhere enormous. If McDonalds is willing to pay the top price for a historic location, it is likely to get it (as much Western experience also shows). Thus choice inner-city sites are likely to be developed to their maximum physical capacity, to the extent that there is demand. On the other side, investors in those enterprises needing extensive land, or where land costs are a significant part of business expense, have been looking at fringe city and suburban locations for new construction possibilities. Sprawl is thus growing. No regional planning or land-use controls are in place in any of the Eastern Europe countries to date that effectively regulate this type of activity; only limited demand has thus far limited development. In Eastern Germany the pattern is particularly visible because of the rapidity of the development, demand from Western German firms being strong (see Haussermann, chapter 7, this volume). Discount stores, do-it-yourself lumber yards, and automobile dealers, all bringing new types of business into areas unused to them, have acquired land (since it is for business use) cheaply, either from private owners or from the state. In Moscow, the bulk of new housing construction is on land at a substantial remove from the centre of the city, replicating or extending the much-criticized pattern of earlier socialist development.

Historic preservation has, however, got significant political force behind it, coupled as it so frequently is with national history and traditions in a period of strong nationalist interest. Thus, for buildings known and widely appreciated for their historical value or symbolism, substantial impetus lies behind preservation. It has been effective, to date, more in influencing discretionary decisions as to sale or development than in the passage of any comprehensive laws dealing with historic structures.

Comprehensive housing policy formulation

Housing is probably the area where property rights most directly affect consumers. Ideally, the handling of property rights in residential land and housing should be integrated into a comprehensive housing policy; the goal of adequate housing provision should be at least one of the goals of policy formulation as to property rights. Further, ideally, comprehensive policy should be formulated before individual governmental actions are taken. Given present conditions, no country in Eastern Europe has followed this path, not only because of pressures of change, but also because the possible impact of an integration of housing with property rights policies is likely to restrict some individual or group property rights and interests. For instance, in Slovakia, which has begun to consider comprehensive housing legislation, it is expected that 20 per cent of the existing stock of socially owned rental units will be set aside, that is, not privatized, to keep it available to meet social needs (Faltran, 1994: 7).

This is the general outline of how constitutional and legislative provisions affecting residential land and housing have developed. It is a fairly consistent general model. What happens on the ground, however, is not so consistent. Conformity to law, particularly new and unfamiliar law, is not a hallmark of rapid change. Other laws, some of them older, severely limit the application of new rights; *propiska* regulations, for instance, for some time practically limited the rights of non-residents to acquire rights in a city if they had no legal right (no *propiska*) to be there. But neither such laws nor their repeal are uniformly respected; in Russia, one commentator notes, 'laws are routinely enacted at the federal level and ignored at the local level' (S.B. Butler and O'Leary, 1994a); in Moscow the constitutional court's invalidation of the *propiska* system is, for instance, often simply ignored. The conflict between presidential decrees and laws passed by the Duma complicates the issue further. But the general tenor of the legislative outline here summarized will probably become more and more the prevailing practice as time goes on.

SUMMARY AND INTERPRETATION

When the murky concept of privatization is analysed and traced in its historic meaning, then, a picture full of understandable tensions emerges. Privatization of land and housing in Eastern Europe is not simply a matter of replacing a discredited system of state socialism with the proven laws and procedures of Western capitalism. Rather, it begins with an existing system, established over a period of from 40 to 70 years which has distributed rights and obligations as to the use of land and housing to benefit certain groups, at the expense of others. In the process, that system created distinctions among types of use and types of property and types of 'owner'; limited certain attributes of ownership, such as the right to make profit from it; and distributed controls among users and government and courts, all in ways very different from those developed in the West. The process of change in property rights thus becomes not only a redefinition but also a redistribution of rights from one set of social locations to others. The history of the change shows the interaction between these two aspects: redefinition and redistribution. In some cases, the concepts take on a life of their own, become ideologically invested (the 'ownership' of land); in other cases, it is a simple conflict of interest (eviction procedures between landlord and tenant). The new directions towards which Eastern European countries are moving thus involve both changes in ideology and changes in the distribution of power. The result has been seemingly neat general declarations about 'the rights of private property' adopted in constitutions and legislation, followed by more specific but often contradictory legislation regulating specific aspects of property rights (such as housing, land, investment, planning and zoning, agriculture, restitution), followed by even more concrete and even more contradictory administrative actions, sometimes pursuant to such legislation, sometimes in contravention of it. Consistency becomes of less importance as the complex impact of changes in property rights on specific interests become clear. That is the general pattern that emerges, I believe, from the account here presented.

Law, and especially dominant systems of property rights, must be seen as reflections and reinforcements of social relationships among individuals and groups. Yet much of the present discussion, in both Eastern and Western circles, assumes that changes in laws are not only a necessary but also a sufficient condition of fundamental change. There has been, as Leonid Abalkin, a prominent reformer in the Soviet Union, commented, 'a euphoria of law creation, . . . a romantic belief in the strength of decrees on State power' (quoted in Charley, 1992: 29). As Charley (ibid.) cogently says, '[There has been] an attempt to create a theatre whereby the contradictions of contemporary Soviet society could be resolved within a set of laws rather than running the risk of exploding into a social struggle that would [threaten] the authority of the bureaucracy. This is tantamount to the reliance on the creation of laws to ensure social transformation.' Property rights reform is unmistakably an issue involving the transfer of power and wealth. It involves the distribution of basic rights and privileges in society. While it is technically complex, it is not this complexity that creates social tensions, but the impact of such reform on real interests, real people. It is not 'clarification' of property rights that is being fought over in Eastern Europe, but what constitutes a just and socially acceptable distribution of the bundle of rights and obligations that constitutes 'ownership'. And that is a challenge in the West as well as the East.

NOTES

1   'Eastern Europe', 'the East', 'state socialist' and 'Soviet' are used inter-changeably, even though none is completely accurate, to refer to the countries of the former Soviet Union, Bulgaria, Romania, Yugoslavia and Czechoslovakia and their successors, the German Democratic Republic, Hungary, Albania and Poland.

2   Drago Kos (1994: 1) refers to the belief, which he holds to be common in Eastern European countries and supported by Western 'experts', that the 'transition is nothing but the transmission of already completed social institutions from the West to the East'.

3   I have explored the implications of this analysis, in terms of the incidence of ownership in housing, in P. Marcuse (1994a).

4   Some Soviet formulations were indeed not so far removed from the 'bundle of rights' analysis used here; they spoke, for example, of the three primary rights of ownership as the rights to 'possess, use and dispose of property within the limits established by the law' (see Schneider, 1990: 449).

5   For the argument that Soviet Marxist theory internally reflected the course of actual practice in the Soviet Union, see H. Marcuse (1958).

6   This later position was laid down by Lazar Kaganovitch in 1931; see Ruble (1990: 7) and Bater (1980: 26).

7   See for example his *Theories about surplus value*. I have discussed this question at greater length in P. Marcuse (1992).

8   Discussion of this passage has been enormous. For a recent comment, focusing on the changing relations between base and superstructure, see Sweezy (1992: 56ff). It is ironically an analysis with which those concerned with changing the socialist legal systems in Eastern Europe today would completely agree.

9   Translation in Hazard et al. (1984: 7) of passage from S.S. Alekseev, *The general theory of law* (vol. 1), published in Russian in Moscow 1981.

10 Although some of the privately owned, multi-family housing in particular was publicly administered, and the absentee owners had no benefit from its ownership (P. Marcuse and Schumann, 1992: 84, table 10.3; for agricultural land see ibid.: 88ff). For the distinction between personal and private property see below.

11 The right to interest on deposits in the State Bank, and on government bonds, was an exception and a theoretical anomaly (Stephan, 1991: 43).

12 The legal basis for the following description is the Constitution of the USSR (1980), articles 10–14 and 17. See W.E. Butler (1988); Schneider (1990: 448).

13 A distinction is made in the USSR civil law and in some of the republics' codes between personal property used in production and 'pure' personal property: the latter could be acquired without limits, while the former was narrowly defined and much more subject to scrutiny. The maximum size of a dwelling unit, the maximum amount of land allocated to it, and the maximum number of livestock which might be in personal possession were to be specified by each republic, but in any event only one dwelling house could be in 'personal ownership'. See Stephan (1991); Hazard (1939: 228). Under the Decree of the Supreme Soviet of the USSR of 26 August 1948, for instance, the figure was set at 60 square meters of living space, and land at 300–600 square meters in urban areas, 700–1,200 in rural areas. In Hungary one home and one vacation home were included; if another was inherited, it had to be sold (Gray et al. 1992: 8).

14 Decree no. 4 of the Plenum of the USSR Supreme Court, 31 July 1981, quoted in Hazard et al. (1984: 46).

15 'Ministries . . . shall facilitate the expansion of the construction of individual dwelling houses (including multiple apartment structures) . . . , with the right of ownership of each builder to the house (or part of the building), for employees of subordinate enterprises, institutions, and organizations, and also for other citizens', quoted in Hazard et al. (1984: 123).

16 See Hazard et al. (1984: 229). Alexeev (1991: 5) estimates from official sources that 2.9 per cent of all urban dwellings were privately rented in the USSR in 1990, but that this estimate is low, because many private rentals were not registered or were technically illegal, either because andlords received more than the permitted rent (see below) or because the tenant did not have the required *propiska* (residence permit).

17 For a general discussion see W.E. Butler (1985). This is not the place to go into the issue, but most observers would agree with Prof. Duncan Kennedy of the Harvard Law School that 'private law [in Western societies] is a crazy quilt, rather than a pyramidal structure of rules derived from general principles . . . within the private law regime the principles of solidarity and participation are just as constantly honored as they are constantly disregarded'.

18 Distinctions are of course made, such as those between fungible and non-fungible property in contract law, between real and personal property in actions for specific performance, etc. But these are either simply responses to practical problems or vestiges of historical differences of declining current importance.

19 Renaud (1991: 43) lists under 'main problems with existing tenure systems [in state socialist economies] an additional layer of ambiguity and therefore inefficiency . . . created by the division between rights to the structure and rights to the land'. But such a division is hardly unique to socialist economies, and its abolition would cause a crisis in many Western real-estate markets; New York City real-estate development would be very different without it. The objection is to the vesting in the public of more of the bundle of rights to control land than are

publicly held in the West, not to the separation out of rights to land from rights to structures, or to 'ambiguity' in where those rights lie.

20   For an effort to carry over such concepts even after the transition, see the concepts of 'hereditary life tenure' and 'permanent use', discussed (with some puzzlement!) in Sanger (1992).

21   Article 10 of the Soviet Constitution of 1936 provided that 'the right of personal ownership . . . shall be permitted'; the 1977 Constitution went further, and in Article 13 provided that the right of personal property is 'protected by the state'. (The draft had said 'protected by law': Hazard et al., 1984: 227).

22   Preamble article 1, section 2 and article 4, emphasis added. For an excellent discussion raising a range of questions about the meaning of the law, which is to be implemented by a codex still under discussion at the time of writing, see S.B. Butler (1992).

23   See Stevens (1980). The English common law public trust doctrine has antecedents in Roman law. The leading US case is *Illinois Central Railroad* vs. *Illinois*, 146 U.S. 387 (1982). A number of useful articles, attesting to a renewed interest in the concept, are in Albany Law Center (1992).

24   In a World Bank staff working paper, for instance, an observer knowledgeable on legal issues in Eastern Europe comments: 'formerly-socialist economies of Central and Eastern Europe . . . need[s] to *rethink the many controls on the use of real property that [they have] inherited from the socialist period* . . . For example, Slovenia . . . has long protected agricultural land from "misuse" through strict zoning regulations . . . existing regulations require a long list of required permits that are likely to be over-restrictive, ill-designed, or redundant in a private market economy . . . they are likely to . . . hamper the emergence of a private construction sector' (Gray and Stiblar, 1992, emphasis added). The World Environmental Summit in Rio de Janeiro, hardly a socialist gathering, was centrally concerned with protecting agricultural land from misuse (not in quotation marks), and saw zoning as one feasible means to that end. The tension around the issue is not confined to one system or another.

25   There remain, of course, conflicts between different individual users of personal property, and the Soviet courts heard many of them. But they were on nowhere near the scale familiar in the West.

26   The blurring of the distinction, and frequent opposition, between 'residents' and 'the private sector' should also be noted. Other examples could be cited. Andrusz (1993: 16) speaks for instance, of the 'absence of rights to land ownership' in the Soviet Union; more accurately, it should be the absence of *certain* rights of land ownership, or the absence of private rather than public rights, or the failure to enforce rights.

27   Renaud (1992); the 'clarification' formulation is often used more innocently, that is to say, without under its aegis proposing a radical restructuring of rights; see for instance the essentially sympathetic account by

John Sanger (1993) of the situation in Kazakhstan, or Ray Struyk's use of the term in describing the history of housing reform in Russia (Struyk 1994, 10).

28   There are, of course, producer interests in housing also, as outlined below; and there are ultimately individual consumer interests in almost any form of production (possibly excepting military expenditures). But the directness of the connection in the one sphere, and the remoteness of the connection in the other, establishes politically a qualitative difference between the two.

29   The estimate in East Germany, for instance, is that 1.14 million dwelling units, almost evenly divided between single-family homes and apartments in multi-family buildings, are subject to restitution (figures cited by Wolfgang Jahn, *Neues Deutschland*, 7 February 1994: 9). The problem is less in some countries (such as Poland, where nationalization went less far, or the pre-1940 Soviet Union, where 70 years have elapsed since nationalization) and greater in others (such as Tallinn in Estonia, where almost half the housing stock is subject to such claims). For a more detailed look at the situation in each Eastern European country, see below.

30   This grouping seems to have been the first to organize in many countries, such as Estonia and East Germany, perhaps because its members are frequently older and possibly better educated or more sophisticated, having frequently chosen to live in more urban settings in older inner-city housing (based on personal interviews).

31   See for instance a whole set of proposals and commentaries by Ray Struyk and others of the Urban Institute of Washington DC: a good example is Struyk (1992).

32   Brie (1990: 10); the very title, 'Who is "owner" under Socialism?', betrays the new concern.

33   Taken from various presentations made by Natalia Kalinina, of Moscow, at conferences in Moscow, Budapest, Gavle, and Washington DC: Kalinina (1989, 1991). I do not believe that they had wide circulation in the Soviet Union, but, given the increasing fragmentation of discussions there, neither did any other single set of ideas. Kalinina's proposals indeed themselves fluctuated, and were in part internally contradictory. They are cited here as an example of the range of thinking during this 'reform' period.

34   Apparently not so radical a proposal; it was included in the official Communist Party program in 1961, under Khrushchev, to be implemented by 1980 (Andrusz, 1993: 8).

35   The proposal was made by some at the National Academy for Housing and the Communal Economy, and is cited in Andrusz (1993: 20). The interpretation is mine. Proposals fixing sales prices for housing in Estonia today based on years worked carry a similar logic.

36   The Round Table in Germany, set up by the dissident and reform movements in the GDR in January of 1990, after the Wall had been opened and the SED leadership overthrown but before West German

domination and unification of the two Germanies had become an established fact, perhaps best expressed the ideals of the socialist reformers. The constitution drafted by the Round Table during this brief period, known to everyone in Germany as 'Die Wende', 'The Turn', deals, in article 29, section 2, with 'personally used and co-operative property' (*Eigentum*; literally, ownership) as well as 'claims to, and expectations of, income arising out of the claimant's own performance' (*Leistung*). That section provides that such ownership as to housing and plots for housing is to be especially supported. Section 3 then provides a series of protections for ownership, but singles out 'personally used property' for special protection. All property may be taken by eminent domain; personally used property only 'if the grounds are pressing'. There must be compensation for such takings; only in the case of personally used property does the amount have to compensate for the owner's losses in full (Arbeitsgruppe 'Neue Verfassung der DDR' des Runden Tisches, 1990). The Round Table's proposals did not get far. By the time of unification, those most involved from the Eastern side were concerned to use unification as an opportunity to improve the West German constitution. (Actually, this is not a constitution, this is but a 'basic law', *Grundgesetz*, the thought being, at the time of its adoption in May 1949, that a real constitution could only be adopted when the division of Germany and the rights of foreign powers over it had ended. That history gave impetus for a movement, after unification, for a new constitution. It has, however, proven abortive thus far.) Its position had by 1991 retreated to the simple statement that 'personal ownership is particularly protected by law', a provision remarkably similar to that of the Soviet Constitution of 1977 and like it devoid of the detailed protection of the Round Table's draft. It was proposed that the 1949 provision: '[T]he duties of ownership. Its use should simultaneously serve the public welfare', should be replaced by: '[o]wnership has social responsibilities. The laws shall guarantee that its use will simultaneously serve the public welfare, in particular the protection of the natural bases of life.' A proposed addition was that 'the state protects the right of every person to an appropriate dwelling', but without creating an enforceable right to housing. No fundamental change in property rights was any longer contemplated; and even the modest changes proposed in 1991 were not taken seriously in the West.

37   See Stephan (1991: fn. 79); Schneider (1990, fn. 6). The Supreme Soviet then passed new laws taking a similar direction, centrally the Law on Property; the Law on Land (for both see Schneider, 1990); and the Law on Leasing (see Stephan, 1991, 57ff). A translation of the constitution as amended to mid-1990 may be found in Feldbrugge (1990). The Law on Property is discussed, and portions translated, in Schneider (1990). The Law of Land is discussed in detail, and translated in an appendix, in Floroff and Tiefenbrun (1991). See also Maggs (1990).

38 In fact, rights were differentiated according to three criteria: the type of property, the persons or entities possessing the rights, and the nature of the use (S.B. Butler and O'Leary, 1994b: 547) – conceptually a quite logical schema.

39 '[L]and, subterranean resources, water resources, and plant and animal life in their natural environment are the inalienable property of the people inhabiting a given territory' (article 10 of the constitution, as amended 1990, quoted in Schneider, 1990: 469). The Law on Property, however, includes land as a form of property; the Law on Land treats it separately, and presumably prevails, although conflicts may result (see Schneider, 1990: 464). In Russia, the Law of Ownership and the 1991 Land Code now constitute the prevailing law.

40 '[T]he state's obligation to provide housing can be satisfied by the household's purchase or construction of housing at its own expense, . . . through a social housing contract, through payments of housing allowances, or subsidies for construction, maintenance or rehabilitation of housing' (Struyk, 1994: 18).

41 The best overview of past practices with respect to housing is B. Turner et al. (1992). Among the overviews of what is happening during the current transition, see Telgarsky and Struyk (1990) and Struyk, chapter 6, this volume. On legal aspects of the transition, the bulletin of the Parker School of Comparative and International Law at Columbia University, *Soviet and East European Law*, is current and informative. *Transition*, published by the Socialist Economies Unit of the Country Economics Department of the World Bank, is also a valuable source of information and references.

42 The decision of the GDR government, made on 21 December 1989, to convert all state-owned enterprises into private corporations was explicitly repudiated.

43 The above details are taken from *Transition*, 1(9), December 1990: 1; and 2(5), May 1991: 3. Employment figures are as of spring 1991.

44 Subject, of course, to the obligation to return expropriated property to its rightful owners or, where other priorities dictate an alternative form of disposition (as, for example, uncertainty of ownership or business considerations), provide compensation for the expropriation.

45 In Germany attempts are now being made to work out compromise formulae to handle some of these problems. For instance, the level of compensation for former owners is proposed to be set at 1.3 times the 1935 values, obviously far below current market values; those former owners obtaining a return of their property rather than compensation for its loss would be required to pay a contribution, essentially a tax, which is proposed for residential rental property, for instance, to be one-third of the value of the property, calculated at six times its 1935 value (*Suddeutsche Zeitung*, 7/8 March 1992).

46 There is a great deal of discussion in the press about how uncertainties of title are hindering more extensive West German investment in the East. In many of these cases, the real culprit may be lack of anticipated

profit for investment, rather than legal difficulties; where there is real demand, legal difficulties, as suggested in the text, have been overcome.

47   This account is based on the author's own experience and conversations with private individuals in East Germany.

48   Adopted on 18 October 1989, and envisaged as a transition document, it was a compromise that has proved relatively stable, although amended a number of times since adoption (see Gray, 1992a).

49   Sections 13 and 14 of the 1989 constitution in effect elevated a provision of the civil code to constitutional status. Coupled with the creation of a constitutional court, the change is significant.

50   But see discussion of the ambiguous rights of foreign-owned corporations in Gray et al. (1992).

51   Czechoslovakia was one of the few socialist countries that explicitly permitted private property, as opposed to the more conventional permissibility of personal or individual property.

52   The original socialist constitution was adopted in 1948. A new constitution was adopted in 1960, and amended in 1968. Technically, it remained in effect after the end of the socialist regime, because of failure to agree on a new text.

53   Including absentee owners, who may have owned up to 50 per cent of all agricultural land (Frydman et al., 1993: 54).

54   See Frydman et al. (1993) and Gray (1992b: 5, 6). Gray estimates that 70,000 properties are involved, and suggests privatization was 'primarily' restitution in kind.

55   Figures from World Bank aide memoire on Poland, prepared for the mission of 8–19 January 1990.

56   The movement towards market practices, including a sufficient set of property rights to make them feasible – that is, rights to use and sell at a profit, if not to give security and foreclose – was also well under way before the changes of regime, most notably in Hungary (the phrase 'goulash communism' goes back to the mid-1960s), but also in Poland and other countries. Yugoslavia's experiments with forms of ownership prior to the collapse of socialism there are well known, and place it in a category by itself among Eastern European nations.

57   The logic was suggested at an early stage by Herbert Marcuse (1958); see also P. Marcuse (1994b).

58   Only in Kazakhstan (to my knowledge) does the constitution maintain all land in public ownership: see Sanger (1993). Sanger attributes the fact 'not as may be presupposed [to] the Soviet system, but rather [to] strong Kazakh tradition'. Nomadic traditions, internal rivalries, and concern about possible Russian ownership in the event of privatization may be relevant also. But national ownership was at the least supported by the former Soviet system as well.

59   As Andrusz (1984: xiv) points out, 'a crucial characteristic of bureaucracies is that they behave like private owners vis-à-vis resources.'

60   I am unaware of any public discussion or action as to such claims for

urban land or housing in the pre-1939 Soviet Union, presumably because of the length of time since nationalization, but it is likely that
there will be at least individual claims made in some republics.

61   As Stephen Butler writes, there are 'charged political and emotional
issues that surround the debate over how or whether to privatize land'
(S.B. Butler and O'Leary, 1994a: 1).

62   For example, 'public opinion surveys indicate that 66% of the Slovene
population agree that land shouldn't be sold to foreigners' (Kos, 1994:
4, citing a Slovene public opinion survey).

63   In the case of the United States the 'due process' clause of the constitution has been interpreted to protect a broad range of personal
property rights, and the Slaughterhouse cases have extended the protection to corporations. The most recent case at the time of writing,
still the subject of major controversy, is *Lucas* vs. *South Carolina Coastal
Commission*, 60 U.S.L.W. 4842, overturning a South Carolina prohibition on building on a property within a coastal zone.

64   Some legislation exists, of course, such as the Russian Law on Urban
Planning, adopted in June 1992 (see Struyk and Kosareva, 1993). In
Poland the land-use planning system was recently described as being
'in limbo', although a 'Spatial Planning Act' was under consideration
(Gray et al., 1992: 292).

6

Housing Privatization in the Former Soviet Bloc to 1995

Raymond J. Struyk

The political and economic transformation of Eastern Europe and the former Soviet Union (FSU) is one of the seminal events of the second half of the twentieth century. The breadth, extent and speed of change make it difficult to follow many of the developments, especially those beneath the headlines of broad economic indicators and the results of major elections. As noted elsewhere in this volume, the changes under way will have profound impacts on the cities in the former Soviet bloc. This chapter focuses on a particular change in the housing sector which will contribute importantly to the restructuring of cities that will continue over the next quarter of a century or more: the privatization of the state housing stock.

Privatization is the single most distinguishing feature of the transformation of the housing sector from the Soviet, centrally planned model to a more market-oriented system. Under privatization, sitting tenants have the right to purchase their unit from a local government or state enterprise, typically at a substantial discount or, in a number of cases, for free except for a nominal processing fee.[1] When the new owner receives title to the property he or she has the full rights of disposition: he or she can sell or rent the unit on the open market without restriction, if he or she wishes. Most of the housing involved is in multi-family apartment buildings, and in a number of countries the new owners do not automatically receive the right to take over maintenance and management of the building. (This is discussed further below.) So the rights given to the new owners are very substantial but usually not as comprehensive as those of a condominium owner in Western countries.

The initiation of the privatization programmes was politically important. As Mandic and Stanovick (forthcoming) state in an essay about reform in the Slovenian housing sector:

> Because social ownership was the vital point of the previous institutional and ideological order, it had a very strong symbolic meaning which can hardly be over-emphasized. It was the sale of social rental accommodation which signaled that the fortress of social ownership was definitely cracking down and was giving way to radical changes which would be beyond possible speculation even a couple of years earlier.

This argument is supported by statistical modelling for Russia which found that enterprise privatization influenced voters to support economic reform when it was subject to a referendum in April 1993 (Boycko et al., 1993: 178–80).

But there were other motivations as well. The transfer of housing wealth from the government to the people was clearly popular. Governments also saw privatization as a way to rid themselves (eventually) of the nearly crushing burden of subsidies for maintenance and communal services – subsidies that were accelerating as inflation became common and rents continued to be severely controlled in the early years of reform. In those countries of the former Soviet Union with very high shares of state rentals, it was clear that a housing market could not be created without a larger share of units being in private ownership and thus being potentially in the market for privately negotiated purchase and rent. In a real sense, unless privatization went forward, there could be no true reforms. Finally, but certainly not least importantly, there was a consensus that giving tenants ownership of their units would heighten their sense of responsibility for the maintenance and rehabilitation of the common spaces in their buildings, that is, increase their monitoring of the performance of maintenance companies and (eventually) their willingness to pay for improvements.

On the other hand, one should not underestimate the resistance of local officials to giving up the prestige and power associated with owning and controlling a large housing stock: the ability to allocate units made a handful of local officials extremely powerful and afforded them ample opportunity for special treatment in the community.

Why is privatization so important for market formation? It is critical to understand that privatization accompanied the restoration of full property rights to housing owners. Under the Soviet model, owners could only sell their units under highly constrained conditions: a state appraiser would set the price of the unit (well below a true market value) and very likely the local government (or legislature) would decide who would purchase the unit. Renting one's unit was forbidden, except under special circumstances, such as being posted overseas; and then the owners could only charge the same rent as was being charged for state rentals. Restoration of full property rights was the *sine qua non* of privatization. It was also a precondition for the formation of a real market in which units are openly sold and rented.

Housing privatization has accelerated the formation of the market by increasing the number of units potentially for rent or sale by several orders of magnitude. Equally important, the way of thinking about one's dwelling has changed even for those who did not consider renting or selling their unit; the unit gradually became thought of as a commodity with value in the market rather than an asset that only had value as long as you could keep it in the family by bequeathing the occupancy rights to other members of your family registered as living there.

More units on offer means increased residential mobility, which in turn means price signals are sent to private developers about what type of housing and which locations are highly valued; and this is where new construction will occur. Hence, privatization will facilitate the process of redevelopment of the city. Simultaneously, the decline in the size of the rental sector – particularly a (price-controlled) social rental sector – may have unfavourable consequences for lower-income families and newly formed families; and these need to be understood.

This chapter reviews the experience with privatization from 1989–91 to 1994 in nine countries. The starting date depends on when the general economic and political transformation really began – 1989 for the earliest of the East European nations, late 1991 for the republics of the FSU. The countries were chosen to include those formed out of the 15 constituent republics of the FSU and the countries of Eastern Europe which were members of the Council of Mutual Economic Assistance and the Warsaw Pact. In the first group are the Russian Federation, Estonia and Armenia. In the second are Bulgaria, Hungary, Poland, the Czech Republic, the Slovak Republic and Slovenia. Principal criteria for country selection were the economic and political importance in the region and the desire to include a range of experience. Inclusion of some specific countries depended on the author knowing an analyst there willing to provide the necessary data.[2]

The essay consists of five sections. The first documents the distribution of units by tenure from about the time of the beginning of the transition. The second reviews briefly the decentralization of the ownership of the state housing stock from central to local governments which universally occurred at the start of the transformation period. Hence, it was the local government that sometimes set the terms or conditions and in all cases was the owner from which units were purchased. The third documents the extent of privatization to the time of writing, and the terms on which units have been conveyed. The fourth outlines some of the implications of the change in ownership produced by the privatization programmes. The final section offers brief conclusions.

TENURE DISTRIBUTION UNDER THE SOVIET SYSTEM

The hallmark of the Soviet housing system is the high share of units owned by the state.[3] The figures in table 6.1 on the distribution of unit ownership in the various countries illustrate the much greater degree to which the Soviet system was actually implemented in the republics of the Soviet Union than in the countries of Eastern Europe. To help focus on the differences between the two sets of countries, this and the other tables in this chapter are organized with the constituent Soviet Union republics appearing first and the countries of Eastern Europe second.

The table lists four categories. The first, 'state rental', includes both municipal rental housing and enterprise housing leased to workers.[4] Directly or indirectly, the state paid for the construction and maintenance of both types. The two systems of developing, maintaining and allocating housing existed side by side. The development of the 'enterprise channel' was part of the centralized industrial policy that allocated more resources, for everything, to favoured industries. Priority sectors received not only more inputs and funds for expanding productive capacity but additional resources for housing, clinics, rest houses and other benefits to attract and retain better workers. On the other hand, for municipal housing the level of funding depended in part on the bargaining ability of regional leaders with the central planning and housing ministries.

Table 6.1   Tenure distribution of the housing stock (percentages) prior to reform

Country	State rental[a]	Co-operatives	Individually owned	Other[b]	Total
Russian Federation (1990)	67	4	26	3	100
Armenia (1980)	53	4	43	–	100
Estonia	60	12[c]	26	2[d]	100
Bulgaria (1985)	16	[e]	84	–	100
Czech Republic (1988)	38	18	41	3	100
Hungary (1990)	23	6	71	–	100
Poland (1990)	35[f]	25	40	–	100
Slovak Republic (1988)	25	20	53	2	100
Slovenia (1991)	33[g]	–	67	–	100

[a] Includes enterprise – and government – agency – provided housing.
[b] Includes units owned by farm co-operatives, unions and other special categories.
[c] And other entities.
[d] Foreign state-owned.
[e] Less than 1 per cent.
[f] Includes 4 percentage points of private rental.
[g] 'Social housing'; includes a small share of private rentals.

Enterprise housing was especially important in the constituent republics of the Soviet Union. In the Russian Federation, for example, in 1991 it accounted for 42 per cent of all housing units, compared with 25 per cent for municipal housing. Yugoslavia is a unique case in this regard, because enterprises were assigned a broader housing role. In effect, enterprises were made the primary provider of social (not strictly state) housing. Of the total social housing stock in Slovenia, for example, state enterprises accounted for 68 per cent in 1990, with the balance divided between municipal housing (30 per cent) and state housing (2 per cent) (Mandic and Stanovick, forthcoming).

Cooperative housing, while heavily subsidized, generally required significant contributions from purchasers. Cooperative housing occupies a middle ground between owning and renting, since in Eastern Europe the difference between living in a cooperative and a state rental was often slight. Cooperative 'owners' had quite limited property rights, including restricted rights of disposition. 'Individually owned' units were almost exclusively single-family units in smaller cities, towns and rural areas. Private rentals did not exist for practical purposes, although in every country there was an illegal market in subleases of state units.

Table 6.1 demonstrates the enormous diversity in tenure patterns prior to the transition. Evident is the extreme state ownership of housing in Armenia, Estonia and the Russian Federation compared with the countries of Eastern Europe. Armenia, with 53 per cent of its housing in state rentals, has the lowest share among these three FSU republics – presumably because it is less urbanized; in Yeravan (capital of Armenia) nearly 80 per cent of the housing was state rentals. At the other end of the spectrum, one is struck by the extraordinarily high homeownership rates in Bulgaria, Hungary and Slovenia – all over the 65 per cent level of the United States, which is often viewed as the quintessential country of homeowners. The high rate in Bulgaria was due to its long-standing policy of privatization of state rentals, a policy which continually fed units from rental tenure to homeownership. In Hungary and Slovenia, on the other hand, high ownership rates resulted from a combination of high consumer preference for single-family units and a government policy to encourage private investment in the sector (to lessen government financial responsibility for fulfilling 'right to housing' articles in their constitutions). Development of cooperatives became a very important element in the housing strategies of Czechoslovakia and Poland in the 1980s, and is reflected in their comparatively large share of these units.

POWER TO LOCAL GOVERNMENTS

The policies of decentralization of ownership and privatization have in common that they afforded national governments the chance to respond to popular demands for reform on the cheap – at least in the sense of avoiding current expenditures from the budget. The shift in ownership of the state housing stock to local governments was a clear response to the overcentralization of authority endemic under the previous regimes. The reallocation of state assets was typically one of the first acts of the newly elected reform governments, and it was accompanied by a parallel shift in the responsibility for formulating policy and financing housing subsidies. The predominant view was that giving responsibility in this sector to governments closer to the people would result in a better matching of services with consumer preferences (and a corresponding gain in the efficiency of subsidy expenditures).

Occasionally, decentralization went too far. For example, within Budapest, ownership and policy responsibility was devolved by the national parliament to the city's 22 districts with very little policy responsibility at the municipal level – from 1990 to 1995 it was actually possible for different parts of the city to have different policies on the rents to charge in state housing and on price discount offered on units being privatized.

The broad pattern in the early years of reform has been for the responsibility for housing to be shared between the national and lower levels of governments, with the national government creating the general policy framework and providing limited subsidies, while local governments have the opportunity to refine the broad policy directives and the responsibility for implementation. Concrete examples abound:

- In Hungary, local governments were given the right to set the price discount on state units being sold to their occupants (privatization) and they had the opportunity to raise rents.
- Both *oblast* (regional or county) and local governments in the Russian Federation had the responsibility for setting some parameters of the housing allowance programme and for deciding how quickly rents would be increased.
- Local governments in the Slovak Republic control the terms on which units are privatized.
- In virtually all countries, local governments control which firms will maintain the housing remaining as state rentals and the terms under which firms will be hired, including whether simply to continue to employ state enterprises.
- In several countries, the rules governing waiting lists for social housing are set by local governments, instead of following a unified national system.

In fact, in many cases local governments have been reluctant to use their new power and have preferred instead to follow the lead of the national government. This is an interesting development, since one of the primary motivations for reallocating the ownership of state housing was the desire of national politicians to avoid dealing with contentious housing issues.

Typically, the early stages of reform involved massive cuts in the national subsidies for housing, particularly for new construction. Local governments were left on their own. Almost never did they have the capital resources to replace national budget funds for housing development. Moreover, the overall reallocation of both spending responsibilities and revenue bases among levels of government often left localities in a worsened fiscal position, which necessitated cutting subsidies for housing maintenance.[5]

It is too early to judge the consequences of decentralization on housing policy and on the provision of housing services. However, local governments in several countries have not been comfortable with their expanded responsibilities. Still, the policy and fiscal relationships of this 'new federal' system continue to evolve. There are signs that both national and local governments recognize that there may have been excessive devolution of policy responsibility. In Hungary, for example, the parliament modified the law governing Budapest to give the municipality more control over policy at the expense of city district governments. In addition, local governments' power over privatization was restricted in 1993 legislation. In other countries, local governments struggle with parliament less energetically now than earlier for the right to set rent policies locally. Similarly, federal governments have shown willingness to cover some new housing expenditures, such as the cost of housing allowances.

THE RECORD ON PRIVATIZATION

Before documenting the record on privatization, it is worthwhile first thinking about how households view this opportunity. The standard economic model of tenure choice casts the household's decision to become a homeowner in terms of the flow of the costs (positive and negative) of renting and owning. Traditionally, there was difficulty in simultaneously analysing investment and consumption aspects of the homeownership decision. The user cost of capital formulation solves this problem by constructing a comprehensive price of owning (Megbolugbe and Linneman, 1993: 668). The net present value of any capital gains expected from owning can be capitalized into a monthly amount. Together with the other monthly pro-rated costs, such as maintenance and taxes, the expected capitalized investment (less appreciation) is part of total monthly housing costs. The costs to the household of gross rent (as a renter) is compared with capital and operating costs less appreciation (as an owner) (see, for example, Malpezzi and Mayo, 1987; Grootaert and Dubois, 1989; Goodman, 1988). The household is likely to choose the cheaper alternative.

In most Soviet-bloc nations, since housing privatization has been at very low cost or free of charge, a tenant's gain from the transfer of ownership is essentially the full value of the unit. Unlike a household purchasing a unit, there is approximately no expenditure associated with unit acquisition, although the privatizing tenant may have to pay for rehabilitation in the future. By comparison, in Hungary under the old system, households could effectively purchase occupancy rights from sitting tenants and move into the units; the gain to these households from privatizing would be the current value of the unit minus the payment made to the prior tenants (Hegedus et al., 1993). In most countries the value of the privatized unit should be a clear and powerful determinant of the decision to privatize: those living in higher-value units are expected to have a higher likelihood of privatizing.

There are other demand-side forces at work. Most notably, pensioners have a special motivation to privatize. Under the regime of state-provided housing, the rental contract (for example, the Russian *naym* social agreement) gave tenants very strong rights. It was (and is) essentially impossible to evict them, and their occupancy rights could be bequeathed to certain family members who were registered as living in the same unit. Those not registered as living in that particular apartment, however, could not receive the unit. Hence, pensioners are motivated to privatize in order to be able to pass their unit to their non-resident relations. They will privatize to 'cash in' their right to bequeath the unit to someone. Pensioners may well be motivated to privatize for the sake of their heirs, when they would not make the same decision if they were to continue living in the unit for a much longer period. Another group very likely to privatize is that of families planning to relocate to other cities or wishing to use the equity in their current unit to purchase another unit locally. Privatization is the initial step, that is, obtaining cash for acquisition of the next unit.

There are, however, factors that discourage privatization. As noted, extremely strong tenants' rights provide owner-like security and reduce such gains from privatizing. In addition, if the operating costs, such as maintenance fees and property taxes, of owning are higher than those of renting, the likelihood of privatization declines as the relative advantage of owning is diminished. Various countries deal with this differently. The government of the Russian Federation acted to encourage privatization. The Law on Privatization declares that during an undefined 'transition period' those who privatize will pay the same maintenance and communal service fees as renters. However, those purchasing a privatized flat must pay the full fees – thus suggesting that in the future those privatizing could also be required to pay the full amount. In some other countries, those privatizing are required to pay full maintenance fees from the time they receive title. The property tax is another factor. State rentals are not subject to this tax, but privatized units are. This clearly reduces the attractiveness of privatizing. There is a final disadvantage to privatizing. Many units already need rehabilitation, and deferred maintenance is accelerating the size of the inventory with such needs. Those privatizing their units may well assume that they will have to bear these costs in the future and weigh them more heavily than the gain in property value that should result from this investment.

The experience with privatization programmes is summarized in table 6.2. The first point is the large share of units transferred to private ownership in some of these programmes. For reference one can note that the much-heralded British 'right-to-buy' programme sold about 1.2 million units or about 20 per cent of social housing during the 13-year period 1979–92, in part by offering tenants large price discounts (Whitehead, 1993). The entries in the table show that most countries in the former Soviet bloc have bettered the British record. Bulgaria and Estonia have 'sold' about nine out of ten state units, and Hungary, the Russian Federation, Slovenia and Armenia have conveyed 35–45 per cent of their units to sitting tenants. Only in Poland and the Czech and Slovak Republics has little happened in the way of privatization. Indeed, privatization was just getting under way in these countries in late 1994. In the Czech and Slovak Republics this is part of a more general pattern to leave the housing sector until a second phase of reform and concentrate on economic restructuring in the first phase. These countries did, however, carry out quite large-scale housing restitution programmes; and these contributed to the delay in launching privatization. Housing reform was a higher priority in Estonia and a good deal has been accomplished, although after some initial delay. In this case restitution of residential properties to their former owners took temporary precedent over privatization, but then privatization moved with alacrity.[6]

The impact of privatization on the size of the rental sector in those countries with active programmes is impressive, as the figures in table 6.3 attest. As a result of this transformation in tenure form, these countries have a lower share of their housing in the rental sector than the typical country in other parts of Europe.[7]

A nearly universal characteristic of privatization is the deeply discounted dwelling prices offered to tenants relative to market prices. Free privatization is in effect in Armenia and the Russian Federation. Deep discounts exist everywhere else with the possible exception of the Czech Republic and Poland, where local governments are setting the prices and our information about pricing is sketchy.

Table 6.2 Housing privatization: conditions and results, up to 1994

	Russian Federation	Armenia	Estonia
Housing units sold:			
Period of sale	1988–[b]	1989, 1993–[c]	1993–5
Fixed end date? When?[a]	No	9/95	5/95
Units sold (thousands)	11,000	148	N/A
Units sold as % state housing stock at start of privatization	36	38	85–90[d]
Terms/conditions of sale:			
Price basis	Free	Free	Fixed amount
Price discount			90%
Financing or instalment sale available?			Vouchers[e]
Minimum share of units in building required?	No	No	No
Condominium association required?	No	No	No

	Bulgaria	Czech Republic	Hungary
Housing units sold:			
Period of sale	1958–	7/94–	Mid-1980s–
Fixed end date? When?[a]	No	No	11/95
Units sold (thousands)	N/A	N/A[f]	306
Units sold as % state housing stock at start of privatization	Over 90		39
Terms/conditions of sale:			[g]
Price basis	Fixed tariff	Market value	Net market appraisal
Price discount	80–90%	Local decision	50–85%
Financing or instalment sale available?	Yes	Local decision	Instalment
Source of financing	State savings blank		
Loan interest rate	Standard lending rates		3%
Loan term years	30		10

Table 6.2 *Continued*

	Bulgaria	Czech Republic	Hungary
Minimum share of units in building required?	No	50%	35%
Condominium assocation required?	No	Yes	Yes

	Poland	Slovak Republic	Slovenia
Housing units sold:			
Period of sale	Mid-1980s–[h]	1994	1991–
Fixed end date? When?[a]	No	No	1993
Units sold (in thousands)	395	N/A[f]	135
Units sold as % state housing stock at start of privatization	11.5	N/A	44
Terms/conditions of sale:			
Price basis	Variable	Construction cost	Book value
Price discount	Variable	2%/year since built	85–90% maximum
Financing or instalment sale available?	Sometimes	No	
Minimum share of units in building required?	No	50%[i]	
Condominium association required?	Yes	Yes[i]	Instalment

[a] For privatization favourable terms; countries with fixed time limits continue to permit sale at market prices.

[b] The major programme was passed into law in July 1991; significant transfers began in 1992.

[c] There was an earlier programme which included some payment for units; the description here is for the new programme which was enacted in 1993.

[d] Anticipated in spring 1995.

[e] A combination of low prices and large number of vouchers per households means most tenants require their units without charge.

[f] In Czechoslovakia a substantial number of units were restored to their owners prior to the time of nationalization of the housing stock.

[g] Hungary changed the terms of privatization in May 1993 to institute a 'right-to-buy' programme which limits local government's ability to restrict sales and set terms of sale; a time limit for the right-to-buy programme was also established through the law and subsequent court decisions.

[h] Structure of the programme is determined by each local government and variation is great. The programme description is for that in operation in 1990–4.

[i] Not a matter of law, but the programme is being administered in this way.

Table 6.3   State rentals as a percentage of all housing

	Before transition	1994
Russian Federation	67	43
Armenia	53	33
Estonia	60	10*
Hungary	23	14
Slovenia	33	19

*Estimate for mid-1995 by B. Turner and Victorin (forthcoming).

Changes to privatization programmes once launched have been rather common. (Table 6.2 shows the most recent programme at the time of writing.) Examples include the following. After beginning with low-cost privatization using complex formulas, both Armenia and the Russian Federation shifted to free-of-charge privatization to accelerate the process. In Hungary, local governments were given the opportunity to change the initial terms set by the national government, but few took advantage of this chance. Then in 1993 the parliament again set terms on a national basis – the 'right-to-buy' programme – and set a time limit for the programme, after which local governments again will set conditions. Four of these countries have already imposed time limits for the current privatization programmes: Armenia, Estonia, Slovenia and Hungary. By the end of 1995, privatization on the current terms will be over in all of these; indeed, it ended in Slovenia in 1993. In some cases, tenants will retain the right to buy their units, but at market prices or on terms set by local governments. It seems probable that more countries will impose time limits in the near future in order to be able to define which units will remain the responsibility of local government. During the privatization period, local governments are understandably hesitant to make significant investments in buildings which may soon move off their balance sheets.

Interestingly, most privatization programmes permit individual units in multi-family buildings to be privatized, that is, it is not necessary for a certain share of all tenants in a building to apply for privatization before the process can begin. Similarly, the rule is to permit privatization without a condominium association being in place. Only three countries – the Czech and Slovak Republics and Hungary – required condominium associations to be in place and a minimum share of owners in a building to apply before proceeding with the privatization of the first unit. In Hungary, the provision concerning a minimum share of applicants required was set aside in 1993 by new national legislation.

The effect of unit-by-unit privatization programmes is that new owners receive attenuated property rights: they receive the right to dispose of their property freely but they do not receive control of the management of their building. Management remains with the state firm until an association of owners is formed. Shared ownership of the units in a building by the municipality (of those units which have not been privatized) and by the new unit owners can produce knotty governance problems when the condominium associations are formed. In most countries these difficulties were only being recognized as the initial associations are created in late 1994 and early 1995.

The results to date for privatization certainly suggest that in some countries a sizable share – perhaps more than half – of state rentals will not be claimed by their tenants. Why not? Surveys indicate that tenants have reasonable concerns about the extensive repairs and rehabilitation many buildings require and the magnitude of future property taxes and maintenance fees they may have to pay as owners (data for Russia, for example, are presented in Daniell and Struyk, 1994). In short, they recognize the potential liabilities in these units and proceed cautiously. The experience, in fact, is that it is the better units that are being privatized. Analyses for Hungary and Russia show that early in the privatization process the probability of a tenant privatizing his or her unit is significantly related to the value of the unit (Hegedus et al., 1993; Daniell and Struyk, 1994). With a single exception, the demographic and economic attributes of tenants were found to play little part in the privatization decision. Elderly persons or couples living alone are significantly more likely to privatize than other tenants, after controlling for the value of their unit. The explanation is clear: they could only pass on the equity in the unit this way, since no other family members are registered as living there.

A fascinating question which remains unanswered is why so much more privatization occurred in Bulgaria and Estonia than in the other countries. Were these countries more successful in allaying the fears of potential owners about increased fees for maintenance and property taxes? This could be the answer in Bulgaria, where privatization has such a long record. Or is it simply a matter of 'herd instinct', which takes over as the privatization rate reaches some critical level?

Still, the story is not over, as privatization continues in many countries. One might see a surge in the rate of privatization when a deadline is imposed for deeply discounted privatization, as it will force the decision on the numerous tenants who have been watching developments on maintenance fees and property taxes and are still considering privatizing.

Privatization programmes are not without controversy. Some analysts argue that the deep discounts mean that cities in countries with a large, existing homeowning population are giving away valuable assets and should be more patient in making sales. The World Bank (1991) estimated that the value of state units in Hungary was greater than the assets of the entire financial system. Revenues from sales could be large and could, for instance, support development of badly needed residential infrastructure. In the meantime, the reductions in maintenance subsidies could be controlled or eliminated through a programme of rent increases coupled with the introduction of housing allowances (Katsura and Struyk, 1991). Others argue that cities should take decisive action to shed their housing stock (Buckley et al., 1992).

A second controversy centres on the inequities of privatization. One aspect is that, among those eligible to privatize their units, the best units are occupied by the former nomenklatura and apparatchiks – hardly the groups that the post-Soviet regimes want to reward. Another inequity arises between those on the waiting list to receive their unit and those who have already received one. With the fall in production of new state rentals and substantial privatization, comparatively few units are now becoming available for those on the waiting lists. Many may never receive a unit. Moreover, it seems likely that the whole deep-discount privatization policy and the inherited policy of distributing units with life-time, even inheritable tenancy with very strong occupancy rights will eventually be replaced. Hence, those on the waiting list now and in the future will not receive the type of wealth transfer obtained by those who privatized their units. Another inequity is between those who paid for their own housing – or received less help acquiring it, such as those who joined cooperatives – and those who privatize. Overall, younger households appear disadvantaged relative to older ones; the nomenklatura benefited compared to others; and higher-income families received larger wealth transfers.[8] There is no denying these inequities. Put simply, transformation at the pace at which it is happening in the former Soviet bloc is unlikely to be elegant. The inequities can only be justified by the imperative of the moment to rid these countries of the vestiges of the old regime and to create and reinforce the preconditions for the operation of a housing market.

BROADER IMPACTS

Three effects of privatization are prominent: the impact on the rental sector, the potential stimulation of residential mobility, and the effects on the quality of maintenance to the residential housing stock.

The future of the rental sector

A scenario for the future of the rental sector in the former Soviet bloc formulated by some experts is as follows:[9] the former state housing stock is largely privatized; the remaining small inventory has little turnover as units are passed among family members; state units are allocated to the poor and this inventory becomes 'marginalized'; only a small number of private units from the existing stock enter the rental market; and there is little new construction of market-rate rental units because most households cannot afford the rents needed to make them profitable. Hence, the rental sector is small, and newly formed households have little chance of living independently because they cannot afford to purchase a dwelling. From the foregoing, one can draw the conclusion that the state must again subsidize the construction of rental housing, either through construction subsidies or through housing allowances with 'normative rents' set high enough to pay for newly built units. Compelled by such reasoning, the governments of Poland and Slovenia have created new programmes to create new social housing.

While this scenario and the policy conclusion are in many ways appealing, it is by no means certain that they are correct or that many governments will move in this direction. First, there is too much uncertainty to justify the policy conclusion. There could be a substantial growth in private rentals fed by the existing housing stock. Private rentals are almost exclusively existing units, that is, there is little construction of new housing explicitly for rental, although a smattering of new units ends up as rentals. The main source of these rentals is families that have acquired multiple privatized units, either by various family members obtaining occupancy rights under the old system and privatizing the units, or by inheriting a privatized unit, or by other means. With real estate generally being a good investment, the 'extra' units are kept and rented out rather than being sold. In the cases of particularly desirable properties commanding high rents, elderly persons living alone may move in with other family members in order to realize the rental income.

In short, the rental market is generally being fed by amateur investors. Based on recent household survey data from Budapest and seven Russian cities and on other information, our sense is that all the countries of the former Soviet bloc have a large share of urban units (on the order of 15–20 per cent or more) occupied by elderly pensioners. This creates the potential for an expansion in private rentals. The extent of the actual expansion is heavily dependent upon the share of those inheriting the units who need another unit to permit them to 'uncouple' from other relatives, whether housing continues to be an attractive long-term investment, and the inheritors' cash needs. Moreover, the source of 'inherited units' may be significantly expanded in the years ahead, by families that are enjoying real income growth building new units for their own use and renting out their former unit.

Second, most governments want very much to avoid the costly budget outlays for new construction of rental housing and the continuing responsibility for its maintenance. It seems more likely that subsidies will go to expand the overall housing supply by offering shallow subsidies to those who purchase new units. This approach is clearly consistent with the 'conversion of existing units into rentals', or 'filtering', argument made above. The real question may be whether governments will be able to wait the five to ten years for the results of such a policy to be clearly evident.

Residential mobility

The Soviet system was characterized by a low degree of residential mobility, although careful analysis is difficult to locate. Once a family had received its unit from municipal authorities or its enterprise, it had little incentive to relocate. Swaps of state rental units were permitted, but they were difficult to arrange, despite the presence of official brokers for this purpose in some cities. Logically, a principal impact of more units being in private ownership should be more units on offer and, hence, an increase in residential mobility.

This expectation appears to be borne out by data on residential turnover rates computed using household survey data collected in early 1994 in seven Russian cities. Table 6.4 presents data on turnover rates in 1992 and 1993 for these cities.[10] Since 1992 was just at the beginning of the transition period in Russia, the rates for this year can reasonably be taken as representative of those under the old

Table 6.4 A comparison of 1992 and 1993 search and mobility factors[a]

	Moscow	St Petersburg	Five cities[b]	All seven cities
Turnover rates:				
1992	2.0	1.4	2.0	1.8
1993	6.2[c,d]	4.3[c]	3.4[e]	4.6[c]
Movers new to the city (%):				
1992	7.1	20.0	48.8	19.7
1993	17.0	12.7	44.6	20.5
Movers who used market search method (%):[f]				
1992	47.4	29.4	35.1	40.7
1993	62.5	68.3[c]	44.5	61.1[c]

[a] If the respondent indicated that he or she had lived less than or equal to one year in the unit, he or she was designated as moved in 1993, even though he or she could have moved in December 1992, since the survey was administered in December 1993. Likewise, if the respondent had lived in the unit less than or equal to two years, he or she was designated as moved in 1992.
[b] Weighted sample taken from Nizhni Novgorod, Rostov-on-Don, Barnaul, Tver and Novgorod.
[c] Significantly different from 1992 at the 0.01 level (chi-square test of proportion or chi-square test of independence of variables).
[d] The 1993 mobility rate for Moscow was adjusted by 1.8 per cent to account for the fact that the survey sample did not include units constructed in 1993 (56,000 units).
[e] Significantly different from 1993 at the 0.10 level (chi-square test of proportion).
[f] A respondent is defined to have performed a market search if he or she responded to the question 'How did your family find your current flat?' in the following manner: advertisements in newspaper/magazines; advertisements on exchange bulletins; through a firm; through an individual agent; through friends, acquaintances; by placing own advertisement; by building it himself or herself. The 'Other' category was defined as: from the waiting list, or provided state housing on emergency basis; through an exchange among relatives; other.

regime. The table shows a distinct increase in mobility between the two years: on average, turnover rates increased from 1.8 to 4.6 per cent. The biggest increase was in Moscow, where privatization got off to an unusually fast start. The final panel of the table also illustrates a sharp change in the way in which households located their new unit. In 1992, 41 per cent of those who moved used 'market search methods' (see notes to the table) to find their unit. Stated differently, they did not receive their unit by having their name taken from the waiting list or through an exchange of units within their family. In a one-year period, this figure rose 20 percentage points to 61 per cent.

It is impossible to know whether mobility rates will continue to increase. Pent-up demand may have produced the jump in turnover rates from 1992 and 1993, and some reduction could even occur in later years. But more privatization may beget more mobility. Similarly, 20 per cent of movers in all seven cities were new to the city in both 1992 and 1993. We do not know how this compares with earlier years, but this number seems high and could certainly result in part from Russians returning from other republics of the former Soviet Union and loosening of residency permit (*propiska*) requirements. On the other hand, sustained high mobility from economically declining to expanding regions is anticipated. In sum, the shift to more 'market sources' of housing is permanent and will most definitely continue to increase in importance in the years ahead.

Maintenance in multi-family buildings

A very long-standing problem in the Soviet housing system was the inadequate maintenance of the state housing stock. The problems were at least as much those of incentives as of funding. During the transition, countries have differed in their aggressiveness in dealing with this problem. Slovenia is the leader among countries studied in implementing the procurement of maintenance services on a competitive basis.

There have been experiments to improve maintenance by breaking the monopoly of the state-owned enterprises responsible for maintenance and replacing that system with one in which firms (both public and private) compete for contracts to maintain parcels of state-owned buildings. Prague began such contracting early, but the practice did not catch on in the Czech or Slovak Republics. The Russian Federation has on-going experiments in which a typical contract covers a few thousand units. By spring 1995, Moscow had 100,000 units under such contracts, and similar systems had been launched in another four or five cities.

While these developments are a step in the right direction, the real hope for improved efficiency in maintenance probably lies with the creation of viable condominium or cooperative associations that will take over management of their buildings from city agencies. This may be the only way to solve the difficult agency problem involved with public officials taking on the role of 'owner' in contracting with private maintenance firms in the case of state housing (see the discussion in Struyk et al., 1991). Again, the record on the incidence of really working condominium and cooperative associations is hard to pin down, and the available evidence suggests the record is variable. Most of the former Soviet-bloc countries now have condominium laws on the books, but the number of associations is small, as they are arising out of privatized buildings. The clear exception here is Hungary, where condominium associations had to be formed prior to any units in a building being privatized. Whether many of these associations have taken real initiative to manage their buildings is unknown. In Slovenia and Bulgaria, it is known that condominium associations are either self-managing or hiring private firms; often it is a combination of the two, with private firms hired for more highly skilled tasks, such as elevator maintenance. Realistically, throughout the region one can expect a several-year process of condominium associations being formed and tenants really taking control of the upkeep of their buildings, and improving the quality of maintenance demonstrably.

CONCLUSIONS

Housing privatization is a universal feature of the restructuring of the housing systems in the countries of the former Soviet bloc. At the same time, the programmes being implemented vary sharply from country to country, and the share of units privatized to date ranges from a few per cent to 85–90 per cent of the eligible stock. It appears that in most countries around half or so of the eligible units will be privatized, with the residual state rental stock containing the less valuable units. An important open question is whether this stock plus additions over time to the rental stock from private sources, including privatized units (among them conversions of some illegally sublet state units), will be sufficient to meet the needs for rental units.

Privatization plus the reconfirmation of property rights will be a major force in reshaping cities. By promoting residential mobility, a more efficient matching of the housing stock with household demand will be achieved. Moreover, the price signals generated by a significant volume of transactions will help direct private development to where it is most valued. Another impact of privatization will be on the quality of building upkeep. New owners, acting through condominium associations, will take control of the maintenance and management of their buildings from the state companies, which were poorly motivated for these tasks. Acting in the self-interest of protecting and increasing the value of their property, condominium owners can be counted on to improve the conditions in the public spaces of their buildings. Naturally, this will take some years to accomplish; but one has every reason to expect it to happen.

Overall, housing privatization, which may have been motivated chiefly by the political objective of increasing the population's stake in reforms and the desire of the central government to rid itself of the responsibility for maintenance subsidies, has turned out to be a key element in the strategy of transforming the Soviet housing system to a more efficient model.

NOTES

The author is a Senior Fellow at the Urban Institute and Resident Director of the Housing Sector Reform Project in the Russian Federation. He acknowledges support from the foundation grants to the Urban Institute for the preparation of this chapter. The opinions are those of the author and do not necessarily represent those of the Urban Institute or its sponsors.

1   This is a narrow definition of privatization in the housing sector. One could also discuss the shift to private ownership of the maintenance firms providing these services, construction companies and developers, and banks making construction period loans and originating mortgages. See Struyk and Kosareva (forthcoming) for a discussion of this broader concept. For a general discussion of housing privatization, see Linneman and Megbolugbe (1994).

2   Most of the information on privatization presented here comes from chapters on nine countries in the book on housing reform in the former Soviet bloc edited by Struyk (forthcoming). These chapters are all listed in the bibliography.

3   A couple of Western European countries, the Netherlands and the United Kingdom (prior to its privatization initiative from the end of the 1970s), have 30 per cent or more of their housing stock in social housing. However, this housing, while heavily subsidized by the state, is owned and operated primarily by non-profit organizations.

4   In addition to these forms, some government agencies had housing for their workers. However, such housing constituted only a few percentage points of the total stock, at most.

5   For documentation in the case of the Russian Federation, see Wallich (1994).

6   Three of the countries included in the survey (Estonia and the Czech and Slovak Republics) adopted policies of returning private property, including residential property, to owners from whom the state had expropriated it. Ultimately, these policies resulted in large numbers of buildings being returned to their owners, but specific data are lacking.

7   Based on data on the percentage of housing in the rental sector in 16 European countries reported in Maclennan (1993: 531). The unweighted average for these countries is 40 per cent.

8   The last point is supported by analysis for Hungary and Russia noted in the relevant chapters of Struyk (forthcoming).

9   For example, at a seminar at the Metropolitan Research Institute in Budapest in January 1995, when 20 housing experts from Eastern and Central Europe were convened to discuss the development of appropriate statistical indicators of housing developments in the region, the plight of the rental sector was discussed in terms very similar to those stated in the text.

10 The cities are: Moscow, St Petersburg, Novgorod, Rostov-on-Don, Barnaul, Tver and Nizhni Novgorod. The information presented here is from Struyk et al. (1991).

7

From the Socialist to the Capitalist City: Experiences from Germany

Hartmut Häussermann

The development of cities in the German Democratic Republic occurred under completely different circumstances to those affecting urban development in the Federal Republic of Germany. Property was state-owned, all investments were centrally controlled, and municipal independence was only a formal facade. Throughout the GDR, townscape, urban structure and living conditions could therefore be 'shaped' in a standardized, homogeneous manner. However, the integration of the GDR into the political and economic system of the Federal Republic of Germany has now fundamentally altered the terms for urban development.

Although a uniform idea of what a 'socialist city' was supposed to look like did not exist, it is possible, by reference to what were seen as the negative aspects of capitalist cities, to infer some characteristics. In socialism, the structure of urban land uses did not result from the profit-seeking concerns of private property owners, but from political decisions. The housing system were not to reproduce social divisions, but to enable all inhabitants to follow the 'socialist way of living'; the city structure was to be compact, so that collective infrastructure and public transport were easily accessible.

DIFFERENCES IN URBAN DEVELOPMENT

The development and land-use structure of socialist cities differed fundamentally from that of capitalist cities. Whereas under market conditions a city is formed by many different factors and actors, the locations and types of investment in socialist cities were controlled centrally.

In the capitalist city the decisions of private property owners play a dominant role. Although their interests may not be completely identical, in general terms the aim is to achieve the most profitable use of land. The political input to determining the structure of a city can be described as involving 'public planning on private land'. Although intervention and planning by local administrations have increased, considerably if gradually, since the massive expansion of cities caused by industrialization in the nineteenth century, urban development is always the outcome of a compromise between private and public interests. Whereas from a legal point of view public planning may seem strong today, in practice it is highly restricted, since private property rights are strongly protected by law.

In Germany in the middle of the nineteenth century, the liberal approach to urban development was wide-spread. Particularly after the creation of the bourgeois constitution, local authorities (dominated by real-estate interests) thought it be best if every owner pursued his or her own interests. This type of 'city production' was successful as long as most inhabitants were also property owners. It would fail, however, if masses of people without such means moved into the cities. Under these 'pure' market conditions, living standards were created that were widely perceived as a danger to political and moral control, as well as to the health of the inhabitants. Since that time, public planning provides investors with a strict framework of rules, which nevertheless has to be flexible enough for investors to accept it. Hence the result, as noted above, that urban development necessarily includes making compromises. This type of urban development involves many actors who interact in a fragile and complex network of power. Rights are differentially established (with respect to legal titles to property and participation rights), and this results in complex decision-making and co-ordination processes. The capitalist city is developed by many decentralized, individual decision makers; the influence of public planning on patterns of land use and social uses is therefore limited.

By contrast, the socialist city developed in a completely different framework; private property did not exist, all investments were state-controlled, decision processes were organized strictly hierarchically and were centrally co-ordinated. The functions of the city, the timing and the extent of investments, were completely a state matter – these were ideal prerequisites for urban planning. The final product (the city) could be designed according to theory and thereupon be realized according to the plan, for the state was in charge of all the means necessary to implement it.[1] In former times, not even the sovereign rulers disposed of such great power over urban development. In this context, the term 'urban development' is basically not applicable to the socialist city, since it normally implies a process in which the actions of different (semi-)autonomous performers and/or systems can only partly be guided. In order to understand what the 'socialist city' is, or what it was supposed to be, we shall examine two dimensions of urban development: its guiding principles and its power structures.

THE GUIDING PRINCIPLES OF THE 'SOCIALIST CITY'

Under the terms of 'democratic centralism', the guiding principles of architects and planners regarding urban development had a much bigger influence on the development of cities than in other Western countries. Where there is private control of land, such principles only set out a framework to guide the investments of the various actors. Generally, these guidelines can therefore only partially be realized.[2] In socialism, urban plans could immediately be put into practice. During the first years of the GDR, the guiding principles for architecture and urban design were influenced by anti-capitalist and/or anti-Western attitudes. However, from the 1960s onwards, urban design was increasingly dominated by the technical regulations for prefabricated housing construction.

Drawing on the literature on urban development (Topfstedt, 1988; Hoscislawski, 1991; von Beyme et al., 1992; Hain, 1992) and from the nature of existing examples, it is possible to define some characteristics of the 'socialist city', though in the 'purest' sense these can only be found in certain 'socialist ideal towns'.[3] Some of the characteristics are: a clear order, axes of development, central squares and monumental enclosures. Centres were to be emphasized by locating a skyscraper there, which would underline the 'size and dimension of socialism's victory' in Germany – a symbolic competitor to cathedral-building in the pre-industrial city. The street was supposed to belong to the 'people'. Boulevards and central squares, the tools of the absolutist city-builder, were constructed for parades and demonstrations. This approach contains characteristics of a representative, traditional art of 'urban design', which was at its peak in the GDR in 1953.

In 1950, Walter Ulbricht, the later leader of the governing party, proclaimed a return to 'national traditions', without any attempt to avoid resemblances to fascist urban development. Already in 1949, it had been decided that the centre of the destroyed city of Berlin was to be rebuilt as an 'urban metropolis' – with broad avenues and solemn squares, with high-class facades and monumental buildings, according to national building traditions – in contrast to the idea of the 'landscaped city' then current in the West. Then, in 1954 Khrushchev ordered a change from this conventional, pompous construction to a modern, industrial house-building. Accordingly, and after the incidents in June 1953, in 1955 the GDR changed its course. In fact, the pompous architectual style of the big urban projects and the general deterioration of the housing supply situation had created many problems. The new trend approach to urban development and housing was thus seen as better, cheaper and faster. It was on this basis that the use of prefabricated building originated, and it therefore also shaped the appearance of the newly constructed estates.

City structure

A principal characteristic of the socialist city concept is the dominance of the city centre. Its special significance is outlined in the *Sixteen principles of urban development*, established by the GDR government in 1950. These state:

> [t]he centre is the heart of the city, it is the political centre for its citizens. The most important political, administrative and cultural establishments are in the city centre. On the central squares, political demonstrations, parades and festivals on public holidays take place. The city centre with squares, main avenues and voluptuous buildings (skyscrapers in the big cities) determines the architectual silhouette of the city. Squares are the structural basis for urban development.

The fact that such principles were determined by the government is a clear sign of centralism to which urban development in the GDR was subordinated. The homogeneous construction of the centres therefore portrayed the new economical and political system. Finally it was possible, unhampered by capitalists' sectional interests, to enforce 'artistic' urban design concepts whose purpose was to portray socialism's victory. Instead of single, privately owned buildings there would be blocks of socially owned establishments, designed according to a single concept, which represented the team spirit of the socialist community, in contrast to the contradictory and fragmented capitalist community. The ornate buildings should encourage the inhabitants to identify with their city and with socialism.

In a functional sense, as in any capitalist city, the socialist city centre contained administration, cultural, trade and service establishments (Hofmeister, 1980; Friedrichs, 1985). Retailing and the service sector were strongly concentrated in the centre, and 'social establishments' also played an important role. It was not primarily differences in the mixture of land uses which marked the difference from the capitalist city, but degree of diversity within each of these functions. As there was no competition and there were scarcely any private companies, the diversity and mixture which is typical of city centres in Western countries was missing.

The trend in capitalist cities, by which changing land-use patterns led to a constant decrease of inhabitants in the central city, did not occur in socialist towns, where neither land prices nor the inhabitants' purchasing power for housing were relevant. As there was no competition from an expanding service sector, new housing could be built in the city centre. In 1989, the number of housing units in the centre of East Berlin, for instance, was higher than before World War II.

After 1945, Western cities planned to increase their open space and decrease their population density. The Eastern European principles for urban development were in sharp contrast to this. The *sixteen principles of urban development* stated, 'in the city one leads a more urban life style, in the suburb the life style is more rural. The multistory construction method is more profitable than the single or double story one. Also, it corresponds to the character of a large city.' This was a clear endorsement of the compact, dense city, leading to high-rise building. Since private housing ownership did not exist in the socialist city, suburbanization, the 'Western type' of urban development after 1945, was completely absent. Suburbanization in socialist towns occurred only in the sense of new high-rises on the city border, but within the city limits.

Urban development under socialism reconstructed the capitalist city in two respects: first, the city centre was interspersed with representative 'socialist' buildings and parade squares; second, housing was constructed on the periphery of the city in which the 'socialist way of life' could find its expression. In the 1970s and 1980s, an extensive housing programme was implemented and thousands of prefabricated units were built. Meanwhile the historical town centres were left to decay.

Dealing with pre-war dwellings

Thus the pre-1945 city was largely neglected. There were several reasons for this. First, quarters which still contained old tenement houses were a reminder of capitalist living conditions, which were supposed to have been overcome by socialism. Therefore, in the large cities there began the removal of the old buildings (urban renewal). In the new residential areas, the 'power of socialism' could be self-evidently demonstrated. The pre-war buildings remained with amenity levels at early twentieth-century standards (stove heating, exterior toilets, no baths), and through decay more and more of them became uninhabitable (the number of apartments in old housing declined from 5.4 million in 1961 to 3.9 million in 1990; in 1989 in the GDR, 200,000 residences were vacant). After 1970, some dwellings were renovated, but their number was marginal. The new buildings were in comparison very attractive: they were weather-proof and equipped with modern facilities. Also, the necessary infra-structure was provided (day-care, schools, shopping for daily goods, etc.).

Second, after 1945, the old tenement houses were still mainly privately owned, so the GDR government was not in the least inter-ested in renovating these properties and thus turning them into profitable or even attractive residences. Handicraft-based building companies constantly fell in number, as building policies were in-creasingly focused on the development of industrialized housing. Rents had been fixed at such a low level that repair and maintenance could not be covered by them. The municipal housing administra-tions often refused to accept pre-war dwellings even as a gift, as then they would have had to carry the burden of their maintenance (Dahn, 1994).

Finally, the authorities responsible for urban affairs believed in the cost-lowering effects of industrialized building (which, however, never occurred). So they preferred constructing new buildings to rehabilitating old ones, as the former was considered to be economi-cally rational.[4]

This rigid policy in favour of new construction was increasingly unacceptable to inhabitants and to dissenting urban planners. But even in 1989, residents of an old inner-city area in Berlin were still having to fill in holes during the night, which demolition squads, consigned to clear this historical part of the city, had drilled during the day. Such local resistance was a sign of disagreement with the modernization plans. Some urban sociologists, who had uncovered these public feelings through empirical investigations, go so far as to identify the dissatisfaction with the decline of old towns as a principal motivation for the revolt of 1989.

Social segregation

These old buildings had also been used as dumping grounds for those social groups which were not highly valued by the ruling party: non-conformists, dissidents, 'trouble makers', elderly people, and unskilled workers in the less important branches of industry. This is one indication that some social segregation did in fact occur. And yet the 'assimilation' of the classes was a top priority, a constantly emphasized goal in the GDR's social policy. This was most apparent in housing. Social segregation in the residential areas was considered as an expression of a capitalist class society, and the removal of class differences in residential areas was an essential, perhaps even deciding factor in the socialist structure of cities (Werner, 1981).

In the cities, an increasingly small share of flats was privately owned, and virtually all flats were run by a local authority, the 'community housing agency'. Since rents were extremely low and did not vary much according to position and quality of dwellings, income did not play a role in the choice of residential area. Flats were allocated according to various criteria, on the basis of one person, one room.[5] However, companies, public organizations and branches of public administration had their own quotas, and clearly segregated groups thus became established in blocks of 'contingent share apartments' (apartments from the stocks reserved for their own allocation, according to their own priorities). In contrast to the discriminatory exclusion of fringe groups at the lower end of the social hierarchy in the GDR, as mentioned above, the upper class, the nomenclatura and the intelligentsia experienced privileged living conditions. Generally, however, the bulk of the population lived comparatively unsegregated in socio-spatial terms, because social differences in the GDR were generally very slight. As in all communist states, segregation by age was practised, because young couples were preferred in the allocation system for new housing.

THE LOCAL POWER STRUCTURE

In the GDR, municipalities had in reality no independent political status (cf. Neckel, 1992). The law gave the 7,563 minicipalities a legal status as 'local organs' of the state. And, although article 41 of the constitution gave them their 'own responsibilities for their own issues', the state made all the decisions, even those that only affected the local level. The latter was doubly subordinate; first, to the 'direct (state) advisors' and, second, to the 'local parliament'. The state councils and respective departments of the state could not only nullify decisions made by the municipality but could also give them direct orders. Important issues pertaining to the city did not even get to the decision-making process of the municipality. In addition, municipalities had hardly any of their own financial resources or income with which they could have supported some independent decision making. In fact, they were dependent on the resources of local economic enterprises in order to realize any goals. So in practice, they became appendices of the local companies.

Thus the companies and their directors were more important actors on the local level than the politicians themselves were. The companies had power not only over human but also over material resources, which the local administration had to try and obtain in order to pursue its own interests and goals. Thus the local administration had to maintain constant contact with the companies, so that they could build and sustain, for instance, roads and sports facilities. The company also supplied additional labour for projects and services, which was never accounted for internally. Since the companies' construction departments were usually underemployed, the labour force was used for municipal purposes. Also, the day-care centres, social services and medical facilities were mostly the responsibility of the companies. Furthermore, large companies maintained adminstrators who were in control of facilities such as housing and holiday camps. Within the GDR's social system, the company became the focal point for organizing 'the socialist way of life'. The large companies were central distribution points from which social services and cultural events were organized. Whenever possible, trophies and presents were given to members – in short, the company took on responsibilities that traditionally the family fulfilled, and hence, the company had a comparable status to that of the landlord during feudalism (Illner, 1991).

Thus, although the institution of an elected government and its legal framework existed and these provisions were closely similar to those of the bourgeois tradition, in practice local self-government was non-existent. Generally, self-government was impossible because the decision-making process was controlled by the state councils and the companies, which, in turn, were part of a vertical structure that was guided by the central planning commissions, because everyone was dependent on the party, there were no free elections, and instead local mayors were choosen and controlled by the party; because there were no autonomous local financial resources, so localities could not undertake any investments; and because the middle class which had traditionally sustained self-government was systematically destroyed and excluded from the decision-making processes. Furthermore, since private construction was terminated, by legal and economic means, all the dynamic elements of municipal self-government were neutralized.

THE TRANSITION TO A 'CAPITALIST CITY'

As we have described, the key characteristics of a 'city in a socialist society' are:

- a dominant and 'artistically' designed urban centre, with a high concentration of publicly organized amenities based on an unlimited power over real estate;
- the city being a compact entity, with suburbanization only in the form of large buildings;
- visible deterioration of large areas of buildings constructed before World War II;
- the absence of classical forms of segregation (that is, by income), but discrimination by politically distributed privileges and by age;
- a fragmentation of local decision making between the party, the central state and industry; the non-existence of local self-government.

All five characteristics show the powerful influence of the central state. The absence of private real estate and other forms of private property allowed the city centre to become a place for the entire population and for public services. The state as a central planning entity was able to concentrate people in mass dwellings and thus prohibited Western-style suburbanization. And finally, the socialist doctrine did not support class differences, thus no social segregation occurred.

With the downfall of socialism, this framework inevitably collapsed. The state was no longer able to form cities according to its political ideology. The land that used to be public has been privatized and therefore the state has lost the material basis for its authority. The cities and suburbs are now in direct competition with each other, their financial resources determining their role. Furthermore, mass housing is no longer provided and guaranteed by the state, and the introduction of market-conditioned rents creates a new relationship between the landlord and the tenant. The re-establishment of local self-government also imposes new tasks on the municipalities: they are now responsible for labour-market policy, finances, social services, environmental issues and urban planning.

With reunification, these changes formally occurred overnight – but in reality they are developing step by step. Only slowly are the social and political institutions and spatial structures changing and adapting. And the human mentalities take time to adapt to the new situation. All these changes are most visible on the real-estate market, where land prices and new projects gain a speculative character. Given the release of property into the free market, such speculation could not be avoided. In fact 'real-estate capitalism' has been the first form of new economic activity, while in manufacturing hundreds of thousands of jobs have been lost. In those municipalities in areas lacking future profit expectations, less change has so far happened than was expected earlier. Socio-spatial and functional changes are most visible in towns where significant growth is expected (such as Leipzig and Dresden). So change and growth are occurring at different speeds in the different eastern German cities: some are developing a speculative character, whereas others remain in a situation of stagnation and depression. Generally, the slow progress with maintaining and modernizing housing in the former GDR is viewed by many as a failure of reunification.

One pecularity of this transitional phase is the persistence of traditional structures, habits, mentalities and political orientations alongside a totally new institutional and legal framework. Does this mean that different urban realities will emerge in the East to those in the West? In former East Germany, different values are held concerning social justice to those in former West Germany. This affects issues which are relevant to urban policy; for example, regarding the right to security of tenure for tenants, the newly instituted power relationship between the landlord and the tenant is viewed only by a few East German property owners as something positive (Dahn, 1994). Furthermore, the fact that an individual's income determines the quality of housing occupied and that homelessness is an unavoidable result of an 'efficient' housing policy are two aspects which have not been acceptable to many eastern Germans. Will this type of socio-ethical orientation shape eastern German municipalities in the future, or is the framework for urban and local policy possibly too restrictive, so that the present policies will have to adapt further to Western standards?

New landlords for old

Whereas the 'city in a socialist society' was owned by the central state and the party, the 'capitalist city' is owned by various social actors. Local representatives and mayors are freely elected and have to cooperate with numerous social organizations and interests that are legally involved with urban development. These organizations and interests include associations, developers, investors, private land owners, political departments such as the labour office, housing authorities, political parties and, last but not least, the local and national public. Urban planning policy has become urban management, since a complex network of interrelated entities with various interests has to be managed effectively. Towns have not only to act quickly but also to move in the 'right' direction. This is the new challenge eastern German municipalities and towns are confronted with. Under these circumstances it is therefore not surprising that, on the one hand, many opportunists used this period of uncertainty as a chance to fullfil their self-interested goals, and, on the other hand, the excessively complex structures led in some areas to stagnation. This new and complex system with its numerous actors has confused many eastern German municipalities and towns. The situation was that 40 per cent of all East German municipalities had fewer than 500 inhabitants and another 40 per cent had fewer than 5,000 inhabitants. Up to 1993, it was almost impossible for these municipalities to make any wise long-term decisions, since they had neither any politicians who were aware of new regulations nor any professional personnel.

In the large East German cities, a different scenario developed. After 1990, the political positions were filled by experienced West German officials, who used this opportunity to act in the interest of their political affiliations. They were familiar with the techniques and legal regulations relating to urban policy, imported from the West since unification, whereas local East German politicians were confronted with West German bargainers, whom they could not trust and with whom they could not compete. This applied not only to those buying up housing and to business people, but also to the consultants, developers and urban planning companies, which offered to act in the interest of the municipality. Land-use plans had to be developed, applications for financial grants had to be filed, and investments had to be planned. At the same time, East German authorities on the state level were confronted with the same problems, and could not correct mistakes that were made on the local level. For instance, many towns constructed oversized sewage plants –

just one example of inexperienced decision making. So how could one expect them to know how to attract the right investors, understand the building laws, and know what financial incentives were available? It was therefore not surprising that many Western opportunists were able to find a niche where they could make large profits as consultants or investors. A brief summary which expresses the viewpoint of East German officials states, '[f]irst the discount stores came to make a quick buck, then the real-estate brokers and attorneys arrived to make requisitions of old properties, then the consultants came who promised a lot, but do not even have any skills, and last but not least the 'qualifiers', who explain to the East Germans what they still have to learn' (quoted in Berking and Neckel, 1992). These problems were also caused by the fact that almost all the high-level and experienced (but politically burdened) leaders were replaced in 1990 by newly elected, inexperienced ones. These new people had mostly not been involved with the previous regime, and therefore did not have any experience in politics.

However, it is not only these recent developments which shape the present situation, but also the social and material structures inherited from socialism. The abolition of private property and of any organization of interests outside the state party by the socialist regime prevented the development of a middle class. Hence, that infrastructure of associations and interest groups which is traditionally the backbone of local self-government had also disappeared. It was the educated middle class with specific interests that historically shaped and sustained local self-government. After reunification, the problematic absence of a middle class become evident, since the only qualified politicians were the East German political elites – too often involved with repressive practices before 1989.

Changing urban structures

The socio-spatial pattern of the 'socialist city' is only slowly changing. In the long run, though, substantial changes will occur. At first the economically weak institutions are the most affected, particularly those in areas located closest to the city centre. These areas are the most profitable for potential businesses. The biggest change in real estate has been caused by new uses for space. The value of commercial space was unknown in East Germany because no land values were determined – prices simply did not exist. Now, prices have been reintroduced, and many shops and public services are unable to pay their rents. However, these changes not only occur in the inner-city areas but also are noticeable further out and in the suburbs, where at the beginning of the transformation phase no building laws existed. Here, large shopping malls and car dealerships have discovered large parcels of land. As a consequence, in some regions more shopping space has been created than is usual in Western cities. And it has also found the consumers. Many eastern Germans, now having cars, are no longer dependent on public transport and can therefore easily travel long distances between their housing and the shopping malls.[6] Meanwhile, the developers have started to redevelop the inner-city properties, creating huge office blocks for tertiary activities.

A second major change is that the suburbanization of housing is in full swing. Real-estate developers and families view the suburbs as the preferable place to live. High tax incentives now make it possible for the middle class to move there. Here too, the competition between the city and the suburb has begun in respect to tax payers.

A third factor is that the renovation of buildings built before World War II is taking longer than was expected in 1990. Because the ownership of these buildings has often not yet been determined, restoration cannot take place. In situations where ownership has been determined, owners are frequently not able to restore their buildings, due to the high costs, so detoriation is continuing.

The effects of the principle of 'restitution rather than compensation'

Today most politicians view the principle of 'restitution rather than compensation' as one of the biggest mistakes that was contained in the Unification Contract (Einigungsvertrag). The goal of this law was to return expropriated East German properties to their original owners. However, this process shows a certain 'retrogressive attitude' since, with the passing of over 40 years, new structures of the built environment and its usage had developed. These had to be ignored in order to enable the original owners the opportunity to regain their old properties. Up to 1992, over 1.8 million requests for restitution of real-estate property had been filed. These requests amount to about 15 per cent of the housing stock, of which 30 per cent is pre-war-buildings (Scholz, 1993). This explains why up to 90 per cent of the properties in certain neighbourhoods are legally entangled due to restitution claims. Berlin and Leipzig are the best-known examples of cities with major problems in this respect.

Returning the properties to their original owners has not always been possible. The exact sites of many former properties are now unidentifiable. However, many such areas still had to be developed so that economic growth could occur. With the experience of these cases, a clause was added to the Einigungsvertrag. It stated that investors with convincing investment concepts could be given priority over a piece of land, even if a claimant existed. In this case, the original owner is compensated. Cities hope that this change will speed up urban renewal, since the negative effects caused by speculators and financially weak property owners are now reduced. Furthermore, small land parcels can now be joined together, thus becoming more attractive to developers.

Although the GDR did not generally allow the private ownership of property, different perceptions of property ownership existed. In some respects, people treated the land that they lived on, in many cases for over 40 years, as their own. This explains why in some cases over 10 restitution claims per property were filed. In addition, because property ownership was not thoroughly documented after 1945, it was difficult to determine the 'real' owner. Moreover, restitution takes time, because the 'offices for restitution' are under-staffed and files are often incomplete. Up to early 1995, less than half of the restitution claims had been decided – and even after a decision is made, a lengthy legal struggle may occur.

The provisions for restitution, however, cannot be viewed just in the light of their practicability and efficiency with respect to future urban development. In fact, they embody deep social-ethical and moral dimensions. After reunification, Germany was confronted with its own problematic history, as many buildings, industries and properties located in the GDR originally belonged to the Jewish community. These properties had been confiscated by the Nazi regime, or sometimes taken by forced sales at incredibly low prices. It has therefore been accepted as Germany's responsibility to prioritize former Jewish ownership and to grant its claims. A special process has been installed for cases where no direct decendant is still alive. If this is the case, the property can be claimed by the Jewish Claims Conference, which in turn funds victims of the Holocaust. In fact, only a few original owners or their heirs have returned to Germany to reclaim and rebuild their old properties. Although this aspect of restitution has caused certain difficulties with urban development, it can be seen as an attempt on the part of Germany not only at reconciliation and reunification with the former East but also to reconcile itself with its own Nazi past.

However, through the sale of a fairly large amount of former Jewish property, a new social structure of ownership has been established. This is the case especially in inner-city neighbourhoods. Here profit-seeking land developers and real-estate firms dominate, rather than individual long-term owners. The size of the land parcels, created by the process of restitution and the consequential transfers of ownership, is larger than those normally found in European cities. Instead, one finds large-scale areas of land, on which 'modern' urban concepts are being realized. Owners of inner-city properties are not any more old traders' and craftsmen's families, but anonymous real-estate funds, international real-estate companies, and speculators of all types.

Real-estate capital has become the urban developer with financial means on a scale which in the past has been unknown in German cities. Corporate land developers have gained an enormous amount of power. They have had the chance to grow rapidly, due to many financial incentives such as tax write-offs. These are unusually generous and mean that calculations of the amount of investment required and the later uses of the developments become an entirely secondary concern. As a consequence, real-estate prices have risen sharply, squeezing smaller, private investors out of the market. Furthermore, this means that ownership becomes anonymous, and therefore long-term vested interests in the locality cannot be established. The former East Germany is even more vulnerable to this type of absentee ownership than the former West Germany is – the reason being the absence of a middle class, and of accumulated middle-class money available for investment. Although local self-government has been reintroduced it will take some time until a middle class with long-term vested interests will establish itself. The whole process of restructuring results in a new structure of ownership, whereby the owners are located mainly in the West.

New structures of social segregation

In 1990, about 41 per cent of the former GDR apartments were in government ownership ('people's owned housing'). Recently, these units have been allocated to 1,200 municipalities and co-operative housing organizations. Following unification, the former GDR is faced with two serious problems. First, the system of rent regulation will be harmonized by mid-1995 with the Western system; second, the housing will not be subject to social housing rules and regulations any longer. Many former East Germans' incomes will be insufficient to enable them to cope with these two major changes.

How the rents in the former 'people's owned housing' will change will be determined by the directors of the co-operative housing organizations and the municipal housing associations. In fact, these directors are in a difficult situation. So far, the rent payments (still regulated by law) have not covered the maintenance costs. Dwellings have been modernized and the costs are drastically increasing. In addition, the housing organizations had to accept an existing debt of DM36 billion when they took the dwellings over. For this reason, the newly created housing associations have been restrained from selling their housing stock at low prices to the tenants or to any other purchaser.

The finance ministry offered these organizations the opportunity to waive 50 per cent of their debt. However, they would then be obliged to privatize 15 per cent of their housing stock. Privatization would allow the present tenants to purchase their apartments for a price of about DM2,000 per square metre. These prices are below the supposed market value but are still too high for a family with an average income in former East Germany. The people who are able to afford these prices will probably think twice about buying, if they can purchase for the same price a better-value house in suburbia. At present, only a few tenants (5–6 per cent) show even an interest in purchasing their apartments. If the above-mentioned 15 per cent cannot be reached within 10 years, the full debt will remain with the housing associations. Hence, both parties, the government and the housing associations, are already thinking of altering the rule: selling not only to the tenants, but also to corporate owners. One can therefore expect a massive change of ownership to occur.

A process feared by urban planners and the housing authorities would then start: social segregation in the large former East German estates, constructed in the 1970s and 1980s. These areas would become segregated, and in the long term only a low-income population would remain, out of whose resources modernization and improvements could not be financed. Today in these areas heterogeneous income and social groups share the same living space, and the average household income is in fact higher than on the large former West German estates created in the same period. But the changes in rents and other matters may now cause better-off households to move out, while others, who cannot afford to move, will have to stay.

The opposite will occur in the old neighbourhoods. Modernization and renewal will lead to the expulsion of inhabitants with low incomes, and their replacement by households with higher incomes. This will occur particularly because the government's financial resources for more socially oriented and publicly regulated renewal are limited, as a consequence of general budgetary crisis in the public sector. This has resulted in deregulation and the introduction of incentives for the mobilization of private capital, a sharp contrast to former West German urban renewal policies. The costs of modernizing these old buildings will cause rents to rise, thus people who cannot afford the new rents will have to leave, and gentrification will occur. Established tenants in old neighbourhoods are legally protected, but they will lose this security in the year 2005, because the special legal regulations which have been implemented for the present transformation period will terminate then.

FUTURE DEVELOPMENTS

Future developments will depend, first, on how income levels and income differences in eastern Germany will evolve and, second, on what kinds of alternative housing and ownership programme are established. If housing associations succeed in privatizing massive numbers of apartments and modernizing the dwellings in such a form that rents will not increase drastically, then less social segregation can be expected. However, if rents increase one can expect many families to leave city centres and establish themselves in suburbia, and old neighbourhoods to be gentrified.

Increasing and increasingly differentiated incomes, the privatization of housing, the modernization of old dwellings, the new construction of family homes, the reuse of property – all these indicate processes which will, most likely, lead to a different socio-spatial patterning of the urban population to that which occurred in the 'socialist' city. An important influence on the future population distribution could be one inherited from the pre-socialist structure of the cities. In capitalism, the size, the standard and the location of an apartment are determined by the demand of specific income groups: on the one hand, working-class neighbourhoods and, on the other hand, bourgeois quarters were developed, complemented by petty bourgeois mixed areas. In the old neighbourhoods, these social structures are signified by specific layouts, amenities, technical standards, architectural designs and types of public space. And these factors cannot easily be changed. One can suppose that the historical 'built social structure' will re-emerge in the pattern of socio-spatial differentiation, when private investments and private renting of housing will again determine the social pattern of neighbourhoods. So far as this occurs, these changes will result in a return to the capitalist city structure.

SUMMARY

The transformation from socialism to capitalism seems to create a new form of urban development. This new form is most visible in the former GDR but is also slowly establishing itself in western German towns. Indicators are: new structures of property ownership, new actors on the real-estate market, the deregulation of housing, and general, drastic financial pressures. All these are changing the framework of urban development in the former GDR. These new conditions are leading to a new type of city in eastern Germany. Increasingly, in the transformation phase of eastern German cities, new capitalist structures are emerging. In the near future, parallel developments will most probably occur in Western German towns too.

NOTES

1   This is an ideal-typical description and ignores the fact that in reality there was competition, conflict and disorganization within and between institutions of the state and the party.
2   The guiding principles for urban development in capitalism become more effective when the terms for development are similar to those of the socialist city: that is, a 'greenfield investment', when large areas are being planned and built by one contractor. This was the case with the development of 'large settlements' in the 1960s and 1970s in West Germany (Jessen, 1987). Which (varying) guiding principles were developed for creating new centres in Western towns are outlined by Gausmann (1994).
3   In the GDR, four new towns were established: Stalinstadt (now known as Eisenhüttenstadt), Schwedt, Hoyerswerda and Halle-Neustadt. On the guiding principles for constructing Stalinstadt, see Kil (1992) and Hannemann (1994).
4   The state economy estimated the cost for a new building at 80,000 marks higher than the cost of renovating a pre-war dwelling. So it would have been possible to create more housing with an adequate technical standard by means of this than by unilaterally favouring new construction. See Pensley (1995).
5   Three criteria determined the distribution of housing. These were socio-political, economic and social. Regarding the latter, large families, young couples without housing and single mothers were given priority. The economic criterion related to the fact that companies had housing nomination rights. The most important criterion, however, was the socio-political one, which resulted in allocations for 'fighters against fascism' and 'persons who have shown eminent efforts to strengthen the German Democratic Republic'.
6   The modal split between private and public transport in the 'old' FRG was 70:30; in the GDR it was 30:70. Now it has nearly equalized.

8

Environmental and Housing Movements in Cities after Socialism: The Cases of Budapest and Moscow

C.G. Pickvance

The aim of this chapter is to discuss the development of environmental and housing movements in 'cities after socialism'. After an introduction, which outlines models of transition and the concepts of citizen organization and social movement, there follow three major sections and a conclusion. The first two major sections describe environmental and housing citizen activity under state socialism, and in post-socialist Moscow and Budapest, and the third examines explanations of social movement development in these post-socialist cities.

INTRODUCTION

Models of transition from state socialism

A chapter on housing and environmental movements cannot avoid the central question in understanding cities after socialism, namely whether the relation between state socialism and what follows is to be understood as one involving radical change or moderate change. It is easy to follow journalistic usage and indeed the usage of some academics in which an overnight change of system is implied. A moment's thought, however, will suggest that the radical change model involves some questionable assumptions.

Firstly the radical change model sees state socialism as 'collapsing', as though all the blood disappeared from the veins of the old body. This then leads to the idea that an economic and institutional vacuum is created where the old body was, in which new structures can easily be built (Stark, 1992a). The task of external agents of change such as the World Bank should thus be relatively easy. This model makes one of two assumptions about the relevance of the legacy of the past to an understanding of the present. The strongest assumption is that no such legacies exist, since the collapse of the former system is total. A weaker and more plausible one is that legacies do exist but are entirely negative, since anything inherited from a system totally opposed to capitalism must be contradictory to a shift towards capitalism. As will be argued below, both assumptions are highly debatable.

The moderate change model, on the other hand, views the metaphor of collapse as inappropriate. It emphasizes three points. First, it draws attention to the divergence between the classical model of a centrally planned economy and the reality of former state socialist societies. This divergence varies between societies. The most 'reformed' countries left considerable scope for private ownership in agriculture and housing and allowed 'second economies' to develop outside but in symbiosis with the state sector (see Stark, 1989; Kornai, 1992; Sik, 1994). Likewise political dissent was tolerated to varying extents in the 1980s.

Second, the moderate change model goes on to argue that retrospectively these 'reform' elements can be seen as building blocks for change to a more market-oriented and democratic system. This is not to say that a change of system was an inevitable consequence of reform elements – such a claim amounts to a teleological re-reading of history – but only that they were relatively compatible with such a change.

Third and following from this, the moderate change model emphasizes the importance of legacies from the state socialist period. Unlike the radical change model, in which legacies are either ignored or seen as forces which act as brakes on social change, the moderate change model is aware both of negative legacies and of legacies which are positive in the sense of anticipating or providing experience of practices and structures of capitalist and democratic societies. As well as the examples mentioned above, one could cite the 'coping mechanisms' developed to overcome some of the rigidities of central planning, which are not far removed from entrepreneurship (Hough, 1969).

Ideally one would like to have a solid empirical grounding for one's choice between the radical change and moderate change models. This is very difficult, since in many cases evidence is hard to interpret or is entirely absent. For example, does data on the extent of private-sector employment indicate the prevalence of market processes, or are some private companies the result of defensive strategies by managers of state enterprises to minimize the development of market-like behaviour (Stark, 1996)? (See also Sutela's, 1994, discussion of 'insider privatization' in Russia.) Similarly one can ask whether democratic elections necessarily bring opponents of communism to power and whether officials are ready to carry out radically different policies. Conversely, the fact that representatives or officials may be ex-communists (Teague, 1994) does not imply that their practices must be understood as attempting to perpetuate 'communist interests'.

It is assumed here that while both negative and positive legacies of the past exist, the former are stronger than the latter and act as obstacles to dramatic change. However, the extent of change varies between societies. For example, in the administrative and political spheres Hungary had probably evolved more under state socialism than Russia[1] and has changed even more since 1989/90.

Citizen organizations and social movements

Before proceeding to the focus of this chapter, it is worth placing environmental and housing movements within the broad category of citizen organizations.

The latter term is used here as a very general one to refer to all groups of individuals who come together to pursue a common interest. It is compatible with a variety of different types of interest and modes of action and is broader than the term 'social movement' (Barnes and Kaase, 1979).

There is no general agreement on the coverage of the concept of social movement (Eyerman and Jamison, 1991). It can refer to a broad, amorphous force or to the specific movement organizations which make up that force. Social movements may be seen as the source of all social change (as in Touraine, 1981) or as a modest source of social change. The approach adopted here is to use the term 'social movement' to refer to 'movement organizations', which may or may not be part of wider entities and which may or may not prove to be significant sources of social change.

What defines and distinguishes them is that they are mobilized groups which make demands which are usually outside the established political agenda, or are highly critical of existing policies, and which rely on non-institutional methods in part. They are distinct from political parties, which are part of the formal political structure. However, over time social movements may become institutionalized as their goals are accepted (in part at least) by the political system. It is therefore possible for the organizational extinction of a movement to be compatible with the success of the movement's ideas. For this reason it is important not to include the impact of movements as part of their definition.

Social movements can therefore be seen as a type of citizen organization. Other types include 'reformist' groups, whose demands are moderate and 'within' the system, and 'co-production' organizations, in which citizens and public bodies work together in the provision of services. It is important to keep in mind such distinctions, since they show how citizen organizations can represent different degrees of threat to existing policies and political systems and will encounter different responses.

In Western societies, the dominant image of citizen organizations is as groups of individuals acting autonomously of the state. This image is partly weakened by the finding that middle-class individuals are disproportionately likely to form citizen organizations. It is more severely damaged by the discovery that some citizen organizations develop close relations with the local or central state – or in extreme cases are even state-sponsored. Clearly then, despite the dominant image, a wide spectrum of citizen organizations exists in Western societies: from social movements whose demands are most hostile to established policies, to reformist organizations which are not averse to reaching compromise, to co-production and state-sponsored organizations whose autonomy vis-à-vis the state is very low. Particular organizations may shift from one category to another throughout their 'careers' or 'life-cycles'.

Under state socialism, however, citizen organizations have a quite different image. Communist Party structures and state institutions are intertwined, and it is a responsibility of the party-state as representative of the people to establish organizations to allow citizens to pursue their interests (Lovenduski and Woodall, 1987). Typically then these are official organizations 'for the people', rather than autonomous organizations 'of the people'. The interests concerned are usually leisure interests which in theory are perfectly compatible with those of the party-state, such as nature conservation. By contrast, organizations which made demands for changes in political structures or even changes in policies would be incompatible with the leading role of the Communist Party.

However, ideology is a poor guide to the actual working of any society, and it would be misleading to take the above picture as adequate. First, just as in Western societies where the citizen character of an organization cannot be taken as a guarantee that it will remain independent of government, so in state socialist societies 'official' citizen organizations may develop a degree of autonomy vis-à-vis the party-state despite their party origins. Second, the totalitarian image of a society controlled by the party-state ignores the space 'between' and 'outside' the formal structures of state socialism, in which illegal and officially disapproved activity developed and was conditionally tolerated, such as human rights activism, samizdat publishing, and the Solidarity movement in Poland. This reflects the gap between the image of state socialism, as a system in which individuals were positively oriented to the regime, and the reality, where passive disaffection was considerable and there were limits to the penetration and effectiveness of party-state structures.

The concepts of citizen organization and social movement are thus strongly shaped by the social context, and it is necessary to be aware both of the diverse types of citizen organization and of the importance of their relations to the state.

ENVIRONMENTAL AND HOUSING ORGANIZATIONS UNDER STATE SOCIALISM

An account of a social phenomenon which traces it back to its 'origins' has an undeniable appeal. It reassures us that the present-day phenomenon is related by organic growth to its predecessors. In the present case, however, such a view implies a model of change from state socialism as a gradual process which, as suggested earlier, is only one possibility.

A strong case about the linkage between present-day environmental and housing movements and their 'predecessors' under state socialism would argue that the latter were also social movements, using the definition given earlier. A weak case would be that present-day environmental and housing movements grew out of citizen organizations whose demands were more moderate than those of social movements. A negative case would be that there is no connection between past and present citizen organizations and that the search for predecessors is chimerical.

Concerning the strong case, it is clear that to say that social movements existed under state socialism is incompatible with the idea that the Communist Party took the leading role in mass organization. However, as already mentioned, opposition forces under state socialism were not always contained within ideologically approved forms. Moreover, in the 1980s there was an increasing tolerance of certain types of citizen organization. The strong case about linkage between previous and current housing and environmental movements cannot thus be completely excluded – though it would be rare. (The weak and negative cases will be discussed below.)

A further problem of interpretation concerns the proposition that any present-day citizen organization which grew out of citizen organizations in the state socialist period must still be under communist influence. This view is in my opinion untenable for two reasons: it adopts a 'totalitarian' picture of the omnipresence of the party-state under state socialism, and it assumes that if the Communist Party was involved in the creation of an organization, its influence continues today. Neither reason is valid: both underestimate the 'play' within state socialism in practice, especially in the more reformed systems in the 1980s, and the tendency of citizen organizations to develop autonomy from their original sponsors.

We now turn to the development of housing and environmental organizations, looking in turn at the period before 1980, and the period of the 1980s. It will be shown that while citizen organization in the environmental sphere is to be found in both periods, in the housing sphere it is absent in both periods.

The period before 1980

In *Russia*, some citizen environmental organizations developed through the activities of official youth organizations and through student organizations. Others were part of organizations such as the All-Russian Society for the Protection of Nature and the All-Russian Society for the Protection of Historical and Cultural Monuments, which had a widespread network of local branches. Both Yanitsky (1993) and Shvarts and Prochozova (1993) draw attention to the Khrushchev 'thaw' as favouring such activity.

However, although these environmental activities were part of official structures they cannot be analysed simply as channels by which the grassroots were managed. The precise degree of autonomy they enjoyed is obviously difficult to assess, and in any case changed over time (for example, it declined in the Brezhnev period). Yanitsky, referring to 'environmental clubs', writes that 'from the moment [they] were formed, a hidden struggle took place within them, a contest between 'directive' and 'initiative' methods of operating, between state policy and the real interests of citizens, between organization and self-organization' (1993: 60). He argues that these clubs developed some autonomy even in the 1960s and 1970s 'because club work lay on the periphery of the system's interests' (1993: 60), because young people had not been fully socialized into the dominant ideology, and because the clubs were run by marginal members of the scientific intelligentsia. Even in the Brezhnev period, according to Shvarts and Prochozova (1993), environmental groups made use of the by-laws of the various inspectorates of nature preservation and drew public attention to breaches of these laws. However, Yanitsky (1993) suggests that environmental activism at this time was limited to the natural environment and excluded the urban.

The precise linkages between these environmental groups and those of the 1980s are hard to trace. Yanitsky (1993) suggests that they supplied experience of struggle and publicly acknowledged leaders. He also suggests that in some cases the later groups were based on a take-over of a local branch of a national citizen organization such as the Society for the Protection of Nature.

Before the 1980s, *Hungary* had a similar experience of environmental organization to Russia's, with official organizations channelling environmental concern with less than complete success. For example, in the 1970s, as environmentalism spread internationally, the People's Patriotic Front (PPF, linked to the Hungarian Socialist Workers' Party) set up an association of GONGOs (government-organized non-governmental organizations) to stimulate action groups. 'Youth organizations, for example, formed action groups in schools, and trade unions organized environmental activities in factories' (Persanyi, 1993: 142). But by the early 1980s, the PPF had been outflanked by the formation of independent groups.

This picture of environmental activism in the 1960s and 1970s within official organizations in Hungary and Russia had no parallel in the sphere of housing. This was not because housing problems were any less serious than environmental ones, but because of the ideological framework within which they were perceived. On the one hand, there was a private housing sector in both Hungary and Russia which was associated with an ideology of self-help rather than making demands of the state. On the other hand, in the state sector housing was seen as a gift for which citizens should be very grateful.[2] As a result, any dissatisfaction that became public took a fragmented form such as letters to the press, or contact with officials, rather than leading to citizen organizations. Nevertheless, awareness of housing inequality and dissatisfaction with long waiting times to obtain housing, with overcrowding, or with slow repairs (but not with rent levels), were considerable.

Beyond the spheres of environment and housing, the 1970s in Eastern Europe saw a growth of activism in areas such as human rights and peace, with international contacts being developed. Samizdat publishing also spread, but all of these initiatives were relatively confined to intellectuals. The Solidarity movement in Poland had much more widely based support and indicated that state socialism was not capable of suppressing all protest.

The 1980s

We now turn to the last decade of state socialism, which saw the emergence against environmental threats of protests not based in official citizen organizations. These can be found sporadically in the 1970s but expanded in scale in the 1980s. Typically they were local protests and the protest groups involved were illegal, since there was no right of citizens to associate outside officially approved channels. That such protest existed at all thus indicates a shift in the balance of forces between state and citizens, supported by the international growth of environmentalism.

In *Russia*, at the start of the 1980s, environmental activism was largely contained within the structures described earlier: official citizen associations, universities and the youth and student clubs they created. From 1986, however, there was an increase in the level of environmental activism (see the chronology given in Yanitsky, 1993). This period saw an increase in independent groups, a concern with the urban environment as well as 'nature', and the rise of commercial activity to help finance environmental groups.

The timing of this change is of course linked to Gorbachev's perestroika policy and the gradual opening up of spaces for citizen action in the interstices of the state socialist system. The late 1980s was a period when the Communist Party was coming under challenge. Gorbachev's reforms were intended to leave communist rule intact. However, for a mixture of reasons they had the reverse effect. On the one hand, the very dynamic of Gorbachev's policies unintentionally undermined the position of the Communist Party. Hence its traditional role of channelling public participation via official organizations came under challenge. On the other hand, in order to pursue his reforms Gorbachev needed a counter-weight to the party elite and appealed to citizens for support over the heads of the party. In doing so, however, he lost control of the reform process (Arato, 1991).

Hence in the late 1980s, a space for citizen action was created outside party structures but lacking any legal basis. This space was the arena for conflict between party structures whose formal position had not changed and informal groups that had responded to the reform messages from above. The inconsistency of state responses towards citizen groups is therefore explicable. State structures were sending mixed messages: they were both agent and obstacle to reform. As also occurred in Hungary, there was a weakening of the power of the party-state and a 'spilling over' of citizen participation into independent groups (Brovkin, 1990).

The rise of independent groups was assisted by some new types of resource which became available in the 1980s. Existing official structures continued to supply resources to official citizen organizations and tried to use their power to restrain the growth of new citizen groups. The new funding was of two kinds. International connections allowed certain groups to gain access to new resources. And commercial activity became increasingly important. This happened to a limited extent in the case of groups which sold their own publications. But activities like monitoring environmental pollution and the preparation of environmental impact appraisals indicated additional possibilities for self-financing. The market for such services had to be created, but the expertise of environmentalists gave them an advantage in meeting the demand. However, running money-making enterprises may displace demand-making if it is very successful, and there is some evidence of such a shift.

An interesting example of a type of environmental organization with commercial activities is the 'environmental centres' described by Yanitsky as existing 'in almost every provincial centre' (1993: 66). The Nizhny Novgorod environmental centre's aims were to support environmental groups, carry out environmental research, advise on legislation and carry out educational work. Interestingly, one of its subsidiaries 'was supposed to grow environmentally clean agricultural produce, but at the moment it's building houses in the countryside' (Yanitsky, 1993: 67). This type of centre exemplifies the changing role of communist power in the late 1980s, which will be encountered again. The environmental centres were set up by Komsomol (the communist youth organization) and the centre's aim of supporting environmental groups makes clear the intention of controlling public participation. However, the difficulty of executing such a role at a time when Communist Party structures were weakening is illustrated by a statement by the leader of the Nizhny Novgorod environmental centre that in early 1991 Komsomol 'demanded all its toys back' (Yanitsky, 1993: 67). Clearly such centres were capable of escaping from Communist Party control.

A final new source of funding for citizen organizations at the end of the 1980s was co-operatives (or small businesses). A 1988 law on co-operatives allowed them to claim tax relief on charitable donations. Unfortunately it is not known how far citizen organizations benefited from this provision.

In *Hungary*, there was a greater development of independent environmental groups. The issues which provoked environmental protests were an oil spill which contaminated a river (at Dunaujvaros in 1974), lead poisoning (at the Metallochemia factory in Budapest in 1978), pollution of water by hazardous waste (at Vac in 1981), dust pollution (at Ajka in 1984), a waste incinerator (at Dorog in 1984), a radioactive waste repository (at Ofalu in 1984), the importation of polluted waste (at Mosonmagyarovar in 1985–7), and last but not least the movement against the Danube dam (from 1984 onwards) (Waller, 1989; Persanyi and Lanyi, 1991; Szirmai, 1993; Persanyi, 1993; Juhasz et al., 1993). These protests were not exclusively local in their impact, and by 1988 Persanyi could list six 'local environmental protests [which] had national reverberations' (1993: 140). By far the best-known of these was the Danube Circle, which will be briefly outlined here.

The Danube Circle

In 1977 the Czechoslovak and Hungarian governments decided to build a dam on the Danube to generate hydroelectric power.[3] The first opposition occurred in 1980, when 400 Hungarian engineers voted against the dam at a professional meeting, and in the following year a journalist, Janos Vargha, published an article critical of the dam in a social science journal. But the movement itself only started in 1984. A public debate between Vargha and a senior official of the National Water Management Office had been arranged, but the official withdrew at the last minute. Instead Vargha gave a talk on the dam, and those present decided to create a movement, the Danube Circle. Its opposition to the dam was based on the dam's expected effects on water purity, habitats, agriculture and landscape and the high cost of the electricity produced.

The movement made extensive use of petitions and was given space for debates by clubs associated with universities and institutions in Budapest. It won so much attention that in 1985 it was given the alternative Nobel Prize, the Right Livelihood award.

The Danube Circle continued its activities in 1986 and 1987, with the police breaking up its demonstrations. In 1988, as the movement again tried to register as an association, the communist-sponsored

PPF set up a rival Hungarian Environmental Protection Union to deny the circle's legitimacy and right to registration. This failed to halt its growth, and in autumn 1988 it held a 30,000-strong demonstration outside parliament, followed by a 140,000-signature petition in February 1989. The televising of parliamentary sessions from 1988 onwards allowed the public to witness the speeches of deputies and acted as a spur to opposition groups.

In May 1989, the Hungarian government announced the suspension of work on the dam and the setting up of parliamentary committees to investigate the effects of suspension. The leadership of the Danube Circle was absorbed into the work of these committees.

A final decision to cancel the agreement was only made in May 1992. The Slovakian government rejected this decision as a unilateral breach and continued work on a partial version of the dam while taking legal action against the Hungarian government. The Danube Circle can thus be seen as successful in helping bring about the 1989 and 1992 decisions, but because there was no counterpart movement in Slovakia, it could not prevent the Slovakian go-it-alone decision.

The expansion of the Danube Circle between 1984 and 1989 was due less to a pure rise in environmentalism than to the coming together of environmentalist and democratic political opposition. To survive, the Danube Circle had to struggle for democratic rights, and this brought it the support of those committed to a fight against the regime. The dam with its destructive effects on nature came to symbolize the regime's suppression of human rights.

Meanwhile the national and international political context was changing rapidly. Between 1987 and 1989, three opposition parties were set up, Kadar was deposed, and the conflict between hardline and reform communists succeeded in destroying the Communist Party (Korosenyi, 1992). One of the opposition parties, the Alliance of Free Democrats, drew a lot of support away from the Danube Circle as the democratic opposition turned its efforts towards electoral politics. The dismantling of the Berlin Wall and Gorbachev's lifting of the Soviet threat to intervene provided external support for the process that led to the holding of the spring 1990 elections and the coming to power of a conservative nationalist government. The Danube Circle found itself marginalized by these events but has continued to exist, on a much smaller scale, keeping its distance from political parties.

The period since 1980 can thus be seen as one in which state socialism weakened in Hungary. Local groups were able to undertake protest action outside the confines of official citizen organizations.

The Danube Circle was the most highly developed example of such protest and clearly merits the term 'environmental movement'. The confluence of environmentalist and democratic protest seen in Hungary (and elsewhere – see Waller and Millard, 1992; Fisher, 1993) was a characteristic shared with other authoritarian societies where environmental or urban protest has been tolerated in the final period before a democratic transition, such as Spain, Portugal, Brazil and Hong Kong, as will be shown below.

Conclusion

This section has shown that in the last decade of state socialism there was a growth of citizen action on environmental issues outside the official organizations set up to channel public participation. This ranged from localized protests over various environmental threats to the example of the Danube Circle, which was much broader and combined environmental and pro-democracy demands.

The existence of such action must be neither ignored nor exaggerated. That citizen action existed at all outside official structures indicates that, de facto, party control was incomplete and the costs to the state of repressing every type of action outweighed the benefits. This can be interpreted as a real tilt in the balance of power between party-state and people – in Hungary, this shift came earlier and was larger than in Russia. On the other hand, the citizen action which did exist was insecure, since it took place in the absence of any legal right of association. There was no guarantee that the toleration of such action was anything but temporary and reversible.

The emergence of environmental movements as well as more moderate types of citizen organization in the 1980s had almost no echo in the sphere of housing. Housing activism will be discussed in the next section.

ENVIRONMENTAL AND HOUSING ORGANIZATIONS SINCE 1989/90

This section will follow the development of citizen organizations into the post-socialist period by presenting some examples of organizations active in Moscow and Budapest. The next section will examine the main propositions which have been advanced to explain the way the changing context affects citizen organizations.

Moscow

Two types of citizen organisation will be described: neighbourhood self-management committees and housing partnerships.[4]

Neighbourhood self-management committees

An important category of citizen organization in Moscow is the neighbourhood self-management committee (SMC).

The idea of self-management by citizens in Moscow made its appearance in 1985, at the start of the perestroika period, with some successful initiatives by tenants to improve their neighbourhoods or residential blocks. The best-known case is Brateevo, a suburban area where, in 1988, a group of residents succeeded in getting a building project which threatened the neighbourhood stopped and in obtaining an allocation of 1 million rubles to improve the area. Also in this period, in the central areas of Arbat and Presnya, residents' groups were formed and achieved modest improvements in their areas. The leader of the Presnya group was active in promoting the concept of self-management, and this was a factor in the decision in 1989 by the Moscow Communist Party leadership to encourage district councils to set up neighbourhood SMCs.

By 1991, over 100 such committees had been created, and by 1993, 250 existed. There was often continuity with previous groups of activists, as in the case of the three examples mentioned. What was significant for their viability initially was their financing by the district councils. This was sufficient in scale to enable them to employ two or three staff each. The stated aims of the SMCs were to deal with local residents' individual and collective problems.

To understand SMCs, it is necessary to separate their origins from their subsequent development. Initially they were intended as virtual extensions of the party-state apparatus to the neighbourhood level. The motivation for their creation was the Communist Party's desire to keep some grip on the local population at a time when its power was being challenged through Gorbachev's reform policies (Sazunov, 1991). The holding of local elections in March 1990 provided an additional spur, since SMC activists could be expected to gain a local reputation and hence be nominated as candidates. In this way, the Communist Party could hope to secure the election to local councils of supporters who did not stand under the party label.

In reality, SMCs were more than a relay for party interests, and in many cases they escaped completely from party control to become neighbourhood representative associations. This occurred for three reasons. First and most important, the Communist party lost control of many SMCs. This in part reflected the weakening of the party-state structure in general and the development of conflicts between (and within) different levels of the structure. The concept of 'party interest' thus lost its meaning. Second, SMCs became open to groups at the local level that did not follow Communist Party ideas. As will be shown, SMCs made demands which often opposed the policy of district and city levels of government. Third, once the resource flow from district councils was cut off, many SMCs found new resource bases, such as the renting out or sale of rooms or buildings over which they claimed control. This economic independence made them more autonomous politically speaking. The net result is that despite their origins SMCs developed considerable autonomy from local administrative structures.

Our research revealed a considerable number of cases where SMC members stood successfully as candidates at local elections and/or became employees of local government. By 1993, 40 Moscow city councillors were or had been members or office holders in SMCs. The leader of the Presnya SMC had by 1993 been elected to Krasnopresnensky district council and Moscow city council as a councillor, and two leaders of Brateevo SMC had become respectively a city councillor (and chair of its self-management commission) and a district councillor (and member of the self-management committee of the Russian parliament). Others became officials.

A simplistic interpretation of such trajectories is that they enabled the Communist Party to advance its interest. But this would only be true if the concept of party interest had any meaning (which was denied above) and if individual interests remained unchanged. In practice, according to the 'asset conversion thesis', individuals with strong backgrounds of participation in Communist Party organizations were highly likely to jettison their party identification and to redeploy their resources (finance, networks, etc.) to take advantage of whatever economic opportunities emerged (Levitas and Strzalkowski, 1990). This alternative interpretation is consistent with the general opinion within the SMCs that they had been used as springboards by individuals wishing to pursue their personal interests, and that such people had rapidly lost touch with the interests of the SMC.

As the SMCs developed more autonomy, they increasingly found themselves in conflict with local authorities. It should be noted that these authorities were themselves undergoing dramatic changes. From 1990 until autumn 1991, the district councils existed with their administrations. After that date they were officially abolished, and the 33 local administrations were reorganized into 10 prefectures. In October 1993, Moscow city council itself was abolished, and was only reconstituted in December 1993. There was ample scope for conflict: it occurred among elected councillors (who lacked party discipline, since there were no clear-cut parties), between councillors and officials (who traditionally had executed policy decided without any inputs from elected representatives), between levels of government (over their spheres of competence), and between the mayor of Moscow and rank-and-file councillors (see Fish, 1991; Campbell, 1992; Boyce, 1993; Hanson, 1993). Such conflicts were facilitated by the confusion of authority and conflict of laws. For example, two administrations might both claim the power to dispose of a residential block on the basis of different laws. This confusion was not entirely to the disadvantage of SMCs, since it created 'spaces' which they could exploit. As already mentioned, they were sometimes able to appropriate and sell or rent out property.

The sharpest conflicts between SMCs and local administrations occurred in central Moscow. To understand the issues, a word is necessary about housing privatization and urban renewal.

In central Moscow, there is a concentration of housing in poor condition. The privatization law, which in Moscow transfers ownership to tenants free of charge, allows the authorities to exclude such housing (and historical buildings) from the privatization programme. However, local governments lack the liquid resources necessary to pay for renovation. Moreover, even buildings in deteriorated condition can have a high potential commercial value. The practice was therefore to move tenants out either to permanent housing elsewhere in the city or to temporary housing depending on their 'merits' (for example, tenants without resident permits would at best be rehoused permanently in the outskirts of the city). But since both building firms and local governments preferred to use flats as a resource to pay and be paid for the renovation work, renewal was synonymous with a diminution of the stock of housing available for allocation to tenants. In addition, the economic interest of the local government was to sell renovated flats at a high price rather than rent them at a low rent to the original tenants. The net effect was to displace low-income tenants from central areas and encourage high-income groups – in a word, gentrification.[5]

Given this context, the demands of the SMCs were to rehabilitate existing housing for the benefit of existing residents, to build new housing on vacant plots, to protect residents against eviction, and to allow residents to privatize their dwellings. (In each respect, illegal residents' interests were ignored.) Many SMCs conducted surveys of residents in their areas and even prepared their own redevelopment plans. What their demands have in common is a wish to preserve the existing residents' locational position, to resist their expulsion to the suburbs and to obtain the advantages of privatization. Given the confused and changing legal situation (with competing claims by different authorities regarding the ownership of property) and the economic advantage to local governments of expelling existing tenants permanently, tenants were highly distrustful of offers of 'temporary' housing. The SMCs thus came to be sharply opposed to local governments, in complete contrast to their origins as virtual 'arms' of local government.

This picture of opposition needs qualification in one respect. In a small number of areas, a more co-operative relationship has developed between SMCs and administrations, based on reciprocal benefits. The SMCs reported to the local administration on flats becoming empty and on the illegal renting out of flats and other spaces. They also helped the administration to persuade tenants to move out while their flats were renovated. In return, the SMCs were given influence over the allocation of flats in their neighbourhood,[6] including no doubt the allocation of flats to SMC activists.[7] The reason for these cases of co-operation between SMCs and local administrations is not clear. They occurred in central areas rather than in the suburbs, where there were fewer grounds for conflict between residents and authorities, since cases of restriction on privatization for urban renewal reasons were rare.

To sum up, neighbourhood SMCs were initially officially sponsored service-providing bodies which had aspects both of a neighbourhood level of administration and of a traditional mass-participation organization. They served as springboards for activists wishing to become councillors or officials, but it is likely that this was primarily beneficial to them as individuals rather than to the Communist Party. However, as the privatization process developed and as many central Moscow residents saw that they were being excluded from it and/or risked expulsion to the periphery of the city, SMCs became demand-making groups which entered into conflict with local administrations. In terms of our categories, they developed towards being social movements, since their demands were in direct opposition to the logic of local government renewal policy.

Housing partnerships

A second type of citizen organization in the housing field is the housing partnership. By 1993, there were estimated to be up to 500 in Moscow.

This type of organization is a direct response to the housing privatization process. Under the housing privatization law, local governments have a right to transfer ownership of flats to their tenants subject to the exceptions mentioned previously. The concept of a housing partnership is of a group of tenants who seek to privatize their flats but in addition seek to become owners of the commercial space (such as shops, offices, etc.) in their blocks. This would entitle them to obtain the rents from letting such space.

There is a contrast between Moscow and Budapest regarding the situation of retail space under state socialism. In Hungary, shops could be leased to individuals and were generally seen as separate from the flats in a residential block. With a few exceptions, residents in Budapest have not therefore shown an interest in purchasing shop space. (In 1993, tenants of retail space were allowed to buy it.) In Moscow, by contrast, shops were not leased to individuals and appear to be conceived of by residents as an integral part of the residential block. In particular, their potential commercial value (for example, as a source of rents) makes them an obvious target for privatization by tenants.

Housing partnerships thus have two types of activity. Externally they press for the right to privatize the whole block, including commercial space. Internally they seek to form an economic unit in which all hope to benefit economically from success in achieving their demands. There is an obvious link with 'self-management' since, if such a scheme is to work, flat owners must co-operate in their mutual economic interest.

In addition to housing privatization, a further context for the rise of housing partnerships is the collapse of state funding for housing maintenance and house building. This forces residents back onto their own resources and those which they feel are accessible, namely revenues from commercial space.

Housing partnerships are making a demand which is in direct conflict with local government interests. Local governments are experiencing an economic crisis. Traditionally they have relied on central grants and on taxes on enterprises. As enterprises cut their production levels or go bankrupt, they cease to be a reliable source of tax revenues. Taxes on households have not been levied in the past and, given the decline in living standards, they are not a politically viable source of income. As a result, the sale and leasing of real estate (whether land or buildings – residential, industrial or commercial) becomes a highly attractive concept for local government – especially when hard currency is involved. Hence housing partnerships are demanding control of the very asset which is most important to the economic survival of local governments, namely commercially attractive property.

Housing partnerships have used unconventional methods in pursuit of their objectives and can be placed in the category of social movements. However, they should not be seen as movements of the underprivileged. It is difficult to be categorical about this, since we did not survey a representative sample of housing partnerships, but our interview data suggests they are formed by highly educated people, sometimes with some entrepreneurial involvement, and are in potentially valuable residential blocks.

By 1993, the majority of housing partnerships had not succeeded in their goals. Our interviews with local government officials revealed attitudes ranging from total opposition to compromise (such as a willingness to share income from renting commercial space). There was some suggestion in 1992–3 that the local government stance had become more co-operative towards housing partnerships. However, two cases of provisional success can be mentioned.

The first housing partnership to be created was Our House in Solyanka Street. It was founded in early 1990 by a couple who ran a theatre in a run-down block in central Moscow. The stimulus for its formation was urban renewal, which threatened to lead to the expulsion of existing tenants and users of commercial space (such as the theatre). Although the housing partnership embraced many of the tenants, it was clearly led strongly by the theatre owners. Initially the resources of Our House were those of the founders (and members). Later the group also obtained rents from letting commercial space. In addition, the wife of the couple was elected as a local councillor in 1990 – though as for most councillors obstacles were placed in her way by the local administration.

The Our House group was actively involved in struggles on two fronts: internal and external. Within the block, rehabilitation work was started by a state building firm. This prompted Our House to make representations to the city authorities. In June 1991, the vice-mayor of Moscow gave the group a 25-year lease on the block. But this lease was not recognized by the rehabilitation agency, which refused to stop work. Our House therefore hired a private security firm, which blocked access to the building workers for 20 days. In August 1991, the state building organization persuaded the mayor of Moscow to overturn the previous decision as 'illegal'. When some new tenants arrived to occupy their flats, the tenants blocked the entrance and a violent situation occurred. The result was that most if not all the flats were allocated to tenants approved by Our House rather than those with 'permits issued by the now non-existent

Kalininsky district executive committee'. Whether Our House is a permanent success depends on legal processes which in 1993 were still pending.[8]

The second provisionally successful example of a housing partnership is Domostroi (Housebuilding), which was formed in April 1990 by a group of families who had previously belonged to an organization of large families waiting for flats. Starting on 16 April 1990, they carried out a 60-day sit-in at Kievsky district council, demanding that an incomplete block of luxury flats being built for Communist Party central committee officials be transferred from the city council to the district council. This sit-in started just after the local elections and just before the first session of the city council, and was successful in achieving the transfer they wanted. The group considers that this 'wave of democracy' period was important to their success.

The group's initial aim was to get work on the block completed and secure the allocation of the 58 flats for their members. Transfer of the block to the district council was thus a first step towards their goal. The group kept guard on the block and did some minor building work themselves, but initially failed to persuade the district council to contract builders to complete work on the block.

In April 1991, with the idea of housing privatization spreading, Domostroi leaders read a newspaper article about Our House and decided to create a limited company, with the intention of forming a housing partnership when (and if) they moved in to the block. Registration of this company allowed them to gain access to the funds of the organization of large families they previously belonged to.

Within the district, there was strong opposition to Domostroi. Local residents and the Arbat SMC preferred a more 'social' solution, namely to sell the luxury block and use the proceeds to build four standard blocks. Domostroi responded by stressing that, as large families, they needed large flats. They also promised to provide facilities for children in the neighbourhood once the block was completed. But this offer failed to win over the public.

Meanwhile the central prefecture (now theoretically owner of the building) was reported to be offering the block for sale. In the end, in October 1992, the district authority allocated the block to Domostroi, together with 30 million rubles, and arranged the finance of the completion of the building by two banks linked to the authority. In exchange, the council and two banks would obtain some of the flats. The precise reasons for this change of policy are not clear. However, by investing a relatively limited sum, the authority would gain control of flats with a much greater value, which it could sell or let.

In mid-1993, building work was going ahead but the group was fearful that, as completion neared, vultures would descend and seize the long-awaited flats. For example, the mayor of Moscow still had designs on the block. According to the leader of Domostroi, 'The Mayor's office doesn't recognize the [district] executive committee. They consider it non-existent. In the meantime, the executive committee is alive and taking decisions. The district council is also alive and also takes decisions' (interview, May 1993). Clearly both Domostroi and the mayor are interpreting the legal situation in ways favourable to themselves. The divergence of their interpretations makes clear how contested is the jurisdiction of different authorities with claims over real estate. Given this confusion, only the publicity surrounding the case gives Domostroi any confidence that they will eventually achieve their aim of owning flats in the block.

Domostroi can thus be seen as provisionally successful in its goals but as facing a very vulnerable period once the flats are finished. There is some evidence that members of the group are moderately well-off. They can thus be seen as a relatively advantaged group seeking to maintain its advantages. Their use of dramatic methods (a threatened hunger strike, as well as a sit-in) indicates that social movements are not necessarily the creation of the oppressed.

Budapest

Outlines are now presented of three organizations in Budapest: the homelessness movement, the Tenants Association, and Green Future, a local environmental movement.

The homelessness movement

The issue of homelessness emerged in 1989/90 in Budapest (Györi, 1991).[9] The origin of the mobilization lay in a protest against rent increases in council-owned workers' hostels in Budapest in autumn 1988. One of the residents contacted the media and the newly formed independent trade union. As a result, a sociologist who belonged to the trade union and who specialized in homelessness wrote to the council in protest and used his contacts with the media to draw attention to the issue – the journalists involved took risks in publicizing the issue. Support and expertise were also drawn from members of the Family Help Service, a small inner-city organization supported financially by the local authority.

In January 1989, negotiations were held between hostel movement representatives and supporters and the council, but the council refused to rescind the rent increases. The movement then decided to re-form itself into the Social Committee for the Homeless (SCH). The emphasis on 'for' is crucial, since the body was explicitly set up as an advisory and lobbying one, and homeless people who wanted to join were not allowed to. By February 1989 the SCH was meeting every fortnight. It gained a lot of media sympathy for the homeless, whose number was increasing, and considers it achieved improved attitudes in hostels and less police harassment of the homeless, and helped get more hostel provision for the homeless. The SCH also became mediators between demonstrating homeless people and the council.

The SCH illustrates several key points: it was led by intellectuals with an expertise in the field; it was a social movement which used demonstrations and petitions; it was a movement *for* rather than *of* its target group; it was ready to discuss with the council (and even took on a mediating role) rather than taking an oppositional stance; and finally it achieved results (helped by the wider changes in 1989, as the old regime declined and citizen initiatives expanded).

The Tenants Association

The Tenants Association shows many similar features. It was launched in September 1988, prior to the passing of the 1989 act allowing the formation of associations. The first members were all personal contacts of the journalist who became its first secretary.

Its initial aim was to defend tenants against the local council real-estate maintenance organizations (IKV), which are responsible for the repair of state flats. The main complaint against these organizations concerned the slowness and poor quality of their work (Hegedus et al., 1994). The government supported the association's criticisms of the IKV. In 1988, tenants took over responsibility for repairs within the flat, but the IKV remained in charge of external repairs. This allowed councils to reduce their expenditure on flats. The ambiguous position of state bodies in a transition is seen by the fact that the (old) Budapest city council, which was formally responsible for the IKV, gave the association 2 million forints (£15,000) in 1990, which allowed it to set up 14 district offices as well as branches in other cities. Individual advice was provided through these offices.

The aims of the association later broadened as housing privatization spread. As early as 1969, councils were given the right to sell flats, but in practice could make little use of it. In 1989, restrictions were eased and the availability of large discounts made purchase an attractive option for those tenants who occupied a good-quality, reasonably maintained flat and who could afford to buy it. As a result, by spring 1993 the figure of purchasers of state flats rose sharply to reach 30.2 per cent of all households in the city (Pickvance, 1994).

For the Tenants Association this posed two issues. First, tenants needed advice on whether their flat was worth buying – this required careful examination of the contract prepared by the local government as well as knowledge of the condition of the building. Tenants wanted to know whether they were acquiring an asset or a liability. To meet these needs, the association provides legal advice to tenants in exchange for a small fee (£1). Tenants who receive advice become 'members' of the association.

The second issue posed by privatization was the threat that, as tenants became owners, the recruitment base of the Tenants Association would gradually disappear. The association therefore changed its title to embrace flat owners as well as tenants.

In addition to its work dealing with individual tenants' problems about repairs or privatization, the Tenants Association central office has also sought to influence national housing policy. It was consulted by the ministry of social affairs in the 1992–3 period about plans for housing reforms, and was paid for this advice. The association also received a grant from parliament.

However, there is evidence that the association may have been co-opted. The association's secretary was keen to have good relations with the government in order to influence housing policy, and to obtain material support for the association. This led the association's central level to concern itself more with changes in the conditions of privatization (the subject of the policy being elaborated in 1992–3) than with the situation of those who continued to be tenants, that is, those who could not afford to buy their flat. This had a divisive effect on the membership. In addition, the secretary took control of contact with the media in order to protect his position vis-à-vis the government, which led to criticisms that he had ceased to represent members' interests. Finally, when responsibility for housing policy formation was transferred from the ministry of social affairs to the ministry of the interior, the Tenants Association lost its influence on government, since its contacts were with the former ministry.

To return to the earlier conceptual discussion, the Tenants Association does not have the characteristics of a social movement. At least until 1993, it combined the provision of a service to clients with pressure on government. It did not engage in mass action using unconventional methods. It was ready to co-operate with and possibly be co-opted by government. The homeless mobilization, on the other hand, was shorter-lived and did involve some mass action. But like the Tenants Association, it was ready to sit down with government to discuss solutions.

From 1988, Budapest thus witnessed citizen organizations in a new sphere, housing, as happened slightly later in Moscow. The case of an environmental group is now examined.

Green Future

In contrast to the last two groups is a local environmental group, Green Future.[10] This is based in an industrial suburb on the southern edge of Budapest which is the location of Metallochemia, a metal-processing plant. The existence of lead pollution caused by the plant was known in the 1970s and attempts were made by local people to get the plant closed, but without success.

The origins of Green Future lie in a coming together of three groupings. In 1989, local intellectuals, doctors and employees of a local community centre concerned with residents' health problems formed a local 'social environmental council' following a public meeting about environment and health. This council then linked up with the 'M0 group' (opposed to a motorway ring which would cut through the district) and an environmental group linked to the local branch of the HDF (the largest party in the governing coalition nationally from 1990 to 1994) to form Green Future, which was registered in February 1990.

In 1989, like the Danube Circle, the movement attracted a lot of opponents of the regime, but by 1990 they had mostly left. By late 1991, the movement had 60 members including 8–10 main activists. However, it has a larger support base and its actions have attracted 500–1,500 people. Initially Green Future relied on the resources of the community centre (office, meeting hall, phones, computer). However, it later applied to the local council[11] for a grant to enable it to operate more effectively and pay two full-time employees. The council was only willing to agree on condition that Green Future gave up its autonomy, a condition it rejected. The activist-employees of the community centre were sacked and Green Future was prevented from using the centre, making life more difficult for it. Its other resources are from the George Bush Foundation, the Parliamentary Environment Committee, and membership fees (a very small proportion). (In late 1991, the group had 4 million forints – £30,000.)

The movement has directed its demands to the local council and the national government (especially the health and environment ministries). In May 1990, the group held a protest march and handed a 3,000–4,000-signature petition to the local council, listing 22 complaints about the environmental situation in the area. It also wrote to the prime minister asking for the area to be declared a disaster area. It has used both public and behind-the-scenes approaches.

The success of Green Future has been mixed. First, its demand for the closure of the Metallochemia plant has been successful. However, this may not be entirely due to its campaigns to get the local council to act. The owners of the plant (who also owned a similar plant in East Germany) may have had economic reasons for not resisting the pressure for closure. Second, the demand for closure was accompanied by further demands including removal of polluted soil from inside and outside the plant, rehabilitation of the plant, and compensation for those affected by the pollution. These demands (like the demand to divert the M0 motorway – which failed) go beyond the competence of the local authority and would require large spending by central government.

The government set up an inter-ministerial committee to enquire into the pollution problems of the area. This is a tribute to the influence of the movement (including its president, who was elected as HDF MP for the area in 1990), since there are numerous other polluted areas about which no such committee has been set up. The committee funded a Dutch investigation into pollution levels and held a competition for solutions. This was won by a proposal to make the plant a storage place for industrially polluted solids (*sic*) which would be encased in concrete. However, no large-scale funds have been promised, and the committee can be seen as a way of dealing with the problem at low cost. In 1993, the local MP was moved from the parliamentary environment committee to its cultural committee.

Green Future has lost some momentum since 1991. This is mainly due to the scale of the goals it has adopted and the resulting conflicts over how they are to be achieved. These conflicts centre on whether to co-operate with local government or not. Green Future's earlier rejection of local government grants because of the strings attached has now been replaced by a more co-operative relationship. But this has been achieved at the expense of internal division and the departure of those who rejected co-operation. The movement has decided that it cannot be the plaintiff in a law suit against the plant's owners and government for compensation for environmental damage. It therefore agreed that the local government (a Free Democrat–Young Democrat coalition) should take it on. It did so, and in March 1993 launched a 5.6-billion Forint (£40-million) claim for compensation.

The potential economic and political advantages of this to the local government are clear.

Green Future is an example of a social movement which advances challenging demands and adopts unconventional as well as conventional methods. Its goals are more concerned with individual health than with a 'deep green' demand for a sustainable economy.

EXPLAINING THE DEVELOPMENT OF HOUSING AND ENVIRONMENTAL MOVEMENTS IN THE POST-SOCIALIST CITY

Having outlined some examples of environmental and housing movements in Budapest and Moscow since 1989/90, we now examine some of the competing explanations. They concern the effect of regime transition and the development of political parties, the election of activists as councillors and MPs and their movement into official posts, administrative reorganization, the availability of resources to citizen organizations, and changes in state responsiveness. The range of theories in this area is considerable and no claim to comprehensiveness is made here.

Regime transition and the development of political parties

Previous research on the 'democratic transition' in authoritarian regimes has shown that four periods can be distinguished:

1   a period of low or nil social movement activity (corresponding to an effective authoritarian regime);
2   a period of mushrooming of social movements in 'non-political' spheres (such as the environment, urban) as the regime's grip on power starts to weaken;
3   a period of decline in social movements as political parties are tolerated;
4   a period of 'normal' moderate social movement activity (Pickvance, 1985, 1995b).

This pattern has been observed in southern Europe (Castells, 1983; Gaspar, 1984), in Latin America (Mainwaring and Viola, 1984) and in South-East Asia (Castells et al., 1990). Although it fits numerous examples of regime transition, this does not imply that all societies converge to a level of social movement activity which is normal for *all* democratic societies. There is a considerable literature which demonstrates persistent divergences in social movement activity in democratic societies due to differences in the openness of political institutions, what Kitschelt (1986) calls their 'political capacity', the acceptance of movement demands by political parties, etc. (see Kriesi et al., 1992; Rootes, 1992; Pickvance, 1995a).

In applying this hypothesis to Hungary and Russia, one is immediately struck by the difference in conditions surrounding the transition.

In the case of Hungary, a stable set of political parties was in place by 1990 and has remained. The main party attractive to activists was the Alliance of Free Democrats (AFD), which formed in November 1988. Its support was drawn from the democratic opposition which was the focus of samizdat activity and, as described earlier, played a large part in the success of the Danube Circle. The suspension of the Danube dam in May 1989 and the subsequent decline in Danube Circle activity coincided with the run-up to the first free general elections in spring 1990. Although the AFD formed part of the opposition in national government, it won control of almost all district councils in Budapest at the local elections later in 1990. Hence its potential impact in drawing off movement activists was considerable.

In Russia, on the other hand, the prospect of the first free general elections (in April 1989) and local elections (in March 1990) did not stimulate the creation of stable parties. Rather, candidates stood either as individuals or under the names of groupings which proved ephemeral. The lack of party organization was crucial to the subsequent ineffective functioning of all elected bodies (McAuley, 1992).

It is undoubtedly the case that the formation of stable political parties in Hungary provided an alternative channel for activists and contributed to the decline of social movement activity from its peak level. However, it cannot be ruled out that the non-crystallization of parties in Moscow had the same effect, since it is likely that the short-lived electoral groupings formed at election time also absorbed some activists.

The election of activists as MPs and local councillors

The election of activists as MPs and local councillors is hypothesized to have two effects: a negative effect of depriving movements of leaders and a positive one of helping them achieve their goals as their demands are carried into the institutional arena.

We have no systematic data on the extent of such trajectories.

However, there are numerous examples. They include the subsequent mayor of Budapest, the current minister of the environment, and the president of the group Green Future, who became an HDF MP. In Moscow, as mentioned earlier, numerous neighbourhood SMC activists became MPs or local councillors.

Likewise, many activists have taken up employment in local or central government. In Hungary, the AFD is a party of urban intellectuals and has 'enough experts for three governments' (Lengyel, 1992: 38). Many of these were drawn into government. Similarly, our interviews in Moscow revealed many cases of activists in SMCs taking up jobs in government.

Turning to the question of whether ex-activists advance the cause of movements once in elected or official posts, our evidence suggests that on the whole they do not. Szirmai (1995), summarizing the situation in Hungary, writes that:

> many had advanced to positions of power from various movements ... after the transition. This has led many to think that the environmental issue is in safe hands, as it is 'their people', those with whom they protested against environmental threats and for a new civil society, who are represented in power, in the Ministry of Environment, the [Budapest] local government, the opposition parties in Parliament, the environmental committee in Parliament.

In fact Szirmai argues that such ex-activists often provided support on an individual basis but were absorbed into structures which had other priorities and over which they had little influence. Hence the frequent perception among continuing activists that their former co-activists had abandoned their ideals. In Moscow a similar comment is justified, but the situation there is different due to the drastic reorganization which curtailed the power of elected representatives, as explained below. In brief, it would appear that, whatever the ideals of former activists, they are unable to bring about rapid changes in structures which have other priorities and great inertia and where financial constraints are very tight.

Administrative organization

The third way in which the post-socialist city may be expected to shape housing and environmental movements is through changes in administrative organization. The model is that of a centralized state socialist administration giving way to a decentralized one in which there are more openings for external groups to press their demands. The situation in this respect is totally different in Budapest and Moscow.

In Budapest, the former centralized structure was replaced by a weak city government and 22 district governments. This was a deliberate response to the belief that 'redistribution by central authority creates inequality' (Rév in Ladányi, 1992). It underestimated the inequality which could arise through decentralization, as can be seen in the US experience of local government (Ladányi, 1992).

The success of the AFD in the autumn 1990 local elections in Budapest partly reflected the relative concentration of support for the party in the capital, and was partly due to public dissatisfaction with the first six months' performance by the national government. In principle, the success of the AFD should have helped citizen organizations to have an influence on policy. It is difficult to be categorical about whether this effect occurred. On the one hand, AFD councils were the natural allies of citizen groups. On the other hand, environmental issues had a low priority and, as shown, some citizen housing organizations quickly took on a service-providing role. Some interviewees even argued that the old, centralized Budapest city council had more resources and acted as a magnet for demand making, whereas decentralization had the effect of fragmenting the efforts of citizen movements.

In the case of Moscow, the March 1990 local elections were fought within an unchanged local government structure: a city government and 33 district governments. Previously this had operated in a centralized way, since the district governments were tightly controlled by the Communist Party apparatus. But events were to show that this apparently decentralized structure (compared with the pre-1990 Budapest one) did not have the expected benefits for movements.

The key issue was not the decentralization of powers alone but how open the district local governments were to movement demands. The newly elected 'democratic' district councillors in March 1990 were keen to show that they could change the way decisions were made. They immediately became enmeshed in battles about procedures and competences (especially the division of powers between city and district governments), as well as the expected conflicts over political issues and between the mayor's clique and ordinary councillors. This was a period in which new councillors' hopes were high but where they were hampered by their inexperience (Boyce, 1993) or lack of party discipline (McAuley, 1992). After an initial 'democratic' period where the new councillors achieved some success, there followed a tightening of control by the city government and by the officials over elected members (Fish, 1991). This culminated in autumn 1991 in the abolition by the city government of the 33 district councils and the creation of 10 prefectures under its direct control (Campbell, 1992). This eliminated challenges to the city's powers, weakened the political forces influential at the district level, gave the city control over the housing and other real estate owned by the districts, and strengthened the (directly elected) mayor of Moscow's position against elected councillors on the city council.

It would be wrong to treat the conflict between city and district governments in isolation from the wider changes in the Soviet Union in 1990/1 leading to its break-up. The city government was engaged in simultaneous conflict with the republican government, and its drastic action vis-à-vis the district councils can be seen as an attempt to solidify its own position in this higher-level conflict. At the same time, as Communist Party structures lost their efficacy, a struggle for control of all resources was taking place (McAuley, 1992), and the elimination of opposition from district governments and the appropriation of their resources were part of this process. But the city council's success was short-lived, since it was itself abolished by presidential decree in October 1993 following the storming of the White House (parliament) and as part of a shift towards a more presidential regime.

The effect of these conflicts and reorganizations was to shift resources away from district councils and hence reduce their capacity to satisfy movement demands, and to create uncertainty among activists about the precise locus of responsibility. The overall effect was demobilizing. The 'political capacity' of district local governments was weak and declining, and until the tightening-up period, a lot of democratic councillors' efforts were devoted to procedural and organizational issues. In brief, the context of protest movements became increasingly negative over time – in contrast to the situation described in Budapest. However, as will be seen, this negative context was not sufficient to discourage all movement activity in Moscow.

Resource availability

The fourth influence on social movement development is the availability of resources. The hypothesis is that, whereas under state socialism those non-official citizen organizations which did exist, and which were repressed or at best (in the 1980s) tolerated, were forced to rely on members' resources, after state socialism new resource channels open up facilitating social movement development.

The term 'resource' is a wide one. It refers both to assets possessed by members of a group and to those held outside it which can be reached through individuals' work and other roles. Resources thus range from the time, energy, commitment and expertise of members to access to equipment, office space and sympathetic media attention. The focus here is on finance, but this is not to deny the relevance of other resources such as office facilities, whose loss, as we saw in the case of Green Future, can weaken a group.

In Budapest, we encountered a wide range of financial resources. Central and local government grants, support from charitable foundations (such as Soros, which also made a mass purchase of photocopiers in the mid-1980s), and international awards (the Right Livelihood award) are mostly obtained via competition. In addition, the production of periodicals (and sale of advertising), membership fees, and support from the media and quangos (such as road-safety promotion agencies) were also relied on. The availability of these resources obviously varies according to the organization. Nationwide citizen organizations are favoured by central government. Environmental groups were successful in attracting grants from health, safety, public transport and environmental agencies, since the groups could be seen as aiding the aims of these agencies. Housing movements had fewer sources of help.

On the one hand, then, a considerable range of resources is now available which, together with media support, are important to movement development. However, there is no cut-off point in 1989/90, as the hypothesis suggests. In the 1980s and especially the period from 1985, there was a growth in sources of financial support for social movements. And around 1988/9, we came across a number of instances of government provision of financial support to movements that were moderate in their demands.

In Moscow as in Budapest, there was no sharp difference on either side of 1989/90, but the availability of resources to social movements in Moscow is much less, as has been noted by previous writers (Butterfield and Sedaitis, 1991; Yanitsky, 1993). Scientific expertise is as available as in Budapest but grants from government and charities are poorly developed. (International links provide a little support.) This means that movements are more dependent on their internal resources, which in turn means either that they find it difficult to develop at all, or that they need to rely on commercial activity too.

This is one reason why housing partnerships and neighbourhood SMCs relied on rents. Lastly, media interest was much less in Moscow than in Budapest.

In brief, the contrasts between post-socialist Moscow and Budapest are as striking in respect of resource availability as they are concerning political party development and governmental organization.

State responsiveness

This leads us to the fifth and final influence on social movement development: state responsiveness. This can vary from the strongly negative (repression) through overt manipulation (setting up rival organizations, refusing information or meetings with representatives) and co-optation to co-operation (granting movement demands, supporting co-production organizations). To some extent such issues have been touched on before, as when discussing the provision of grants, but state responsiveness is such a key concept that it merits separate treatment.

State responsiveness influences the likelihood of success of a movement with given demands, but also acts as an incentive or deterrent to the formation of new movements. In part, it is structural, relating to historical traditions of state–citizen relations, and in part conjunctural, due to the economic and political conditions of the moment. Although it can be hypothesized that, in the post-socialist city, state authorities are more responsive than before to movement demands, the evidence from Budapest and Moscow does not seem to conform to such a simple pattern.

In Hungary, we encountered some evidence of good relations between authorities and citizen organizations. Weak ministries (like that for the environment) welcome external pressure to strengthen their own position. The Danube Circle and Tenants Association had both received funding from central departments in exchange for consultancy. This can be seen either as a 'favourable response' or as co-optation (implying that the movements' demands were moderated), as we argued in the case of the Tenants Association. Other groups such as the homeless movement had benefited from grants for 'pilot professional projects' given by the ministry of social welfare, through competitions. There was also a disposition on the part of the government to reach compromises with social movements, as in the case of the homeless movement.

On the other hand, there is also evidence of conflict. Green Future's application to the district council for a grant to allow it to expand its operations was rejected. And another environmental group, a coalition called the Air Group, sees the environment ministry as envious of the group's environmental information and advice service, while the ministry criticizes it for demanding funding to train experts which will rival its own (Szirmai, 1996). An activist of the Air Group even argued that the ministry of transport was more responsive in the past: 'They asked us what we intended to do, they obeyed at once and did something, in order to avoid negative publicity . . . they came and paid a visit regularly . . . and were very anxious to justify themselves. Similar eagerness is unimaginable today' (Szirmai, 1996). This comparison is in fact with the immediate past when, in the 1988/9 period, state authorities were particularly attentive to demands from local groups. (One interviewee referred to it as an 'anarchic period'.) This was not characteristic of state socialism but was specific to the final period of weakening authority, when government was taking some quite novel steps towards groups in 'civil society'. This reflected the insecurity of the authorities as the Communist Party lost its previous monopoly of power.

In brief, in the last year or two of state socialism in Hungary, state responsiveness was particularly high, relatively speaking. After 1989/90, there was continued evidence of a willingness to meet protest groups and reach a compromise in some cases, though in others movement demands were rejected.

In Moscow, the situation is very different. State responsiveness is on the whole lower and movement demands are far more likely to be rejected than in Budapest. This also creates disincentives to movement formation, but does not act to discourage movements totally.

The reluctance to compromise is related to a more authoritarian tradition of state–citizen relations. Different authors link this to the length of communist rule or even to a pre-1917 authoritarian tradition. In addition to this structural factor, conjunctural factors are also relevant. As explained earlier, because of the coincidence of the transition with the collapse of the Soviet Union and the conflicts between levels of government over their jurisdictions, state institutions were fighting for their own survival. Movement demands were seen as an unwanted source of additional pressure. In the rare cases where movements achieved success, this was provisional, or else was linked to a particular political conjuncture, such as the period immediately around the first free local elections. In general, the evidence considered here would suggest that state responsiveness in Moscow today is low and creates a larger hurdle for movements to overcome than in Budapest.

In this section, five conditions have been considered which are hypothesized to characterize the post-socialist city and to influence movement development. The most striking finding is that only one of these conditions (the absorption of activists into elected bodies and official posts) proved to be present in both cities. The other four – the development of stable political parties, administrative decentralization, greater resource availability for movements, and greater state responsiveness – were shown to be present in Budapest but not in Moscow. It is these four features, therefore, which are potential contextual explanations of differences in the level of social movement activity in the two cities. However, only the last three are hypothesized to favour such activity: the development of political parties acts as a counter-magnet to activists. Ideally, to test these hypotheses, there would be needed (1) some indication of the relative weights of each contextual feature and (b) time-series data on social movement activity. The former is lacking, and on the latter it appears that environmental movement participation in both cities has followed the four-phase model identified earlier and is now in a period of low to moderate activity. Housing movement activity is undoubtedly higher in Moscow than in Budapest, but has started so recently that the four-phase pattern is not applicable.

Since our contention is that the Moscow context is in all but one respect less favourable to citizen organization than that of Budapest, the high level of housing partnership and neighbourhood self-management-association activity in Moscow needs explanation. In my view, the key to this lies in the stakes associated with housing privatization. Those who take part in these two types of housing organization are (1) those who have been excluded from the housing privatization process due to the run-down nature and/or potential high commercial value of their blocks, and (2) those who are seeking to obtain a rent income from commercial space in their apartment buildings. In both cases, the potential gains are sufficient to sustain participation in housing movements despite the hostile political context. Moreover, since these gains will only be realized if a changed decision is made about the whole block, the need for collective action (as opposed to approaches by individual tenants to officials) is obvious. This demonstrates the need to pay attention to participants' motivation as well as contextual influences in understanding social movement activity. The context creates a structure of incentives to participation but does not determine it. (A parallel point has been made in respect of altruistic motivation in sustaining participation in movements like CND when the prospects of success were low.)

In brief, the five contextual features discussed in this section go a considerable way towards explaining the level of citizen activity in the environmental and housing fields, but it would require a comprehensive over-time study to resolve their precise influence, and that of participants' motivation.

CONCLUSION

This chapter has tried to give a sense of environmental and housing movements and the conditions affecting them in two very different post-socialist cities.

Citizen organizations before 1980 almost all took the form of officially sponsored organizations, but some of them developed an element of autonomy. There is a danger of exaggerating this element in order to claim continuity between past and present organizations; but that it existed at all is interesting. The 1980s, however, saw an increase of local protest in the environmental sphere in both Russia and Hungary (but especially in the latter), which occurred independently of official citizen organizations. Some of these protests fall into our category of social movement. However, in the sphere of housing, discontent took individual rather than collective form.

With the transition from communist regimes, environmental action declined (but did not disappear), while housing became a focus for activism for the first time. The link between housing activism and new stakes, such as housing privatization (and exclusion from it) and homelessness, is very clear. There has been no attempt here to give any quantitative index of the extent of citizen organization in the two fields. But the discussion in the previous section has sought to capture the combined influence of contextual features and participant motivation on citizen organization.

A first conclusion is therefore that the 'post-socialist city' does not imply a common pattern of social movement activity. The post-socialist city is not a homogeneous reality. There are big variations between the two cities studied. This is partly because they represented different variants of state socialism, and partly because transition processes in the two countries have differed greatly. It should not therefore be surprising that they have witnessed different patterns of citizen activism. Capitalist cities also exhibit persistent divergences due to their distinctive political, social and economic structures.

A second conclusion is that, in thinking about the political aspects of the transition process, the obvious assumption that a system closed to citizen inputs was replaced by one open to citizen inputs is misleading. The argument here is that, in the final pre-transition phase of uncertainty and hesitation, when the authorities are themselves divided, they could prove unusually open to demands from civil society. We observed this in Budapest in the late 1980s and in Moscow in 1990, times which were referred to as 'anarchic periods' and 'waves of democracy' respectively. These moments coincide with periods of uncertainty, when authorities lose confidence and depart from their scripts in order to try to consolidate their power positions. Conversely, the 'openness' of post-socialist authorities cannot be taken for granted.

Finally, we would conclude that if the concept of transition entails a model of radical change it is misleading, since it prejudges the outcome of an analysis. The choice of cases in the present chapter has made this particularly clear. As it has shown, the starting points and end points of change in the fields of social movement development and state response are different in the two cases studied. It has also been shown that there are some continuities across the transition. Reforms in the 1980s led to a tilt in state–citizen relations before the 1989/90 transition. Only a model which allows for a mix of degrees of change in different spheres is compatible with the conclusion drawn here, namely that in two 'cities after socialism' housing and environment movement development take very different courses.

NOTES

1   For simplicity 'Russia' is used to refer to the Russian Republic of the USSR up to 1991 as well as to independent Russia.

2   The very low rents encouraged this view. They did not of course mean that housing cost almost nothing to produce, but that state housing production was financed out of undistributed surpluses rather than out of personal disposable income. The counterpart of apparently cheap housing was therefore lower personal incomes (see the discussion of Bessonova's ideas by Andrusz, 1990).

3   The following paragraphs are based on Fleischer (1993), Galambos (1993) and Szirmai (1996). Although the Danube Circle continued into the 1990s, it is described here as a movement of the 1980s, since this was the period of its greatest influence.

4   This section is based on research by Yelena Shomina, who collaborated in the ESRC research project 'Environmental and housing movements in Hungary, Estonia and Russia' carried out at the University of Kent at Canterbury from 1991 to 1994 by C. Pickvance, N. Manning, K. Pickvance and S. Klimova. The reports by the five collaborators are available in Láng-Pickvance et al. (1996). The present section is based

on Shomina (1996) and on the original interviews on which that report is based. I would like to thank Nick Manning and Katy Pickvance for their stimulation and helpful comments on this paper. Responsibility for the interpretation and any errors are mine. (A list of project publications is available from the Urban and Regional Studies Unit, University of Kent, Canterbury. A monograph is also in preparation: Láng-Pickvance et al., forthcoming).

5   Local government could also convert flats to commercial space attractive to private firms.

6   Despite the centralization of flat ownership as part of the 1991 local government reforms, responsibility for most flat allocation remained with the local-level administrations.

7   Under state socialism, it was not unknown for people to try and jump the housing queue by taking jobs in housing departments or doing volunteer work in the housing sphere. This pattern has continued and has encouraged participation in local government housing committees by local councillors and co-optees. An organization calling itself the 'trade union' Muscovites was set up by a Moscow city councillor as a personal fiefdom and appears to have attracted participants who hoped (perhaps correctly) that, through sufficient volunteer work, they could improve their own housing situation.

8   The founders of Our House also operated on a wider scale. In October 1991, they registered the All-Russia Fund for the Liquidation of Communal Flats (and Promotion of Individual Flats). Its aim is to help create housing partnerships by providing legal and other advice in exchange for a 5 per cent levy on their subsequent profits. The fund is based at the Solyanka Streat building, where Our House provides office space, equipment and a salary. The fund has helped spread the idea of housing partnerships in Moscow and has created 11 branches elsewhere in Russia. Like housing partnerships, it embodies a combination of mutual support, commercial activity and political demands. It has adopted unconventional methods such as demonstrations and picketing.

9   The discussion of the homelessness movement and the Tenants Association is based on project interviews by Peter Györi and on his report (Györi and Matern, 1996).

10   This discussion is based on project interviews by Viktoria Szirmai and on her report (Szirmai, 1996).

11   Green Future has two representatives on the local council's environment committee. However, the committee has only advisory status and environmental spending does not have a high priority.

9

A New Movement in an Ideological Vacuum: Nationalism in Eastern Europe

Klaus von Beyme

Western scholars pretend to be surprised by the sudden resurgence of nationalism in Eastern Europe. It is this author's hypothesis that nationalism as an ideology was the consequence, first, of the decline of the socialist 'empire' and, second, of its multi-ethnic ideology, which disguised the factual dominance of one ethnic group. This chapter summarizes certain research on nationalism in the West and attempts to test the findings in Eastern Europe. Following this, typologies of nationalism in Eastern Europe are suggested. Indicators of nationalism are then tested against the results of a comparative survey. Finally, the chapter outlines the first steps towards a just solution to ethnic conflict in post-communist, multi-ethnic societies.

THE CONTINUITY OF NATIONALISM IN EASTERN EUROPE

Although Western Europe experienced a wave of nationalism of varying degrees of aggressiveness by what might be called 'sub-nations' during the 1970s and 1980s (Scots, Basques, Corsicans, South Tyroleans and others), none the less the new wave of nationalism in Eastern Europe which followed the collapse of state socialism in the region came as a surprise to many observers. However, this was not really a revival of nationalism, since it had never actually disappeared. Rather, national aspirations had temporarily been suppressed under Soviet dominance (Brown, 1991: 35).

Some Western politicians after 1989 welcomed the re-emergence of open nationalism in Poland and Romania, as it was considered an element of 'realism' grounded in facts rather than on the illusions of a multi-ethnic communist ideology. The new nationalism after 1989, on the other hand, was considered a dangerous ideology. Indeed, ideological obscurantism grew. 'Nation' and 'nature' were considered to be two concepts sharing a common origin, as a Russian discussant revealed during an allegedly scientific debate.

After the collapse of communism, imperial ideologies could no longer be relied upon. The three multinational federations in the region – the Soviet Union, Yugoslavia and Czechoslovakia – collapsed due to the decades-long abuse of a counterfeit federalism. The Russian intelligentsia continued to confuse, through their synonymous usage, the notions of 'Russian' and 'Soviet'. The new Slavophile ideologies had a deterrent effect on the non-Slavic nations because they prevented them from being treated equally. The traditional fixation on Russia as the 'leading' nation meant that the 'new thinking' which accompanied 'perestroika' had little to say to the non-Russian peoples (Geyer, 1989: 310). Surveys conducted after the collapse of the Soviet Union revealed that the identification of Russia with the Soviet Union was even stronger among the elites than among the average citizens, since the former apparently identify more than other social groups with the existing power structures from which they benefit (Ivanov, 1993: 64). The Russian Federation (RF) has perpetuated the problem, though on a diminished scale. For instance, the constitution of the RF adopted under President Yeltsin can hardly be thought to inspire confidence among the smaller nations when article 3 postulates that, in cases of doubt, the notions of 'Rossiiskaya Federatsiya' and 'Russia' should be considered identical.

After the demise of the old regimes in 1989, there was no ideology sufficiently strong to counter nationalism. That offered by the old intelligentsia, namely the concept of 'civil society', was unrealistic, for it failed to accept its Anglo-Saxon connotations of Locke and the federalist papers, including not only the 'citizen' but also the 'bourgeois'. In Eastern Europe this concept soon deteriorated into a new ideology which was apolitical and anti-market economy. Of greater significance than the fact that nationalism grew following the erosion of the old hierarchical power structures is that nationalism did not itself play a major role in the disintegration of the system.

Although theoreticians of totalitarianism had not foreseen that the system would collapse from the inside (as a consequence of internal contradictions), writers on nationalism, such as Carrère d'Encausse (1978), considered that the disintegrative power of national aspirations would eventually precipitate the demise of the system. However, their choice of the catalytic factor responsible for collapse was incorrect. In the final analysis, the Soviet Union broke up because the nomenklatura was incapable of solving its principal economic problems. With the exceptions of the Baltic Republics, the nationalist impulse of the sub-nations – that is, those not belonging to the dominant ethnic group – led them to abandon the Union only when the economic failure of the whole system could no longer be overlooked and local elites preferred to try their hand with their own national sovereignty.

When it did collapse, the ideologues of the independent republics frequently argued about 'exploitation by the Soviet Union'. They preferred not to take into account that some of the poorer republics had actually benefited from the Union: 'political imperialism' had as a concomitant a certain 'welfare imperialism', a notion which strengthened the case of the Slavophiles, who argued that Russia had for too long borne a close equivalent to the 'white man's burden' – one which it ought to relinquish as soon as possible. The new ideologues were not slow to notice that it was precisely some republics where nationalist sentiment and mobilization were strongest, such as Lithuania, that had developed more quickly and prospered more visibly than most of the other Union republics under the Brezhnev regime (cf. von Beyme, 1988: 170ff). In general, throughout the region, separatist movements proved in many cases to be strongest in the more prosperous parts of federations (Slovenia, Croatia, the Baltic States and the Czech lands). In other words, it seems that, in some cases, economic collapse and falling living standards gave rise to separatist movements, while in other cases, the impetus to achieve national sovereignty came from a wish by the better-off regions within federations to cease subsidizing poorer areas.

THEORETICAL APPROACHES TO NATIONALISM IN EASTERN EUROPE

Nationalism played little or no part in the basic premises of modernization theories. Both functionalism and Marxism were optimistic that growing modernization would herald the withering away of national conflicts. In contrast to this deterministic stance, the advocates of the new ethnic movements developed theories of internal colonialism, which seemed to be applicable to many East European countries. The dominant nations were accused of exploiting the periphery. With the rise of nationalism, modernization theories were in the main unable to explain why the more assimilated elites of the sub-nations suddenly turned to a militant nationalism. Theories of internal colonialism, on the other hand, failed to explain why some richer areas (the Basque country, Catalonia, South Tyrol) developed the most militant nationalism.

The growth of neo-nationalism in Eastern Europe fits into the experience of earlier democratization theories, such as that formulated by Stein Rokkan (1970: 47). Western Europe too has experienced ethnic mobilization around nationalist symbols and slogans when a certain autonomy has been given to the sub-nations as a consequence of increased democratization in the society. What Rokkan called a 'penetration crisis' – that is, when the centre of power loses control over the periphery – came to the fore when the communist nomenklatura lost control in the formerly socialist countries. A distribution crisis between the rich and poor areas of the federations explained a further disintegration of the former multinational states.

Most theoreticians of modernization, who abandoned the old optimism that modernization would in itself make nationalism an anachronism, contrived a variation of these theories which has been called *reactive nationalism*. According to some thinkers, class and ethnic conflicts accumulate more frequently in Eastern than Western Europe because, in the case of the former, the various ethnic groups have not such clearly defined territorial boundaries (Gellner, 1969; Hechter, 1975). Thus, in this view those who actively mobilize are not to be seen as undeveloped 'hillbillies', incapable of modernizing and nation-building. Members of the dominant nation have penetrated the life sphere of the sub-nation (as did the Italians in South Tyrol), and its (regional) economy has been made into an appendix of the national economy. The economic life-chances of classes and ethnic groups are distorted, making conflicts seemingly inevitable.

Reactive nationalism develops most frequently in areas where the economy is in decline. In some cases, such as in Belgium, the two major ethnic groups compete in nationalistic terms. Wallonia was once the industrial centre but later declined to a 'black country'. The Flemish-speaking parts, on the other hand, developed from being agrarian-based into the loci of modern industries. Then in the 1980s the former dominant group, the Walloons, began to feel like a suppressed minority. Nevertheless, the now dominant ethnic group, the Flemings, retained their militant, nationalist attitude since they felt culturally inferior. It is possible that the Ukraine might develop along this path.

Reactive nationalism can be linked to a model of *ethnic competition.* Modernization does not extinguish feelings of national identity. On the contrary, it is only when modernization has succeeded in overcoming family and parochial loyalties that sub-nations are able to begin discovering their identity. Ethnic mobilization is more important than is suggested by deterministic, evolutionary theories of the modernization process, which assume that history takes its inevitable course. Mobilization occurs when the pressure of the forces of modernization give rise to competition between identifiable ethnic units for jobs, housing and other benefits.

For political scientists who have an interest in actors and not only in autopoietic processes of self-development, a *resource approach* to nationalism can be most fruitful. Ethnic groups need to be of a minimum population size and possess organizational resources if they are to enter into competition with other ethnic groups (McCarthy and Zald, 1977). Although the resource theory has been developed in the study of wealthy countries, elite fractions in developed countries who have not been sufficiently absorbed by the system also organize protests over resource allocation. Such elites, drawn in part from the declassés of the old regime and in part from the membership of former dissidents, existed in the new democracies of Eastern Europe. After the collapse of the extremely centralized structures of the old system, the rise of new regional and municipal institutions served to reinforce the organizational resources of the new elites. Changes in the power structures gave rise to new opportunities for the new elites, whose demands also grew.

But resource mobilization is only one factor which explains the growth of nationalism in Eastern Europe. Competition between the former nation state and the sub-nations is a consequence of the launching of the new market society. With the collapse of the state socialist distributional system, a relentless competition for jobs, housing and life-chances aggravated the underlying ethnic conflicts. Certain preconditions have to be met before ethnic competition (Olzak and Nagel, 1986) gives rise to ethnic mobilization, one of the most important of which is urbanization.

Socialist systems were biased in favour of the development of heavy industry, which was accompanied by rapid urban growth. Ethnic segregation in the cities was avoided. But with the new market system, segregation of ethnic groups has begun to grow rapidly in the larger cities, such as Moscow. The rise of bazaar capitalism has reinforced these tendencies. Only the underdeveloped housing market has prevented this reshuffling of populations within the cities from becoming even more brutal than in American cities, where similar processes have been in evidence for decades.

The new market society leads to a *tertiarization of the job market*. The differentiation of services, which were totally underdeveloped in socialist countries, have aggravated competition and tension between ethnic groups. Under the socialist system only certain minorities, such as gypsies, occupied specific niches in the job market. With the collapse of socialism, other ethnic groups started to compete with the gypsies for the niches which they had secured (such as street cleansing, repair work), which led to a growth in anti-gypsy sentiment.

Systemic change in Eastern Europe has been accompanied by class differentiation, which has led to more militant ethnic mobilization. Dominant ethnicities, such as Russians and Serbs, were threatened by a relative decline in their status and, arguably, their market situation. Hitherto minorities which suffered from discrimination at least had an equal chance in the market. Jews who occupied top positions in many of the system's hierarchical structures had limited chances. After democratization, although these limitations were abolished, more competition in certain hierarchies reinforced growing anti-Semitism. The overnight transition to a market society led to an enormous emigration. Earlier theories of social deprivation regarded emigration from certain ethnic regions to be the cause of a very serious threat to ethnic balance. Yet now, small regions which are currently enjoying a boom period and, as a result, attracting immigrants are in even greater danger of experiencing ethnic conflict.

The likelihood of ethnic stress manifesting itself depends on a number of factors such as the size of the sub-nation, the strength of the language basis of an ethnic group, the relative wealth of a sub-nation, and the growth or decline of a region (Ragin, 1989: 139ff). In Eastern Europe the probability of ethnic mobilization occurring can be predicted on the basis of the presence or absence of constellations of factors:

1   A small group with a weak linguistic basis and low relative wealth normally leads to little ethnic mobilization (North Frisians in Germany, Basques in France). Some parts of Eastern Europe deviate from this norm: for instance, ethnic mobilization among the Chechens and Ingushians in the north Caucasian parts of Russia, the Gagausians in Moldova and the Abkhazians in Georgia (also in the Caucasus) led to civil war. During a period of transition, when ethnic elites are demanding the redrawing of arbitrary and artificial boundaries between territorial units, mobilization can in part be explained by the involvement and manipulation of the situation by outside forces (foreign states).

274   *Klaus von Beyme*

2   A large ethnic group with growing economic wealth but weak linguistic
     cohesion tends to respond with a kind of reactive nationalism, as
     witnessed by the Occitanians in France). In the East, the Ukrainians
     and Belorussians come close to the reactive model. The state socialist
     policies of equalization and oppression had left a mood of latent reactive
     nationalism in most areas where ethnic problems remained unsolved.
3   Major ethnic groups with relative wealth and strong linguistic cohesion
     tend to find themselves forced into ethnic competition. Examples of this
     and, in Western Europe the Alsatians in France and Basques and
     Catalans in Spain, and, in Eastern Europe, the Baltic States and the
     Slovaks.
4   Economic decline when combined with a fairly high level of develop-
     ment in the area can lead to ethnic mobilization, as in the case of
     Slovenes, Czechs, Estonians and Latvians. The conventional theory of
     development, which closely links economic growth with a declining
     pertinence of nationalism, in this case continued to have a prognostic
     value.
5   The last group is found where a former dominant group begins to
     perceive itself to be a minority, such as Russians in Kazakhstan. The
     Ukraine might be placed in this category, as might the conflict between
     Serbs and Croats.

Neither theoretical concepts nor research findings on the causes
of ethnic conflict in Western Europe adequately explain all the mani-
festations of ethnic stress which have emerged since the collapse of
socialism in Eastern Europe. A number of unique factors which have
contributed to ethnic conflict here did not play a major role in
Western Europe (cf. Offe, 1992: 26ff).

First of all, the state experienced a general crisis during the early
phase of the transformation process. It proved itself incapable of
protecting ethnic minorities and sub-nations within its borders
against attacks from the outside. With the erosion of the socialist
state, it became evident that the process of nation-building, which
had evolved over centuries in Western Europe, had never been completed in the majority of East European states. Apart from Russia and
Hungary, few ethnic groups had a continuity of statehood. If a matrix
is constructed with ethnic consciousness on one axis and continuity
of statehood on the other, Eastern Europe offers a very diversified
picture (see figure 9.1).

According to figure 9.1, long state experience combines with low
ethnic identification only in old historical systems. Sometimes a fairly
recent state, such as Belgium, shows an increasing division over
ethnic loyalties, as happened in Czechoslovakia. Some newly independent states, such as Moldova, are difficult to classify, since their
loyalties are divided. In this particular instance, Moldovan citizens
are divided on whether they want to be integrated (wholly or partly)

Ethnic consciousness

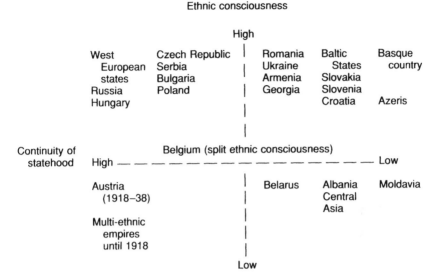

Figure 9.1 Ethnic consciousness and continuity of statehood

into Romania or to become an independent state. The indications from some surveys are that many Moldovans are, for tactical reasons, against reunification with Romania at this point in time.

The matrix in figure 9.1 also suggests that the countries in Eastern Europe form into three groups:

1 nations with long state continuity, highly developed ethnic consciousness and relative ethnic homogeneity – Russia, Poland, Czech Republic, Hungary;
2 late historical nations with low ethnic homogeneity but strong ethnic nationalist mobilization – Serbia, Croatia, Romania, Slovakia, Ukraine, Caucasia (with the exception of Armenia);
3 new nations with little experience of independent statehood and low ethnic homogeneity – Albania, Macedonia, Belarus, Baltic States, Moldavia, Central Asia.

Nations are political artifacts and grow through the grasping of political opportunities. While continuity of experience with independent statehood supports nation-building, it does not fully explain militant aspirations to national independence. Traditionally, 'astatal' groups quickly come to assert a claim to sovereign statehood when the national elites do not see any other alternative to satisfy their needs for power and co-determination. As the constitutions of the new democracies have shown, the historical factor also plays a role in nation-building even where little continuity exists. Russia and Hungary do not need prompts about their historical justification. Even Poland, despite a long period without statehood, is conscious enough of its historical identity to have no need of 'constitutional poetry'.

On the other hand, latecomers to the nation-building process need historical treaties to justify their existence. This was shown to excess in the case of Croatia. The shorter the period of independent statehood, the more strident are the invocations of a historical past. Lithuania stressed its 'foundation centuries ago'. Slovenia referred to its centuries of struggle to become an independent state. The Czech Republic perceives itself as representing continuity for the 'lands of the Bohemian crown', while Slovakia returned to the Grand Moravian Empire to find some precursor for its independence.

In Eastern Europe, such historical reminiscences are dangerous because they could lead to the raising of unjustified territorial claims. Most borders in Central and Eastern Europe are arbitrary, either because of the peace treaties drawn up in the suburbs of Paris after World War I or because of the internal dispositions of dictators such as Stalin or Tito. Virtually nowhere are ethnic claims and state borders identical with a rapidly developing ethnic consciousness. In the Czech lands, most educated people were 'constitutional patriots' who were in favour of a bi-ethnic state. Around 1991, the Slovaks switched from statehood to a separate ethnic identity, grounded in the criterion of language (Gerlich et al., 1992: 39).

Second, the borders between East European nations lack the degree of universal acceptability that attaches to borders in the West, although surveys have revealed that even in Western Europe many people preserve some irredentist feelings towards neighbouring territories. The point is that in Eastern Europe these feelings, which were much more generally and strongly held, were intensified in proportion to the arbitrariness of the shifting of borderlines during the state socialist period. The most spectacular case is certainly Khrushchev's gift of the Crimea during the tricentennial commemorations of the unification of Russia and the Ukraine. Tito was frequently criticized for his partisan drawing of the border between Croatia and Serbia in favour of his own Croat nation. There are at least 10 instances where the possibility of territorial conflict remains an open question (Hatschikjan, 1991: 213). In 1991, the Geographical Institute in Moscow estimated that out of 23 borders within the Commonwealth of Independent States (CIS), only three were not disputed.

Third, state history, religion and cultural traditions in Eastern Europe are much more fragmented than in Western Europe. The hiatus between the Greek Orthodox and Roman Catholic churches, combined with the different historical incorporations of state traditions, have divided Serbia and Croatia to such an extent that the similarities in language are of minor importance. According to the Serbian Constitution, only dialects written in the Cyrillic alphabet are recognized as being part of the Serbia ethnic group. Tito's 40 years of propaganda for a Serbo-Croatian language were futile. Although Serbs, Croats and Muslims living in that territory differ little in terms of the language which they speak, mobilized militias determine who belongs to the in-group and who is persecuted as member of an out-group.

Fourth, when the old states withered away, so did their ideologies. Since the concept of a 'civil society' was too apolitical during a nation-building phase, nationalism seemed to be the only integrative ideology which had mobilizing capability. Speeches in favour of democracy as an ideal have tended to attract few listeners, whereas a rally with a strongly nationalist flavour could mobilize thousands of citizens, as Izetbegovic once stated, full of pessimism. Nationalism not only integrated elites and masses, but also served as a means to reintegrate the divided elites of the respective countries. In parochial, traditional societies, as in Central Asia, old tribal rivalries re-emerged after the disintegration of the Soviet Union. The new nationalism in these areas could be said to be having a modernizing effect in so far as it might help to stabilize the new ethnic elite in its struggle against traditional tribal cliques.

Ethnic conflicts in Eastern Europe became increasingly more violent the more nations and ethnic groups perceived themselves in terms of victims and oppressors. The list below shows that even in this respect the picture is more complicated than in the West. The victim in one case can be the oppressor in another (cf. Offe, 1992: 8).

	Minority	Majority
Victims	Hungarians in Slovakia and Rumania, Greeks in Albania	Albanians in Kossovo
Oppressors	Serbs in Kossovo, parts of Bosnia or Croatia	Bulgarians against Turks, Estonians and Latvians against Russians via citizenship laws

INDICATORS OF NATIONALISM

Ethnic conflict in Eastern Europe is more violent than in Western Europe because more nations feel that they have claims on the territory of others. Such claims are rare in the West: Sweden hardly

Table 9.1   Survey data about nationalism (percentages), 1991

	USA	UK	FRG	GDR	Cz	Hu	Pol	Bul	Rus	Ukr	Lit
I am very patriotic	88	72	74	69	70	70	75	75	60	62	63
We should fight for our country whether it is right or wrong	55	58	31	16	28	30	47	53	42	36	39
There are parts of other countries that belong to us	–	20	43	25	39	68	60	52	22	24	46
We should restrict immigration to our country	–	79	70	70	65	68	58	38	45	31	54

Source: Times-Mirror: Center for the People and the Press (1991)

intervenes in favour of the Swedes in Finland, while Germany remains cautious in its support of autonomy for Alsatians in France. Similarly, in the West a 'patron' nation, such as Austria in the case of South Tyrol, supports negotiations for greater autonomy, in this instance within Italy. But in Eastern Europe the constitutions of many countries actually proclaim their support for their ethnic group abroad. A survey published in the *Times-Mirror* (*Times-Mirror*. Center for the People and the Press, 1991) showed that in Eastern Europe there is a widespread opinion that parts of other countries should belong to one's own country. Even in Czechoslovakia, 39 per cent of Czechs expressed such an opinion prior to the country's division (see table 9.1).

Hungary ceded much of its former territory as part of the 1919 Versailles settlement. Therefore it is not by chance that Hungarians more frequently than others display irredentist feelings towards foreign territory (see table 9.1). Even in Bulgaria, 52 per cent of the citizens interviewed expressed discontent over the territorial issue, particularly Macedonia. In Lithuania, 46 per cent of those questioned demonstrated irredentist feelings, although it is not clear what the object of their claim could be: Kaliningrad/Konigsberg? At the time of the survey, in Russia (22 per cent) and the Ukraine (24 per cent) these feelings fell below those recorded in West Germany. Poland recorded a higher score (60 per cent). On the other hand, other surveys undertaken in Poland and Germany show that only tiny minorities favour an active policy to reclaim territory. In Poland, this topic is particularly unpopular because many people are afraid that Polish claims on Belarus or the Ukraine would entail German claims on Poland. Most countries so far have followed a very cautious line, even Romania towards Moldova. Most of the former Comecon countries have signed agreements within the Conference of Security and Cooperation in Europe recognizing existing borders.

Nevertheless, people in many of the new democracies do express distinct feelings of being threatened, although not all of their fears can be explained in terms of territorial claims. Some former ex-socialist states feel threatened by each other, as in case of Bulgaria and Yugoslavia (18 per cent) and Hungary and Romania (42 per cent). However, in most other countries these perceptions of being threatened by a neighbour, which until 1991 was a member of the same defence alliance, remained below 10 per cent (*Times-Mirror* Center for the People and the Press, 1991: Qs 102, 109).

Where other subjective indicators of nationalism, such as patriotism, are used, then it transpires that most East European populations react in the same way as people in Western countries. Only the Germans in both the East and the West fell below the average. East Europeans showed much less willingness than their Anglo-Saxon counterparts to fight for their country regardless of its being right or wrong. In East Germany, only 16 per cent answered in the affirmative.

When it is a matter of measuring levels of national tolerance by testing antipathies against foreign nations and ethnic minorities within the respondent's own nation, on most scales, West Europeans do not provide good models for citizens in the new democracies. Fourteen per cent of the British and 26 per cent of German and Russian respondents displayed anti-Semitic attitudes. Only Poland (34 per cent) was clearly above the average, though there are hardly any Jews left in Poland. The most negative feelings against a minority were restricted to and focused on the gypsies, even in Spain (*Times-Mirror* Center for the People and the Press, 1991: App. Q. 64 – cf. table 9.1).

Each country proves to have its favourite enemy. In France it is the North Africans (42 per cent), in Germany, Poles (49 per cent, Turks 46 per cent). Even a group as close to the British as the Irish were perceived badly, with 21 per cent of those interviewed in the UK expressing negative feelings towards them. In Eastern Europe, the Czechs and Slovaks are the favourite enemy of the Hungarians. The Lithuanians displayed more hostile feelings towards the Poles (30 per cent) than towards the Russians (21 per cent), although according to the 1989 USSR Population Census there were more Russians (9.4 per cent) than Poles (7 per cent) living in the country. In Poland, antipathies are divided among Germans (45 per cent) and Ukrainians (41 per cent). Russians perceive the Caucasians as their favourite enemy. Considering the tensions which exist between Hungary and Romania, the fact that only one-third of Hungarians expressed hostile sentiments against Romanians may be regarded as moderate. Yet too much should not be read into these figures, since both Hungarians and Germans display high percentages of negative attitudes even against their own ethnic group who are moving back to their country of recent or distant origin.

National sympathies underwent considerable change after the collapse of communism. Until 1989, the GDR was less popular in Poland than the Federal Republic (Simiénska, 1992: 208). In 1975, the Russians were more popular amongst the Poles than the French. In 1991, the Americans (68 per cent) and the French (61 per cent) found themselves topping the popularity charts in Poland. Germany remained at the low point previously reserved for the GDR (23 per cent), and in 1990 its reputation declined to 13 per cent, a level close to that enjoyed by the Chinese, Turks and Jews.

In some East European countries, such as Poland and Hungary, survey methods were already well advanced under state socialism. Social psychologists used sophisticated Western techniques, evident in their studies on prejudice. However, verbal nationalism does not necessarily mean preparedness for nationalist action. A willingness to convert ethnic chauvinism into a support for right-wing extremist parties has hardly been studied in most of the countries.

In Western Europe, immigration became a test case for ethnic tolerance, while Eastern Europe, in this respect, is a latecomer to the league of national intolerance. Western nations recorded a higher score than East Europeans when asked whether immigration of foreign people should be stopped. An affirmative answer to this question was highest in Italy and France – far ahead of Germany (70 per cent), though Germany had almost ten times as many immigrants as Italy and France. Even though East European countries basically experience a transit migration, there is a growing perception that immigration should be brought to a halt. The Czechs (65 per cent) and Hungarians (68 per cent) were approaching Western values, and even Russia, anticipating that it will increasingly become an immigration country for Central Asia and the Caucasus, recorded 45 per cent in favour of restricting immigration. Ironically, those migrating to Russia from other republics of the former Soviet Union are predominantly Russians. Most of these instant, snapshot opinions do not yet reflect stabilized attitudes; however, growing ethnic mobilization can easily generate more permanent xenophobic attitudes.

APPROACHES TO JUST SOLUTIONS IN
ETHNIC POLITICS

Federalism would seem to be the fairest solution to ethnic conflict. East European elites continue to adhere to certain Marxist tenets, such as the fact that federalism is only feasible in multi-ethnic systems. Even countries which host large ethnic minorities do not define themselves as multi-ethnic. The three multi-ethnic federations in the region did not survive the demise of state socialism. Until the outbreak of overt hostilities between Moscow and Chechenya in December 1994, the RF offered some hope that a fair and just solution might be found, although the term 'sovereign republics' was removed from the draft to which Yeltsin asked the people to agree in December 1993. However, federalism has no tradition in Russian history, despite the huge size of the country, which encompasses land from the Baltic Sea to the Pacific Ocean. Attempts by Khrushchev and Gorbachev to grant greater autonomy to the regions failed (von Beyme, 1988: 29ff). Only the regions of the Far East and east and west Siberia have so far shown any evidence of a regional identity to promise a stable federal unit. Most other Russian areas west of the Urals have yet to develop this kind of regional identity.

Historical experience teaches us that dominant nation states and ethnic minorities or sub-nations tend to conflict with ever greater shows of violence unless the central state makes substantial concessions. Electoral laws which are not proportional but majoritarian normally aggravate the problem. Despite this social fact, not one of the budding democracies in the east has turned to a majoritarian solution. A matrix (figure 9.2) based on the electoral law and the territorial status allows several models to be distinguished.

| | Territorial status | |
	Equal rights	Unequal modified rights
Proportional	Federalism, moderate egalitarian	Modified autonomy, Spain
	Germany, Austria, Russia	
Majoritarian	Equal rights, USA	Devolution, UK

Electoral law

Figure 9.2 Autonomy to solve territorial conflicts

The Russian solution approximates that found in Germany and Austria. But there are strong tendencies in Russia to reduce the rights of autonomy granted to the sub-units. Thus, in the long run, it seems more likely that Russia will develop in the direction of the model of 'modified autonomy', as in Spain. So far, in most of the other countries the myth of a '*nation une et indivisible*' is stronger than pragmatic ethnic-pluralist reason. They have not even proposed the solution of limited autonomy which the Romanian government had granted the Hungarians until 1968. The Hungarian minority in the early 1990s did not dare to reopen the question of its autonomy lest it provide ammunition for extreme chauvinists among the nationalist Romanian parties.

Even in those countries where federalism or far-reaching autonomy is not feasible, a more just ethnic policy should entail a degree of *affirmative action* in favour of sub-national movements as a means of mollifying ethnic conflict. Only in a few countries, such as Bulgaria and Slovakia, do ethnic parties form effective political organizations which already play a part in the forming of governments. For the ex-communists in Bulgaria, the party representing Turkish interests is more attractive as a coalition partner than the Democratic Forum type of party. Though the party of the Hungarian minority in Romania (7.4 per cent of the population) is only slightly weaker than the Turkish group in Bulgaria, its relative weight within the party system is not as impressive, because the hegemonic position of the ex-communists is stronger and alternative coalitions are not yet feasible.

Ethnic parties tend to stand for election as catch-alls which try to integrate all groups and classes of the sub-nation, as do the Swedish People's Party in Finland or the South Tyroler Volkspartei in Italy – groups which for a long time brought together about two-thirds of the potential ethnic group. A sub-nation rarely fragments into various ideological ethnic groups, as has happened in the Basque country following the decline of the PVN (Basque Nationalist Party) from its former hegemonic position. So far, only the Hungarian minority in Slovakia has shown this degree of maturity and differentiation. But even here, electoral laws force the ethnic groups into an alliance (Reisch, 1992: 13ff).

Most Western commentators poorly understood the new wave of nationalism in the East, finding it comprehensible only as a *nationalism of desperation*. Western modernization and neo-Marxist theories tended to perceive nationalist movements negatively, as being 'reactionary'. Only a few modern thinkers, such as Karl W. Deutsch, have always seen nationalist movements as serving a *modernizing function*.

Nationalism in Eastern Europe may be regarded as a third form of developmental nationalism, which succeeds the second failed attempt between the two world wars and is used as an instrument (both defensive and offensive) in the struggle to accommodate to the asymmetric power relations in Europe (Senghaas, 1992: 32; Kolankiewicz, 1994: 486).

Except for Russian nationalism, and for the time being Serbian nationalism, this new wave of chauvinism is more dangerous for the ethnic minorities within the new nation states than for their respective neighbours. Nevertheless, prospects are brighter than between the two world wars, when almost all the new and old states in Eastern and Southern Europe were on the brink of war.

First, in the summer of 1990 the nations of Eastern Europe recognized the rights of ethnic minorities as part of an inviolable set of human rights, and are signatories to guidelines for the treatment of minority groups. The Paris Charter has been solemnly accepted by all the states. At present these declarations are only self-imposed, not binding in international law (Ludwig, 1992: 7). But since most of these countries want access to the European Union and are in great need of assistance from the Organization for Economic Cooperation and Development and other Western organizations and governments, they cannot afford to deviate too much from these declarations.

Second, bilateral agreements between countries, such as that signed by Poland with its neighbours, have become a model for the region. Still, latent fears remain of Hungarian irredentist feelings. Only the Ukraine so far has not rejected the Hungarian declaration on Protective Rights for Ethnic Hungarians Abroad as interfering in Ukrainian state rights (Oltay, 1992: 26). The framework of the Conference on Security and Co-operation in Europe facilitates the multi-lateralization of bilateral agreements between states. Apart from the good wishes of the Entente, between the two world wars there was no comparable body trying to mitigate conflicts in Eastern Europe.

Some countries, such as Poland, had difficulties in passing legislation, preferring for the time being to rely on international law (McQuaid, 1993: 20). During the transitional period, agreements are more easily made and implemented in the international arena, since a treaty can contain profitable concessions when, for example, economic concessions are granted by the West in return for legal concessions made in the East on, for instance, human rights.

Many East European politicians are wary of passing laws in favour of minorities. International experience teaches that affirmative action in favour of ethnic minorities not only does not solve problems, but sometimes creates a pretext for the minorities to mobilize and make further demands for the greater participation and representation of minorities in central institutions. It is not by chance that countries which do not have threatening ethnic minorities within their boundaries, like Hungary, were the first to pass fair minority legislation. Already in the summer of 1990, the Hungarian Constitution was amended, and article 68 now declares that the ethnic minorities are constituent parts of the 'nation'. Affirmative action in favour of ethnic group organizations in Hungary was also very generous, with parliament assigning the equivalent of $2.7 million to support ethnic organizations within the country. Moreover, part of the money was earmarked for the most depressed ethnic minorities, the Roma and Sinti (Reisch, 1992: 17).

Many of the new democracies have also adopted fair ethnic policies in their electoral laws, for example by suspending, as Poland has, its 3–5 per cent ruling on parties wishing to enter parliament as far as ethnic parties are concerned. Other countries have tried to promote affirmative action by symbolic politics instead, such as that instituted by Romania when it created a 'council of national minorities'. Although it was widely perceived as a window-dressing exercise, the Hungarian minority's skilful and moderate use of the council prevented the institution from becoming a mere instrument of government manipulation.

Third, arguably the most important part of any affirmative action programme in favour of ethnic minorities is toleration of ethnic parties. All the countries facilitated access to central representation by choosing a proportional representation electoral law. Attempts have been made to measure the deviation from the arithmetical mean in proportional electoral laws. In Bulgaria, for instance, the deviation was no greater than 7 per cent. But because of the 4 per cent threshold, almost one-quarter of the electorate was unrepresented. However, in Albania the same 4 per cent threshold led to only 1.9 per cent of unrepresented voters (McGregor, 1993: 13). Hungary came after Albania in a low deviation from the possible average. It is, however, difficult to assess whether the less favourable results in regional representational fora in Bulgaria were unanticipated by those who passed the electoral law, or were deliberately created in order to diminish the electoral chances of regional and ethnic groups.

The political chances of ethnic minorities are not easily deduced from electoral laws. Ethnic groups frequently have regional strongholds. Electoral laws can try – as in Hungary – to reduce and equalize the electoral chances of regional strongholds, or to maximize regional representation by additional mandates, as provided for in the Albanian electoral law. Most countries have not followed the Polish example in exempting national minorities from the electoral threshold. Some countries, for instance Croatia, have tried to avoid the disruptive tendencies within their systems by assigning a fixed number of seats to the minorities. This applies mainly to the Serbs (Bicanic and Dominis, 1992: 22). Even Hungary, which is by virtue of its territorial losses one of today's most ethnically homogeneous states in Eastern Europe, has reserved eight seats for its minorities (Germans, Romanians, Serbs, Slovaks, Croatians, Jews and gypsies).

Fourth, a crucial test of the extent to which a country is pursuing a 'fair' ethnic policy is the rules governing national citizenship, bearing in mind that constitutional texts and constitutional reality in Western states do not always correspond. While blatant discrimination and outright ethnic purges occur regularly in some cases, some forms of discrimination of ethnic groups are marginal. For example, in 1993 a Slovak law had to be amended in order to allow the Hungarian minority to escape the 'prescription' that the female form of a name had to end with 'ova', although even this rather minor matter was only achieved following intervention by the European Council on behalf of the Hungarian minority. The Hungarians hailed this concession as a 'step towards reason'. The outvoted minority in parliament, however, continued to argue that even the European Council was not able to change the rules of Slovak grammar. Other forms of discrimination are more serious, such as those found in Croatia. A document called 'Domovnica' – in which citizenship had to be proved – discriminated especially against the Serb minority. Citizenship was frequently denied without reasons being offered.

Fifth, the most important guarantee to ensure a just ethnic policy is the fact that all of the Eastern European states want, to varying and changing degrees (Kolankiewicz, 1994), to enter or have a close relationship with the European Union, and in order to be eligible they must demonstrate their democratic credentials, which include their treatment of ethnic minorities. The Balkanization of Eastern Europe does not necessarily have to lead to new wars and permanent ethnic strife.

10

Cities under Socialism – and After

Ivan Szelenyi

POSING THE PROBLEM

The purpose of this chapter is to explore how much difference socialism made to urban development in Eastern Europe and how urbanization is affected by post-communist transformation. The question about whether cities under socialism developed differently from those in the West has been the subject of scholarly controversy over the last two decades, some researchers answering the above question in the affirmative, and others disagreeing. So this analysis begins with a review of alternative theoretical positions, and the rest of the chapter sides with those who give the affirmative answer. The attempt is to show that urban development in the socialist epoch in Eastern Europe was quite different from urban development in Western countries at a similar stage of economic growth. Or to use 'counter-factual' reasoning: the argument is that urbanization in socialist Eastern Europe followed a different path from what one might anticipate if this region had followed a Western trajectory of development after World War II. The chapter also analyses the changes of the post-communist epoch in order to test to what extent the unique features of socialist urban development may disappear following the collapse of the socialist socio-economic order. The aim is to show that qualitatively new trends seem now to be emerging with the post-communist transformation in the urban scene.

Before we proceed any further, it is important to clarify that no value judgement is intended: the point is not that socialist urban development was better or worse than Western urbanization; the only claim is that it was different. Also these cities are here called socialist not because they necessarily looked the way socialist planners or ideologues wanted them to look, but because they were cities of industrial societies which had abolished private ownership of the means of production. The chapter also tries to demonstrate that what are identified as socialist features were often unintended by socialist planners, and were often even regarded as undesirable by the ideologues of socialism. Nevertheless, they were the consequences of the abolition of private property, of the monopoly of state ownership of the means of production, and of the redistributive, centrally planned character of the economic system.

This final chapter offers an overview of some of the theoretical questions raised by the cities created by a historically unique social formation, and speculates on their future trajectory. It will highlight three uniquely socialist features of urbanization in Eastern Europe. First, in Hungary, Czechoslovakia and Poland, post-World War II industrialization has been achieved with *less urban population growth* and less spatial concentration of the population than in market capitalist societies at the same stage of economic development. The socialist societies of Eastern Europe became 'under-urbanized' during extensive socialist industrialization. Second, we suggest that there was *less 'urbanism'* during the socialist epoch in cities like Budapest, Prague, East Berlin, Warsaw and Bucharest than in comparable cities in Western Europe. These cities may even have lost some of their 'urbanism' with socialist transformations of their societies. The best test case, of course, was East Berlin. Arguably East Berlin became 'less of an urban place' while it was the capital city of the GDR, West Berlin being contemporaneously more 'urban' (as, indeed, was Berlin as a whole at the turn of the twentieth century). Finally, the suggestion is made that it is possible to identify *uniquely socialist 'urban forms'* in these cities. In the socialist cities of Eastern Europe, one could identify an ecological structure which was different from their pre-socialist structure or the ecological structure of Western cities during the same historic period. Rich and poor and ethnic minorities may have been almost as highly segregated in the socialist cities of Eastern Europe as in capitalist cities, but the main point is that their segregation was produced by new, different mechanisms. Slums, for example, were formed at spots which are not typical locations for slums in a West European or a North American city.

From the mid-1970s in some countries of Eastern Europe, there was a significant shift away from the classical model of Soviet-style socialism. Hungary in particular, and to some extent Yugoslavia and Poland, began to move cautiously towards a mixed economy. In 1989, these trends accelerated significantly. At the end of this chapter, there is a review of the effects that post-communism appears to be having so far on the three uniquely socialist features of the East European urban system. The character of urbanization has so far not changed. There has been no exodus from rural areas, but urban–rural tension is building up, and the forecast is for an acceleration of urbanization as soon as the crisis of post-communist transformation comes to an end. However, urbanism has changed radically, so that East European cities now exemplify features of both Third World and West European cities; they could develop in either direction. Urban social geography is also changing. The most characteristically social-ist phenomenon in these cities, namely the mass housing develop-ments built during the socialist phase, are experiencing a deep crisis. These formerly privileged zones are losing their social status, many inner urban areas are stagnating, and there are strong trends towards suburbanization for the neo-bourgeoisie.

So in the mid-1990s, East European urban systems are at a cross-roads: their socialist features are fading, but it is not yet clear whether they are heading towards dependent urbanization or will evolve ur-ban forms akin to those found in the West. It is somewhat too early to assess the full impact of the post-communist transformation. How-ever, this chapter will try to demonstrate that many features of social-ist urban development are now decaying rapidly, and those that still survive are increasingly in contradiction with the emergent socio-economic reality of the region. This is perfectly compatible with the central hypothesis of this chapter: the greater the role of markets (the private sector) in these societies, the less different their cities will be from those in the West, or, to be more precise, from capitalist cities of societies in analogous locations in the world system.

SOCIALIST CITIES: THE THEORETICAL PUZZLE

The two different traditions of urban sociology – the ecological and the historical approaches – give two different answers to our key theoretical question: how much difference did socialism make to urban development?

The ecological approach emphasizes the importance of the imperatives of industrialization in the urbanization process.[1] Economic growth in general, and industrialization in particular, require an optimal spatial concentration of the population.[2] This optimum is, by and large, independent of the socio-political organization or cultural heritage of a society. Or to be more precise, socio-political organization or intervention by planners may deviate from this optimum for some time, but there will be a tendency to correct such deviations. Figure 10.1 expresses the relationships.

The ecological approach was challenged during the late 1960s and early 1970s by the then emergent neo-Marxist and neo-Weberian urban sociology, both of which were more sensitive to the historical and institutional specificities of urban development.

The neo-Marxists argued that the mode of production plays a fundamental role in shaping the process of urbanization (Castells, 1977: 7, 64; Harvey, 1973: 203–6). There is no history of cities; only modes of production have their history. Therefore, cities, urban problems and contradictions have to be analysed as spatial expressions of the contradictions of the mode of production. More specifically, the neo-Marxist urban sociology of the last two decades established an impressive new research agenda for the study of contemporary cities in the Western and Third World capitalist countries by interpreting these as 'capitalist cities', and by explaining their contradictions as contradictions of modern capitalism. Neo-Marxists, in studying urban places, looked at class contradiction, problems of capital accumulation, and the fiscal crisis of the state (see, for example, Harvey, 1985: 1–61; Alcaly and Mermelstein, 1977). Using these tools, they also tried to explain problems of regional restructuring, such as the decline of the Snow Belt and the rise of the Sun Belt (see, for example, Bluestone and Harrison, 1982), and the decay of old urban centres and their consequent revitalization/gentrification (see N. Smith and Palen, 1984). They interpreted the problems of Third World urbanization as expressions of dependent capitalist

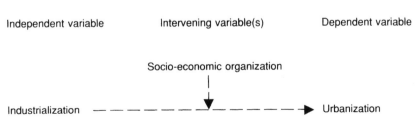

Figure 10.1   The ecological explanations of the process of urbanization

development, not as 'over-urbanization' but as 'dependent urbaniza-tion' (Castells, 1977: 43–63; Timberlake and Kantor, 1983; Roberts, 1978: 36–87).

The neo-Weberian wing of modern urban sociology approved of the Marxist attempt to 'historicize' the object of urban sociological investigation, but objected to what it believed to be an ideological component in the neo-Marxist research project. According to the neo-Weberians, the Marxist claim that urban problems could be blamed on capitalism would only be believable if the Marxists could show that socialism did not produce the same or analogous con-tradictions (see Pahl, 1977a: 154, 163–6; Harloe, 1981: 185–6; Pickvance, 1986). The Marxists were criticized not for having a criti-cal theory of the capitalist city, but for having only an ideology of urban development under socialism. The neo-Weberian position calls for an historical and comparative analysis of the process of urbanization, which does not presume that socialism is the solution to the problem of capitalist cities. Instead, in the tradition of inter-pretative sociology, analysis begins with the hypothesis that societies with different socio-economic orders will produce qualitatively differ-ent urban contradictions.

Despite these fundamental and important disagreements, when confronted with the ecological tradition, neo-Marxists and neo-Weberians have tended to close ranks and advocate the necessity of an historical approach, which explains urban phenomena in connec-tion with the historically specific and concrete circumstances in which the cities under investigation exist. Both neo-Marxists and neo-Weberians doubted the determining influence of the imperative of industrialization, or stage of economic growth, on urbanization. In-stead, they used social organization (Weberians) or the mode of production (Marxists) as the most important independent variable (see figure 10.2).

These differences between the ecological and historical traditions are far from trivial. They identify, in my view, the most important

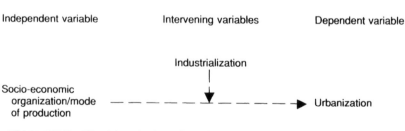

Figure 10.2   The historical explanations of the process of urbanization

issues which urban social research in our times should address. They also have far-reaching policy implications. Let me illustrate the essence of this controversy with a few simple examples.

Those who come from the ecological tradition will argue as follows:

> Look at the problems of urban transportation or issues of environmental protection. If you compared from this point of view what used to be socialist Moscow and capitalist New York you of course found certain differences, but you could have explained these almost exclusively by the differences in economic and technological development between the two societies. As the USSR was becoming wealthier and technically more developed, the density of cars also increased and the planning of the transportation system faced problems very similar to those which urban planners were struggling with in New York at the same stage of economic growth. True, Soviet planners for a while may have suppressed some of the objective forces at work; thus, for a while, they may have pressed for too much public transportation and intentionally restricted the use of private cars, but at one point in time the imperatives of economic growth gained the upper hand and these temporary deviations began to disappear. The post-communist epoch can be understood as such a readjustment from a temporary deviation to the normal state of affairs.

Those who share the basic assumptions of the historical approach will reject this reasoning and may argue this way:

> If you have any doubt that cities under socialism were any different from cities under capitalism, you should have compared socialist East Berlin and capitalist West Berlin. East and West Berlin were strikingly different from each other, and their difference could not be described in terms of one being wealthier and technologically more advanced than the other. East Berlin adapted to ecological challenges differently from West Berlin, and these differences could have been explained more in terms of the organization of their political and economic system than in terms of the differences in their economic growth. Thus, strict limits on private enterprise in East Berlin, with the virtual non-existence of market allocation of land and housing, were the most important factors explaining the kind of housing that was built and where or which social strata had access to certain types of housing or public facilities. The post-communist transformation of East Berlin offers further proof. As the GDR was absorbed into the Federal Republic, East Berlin did not 'take off' as the ecological approach would have expected – on the contrary, it collapsed. East Berlin may not have been an attractive city for many during the GDR times, but it was a viable place, with its own dynamics. Today it is like a dinosaur during the Ice Age – it is dying, or it is already dead.

This chapter adopts a neo-Weberian variant of the historical position and will explain why socialism made a lot of difference to urban development, and why the urban experience of people living under socialism was significantly different from that of those who lived in a similar stage of economic development in capitalist cities.

But before doing this, it is necessary to refine the dependent variable in figures 10.1 and 10.2. 'Urbanization' is a rather broad and somewhat vague notion and, in order to explore our problem in an empirical way, it has to be further specified. There are at least three different ways in which the term 'urbanization' can be operationalized. Or to put it another way, there are three aspects of the urban phenomenon, in each of which socialist and capitalist countries differed.

Urbanization can first be understood as the *growth of urban population*. Here, of course, what 'urban' means still remains undefined. The category is interpreted differently in different countries and at different times. In many countries, settlements with 2,000–3,000 inhabitants are regarded as urban. Elsewhere, for instance in some East European countries, no settlement is classified as urban unless it gains the legal status of city, which rarely happens to villages with fewer than 10,000 inhabitants (sometimes even settlements with 20,000 inhabitants are regarded as 'villages' or as 'rural' places of residence). Despite these definitional problems, it is quite obvious that 'urbanization' means, among other things, a trend towards population concentration in space, that is, the growth of population in larger settlements. Measures such as proportion of population living in settlements with 2,000 or 10,000 or 20,000 inhabitants capture something about such concentration. The question posed here is whether the trend towards population concentration in space under socialism has been identical or similar to capitalist development, if one controls for stage of economic growth. Did industrialization require the same degree of concentration of population in space under socialism as is required under capitalism?

However, large settlements do not always 'look' urban. There are indeed 'large villages' with tens of thousands of inhabitants and 'small cities' with a few thousand inhabitants. Beyond the largely quantitatively measurable tendency of population to concentrate in space, urbanization also implies a *certain quality of social relationships*, or way of life, which is best captured by the term 'urbanism'. Classical authors of urban sociology from Ferdinand Tönnies (1887/1974) and Georg Simmel (1964, first published 1902–3) to Louis Wirth

(1938) caught this element of urban life by defining urbanism in terms of the density and diversity of human interaction (and institutions), anonymity, the breakdown of traditional community and its replacement by 'society', and the tendency of the urbanite to be marginal, detached and creative. While Louis Wirth, inspired by the ecological tradition, tried to explain the emergence of 'urbanism as a way of life' as a consequence of increasing 'size, density and heterogeneity' – as a result of non-historical, ecological factors – those who follow the historical tradition of urban research would anticipate that socio-political organization, class, or ethnic divisions within a society are primarily responsible for shaping the ways in which people live (Gans, 1962). Following in this historical tradition, this chapter will suggest that the socialist societies produced a different kind, and arguably a more limited urbanism than the one we are familiar with in capitalist societies at the same stage of economic growth.

Finally, the ecological approach assumes that *'urban forms'* – the way in which sub-populations or certain institutions are distributed in space within cities or within regions – change in a 'unilinear', evolutionary way. The classical example was of course Burgess's (1925) concentric zone model, which described how the location of the rich and poor, the slums, the suburbs, and certain industrial, commercial and business institutions changes with the growth of the city. Burgess developed his model from empirical studies conducted in Chicago, but he assumed that all cities, if they grow, will produce similar arrangements of spatial structures over time. The urban forms or zonal patterns found in Chicago will tell us how other cities will look as they proceed with industrialization and urbanization. The spatial structure of Rio de Janeiro, Vienna or Shanghai are only different because they are at a lower level of urban-industrial development, and they will follow suit in due course. While the Burgess model was dismissed by geographers and sociologists a long time ago, the logic of his analysis is very much alive. The historical approach – be it Marxist or Weberian – challenges the evolutionism of ecology. It assumes that diverse urban forms are possible; the urban forms of European or Latin American cities are and will remain different from those in North America, for specifically institutional, cultural, conjunctural reasons.

In what follows there is presented evidence – mainly preliminary, in need of further systematic empirical investigation – about the uniqueness of socialist urbanization with respect to the three dimensions discussed above.

URBAN POPULATION GROWTH UNDER
SOCIALISM

In an article first published in 1971, this author argued that East European countries during the epoch of socialist extensive industrialization became '*under-urbanized*' (Konrad and Szelenyi, 1977; see also Golachowski, 1967). The term 'under-urbanization' was coined as the twin of the concept of 'over-urbanization'. The latter was used widely during the 1950s and 1960s to describe what appeared to be a unique feature of urbanization in many Third World countries (Davis and Golden, 1954–5). According to the theory of over-urbanization in the Third World, there is a tendency for urban populations to grow faster than urban job opportunities. Pressures within rural areas are too strong, and people leave their villages even when there are no job prospects in cities. The result is the 'excessive' growth of cities, with a high level of unemployment or under-employment, acute housing shortages, a large urban homeless population, and the growth of shanty towns. Thus, the most general theoretical proposition is that peripheral capitalist countries often produce faster urbanization than industrialization.

By comparing the growth trends of urban industrial jobs to the growth of the permanent urban residents in Hungary, the current author concluded that socialist industrialization in that country, and probably in most other East European socialist countries, followed a very different trajectory from Western capitalist countries in their stage of extensive industrialization. Under socialism, the growth of urban industrial jobs seems to have been much faster than the growth of the permanent urban population. Thus these countries became 'under-urbanized'.

The intention was to use the term 'over-urbanization' and to propose the concept of 'under-urbanization' in a value-neutral way. It is important to note this, since the theory of over-urbanization has been primarily criticized for its real or assumed ideological implications (see Sovani, 1964; and for a defence of the concept of over-urbanization, see Gugler, 1982). The theory of over-urbanization was rejected, particularly by dependency theorists, since it apparently presupposes that: (1) the urbanization pattern followed by the core Western capitalist countries is the 'normal' one, which will eventually be replicated by countries in the Third World; and (2) that over-urbanization is largely, if not exclusively, a result of policy errors and that if those are corrected over-urbanization will be overcome. Such critics of 'over-urbanization' wished to replace it with the notion of 'dependent urbanization'. The theory of dependent urbanization was inspired by the idea of the 'development of underdevelopment', which claimed that peripheral countries are locked into a self-reproducing cycle of backwardness from which no 'proper' government policy can release them. Accelerated destruction of agriculture and village communities and excessive growth of cities are, among other phenomena, expressions of this vicious circle of underdevelopment.

In my view, the notion of 'over-urbanization' can be used in a value-neutral way. In this case the 'over-urbanization' versus 'dependent urbanization' controversy largely disappears. Those who subscribe to the idea of 'dependent urbanization' usually also accept that dependency results in excessive growth of the urban population and the inability of dependent capitalist economies to produce jobs, housing and proper infrastructure for the large mass of rural – urban migrants. At this level both 'dependent-urbanization' and 'over-urbanization' theorists agree on what the unique pattern of urbanization in dependent, peripheral capitalist countries typically is, though they may have opposing hypotheses about what causes this pattern and how it can be managed effectively by state policies.

The concept of 'under-urbanization' was coined in a similarly value-neutral sense. 'Under-urbanization' simply means that under this pattern of industrialization and urbanization, the growth of the urban population falls behind the growth of urban industrial and tertiary sector jobs. It does not imply that this was the result of policy errors, or even that this was an undesirable pattern of urbanization which will be surpassed as policy errors are corrected, or as socialist countries further proceed with their economic growth. One could even argue that the core Western capitalist countries produced an over-concentration of population in space during their industrial epoch and, as they enter the post-industrial stage and the demographic turnaround, a certain degree of deurbanization corrects this mistake. From this perspective one could present under-urbanization as a desirable and rational pattern which avoids such a costly and, in the long run, unsustainable over-concentration of the population.

But, while no value-judgement was intended with the theory of under-urbanization, the attempt was to prove that under-urbanization was a consequence of a socialist-type social and economic structure. It was the result of the elimination of private property and the centrally planned or redistributive nature of the economic system.

A longitudinal analysis of urban population growth before and after the socialist transformation seemed to support this claim. If one looks at the growth of the urban population over the last century in Hungary, for instance, one will note a virtually steady increase in the number and proportion of urban residents per decade. But if one looks at the growth of urban industrial jobs, then the picture is quite different. While from the late nineteenth century until the late 1940s there was a parallel growth in urban industrial employment and urban population, from the late 1940s the growth of industrial employment in cities suddenly exploded. As these two curves departed from each other during the 1950s and 1960s, the commuter population rose sharply. The 'gap' between these two curves, and the proportion of working-class commuters (living in villages and working in cities), measured the degree of under-urbanization. In other words, under-urbanization appeared at that time of history when socialist industrialization began.

But this could be a sheer coincidence. In order to substantiate further a causal link between the socialist character of the economy and under-urbanization, one should be able to identify the mechanism by which socialist extensive industrialization produced a delayed urban growth. It is not difficult to find such a 'smoking gun'. Under-urbanization was the direct consequence of the policy of socialist extensive industrialization, which economized on 'nonproductive' investments – such as those in housing, or other nonproductive infrastructure such as schools, hospitals and even shops – and maximized the volume of investments in industry. The drastic rechannelling of resources away from personal and collective consumption to industrial, and particularly heavy industrial, development was only possible in an economic regime which eliminated private property and in which central planners could effectively redistribute the surplus. In market economies – that is, economic systems based on private property – extensive industrialization occurred with less or no retardation of infrastructural development. Under-urbanization was thus a spatial expression of distinctively socialist economic growth. Since, during the phase of socialist extensive industrialization, urban housing and infrastructure grew slowly, it made sense to try to keep the workforce, which was freed from agriculture and redirected into the newly established industry, in its old place of residence. In this way the existing housing and public infrastructure, no matter how inadequate, could still serve the new industrial working class.

This theory of under-urbanization captured a unique and important feature of urban growth under state socialism. It is indeed quite safe to say that socialist redistributive economies achieved the task of urbanization with significantly less spatial concentration of urban population than market capitalism.

The theory of under-urbanization can be extended, and therefore somewhat modified, in two ways. First, the comparative study of urban growth of different socialist countries, and in particular the comparison of East European experiences with those of 'socialist developing countries' (especially in Asia), proved that under-urbanization was only one of the possible socialist patterns of urbanization (Murray and Szelenyi, 1984; Forbes and Thrift, 1987). All socialist countries, in virtually all historic epochs, seem to have produced relatively little urban growth. But the extent and explanation of this difference varied across countries in different epochs. In the case of post-war Vietnam or Kampuchea, the term 'under-urbanization' is not sufficient to describe the massive decline in urban population which resulted from the attempt of communist elites to consolidate their power and to break the back of, or even eliminate, the urban bourgeoisie or petty bourgeoisie. Vietnam and Kampuchea for a few years thus experienced a significant decline in urban population, or *deurbanization*. This deurbanization was intimately linked to the transformation of class and property relations in these countries, as the victorious communist elite removed the bourgeoisie from the cities in order to consolidate its political power and the hegemony of public ownership and central planning. In China from the early 1960s until the mid-1970s, or in Cuba in the late 1960s, however, the urban population did not decline, but the proportion of the population which lived in towns remained basically unaltered. In China, this was the result of an industrialization strategy which created a significant proportion of the new industrial jobs within the communes in the countryside. During this epoch China and Cuba were not deurbanized, although they followed a strategy of economic growth which could produce an even slower urban population growth than the one identified in under-urbanized Eastern Europe. In one paper, the term 'zero-urban population growth' was used to describe this third pattern of socialist industrialization (Murray and Szelenyi, 1984). In other words, the comparative study of socialist urbanization among different socialist countries demonstrated that under-urbanization was the characteristic only of those East European countries which entered socialism and began the task of socialist industrialization as relatively developed countries. The economically more backward countries were likely to produce even slower urban growth rates, as socialist developing countries spectacularly avoided the pitfalls of over-urbanization.

Second, during the 1980s some of the East European countries – East Germany, Czechoslovakia and Hungary – entered the 'post-industrial' age. This had far-reaching consequences for the character of their urbanization. The following is a brief summary of the experiences of Hungary during the 1980s and a discussion of the novel features of socialist urbanization in this last stage of state socialism. The argument is that, even after the process of industrialization was completed, socialist urban development did not converge with the Western pattern but entered a qualitatively new trajectory, which was as different from socialist under-urbanization as it was from Western post-industrial regional structures.

After the late 1970s in Hungary, the industrial population ceased to increase. Actually, the proportion of blue-collar industrial workers began to decline. So could one expect a 'correction' of under-urbanization under these circumstances? During the extensive indus-trialization period, planners argued that one should not eat the 'goose which lays the golden egg'. In other words, the low level of public investment in urban housing and in the means of collective consumption was promised to be only temporary, and would be compensated for after the productive capacities of the economy were properly developed. Interestingly, nothing like this compensation happened in socialist urban and regional development in the last, post-industrial epoch of state socialism. Public investment in urban housing declined rather than increased, and the population, which during the epoch of under-urbanization retained its rural residence, did not now move into cities. On the contrary, during the 1980s the decline of the rural population, rather than accelerating, slowed down (Enyedi, 1984).

Still, Enyedi (1984) argued that such a slow-down of urban popu-lation indicates convergence. He believed that this proved that social-ist societies follow in the footsteps of Western urbanization and, after an epoch of urban population explosion, by the 1970s–1980s they had entered the stage of suburbanization (see also Enyedi, chapter 4, this volume). This author disagrees, for two reasons. First, in the light of what has been shown above, it is difficult to accept that during the extensive industrialization epoch a real urban explosion took place. Certainly the urban population grew, but its rate of growth fell significantly behind that of the urban industrial workforce. Socialism produced industrialization with exceptionally small urban, and large rural, populations. Additionally, the stabilization of rural communi-ties in Hungary during the 1980s was a very different phenomenon, in terms of its social content, from suburbanization in the United States during the 1950s. The Hungarian villages, in which 40 per cent of the population lived by 1990, were quite *rural* places. About 90 per cent of the residents of these settlements produced agricultural goods, and about half of the rural residents even produced food for markets, significantly complementing their industrial incomes with incomes from part-time family farming (Szelenyi, 1988: 28–32). These settlements were strikingly different places from the suburbs of Long Island during the 1950s and 1960s. Socialist countries, in a quite extraordinary way, entered the post-industrial stage with large and apparently, for the time being, stable rural populations, heavily involved in part-time family farming. This feature of their development was closely linked to the socialist character of the social and economic order. It reflected the inability of the collectivized sector of agriculture to feed the population. It was also a result of a decades-long struggle by the rural new working class to carve out for itself some autonomy in the 'second economy', which was an emergent private sector.

Let me summarize the ways in which the theory of under-urbanization has to be reformulated in the light of evidence from cross-national research and developments during the late socialist period in the economically more advanced countries of Eastern Europe. In different socialist countries, including socialist developing countries, one can find not one but several patterns of urbanization; that is, several different ways in which urban and industrial growth are matched with each other. But all these patterns are different from those which were followed by market capitalist economies at similar stages of growth or which characterize post-communist urban development. All socialist societies industrialized with less spatial concentration of population than market capitalist economies. Furthermore, as this phase of industrialization was completed, socialist societies – as long as they retained the hegemony of public ownership and redistributive or central planning – did not 'catch up' in urban population growth. They did not converge with the trajectory followed by Western societies during the 1950s and 1960s. While in their post-industrial phase, as one can anticipate from figure 10.2, socialist societies produced new types of regional arrangement (after all, economic growth or stage of industrialization *is* an intervening variable!), these arrangements were qualitatively different from those observable in the West in the early stages of post-industrialism.

SOCIALISM AND URBANISM

The notion of urbanism is more vague and therefore its measurement is even more problematic than that of urban population growth. But, despite such measurement problems, scholars such as Simmel and Wirth did indeed capture something important about human experience in cities with the notion of urbanism, in their attempt to define urban social relations as qualitatively different phenomena from non-urban social existence.

With little systematic empirical evidence to support the claims, the following argument rests basically on personal observation. The intention is to show that there was less urbanism in socialist cities than in similar capitalist cities in at least three senses of the term: there was less urban diversity; there was less economizing with space and consequently lower inner-city urban density, including the density of social interaction in inner urban public places; and there was less urban marginality. Let me elaborate and try to indicate that these indicators of less urbanism were consequences of socialist urban socio-economic and political organization.

Less diversity

One of the most striking differences found when crossing the Berlin Wall before it fell was less diversity in the eastern part of the city. To put it more generally, a somewhat mundane but obvious indicator of such a limited diversity was the relative scarcity of urban services, such as shops, restaurants, advertisements and street vendors in socialist cities. The cities of Eastern Europe are, of course, quite different from each other from this point of view, and some of them have also changed quite radically over time. Budapest, or even Prague, demonstrated more of this indicator of urbanism from this point of view than East Berlin or Warsaw (largely rebuilt under socialism), and the least urban places were, of course, the new towns, the so called 'socialist towns' such as Nowa Huta or Dunaujvaros. During the last 20 years of socialism Budapest also altered greatly, but these changes mainly reflected adaptation to the needs of tourists from the West and the emergence of small private business in the retail trade. But even if one takes Budapest, the East European socialist city which probably demonstrated the highest degree of urbanism during the socialist epoch, one could argue that it was a more vibrant place before World War II, or even at the turn of the century, offering a greater variety of shops, restaurants and other services than it did at the peak of its socialist period of development. For a much smaller population, Budapest during the 1930s, or at the turn of the century, had a larger number of retail trade institutions and was more of a 'market place' than it was even by the end of state socialism.

Less economizing with space

Inner urban land was exclusively or overwhelmingly publicly owned in all socialist cities. While land markets operated with relative freedom in rural areas or on the peripheries of the cities, markets could only be 'simulated' in the downtown area during socialism. For some time after socialist transformation, the dominant philosophy was that urban land does not have a value under socialism. Thus, urban planners could operate without the constraints of land prices. After a long time, the absurdity of such a position was realized and attempts were made to install a mechanism which would measure the value of land, simulating its market price if competing owners determined, on self-regulating markets, the prices of inner urban locations. But since the monopoly of public ownership was retained, this remained a somewhat fictitious activity. Thus, urban planners in socialist cities had a significantly greater degree of freedom in finding space for their plans than did those in capitalist cities.

As a result, urban planners in socialist cities typically could be more generous in using space and could pay more attention to aesthetic rather than to narrow economic considerations in their urban design. One good example was Alexander Platz in East Berlin, indeed an impressive development, which expressed some kind of imperial grandeur and responded to certain ceremonial needs of a socialist society. Such a rather luxurious use of inner urban space is not unheard of in a capitalist city either, but the creation of such a public place in a market economy is very exceptional, while it appeared quite normal and functional in a socialist non-market economy.

Another example of the planners' priorities was the debate among Budapest city planners during the early 1970s about high-rise developments in the city. Many of these planners were vehemently opposed to such development in the central business district (CBD) in Pest, basically on aesthetic grounds. Their argument was that one should preserve the beauty of the urban vista one gets of Pest from the Buda Hills, and therefore high-rise buildings should only be constructed around the line of the outer boulevard, to close this vista, rather than to disturb it. Most of the high-rise development in Budapest indeed has been outside the CBD and along the line of the outer boulevard.

It may be a reasonable hypothesis that urban planners in a socialist society were in a much better position than planners in a capitalist society to use urban space in a more aesthetic manner, for the purposes of symbolic, political needs. They were less constrained by narrowly economic considerations. This more generous use of urban space had implications for the degree of urbanism and inner urban density, which, particularly in public places (all other conditions being equal), was likely to be lower in socialist cities.

Less marginality

Robert Park (1928), under the influence of Georg Simmel, argued that one of the most important features of urbanism is the existence of urban marginality, both in its 'positive' and in its 'negative' senses. People living in cities are more likely to be marginal, thus less rigidly controlled by existing norms, and thus more creative. In this sense, urban marginality explains why cities are dynamic and innovative places. Urban tolerance of marginality is also demonstrated in tolerance of innovation. But urban marginality inevitably has side effects too. There is also more deviance, such as crime, prostitution and homelessness, in urban places.

While Park's interesting ideas about the link between urbanism and marginality, and in particular about cities and deviance, have been challenged, it seems quite certain that there is indeed more marginality in capitalist cities than there ever was in socialist ones. Other conditions being equal, the cities of socialist Eastern Europe were relatively safe from crime. There were relatively few of the extreme expressions of poverty, such as beggars or homeless people on the streets, in railway stations and under bridges. And one had to search far longer than in similar cities of Western Europe to find prostitutes or drug dealers.

One can evaluate the relative lack of marginality in different ways. These phenomena can be cited as proof of the success of socialist welfare policies. The societies of Eastern Europe, so much poorer than the United States, could operate with virtually no homelessness. But they can also be evaluated more negatively, attributing them more to the strictness of police control than to the success of the welfare state. In the socialist cities of Eastern Europe, it was illegal to be homeless (or unemployed); thus the police 'took care' of those who tried to sleep in parks, or under bridges, or who just hung around without the address of an employer on their ID card. But irrespective of the evaluation, by and large socialism – with a commitment to provide at least some housing for all, with a stricter system of police surveillance, with the almost inevitable trend towards full employment of a dominantly redistributive economy – produced relatively little marginality in its cities.

However, during the 1980s there were signs of 'convergence' with Western urban development; urban marginality increased, although this was not always greeted with much enthusiasm. By the end of the 1980s, there was more open prostitution on the streets of Budapest, there were people sleeping in the parks and on the railway stations, and there may have been some permanently homeless people. There was also more 'bohemian' marginality, such as street musicians, artists who, for a few dollars, drew your picture, punks and probably also a drug trade. This 'convergence' was a response to Western tourism, the decay of the redistributive economy, and the market gaining ground even in the allocation of labour and housing, thus generating unemployment, for instance. Importantly, this was an indication that Eastern Europe was moving towards its transition to post-communism, in which the totalitarian system of political and police control began to break down and civil society gained at least a relative autonomy from the political state. Thus the convergence in urban marginality coincided with some trend towards convergence with the Western economic and political system.

DID THE URBAN FORMS DIFFER IN SOCIALIST SOCIETIES?

Sufficient evidence has been provided, by ecological research, to establish that the socialist cities of Eastern Europe demonstrated a fair degree of segregation by occupation and ethnicity. While there may be disagreement among researchers about the degree, with some arguing that there was less segregation under socialism than under capitalism, and with others contesting this view, there is not much controversy about the fact that segregation did exist and that it could not just all be blamed on the 'capitalist past'.[3] In the light of the research evidence available, one can conclude that socialist cities, as they operated in their socialist ways, by restricting markets and by regulating regional processes, primarily through central planning, did produce and reproduce the asymmetrical allocation of social classes, occupational and ethnic groups in space.

But was there any difference in terms of the forms this segregation took? Could one identify a spatial structure, zonal or sectoral or some other sort of model, or patterns of segregation which could be linked to the socialist character of these systems? Or were these urban forms universal, the same in former socialist Eastern and in the capitalist

Western Europe? While most research on the spatial structure of East European cities under communism either did not explore this question or, at least implicitly, assumed urban forms were not different under capitalism and socialism, the hypothesis here is that the redistributive character of a socialist economy had consequences – precisely what they were may require further systematic research – for the inner urban spatial distribution of social classes, occupational and ethnic groups, and economic, social and cultural institutions.[4]

Here the analysis again starts with the classical or pure model of state socialism and the practices of urban planning from the late 1940s until the early or mid-1970s. The changes which then occurred until the collapse of state socialism in 1989 were the result of the increasing role being played by markets and private incentives. But first it is necessary to establish whether one can identify any uniquely socialist features of the 'pure model'.

There were two important elements of the urban economy which affected inner urban growth in the classical communist epoch: the prominent role of the state in financing, building and allocating new urban housing, and the highly restricted nature of land markets in inner cities. During the first decades of socialism, private housing construction was tolerated only in villages; all new housing in cities was to be built by the state, with state funding. Moreover, the existing inner-city housing stock, particularly housing in apartments, was nationalized. As mentioned above, there were no functioning urban land markets. Inner urban land could not be bought or sold by private individuals, although, in transactions between state agencies, some market-simulated prices were charged. But these transactions happened within the state sector among firms with soft budget constraints.

Such a dominant role for public ownership in inner-city housing had certain important ecological consequences (see also Haussermann, chapter 7, this volume). The quality of the existing housing stock deteriorated, leading to a physical, and even the social, decay of established neighbourhoods. Furthermore, almost all new building was concentrated in large new developments, typically at a significant distance from the decaying city centres. The nationalization of existing urban housing has led without exception, in all socialist countries, to a neglect of the stock. Housing authorities were under tremendous pressure to keep rents low in order to match the low wages, and to build as much new housing as possible. This policy, with low rent revenues and pressure to use funds for new construction, meant that the existing housing stock was not adequately maintained, and by the late 1960s it began to deteriorate seriously. Signs

of physical decay could be seen in inner cities in the few old neighbourhoods which survived World War II in East Berlin, Warsaw, the
old city of Prague and most of inner Pest.

The laws which regulated the character and location of new housing construction reinforced this effect. First, there was a trend towards concentrating all new housing in larger developments, rather
than spreading it around the urban space. There were several reasons for this. Most importantly, the new housing was built by large
state construction firms and designed by large state planning agencies. Construction firms and planning agencies preferred large building projects consisting of 5,000–15,000 dwelling units rather than
smaller housing projects of low-rise, detached buildings, in order to
reap (supposed) economies of scale. Development by the early 1970s
of construction technologies, especially the introduction of 'house-
factories' (that is, large-scale plants for the production of prefabricated units), which were justified more by the organization of the
construction industry than by economic criteria, further reinforced
this trend towards large-scale construction. When the 'house-
factories' were established, the construction industry was suffering
from labour shortages. But instead of increasing wages and attracting
labour by market means, it was decided to build these factories,
reducing on-site construction work to the mere assemblage of these
elements. In this way, the construction industry in the East European
socialist countries 'economized', by replacing cheap though scarce
labour with expensive technology, while resisting market pressure for
wage increases. This new technology reinforced the attraction of
construction firms and planners to large-scale, new housing development. It appeared to be more rational to prepare land for development, build roads, unload large quantities of prefabricated elements,
and operate cranes capable of handling these heavy elements if the
construction site was extensive.

The restricted nature of land markets also contributed to the
deterioration of old, centrally located neighbourhoods and helped
to rationalize the concentration of most new construction of large
housing developments on the outskirts of cities. Since rents were
below the replacement costs, they did not reflect market prices in any
way (and this was as true for industrial and commercial land use in
inner cities as for residential buildings). There was little pressure on
the city landlord to improve land use in central locations. Thus, as far
as the owner/municipal authority was concerned, there were no
economic limits on the deterioration of old neighbourhoods. By
contrast, the municipality was greatly interested in building new
housing where the least possible urban renewal was necessary. Urban

renewal appeared to have only costs (one had to find new housing for every apartment which was bulldozed) and no economic benefits. Under these circumstances, the new housing estates were built on the first available unoccupied land.

Physically deteriorating inner-city neighborhoods, with new housing estates leapfrogging them and forming a new zone around them, were the major changes in the inner urban structure of East European socialist cities between the 1950s and mid-1970s. This had something to do with population succession as well. For two decades, before the re-emergence of private housing, the urban middle class was overwhelmingly served by the public sector. It had little choice but to move into the new housing estates if it had no previous housing, or if it wanted to escape the increasingly deteriorating inner neighbourhoods. Many such households did so. So until the mid-1970s, the new housing estates had a distinctively middle-class character and the inner-city neighbourhoods began to lose social status. The inner city kept the old and poorer families and began to attract the lower-class immigrants such as immigrant Gypsies, as in the case of several Budapest inner-city neighbourhoods. These neighbourhoods were becoming slums.

This, in many ways, was a fundamental change from the pre-socialist ecological pattern of these cities. Prior to World War II, the East European cities were quite similar to many West European cities, such as Paris. This is certainly very true for Berlin, Prague and Budapest. A significant proportion of the urban bourgeoisie lived in prestigious inner-city neighbourhoods and the immigrant proletariat often had to settle on the outskirts, in the 'banlieux'. As public ownership of the existing housing stock led to the decay of inner-city neighbourhoods and the pressure to avoid urban renewal, all new housing became located in large housing estates on undeveloped land, creating a middle-class or even upper middle-class zone where these working-class 'banlieux' used to be. The ecological structure of these cities has changed significantly.

A mid-1980s study of the ecological structure of Budapest questioned whether the deteriorating inner neighbourhoods created large, geographically identifiable areas, and challenged the view that the new housing developments form a merged zone which encircles these deteriorating areas (Csanádi and Ladányi, 1985). Still, it is likely that no matter how large-scale or how small-scale the process described above was, it did lead to a novel rearrangement of the population, and of high- and low-quality, desirable and undesirable housing in urban space. This new rearrangement was caused, the claim here is, by uniquely socialist characteristics of the urban economy. Thus they presented a socialist urban form, which is distinctively different from the forms we knew in these countries before socialist transformation and equally different from the forms which would be likely to evolve without a socialist reconstruction.

During the last decade, some of these processes were significantly altered, and in Hungary probably more so than elsewhere. The most important change was a major expansion of private housing. Already during the last decade of socialism, some of the old housing was privatized. Also, private housing construction in cities was encouraged from the late 1960s and early 1970s. As the housing market gained ground, public housing contracted. After the 1970s, the urban middle class was more likely to build condominiums (cooperatives) for themselves or their children. They tried to move away from the previously quite desirable housing developments and towards the ecologically most attractive locations, such as in the surrounding hills or along the riverside in Budapest. These developments fundamentally altered, the social status of housing development. As unbuilt-on land nearer to the city centre was all occupied, the newest housing development began to move further out, at excessive commuting distances. These developments were less and less attractive for the middle class, which now had an alternative in condominium development in the previously bourgeois quarters. They disliked the poor location of the housing estates and were increasingly sensitive to living near working-class residents and ethnic minorities, particularly Gypsies, in these developments. Thus the fifth decade of state socialism saw a new trend in population succession, the zone of new housing estates began to lose social status, there was a re-bourgeoisification of traditional bourgeois neighbourhoods, and even the first signs of gentrification of inner-city areas were under way.

CITIES AFTER SOCIALISM

The phenomenon discussed in the earlier parts of this chapter – the 'socialist city' – is about to disappear. In 1989, Eastern Europe began to enter a post-communist phase. These concluding remarks present the most accurate diagnosis so far achievable concerning the current social characteristics of East European societies, together with some speculations about the possible future trends of development, in particular the prospects for urban social change in the region. Since the effects of post-communist transformation are very recent and this author's knowledge of all parts of the region is quite limited, these comments on post-communist urban processes will be mainly restricted to the situation in Hungary.

Eastern Europe in post-communist transition

In the whole region, the three major constituents of the state socialist socio-economic and political order were dismantled:

1   The state monopoly ownership of major means of production was abolished, at least in legal terms. Property laws were introduced, according to which private property is treated as equal to public property (for an extended analysis see Marcuse, chapter 5, this volume). In economic policy, the key slogan is privatization: the aim of the political elites in power is to remove the state from the productive sphere, leaving it as the exclusive domain of private entrepreneurs.

2   The system of one-party rule came to an end. The ruling parties, which had legitimated themselves under the banners of revolutionary socialism and Marxism-Leninism, accepted a multi-party parliamentary democracy, changed their political colours and re-labelled themselves as social democratic, socialist or democratic socialist parties. Multi-party elections were held, which in some countries could be called 'free'.

3   The social structure is also undergoing a sharp change. The classical stratification system of state socialism could have been described as a single-rank hierarchy, with the cadre elite on the top and the working or popular classes at the bottom. Now the cadre elite has been unseated and replaced by a new political class, composed of technocrats, literati, academics and other members of the intelligensia (many of whom played a key role in politics in 1989–90). A new class is also in the making: the class of the neo-bourgeoisie. These societies are in the process of transition from a 'socialist rank order' to a stratification system based on class cleavages.[5]

The description above of structural changes in Eastern Europe specified those three key characteristics that are used to distinguish state socialism, or Soviet-type societies from Western capitalism: state monopoly of ownership of the means of production, the one-party state, and the absence of capitalist class relations. All that is claimed here is that, as these features have disappeared, Eastern Europe is now beyond socialism, or communism. These are deep-seated, far-reaching structural alterations, which are not altered significantly by changes in political fortunes. Thus the electoral victories of the socialist parties in some of these countries (in September 1993 in Poland or in May 1994 in Hungary) do not indicate a return to state socialism. As the Hungarian socialist prime minister, Gyula Horn, put it so eloquently in an interview given to an Austrian newspaper shortly after he won the elections: 'now in Hungary the socialists will build capitalism.' It is, however, also obvious that these countries are not modern capitalist formations, at least not as yet. A number of interesting and provoking theses have been advanced to describe and explain the system which is emerging. Although these cannot be discussed here, two deserve to be mentioned. The first is David Stark's (1990) formulation that in Eastern Europe the transition is from 'plan' to 'clan' (rather than to 'market'). Stark (1992b) has also pointed out that privatization implies a path-dependent transformation of property rights rather than a simple transition from public to private ownership. The second is Michael Burawoy and Pavel Krotov's characterization of the post-communist Russian economic system as 'merchant capitalism' (1992; see also Burawoy, 1992).

Post-communism is hardly a stable formation, capable of self-reproduction; eventually it will move in one direction or another. In 1989–90, modernization theory was again placed on the social science agenda; the fall of the Berlin Wall, it was commonly accepted, indicated the 'end of history'. By the mid-1990s, the final convergence of the whole world under the model of liberal capitalism was thought to be under way. However, many commentators remain sceptical. The first five years of post-communism showed that the evolutionary, path-dependent character of change is strong and the costs of transition to capitalism are higher than expected by most analysts.

After 1989, the whole region entered what Janos Kornai (1990) described as the 'crisis of post-communist transformation'.[6] This refers to one of the most if not the most severe economic crisis in modern history (for further details see Andrusz, chapter 2, this volume). The crisis of post-communist transformation is certainly both deeper and wider than the Great Depression was. By 1994, GNP in the region had fallen by some 30 per cent and industrial production by some 40 per cent. Unemployment had increased from virtually zero to 15–30 per cent, the inflation rate was well above 20 per cent, and in some countries it reached up to double this proportion. By 1993–4, however, the more successful economies – the Polish, the Czech and the Hungarian – were bottoming out and showed signs of growth, but even they were not likely to surpass their 1988 levels of economic performance much earlier than the turn of the century. It is quite possible that Michael Burawoy (1992: 784) will prove to be correct: the post-Soviet and East European states, rather than moving towards modern capitalism and catching up with the core of the capitalist world system, may follow the laws 'of a merchant capitalism, or some might say of feudal capitalism – ploughing a third road to the Third World'. For the time being, it is not possible to predict with any precision where post-communist societies will be inserted in the capitalist world economy: how close they can get to the core or how far they go towards the periphery.

The spatial consequences of post-communist transformation

East European cities are already experiencing far-reaching changes in all the three dimensions of urban development where it was possible to detect 'socialist characteristics': the urban–rural relationship which evolved under state socialism is at breaking point and major dislocations of the population may be expected as the crisis of post-communist transformation evolves; the 'urbanism' of post-communist cities has already undergone spectacular changes; changes can also be detected in urban forms and in patterns of social segregation.

An end to under-urbanization?

It is possible that, with capitalist restructuring of the economy, a sharp decline in the size of the rural population will occur. The countries of Eastern Europe reached post-communism with a high rural population: a third or more of their population still lived in rural settlements and was involved in one way or another with food production. One important source of under-urbanization was the inability of the socialist collective farm sector to produce sufficient food to meet the needs of the people living in the towns. So the rural population supplemented the supply from their own smallholdings, which in all countries, but especially in the more liberal ones such as Hungary, generated substantial incomes. These incomes enabled the rural population to achieve respectable living standards and in particular to build good-quality rural housing.

During the post-communist epoch, the state socialist agrarian system has begun to disintegrate rapidly. As the national economies opened up to world market competition and price subsidies were eliminated, the rural economy went into serious decline and, in some instances, total collapse. In Hungary, for instance, if gross agricultural production in 1988 was 100, it decreased to 90 in 1990, 84 in 1991, 66 in 1992, and a devastating 50 in 1993, before stabilizing in 1994 at the 1993 level (Harcsa and Kovach, forthcoming). The decline of agricultural production can be attributed in part to the decline of the domestic market – domestic meat consumption in Hungary, for instance, declined by some 20 per cent by 1992 in comparison with 1988 (ibid.) – to the importation of subsidized West European agricultural goods without tariff protection to East European markets, and to the virtual disappearance of the former COMECON market.

Under these macro-economic conditions, both the former collective farm sector and the small-scale private farm economy crumbled. By the mid-1990s, the decollectivization of agriculture had not resulted in any substantial growth of private farming; it had only led to a restructuring of the (collective) latifundia and a sharp fall in the number of employees of large agricultural enterprises. Thus, for instance, in Hungary in 1994 over 70 per cent of arable land was being cultivated by successor organizations of the former cooperatives – quasi-private large estates; but while in 1988 the cooperatives employed over 1 million people, by 1994 the number of agricultural wage labourers had fallen to 200,000. Small family enterprises were in no better shape, and the rural industry supported by the agricultural cooperatives during the last period of state socialism had also virtually disappeared.

The result is massive rural unemployment. Those regions which are not within commuting distance of urban industrial centres are particularly heavily affected; here the unemployment rate can be two or three times higher than the national average. In Hungary, this is the case in the north and north-east (Borsod and Szabolcs-Szatmar counties) and in the south-west (Vas county), where unemployment can reach 40–50 per cent, or even higher levels in isolated villages.

So far, though, there is little sign of a post-communist *Landflucht* (flight from the land) – under-urbanization continues to be reproduced, even though its socio-economic and political basis has been undermined. The reasons for this are: first, a weak push from the rural communities and, second, an even weaker pull from the urban centres. As a result of the crisis of post-communist transformation, there is a limited supply of jobs in urban centres; industries which are expanding or the growing tertiary sector offer employment to young and better-trained people, not the unskilled and semi-skilled working class which was kept in rural residences as a result of underurbanization. Cities thus have little attraction for the population which is trapped in the villages; at the same time, rural living, while becoming difficult, still appears to be the better alternative. Rural housing is a major consideration. In the 1970s and 1980s, particularly in Hungary but to some extent also in Poland and the former Czechoslovakia, good-quality rural housing was built. Although in

terms of the distribution of work places and other economic opportunities this housing may not be located in the 'right places', none
the less it remains the best-quality housing available for this population. Furthermore, while the agricultural second economy no longer
offers the opportunities it did when it had to compete only with the
inefficient socialist sector, for the rural unemployed access to a garden and the ability to produce food are still a method of survival at
the present time.

In fact, it is not inevitable that a *Landflucht* should occur. With
some luck, and good social policies, the transformation may be man-
ageable. Enyedi's predictions about suburbanization as the next stage
of urban change may be more on target by the turn of the century
than they were during the 1970s and 1980s. Villages which are within
commuting distance of urban industrial centres may be transformed
into dormitory working-class suburbs. In small countries such as
Hungary and Bohemia, a substantial proportion of villages are close
enough to cities for them to become 'rurbanized'. Furthermore,
although most new job creation has so far been centred in cities, rural
industrialization, the development of a rural tertiary sector and tourism may soften the pains of rural post-communist reconstruction.
This author's key hypothesis, however, is that the mismatch between
rural infrastructure, developed according to the logic of state socialism, and economic – typically urban – opportunities, created by
'merchant capitalism', will find no easy solution and sooner or later
may result in major geographic shifts of the population.

Urbanism

Urbanism already shows significant changes. The transformation of
former socialist cities is the most spectacular in this respect. The
number of small shops, restaurants and street vendors is rapidly
increasing. While GNP, industrial and agricultural production have
declined, the tertiary sector has expanded even during the transformational crisis.

There is an increasing ethnic diversity in most East European
metropolitan centres. The centre of Budapest bustles with Hungarian peasants from Transylvania, Polish black-marketeers, Vietnamese
and Chinese smugglers, all offering their goods to tourists. Arab
money changers dominate the currency black market, which the
police no longer tries to control. The city has become almost as
colourful as a Third World metropolis. More generally, Eastern
Europe is becoming a demographic buffer zone between the Third
World and Western Europe. Since the early 1990s, Germany and

Austria have tightened their immigration policies, so now Poland and Hungary have become the destination of a great deal of immigration from the former Soviet states, from other East European communist countries and from the Third World. Just a decade ago, countries like Poland, Hungary and Czechoslovakia were ethnically quite homogeneous – only Gypsies represented some ethnic diversity. This has rapidly changed: now Turks, Arabs, Russians, Chinese, Vietnamese live in substantial numbers in these countries, diversifying their culture, and even their cuisine.

The increase in urban marginality is also striking. Just as it did in the late nineteenth century, Budapest now supplies young women for the West European sex industries (as do Poland, Russia and other Eastern European countries). Prostitutes are now easy to find in East European cities, or even along international highways. As one drives from Vienna to Budapest, if passport control does not alert you to the fact that you have passed the border, you will notice it from the sight of young, and not so young, women offering their bodies for sale along the highway. Pornography is a major business; the Italian pornography industry is well supplied with Hungarian young women, for example.

Homeless people appeared in the parks and streets of Budapest well before the fall of communism. During the 1980s, homelessness was attributed to the easing of police control. Some of the homeless were people who found the city street a more attractive choice than a repressive home environment, and since the police did not bother them they stayed on the streets. However, post-communism has accelerated the process: now people who do not pay rent can be and occasionally are removed from their homes by police and left in the streets.

There is a sharp increase in crime and deviance. Inner-city streets are crowded with Gypsy beggars and pick-pockets, and you have to watch your wallet as closely as in the busiest streets of New York or Mexico City. It is not clear whether it is the privatization or the criminalization of the economy which proceeds faster. Car theft is so common and carried out so professionally that the police do not really want to be bothered with it. International gangs operate; the car stolen in the streets of Budapest is within hours smuggled to the Ukraine or Romania.

Criminalization is helped by the confusion and the legitimacy problem of law enforcement agencies. The police are so concerned to avoid accusations of harassment that they are reluctant even to perform their crime-prevention functions. Border controls, including those by the customs authorities, are lax for the same reasons.

Nuclear materials, drugs and armaments are easily smuggled. Measured by these standards, there is little doubt where post-communist Eastern Europe is heading; it appears to be moving more in the direction of the Near East than that of Western Europe. The boredom of the socialist cities is gone, but so is their safety.

Suburbanization and inner urban decay

Urban forms change more slowly than urban diversity. It is obvious, though, that social inequalities are increasing sharply, and this is beginning to affect patterns of urban social segregation as well.

So far the new rich have tended to move into the traditional middle-class districts, where they have bought up the villas of the old bourgeoisie and renovated them, or built luxurious though often tasteless condominiums or town houses, and in some cases even new villas in their place. As the existing stock of properties in the old middle-class suburbs is gradually bought up, the expanding new bourgeoisie and the professional class – whose living standards are rapidly increasing – are beginning to look for new locations. This may lead to suburbanization or may result in the gentrification of inner-city areas. At present, suburbanization is the dominant trend: not only is the air in the inner-cities too polluted, but with poverty, crime and prostitution flourishing in downtown areas, the rich find it healthier, safer and more pleasant to move into formerly rural villages around the metropolitan centres. There are, for example, signs of this happening around Buda, where areas such as Szentendre and Solymar are beginning to look like Western-style suburbs.

If Eastern Europe successfully closes the gap with Western Europe and local governments can solve the problems of air pollution and ensure inner-city safety, then gentrification of inner-city areas may at least complement the suburbanization of peripheral (formerly rural) villages. While inner-city neighbourhoods in cities like Budapest and Prague deteriorated both physically and socially during the decades of state socialism, they are eminently 'gentrifiable'. There is substantial reasonable inner-city housing, built around the turn of the century, which, like inner-city housing in American cities with histories reaching back to the nineteenth century, could become attractive for Yuppies and the nouveau riche.[7]

The formerly new housing developments are now in sharp physical and social decline. Those built (during the 1960s and early 1970s) closer to the city centre initially attracted the professional class, but this began to change during the last decade of state socialism. Soviet 'house-building factories' flooded most East European cities with low-quality housing. The lack of vacant building plots in the inner areas forced construction organizations towards the periphery. As this happened, the social status of new housing areas began to decline. The process is now being accelerated by the post-communist transformation. Now local governments try to relinquish control over this housing. However, this low-quality housing, located in undesirable neighbourhoods, and poorly served by public transportation and other services, cannot easily be privatized. Only those who are trapped in it would buy it, and, if they do, they will have no resources to pay for the maintenance or renovation (the physical structure of these buildings began to deteriorate within 10–20 years of their date of construction). Those who can afford to move are beginning to escape from them, leaving the poor and ethnic minorities to concentrate in them (a process of residualization familiar in the similar estates on the periphery of many Western European cities). As a result, the whole belt of 'new housing estates' is likely to became the slums of the early twenty-first century. One of the major challenges facing urban planners is how to eliminate these slums. However, if Eastern Europe remains on the periphery of the world system, then their decay may continue and the new rich will escape these cities to their luxurious suburbs, defended by their private police forces and served by high-quality private schools, hospitals and shopping malls.

CONCLUDING REMARKS

If we now ask our initial question again – did socialism make any difference to urban development in Eastern Europe? – we can answer in the affirmative. The East European societies achieved industrialization under socialism with less population concentration in space than they would have had if they had followed a market capitalist path of development. The East European cities lost some of their 'urbanism' during their socialist epoch: they offered less diversity and choice in urban services, less urban stimuli in public places, and less marginality than they had before World War II. And, finally, particularly during the first two or three decades of socialism, the prominence of the state in providing urban housing, especially new housing construction in the cities and the restriction on the functioning of the urban land market, resulted in the concentration of new housing in large housing estates, built a fair distance from the city centres. These developments attracted mainly the middle class and were, at least in part, responsible for the physical and social decay of the traditionally quite prestigious inner-city neighbourhoods. The resulting new social geography of the East European cities was undoubtedly the product of socialist urban planning and a socialist urban management system.

Today it appears that state socialism just proved to be 'the longest and most painful way from capitalism to capitalism' – as a bitter East European joke puts it. But though socialism eventually fell, while the socialist experiment lasted it did produce historically unique patterns of urbanization. Socialism, by eliminating or drastically reducing the role of private ownership of the means of production and private property in urban land and housing, for better or worse, broke the correlation between industrial and urban growth that we knew from the history of Western capitalist development, and created cities which were different from their capitalist counterparts both in the character of their urbanism and in their urban forms.

Now urban research on Eastern Europe has a fascinating research agenda. The dismantling of the inherited socialist patterns of urbanization and urban forms is a historically unprecedented process. How it unfolds will enrich our knowledge of capitalist urban development. Most importantly, the immediate future of Eastern Europe will help us understand whether dependent capitalist development, with its urban consequences, is avoidable or not; which urban policies may prevent such a development; and which policies may lock these societies into the 'development of under-development'. The years to come, just like the decades we left behind, may not be that cheerful for those who live in the cities of Eastern Europe, but they will undoubtedly be very instructive for the scholars of urban processes.

NOTES

This is a significantly expanded and revised version of an earlier paper, written before the fall of communism and published as 'East European cities – how different are they?' in Greg Gudin and Aiden Southall (eds), *Urban anthropology in China*, Leiden and New York, E.J. Brill, 41–64.

1   For the most comprehensive and sophisticated elaboration of the ecological position and for an overview of the current literature see Wilson, 1983.

2   Ecologists often believe in an 'equilibrium state of population concentration', which reflects the level of technology and economic growth (Wilson, 1983: 17; Hawley, 1971; Wardwell 1980).

3   For the most comprehensive analysis of urban ecological structure under socialism see French and Hamilton (1979). For a recent analysis of occupational segregation under socialism see Dangschat (1987).

4   For earlier publications on this topic see Szelenyi (1983, 1987).

5   What is the character of the social formation, which emerged as a result of these changes? The best term I can come up with is 'post-communism'. The concept of post-communism was first coined by Brzezinski (1989), who foreshadowed the fall of state socialism and used the concept of post-communism to describe what he believed to be an evolutionary step between communist totalitarianism and Western-style democracy. I have borrowed the term from Brzezinski, but I apply it in a value-neutral, descriptive way, without subscribing to modernization theory, which underlines Brzezinski's use of the term. The notion of post-communism tells us what Eastern Europe is leaving behind, without specifying where it is heading towards. Like the concepts of post-Marxism, post-structuralism, or post-modernism, that of post-communism defines our subject matter as what it is *not* without implying much about what it is.

6   In 1993, Kornai coined the term 'transformational recession'. In my view the depth of the economic decline is so severe that the term 'recession' is an understatement and the use of the term 'crisis' is in order.

7   For the time being, there is little sign of this happening. Budapest's city planners, for instance, created an enclave around Klauzal Square, a run-down inner-city area with a rapidly increasing Gypsy population. They rebuilt and modernized two blocks of housing (doing a good job of gentrification) and expected that its effect would spread. It did not. The Yuppies, or members of the upper middle class, the gentrifiers in other countries, here still prefer to move to the newly forming suburbs.

Bibliography

Aage, A., 1989, *The soviet distribution of income in comparative perspective*, Copenhagen, Institute of Economics, University of Copenhagen.

ABV, 1994, 'Privat-inform', *ABV* (Almaty, Kazakhstan), 15 March.

ADEF, 1992, *The Russian system of land tenure* (interim report), Paris, Russian Federation/World Bank.

Albany Law Center, 1992, *The use of the public trust doctrine as a management tool for public and private lands*, Albany NY, Albany Law Center.

Alcaly, R.E. and Mermelstein, D. (eds), 1977, *The fiscal crisis of American cities*, New York, Random House.

Alexeev, M., 1991, 'Expenditures on privately rented housing and imputed rents in the USSR', *Berkeley-Duke Occasional Papers on the Second Economy in the USSR*, Durham NC, Duke University, no. 31.

Andrusz, G.D., 1984, *Housing and urban development in the USSR*, London, Macmillan.

—— 1987, 'The built environment in Soviet theory and practice', *International Journal of Urban and Regional Research*, 11(3), 478–98.

—— 1990, 'A note on the finance of housing in the Soviet Union', *Soviet Studies*, 42, 555–70.

—— 1992, 'Housing co-operatives in the Soviet Union', *Housing Studies*, 7(2), 138–53.

—— 1993, 'Housing reform in Russia: the limits to privatisation', in R.A. Hays Jr (ed.), *Ownership, control and the future of housing policy*, Westport CT, Greenwood Press, 75–102.

Anlian, S. and Vanian, I., forthcoming, 'Armenia', in R. Struyk (ed.), *Eco-*

nomic restructuring in the former Soviet bloc: evidence from the housing sector, Washington DC, Urban Institute Press.

Arato, A., 1991, 'Social movements and civil society in the Soviet Union', in J.B. Sedaitis and J. Butterfield (eds), *Perestroika from below*, Boulder CO, Westview.

Arbeitsgruppe 'Neue Verfassung der DDR' des Runden Tisches, 1990, *Entwurf, Verfassung der Deutschen Demokratischen Republik*, Berlin, Staatsverlag der DDR.

Argumenty i fakty, 1994, 'Narodnye igry 94', *Argumenty i fakty*, 26 June.

Atkinson, A. and Micklewright, J., 1992, *Economic transformation in Eastern Europe and the distribution of income*, Cambridge, Cambridge University Press.

Avineri, S. (ed.), 1992, *Communitarianism and individualism*, Oxford, Oxford University Press.

Baar, K.K., 1993, 'Residential landlord tenant law for privately owned flats', MS, Budapest, Budapest University of Economic Science.

Bagnasco, A., 1977, *Tre Italie: la problematica territoriale dello sviluppo italianso*, Bologna, IL Mulino.

Baranovsky, V. and Spanger, H.-J., 1992, *In from the cold: Germany, Russia and the future of Europe*, Boulder CO, Westview.

Barbash, N.B., 1982, 'Spatial relations among places with complementary functions within the city of Moscow', *Soviet Geography*, 23, 77–94.

—— 1983, 'Physical development of infants as an indicator of the condition of the urban environment', *Soviet Geography*, 24, 204–13.

Barbash, N.B. and Gutnov, A.E., 1980, 'Urban planning aspects of the spatial organisation of Moscow', *Soviet Geography*, 21, 557–73.

Barnes, S.H. and Kaase, M. (eds), 1979, *Political action*, Beverley Hills, Sage.

Bater, J.H., 1980, *The Soviet city: ideal and reality*, London, Edward Arnold.

—— 1984, 'The Soviet city: continuity and change in privilege and place', in J.A. Agnew, J. Mercer and D.E. Sopher (eds), *The city in cultural context*, Boston, Allen & Unwin, 134–62.

—— 1986, 'Some recent perspectives on the Soviet city', *Urban Geography*, 7, 93–102.

Benácek, V., 1994, 'The transition of small businesses and private entrepreneurship in the Czech Republic', in *Conference proceedings: democratic modernisation in the countries of Central Europe* (University of Essex, 11–14 May), Colchester, Forum on Central and Eastern Europe and Centre for European Studies, University of Essex, 137–77.

Berezin, M., Kaganova, O., Kosareva, N.B. and Prytkov, A., 1992, 'Housing privatization in the Russian Federation', mimeo, paper prepared for the European Network for Housing Research.

Berking, H. and Neckel, S., 1992, 'Die gestört Gemeinschaft. Machtprozesse und Konfliktpotentiale in einer ostdeutschen Gemeinde', in S. Hardil (ed.), *Zwischen Bewusstsein und Sein: Die Vermittlung 'objektiver' Lebensbedingungen und 'subjektiver' Lebensweisen*, Opladen, Leske & Budrich, 151–71.

320   Bibliography

Berle, A. and Means, G., 1932, *The modern corporation and private property*, New York, Macmillan.

Berman, H.J., 1950, *Justice in Russia: an interpretation of Soviet law*, Cambridge MA, Harvard University Press.

Berry, B.J.L., 1980, 'The urban problem' in American Assembly (ed.), *The farm and the city: rivals or allies*, Englewood Cliffs NJ, Prentice Hall, 36–59.

—— 1981, *Comparative urbanisation*, New York, St Martins Press.

Beyme, K. von, 1988, *Reformpolitik und sozialer Wandel in der Sowjetunion 1970–1988*, Baden-Baden, Nomos.

Beyme, K. von, Durth, W., Gutschow, N., Nerdinger, W. and Topfstedt, T. (ed.), 1992, *Neue Städte aus Ruinen, Deutscher Städtebau der Nachkriegszeit*, Munich, Prestel.

Bicanic, I. and Dominis, I., 1992, 'Tudjman remains dominant after Croatian elections', *RFE/RL Research Report*, 37, 20–6.

Bluestone, B. and Harrison, B., 1982, *The deindustrialization of America*, New York, Basic Books.

Bogetic, Z. and Wilton, J., 1992, 'Bulgarian market reform', *Transition*, 3(6), 5–6.

Bourdieu, P. and Wacquant, L.J.D., 1992, *An invitation to reflexive sociology*, Cambridge, Polity Press.

Boyce, J.H., 1993, 'Local government reform and the new Moscow city soviet', *Journal of Communist Studies*, 9, 245–71.

Boycko, M., Shleifer, A. and Vishny, R., 1993, 'Privatizing Russia', *Brookings Papers on Economic Activity*, no. 2, 139–92.

Brie, M., 1990, *Wer ist Eigentümer im Sozialismus?*, Berlin, Dietz Verlag.

Brovkin, V., 1990, 'Revolution from below: informal political associations in Russia 1988–1989', *Soviet Studies*, 42, 233–57.

Brown, J.F., 1991, 'The resurgence of nationalism', *Report on Eastern Europe*, 24, 35–7.

Brzezinski, Z., 1989, *The grand failure: the birth and death of communism in the twentieth century*, New York, Charles Scribner's Sons.

Buckley, R., Hendershott, P. and Villani, K., 1992, *Rapid housing privatization: pay the special dividend and get on with it*, Washington DC, World Bank.

Burawoy, M., 1992, 'The end of Sovietology and the renaissance of modernization theory', *Contemporary Sociology*, 774–85.

Burawoy, M. and Krotov, P., 1992, 'The Soviet transition from socialism to capitalism: worker control and economic bargaining in the wood industry', *American Sociological Review*, 57, 16–38.

—— 1993, 'The economic basis of Russia's political crisis', *New Left Review*, 198, 49–69.

Burgess, E.W., 1925, 'The growth of a city', in R.E. Park, E.W. Burgess and R.D. McKenzie (eds), *The city*, Chicago, Chicago University Press, 42–62.

Burnham, J., 1941, *The managerial revolution*, New York, Day.

Butler, S.B., 1992, *Final report of activities: legal assistance to the Russian Federation for the housing sector*, Washington DC, Urban Institute.

Butler, S.B. and O'Leary, S., 1994a, *The legal basis for land allocation in the Russian Federation*, Washington DC, Urban Institute.

—— 1994b, 'A survey of the emerging land law of the Russian Federation', *Parker School Journal of East European Law*, 1(5–6), 541–89.

Butler, W.E., 1985, 'Marxian concepts of ownership in Soviet law', *Columbia Journal of Transnational Law*, 23, 281–96.

—— 1988, *Soviet law* (2nd edn), London, Butterworths.

Butterfield, J. and Sedaitis, J.B., 1991, 'The emergence of social movements in the Soviet Union', in J.B. Sedaitis and J. Butterfield (eds), *Perestroika from below*, Boulder CO, Westview.

Calvocoressi, P., 1991, *Resilient Europe: a study of the years 1870–2000*, London, Longman.

Campbell, A., 1992, 'The restructuring of local government in Russia', *Public Money and Management*, 12(4), 19–24.

Carrère d'Encausse, H., 1978, *L'empire éclate: la révolte des nations en URSS*, Paris, Flammarion.

Castells, M., 1977, *The urban question*, London, Edward Arnold.

—— 1983, *The city and the grassroots*, London, Edward Arnold.

Castells, M., Goh, L. and Kwok, R.Y., 1990, *The Shep Kip Mei syndrome*, London, Pion.

Central European Economic Review, 'Investors warm to growing normalcy: fewer risks and more incentives attract foreign money', 1994, *Central European Economic Review*, 2(3), 6.

Charley, J., 1992, 'Perestroika and the built environment: slogans revisited', in *The production of the built environment* (12th Proceedings of the Bartlett International Summer School, Moscow, 1990), London, BISS.

Chavance, B., 1994, *The transformation of communist systems: economic reforms since the 1950s*, Boulder CO, Westview.

Chernomyrdin, V., 1994, 'No exits on the road to market', *Financial Times*, 16 May.

Ciechocinska, M., 1987, 'Government intervention to balance housing supply and urban population growth: the case of Warsaw', *International Journal of Urban and Regional Research*, 11(1), 9–26.

Clark, E. and Soulsby, A., 1994, 'Enterprise restructuring and the community in the Czech Republic: the role of embeddness', paper prepared for the ESRC East–West Initiative Workshop, London, 9–10 December.

Clark, W.A., 1993, *Crime and punishment in Soviet officialdom*, London, M.E. Sharpe.

Coleman, J.S., 1990, *Foundations of social theory*, Cambridge MA and London, Belknap Press.

Csanádi, G. and Ladányi, J., 1985, 'Budapest – A Városszerkezet Történetének És Különbözö Társadalmi Csoportok Városszerkezet Elhelyezkedésének Nem-ökologiai Viszgálata' ['Budapest – a non-ecological study of the history of urban structure and ecological distribution of the population'], PhD thesis, Hungarian Academy of Sciences.

Dahn, D., 1994, *Wir bleiben hier oder wem gehört der Osten*, Reinbek bei Hamburg, Rowohlt.

Dangschat, J., 1987, 'Sociospatial disparities in a "socialist" city: the case of

Warsaw at the end of the 1970s', *International Journal of Urban and Regional Research*, 11(1), 37–60.

Dangschat, J. and Blasius, J., 1987, 'Social and spatial disparities in Warsaw in 1978: an application of correspondence analysis to a "socialist" city', *Urban Studies*, 24, 173–91.

Daniell, J. and Struyk, R., 1994, 'Housing privatization in Moscow: who privatizes and why?', *International Journal of Urban and Regional Research*, 18(3), 510–25.

Davis, K. and Golden, H.H., 1954–5, 'Urbanization and the development of pre-industrial areas', *Economic Development and Cultural Change*, 3, 6–26.

Demko, G.J. and Regulska, J., 1987, 'Socialism and its impact on urban processes and the city', *Urban Geography*, 8(4), 289–92.

Derbinova, M., 1983, 'Leninskii raion Moskvy: Ekologichesky aspekty razvitiya', *Vestnik Moskovskogo Universiteta (geografiya)*, no. 2.

Durkheim, E., 1893/1964, *The division of labour in society*, London, Collier-Macmillan.

—— 1921, 'La famille conjugale', *Revue philosophique*, 91 (cited in Giddens, A., 1971, *Capitalism and modern social theory*, Cambridge, Cambridge University Press, 103).

Economist, 1993, 'Jobless Europe', *Economist*, 26 June.

—— 1994a, 'A privatiser's life', *Economist*, 25 June.

—— 1994b, 'Welcome to capitalism', *Economist*, 9 July.

—— 1994c, 'Good intentions', *Economist*, 15 October.

—— 1994d, 'Russia's crisis of capitalism', *Economist*, 15 October.

Edel'man, N., 1989, *Revolyutsia sverkhu v Rossii*, Moscow.

Eisenhammer, J., 1995, 'Germans pay a price for freedom fire sale', *Independent on Sunday* (Inside Story), 8 January.

Embassy of the USA, USIS, Regional Programme Office, 1993, *Materialy o pastvete ekonomiki. Privlechenie inostrannykh kapitalovlozhenii*, Vienna, Embassy of the USA.

Enyedi, G., 1978, *Kelet-Közep Európa gazdasági földrajza*, Budapest, Közgazdasági és Jogi Kiadó.

—— 1984, *Az urbanizációs ciklus és a magyar településhálozat átalakulása* [*The cycle of urbanization and the changes of the Hungarian regional system*], Budapest, Akadémiai Kiadó.

—— forthcoming, 'Urbanization in East Central Europe'.

Eyerman, R. and Jamison, A., 1991, *Social movements*, Cambridge, Polity.

Faltran, L., 1994, 'Housing policy in Slovakia at the crossroads: between marketability and state interventionism', mimeo, paper presented at the XIIth World Congress of Sociology, 18–23 July, Bielefeld.

Feldbrugge, F.J.M., 1990, 'The constitution of the USSR', *Review of Socialist Law*, 16, 163–6.

Field, D., 1976, *The end of serfdom: nobility and bureaucracy in Russia, 1855–1861*, Cambridge, Cambridge University Press.

Fish, S., 1991, 'The emergence of independent associations and the transformation of Russian political society', *Journal of Communist Studies*, 7, 299–334.

Fisher, D., 1993, 'The emergence of the environmental movement in Eastern Europe and its role in the revolutions of 1989', in B. Jancar-Webster (ed.), *Environmental action in Eastern Europe*, Armonk, NY, M.E. Sharpe.

Fleischer, T., 1993, 'Jaws on the Danube: water management, regime change and the movement against the Middle Danube Hydroelectric Dam', *International Journal of Urban and Regional Research*, 17, 429–43.

Floroff, O. and Tiefenbrun, S., 1991, 'New Soviet fundamentals on law of land ownership', *New York International Law Review*, summer, 4(2), 92–106.

Forbes, D. and Thrift, N. (eds), 1987, *The socialist Third World: urban development and territorial planning*, Oxford, Blackwell.

Forrest, R. and Murie, A., 1988, *Selling the welfare state: the privatization of public housing*, London, Routledge.

Frampton, K., 1985, 'Critical regionalism: speculations on an architecture of resistance', in C. Johnson (ed.), *The city in conflict*, London, Mansell.

French, R.A., 1987, 'Changing spatial patterns in Soviet cities – planning or pragmatism?', *Urban Geography*, 8, 309–20.

—— 1994, *Plans, pragmatism and people: the failure of Soviet city planning*, London, UCL Press.

French, R.A. and Hamilton, F.E.I. (eds), 1979, *The socialist city: spatial structure and urban policy*, Chichester, John Wiley.

Friedmann, W., 1972, *Law in a changing society*, New York, Columbia University Press.

Friedrichs, J. (ed.), 1985, *Stadtentwicklungen in West-und Osteuropa*, Berlin and New York, de Gruyter.

—— 1988, 'Large cities in Eastern Europe', in M. Dogan and J.K. Kasarda (eds), *The metropolis era: vol. 1 A world of giant cities*, Beverly Hills, Sage, 128–54.

Frydman, Roman, et al., 1993, *The privatization process in Central Europe*, Budapest, Central European University Press.

Fukuyama, F., 1989, *The end of history and the last man*, London, Hamish Hamilton.

—— 1990, 'Two sets of rules for a split world', *Independent*, 7 September.

Galambos, J., 1993, 'An international environmental conflict on the Danube: the Gabcikovo-Nagymaros dams', in A. Vari and P. Tamas (eds), *Environment and democratic transition*, Dordrecht, Kluwer.

Gans, H., 1962, 'Urbanism and subarbanism as ways of life', in A.M. Rose (ed.), *Human behavior and social processes*, Boston, Houghton and Mifflin, 625–48.

Gaspar, J., 1984, 'Urbanization: growth, problems and policies', in A. Williams (ed.), *Southern Europe transformed*, London, Harper and Row.

Gausmann, D., 1994, ' "Ein Bild von einer Stadt": Eine Industriestadt auf der Suche nach ihrer Mitte: Das Beispiel Marl', in R. Lindner (ed.), *Die Wiederkehr des Regionalen*, Frankfurt and New York, Campus, 158–83.

Gellner, E., 1969, *Thought and change*, Chicago, Chicago University Press.

—— 1994, *Conditions of liberty: civil society and its rivals*, London, Hamish Hamilton.

Gerlich, P., Plasser, F. and Ulram, P.A. (eds), 1992, *Regimewechsel: Demokratisierung und politische Kultur in Ost-Mitteleuropa*, Vienna, Böhlau.

Geyer, D., 1989, 'Perestroika und "russische Seele"', in J. Heideking, G. Hufnagel and F. Knipping (eds), *Wege in die Zeitgeschichte: Festschrift zum 65. Geburtstag von Gerhard Schulz*, Berlin, de Gruyter, 305–18.

Golachowski, S., 1967, 'Semi-urbanization?', *Polish Perspectives*, 4, 22–30.

Goodman, A.C., 1988, 'An econometric model of housing prices, permanent income, tenure choice and housing demand', *Journal of Urban Economics*, 23, 327–53.

Gorbachev, M., 1987, *Perestroika: new thinking for our country and the world*, London, Fontana.

Gray, C.W., 1992a, 'The challenge of legal reform in Hungary', *Transition*, 3(9), 6.

—— 1992b, *The legal framework for private sector activity in the Czech and Slovak Federal Republic*, Washington DC, World Bank.

Gray, C.W. and Ianachkov, P., 1992, *Bulgaria's evolving legal framework for private sector development*, Washington DC, World Bank.

Gray, C.W. and Stiblar, F.D., 1992, *The evolving legal framework for private sector activity in Slovenia*, Washington DC, World Bank.

Gray, C.W., Hanson, R. and Heller, M., 1992, *Legal reform for Hungary's private sector*, Washington DC, World Bank.

Gray, C.W., Hanson, R. and Ianachkov, P., 1992, *Romania's evolving legal framework for private sector development*, Washington DC, World Bank.

Gray, C.W., Hanson, R.J., Heller, M.A., Ianachkov, P.G. and Ostas, D.T., 1992, 'The legal framework for private sector development in a transitional economy: the case of Poland', *Georgia Journal of International and Comparative Law*, 22(2), 283–327.

Grootaert, C. and Dubois, J.L., 1989, 'Tenure choice and the demand for rental housing in cities of the Ivory Coast', *Journal of Urban Economics*, 24, 44–63.

Gsovski, V., 1945, *Soviet civil law: private rights and their background under the Soviet regime*, Ann Arbor, University of Michigan Law School.

Gugler, J., 1982, 'Overurbanization reconsidered', *Economic Development and Cultural Change*, 3, 173–89.

Gulbinsky, N., 1992, 'A dragged-out 9th Thermidor', *Moscow News*, 1, 5–12 January.

Györi, P., 1991, 'Report prepared on the homeless in Hungary, 1990', *Research Review*, 91/2, 211–24.

Györi, P. and Matern, E., 1996, 'Housing organisations in Budapest', in K. Láng-Pickvance, N. Manning and C.G. Pickvance (eds), *Housing and environmental movements: grassroots experience in Hungary, Estonia and Russia*, Aldershot, Avebury Press.

Hain, S., 1992, 'Reise nach Moskau: Wie Deutsche "sozialistisch" bauen lernten', *Bauwelt*, 45, 1546–58.

Hamilton, E., 1993, 'Social areas under state socialism: the case of Moscow', in S. Soloman (ed.), *Beyond Sovietology: essays on politics and history*, New York, M.E. Sharpe, 192–225.

Hannemann, C., 1994, 'Industrialisiertes Bauen: Zur Kontinuität eines Leitbildes im Wohnungsbau der DDR', PhD thesis, Technical University, Berlin.

Hansen, N.M. (ed.), 1977, *Human settlement systems*, Cambridge MA, Ballinger.

Hanson, P., 1993, 'Local power and market reform in Russia', *Communist Economies and Economic Transformation*, 5, 45–60.

Harcsa, I. and Kovach, I., forthcoming, 'The price of privatization – Hungary', in I. Szelenyi (ed.), *Pathways from collectivism*, Boulder CO, Westview.

Harloe, M., 1981, 'Notes on comparative urban research', in M. Dear and A.J. Scott (eds), *Urbanization and urban planning in capitalist society*, London and New York, Methuen, 179–98.

—— 1995, *The people's home? Social rented housing in Europe and America*, Oxford and Cambridge MA, Blackwell.

Harvey, D., 1973, *Social justice and the city*, London, Edward Arnold.

—— 1985, *The urbanization of capital*, Baltimore, Johns Hopkins University Press.

Hatschikjan, M., 1991, 'Osteuropa – ein nationalistischer Hexenkessel', *Osteuropa*, 41(3), 201–20.

Hawley, A.H., 1971, *Urban society – an ecological approach*, New York, Roland.

Hazard, J.N., 1939, *Soviet housing law*, New Haven CT, Yale University Press.

Hazard, J.N., Butler, W.E. and Maggs, P.B., 1984, *The Soviet legal system: the law in the 1980s*, New York, Oceana Publications for the Parker School of Foreign and Comparative Law, Columbia University.

Hechter, M., 1975, *Internal colonialism: the Celtic fringe in British national development*, London, Routledge & Kegan Paul.

Hegedus, J. and Tosics, I., 1983, 'Housing classes and housing policy: some changes in the Budapest housing market', *International Journal of Urban and Regional Research*, 7(4), 467–94.

Hegedus, J., Mark, K. and Tosics, I., forthcoming, 'Housing reform in Hungary', in R. Struyk (ed.), *Economic restructuring in the former soviet bloc: evidence from the housing sector*, Washington DC: Urban Institute Press.

Hegedus, J., Mark, K., Struyk, R. and Tosics, I., 1993, 'The privatization dilemma in Budapest's public rental sector', *Cities*, 10(3), 257–70.

—— 1994, 'Tenant satisfaction with public housing management: Budapest in transition', *Housing Studies*, 9, 315–28.

Hofmeister, B., 1980, *Die Stadtstruktur*, Darmstadt, Wissenschaftliche Buchgesellschaft.

Hoscislawski, T., 1991, *Bauen zwischen Macht und Ohnmacht: Architektur und Städtebau in der DDR*, Berlin, Verlag für Bauwesen.

Hough, J.F., 1969, *The Soviet prefects*, Cambridge MA, Harvard University Press.

Illner, M., 1991, 'Zwischen Ökonomie und Neofeudalismus', in W. Glatzer (ed.), *Deutscher Soziologentag 1990: Die Modernisierung moderner Gesellschaften*, Frankfurt and New York, Campus, 407–13.

IMF, World Bank, OECD and EBRD, 1991, *A study of the Soviet economy*, Paris, OECD.

Ivanov, V.N., 1993, 'Mezhnatsional'naya naprjazhennost' v regional'nom aspekte', *SocIss*, 7, 59–66.

Jacobs, J., 1964, *The economy of cities*, New York, Random House.

Jessen, J., 1987, 'Die Zukunft der Grossiedlungen in schrumpfenden Stadtregionen', *Archiv für Kommunalwissenschaften*, 52–65.

Joly, D., Nettleton, A. and Poulton, H., 1993, *Refugees: asylum in Europe?*, Boulder CO, Westview.

Juhasz, J., Vari, A. and Tolgyesi, J., 1993, 'Environment conflict and political change: public perception of low-level radioactive waste management in Hungary', in A. Vari and P. Tamas (eds), *Environment and democratic transition*, Dordrecht, Kluwer.

Jung, B., 1994, 'Polish youth and its leisure in a risk society', paper presented at the ESRC East–West Initiative Workshop, 'The Social Consequences of Marketisation', London, 9–10 December.

Kagarlitsky, B., 1989, *The thinking reed: intellectuals and the Soviet state, 1917 to the present*, London and New York, Verso.

Kalinina, N.V., 1989, 'Housing and housing policy in the USSR', mimeo, paper presented at Noszvaj Conference, Hungary, July.

—— 1991, 'Guaranteeing housing in the USSR', mimeo.

Kansky, K., 1976, *Urbanisation under socialism: the case of Czechoslovakia*, New York, Praeger.

Katsura, H. and Struyk, R., 1991, 'Selling Eastern Europe's state rental stock: proceed with caution', *Housing Policy Debate*, 4(2), 1251–74.

Kil, W., 1992, 'Der letzte Monolith: Baudenkmal Stalinstadt', *Bauwelt*, 10, 497–505.

Kingsley, T. and Mikelsons, M., forthcoming, 'The Czech and Slovak Republics: housing as a second stage reform', in R. Struyk (ed.), *Economic restructuring in the former Soviet bloc: evidence from the housing sector*, Washington DC, Urban Institute Press.

Kirkov, P., 1993, 'Regional policy and territorial economic differentiation in Russia: a case study of the Altai Krai in Western Siberia', paper presented at CREES Annual Conference, Cumberland Great Lodge, Windsor, 25–7 June.

Kitschelt, H., 1986, 'Political opportunity structures and political protest: anti-nuclear movements in four democracies', *British Journal of Political Science*, 16, 58–95.

Kolankiewicz, G., 1994, 'Consensus and competition in the eastern enlargement of the European Union', *International Affairs*, 70(3), 477–96.

—— 1995, 'Regime transformation as the rationalisation of social capital', in *Conference for David Lockwood: conference programme and papers* (University of Essex, 18–20 April), Colchester, Department of Sociology, University of Essex.

Kolosi, T. and Szelenyi, I., 1993, 'Social change and research on social structure in Hungary', in B. Nedelmann and P. Sztompka (eds), *Sociology in Europe: in search of identity*, Berlin and New York, de Gruyter, 141–63.

Kolossov, V.A., 1992, *Territorial briefing: ethno-territorial conflicts and boundaries in the Former Soviet Union*, Durham, International Boundaries Research Unit, University of Durham.

Kommersant, 1992, 'Na rynke prodazhi kvartir snova ozhivlenno', *Kommersant*, no. 44.

Komsomol'skaya Pravda, 1994, 'Sbezhavshie iz ada', *Komsomol'skaya Pravda*, 20 July.

Konrad, G. and Szelenyi, I., 1977, 'Social conflicts of under-urbanization', in M. Harloe (ed.), *Captive cities*, Chichester, John Wiley, 157–74.

Kopp, A., 1970, *Town and revolution: Soviet architecture and city planning 1917–1935*, New York, G. Braziller.

Kornai, J., 1990, *The road to a free economy: shifting from a socialist system: the example of Hungary*, New York, W.W. Norton.

—— 1992, *The socialist system*, Oxford, Oxford University Press.

Korosenyi, A., 1992, 'The decay of communist rule in Hungary', in A. Bozoki, A. Korosenyi and G. Schöpflin (eds), *Post-communist transition*, London, Pinter.

Kos, D., 1994, 'Hypercomplexity of the transition', mimeo, available from Edvard Kardelt University, Faculty of Sociology, Ljubljana, Slovenia.

Kosareva, N., Puzanov, A. and Tikhomirova, M., forthcoming, 'Russia: fast starter', in R. Struyk (ed.), *Economic restructuring in the former Soviet bloc: evidence from the housing sector*, Washington DC, Urban Institute Press.

Kriesi, H., Koopmans, R., Duyvendak, J.W. and Gingni, G., 1992, 'New social movements and political opportunities in Western Europe', *European Journal of Political Research*, 22, 219–44.

Kutsev, G., 1982, *Novye Goroda (Sotsiologicheskie ocherk na materialakh Sibirii)*, Moscow: Mysl'.

Ladányi, J., 1989, 'Changing patterns of residential segregation in Budapest', *International Journal of Urban and Regional Research*, 13(1), 55–72.

—— 1992, 'Local government reorganisation and housing policy in Budapest: a round table discussion', *International Journal of Urban and Regional Research*, 16, 477–88.

Lane, D., 1992, *Soviet society under perestroika*, London, Routledge.

Láng-Pickvance, K., Manning, N. and Pickvance, C.G. (eds), 1996, *Housing and environmental movements: grassroots experience in Hungary, Estonia and Russia*, Aldershot, Avebury Press.

——, forthcoming, *Citizen action on housing and the environment in Hungary, Estonia and Russia*, Oxford, Oxford University Press.

Lengyel, L., 1992, 'The character of the political parties in Hungary (Autumn, 1989)', in A. Bozoki, A. Korosenyi and G. Schöpflin (eds), *Post-communist transition*, London, Pinter.

Levitas, A. and Strzalkowski, P., 1990, 'What does "uwlaszczenie nomenklatury" [propertization of the nomenklatura] really mean?', *Communist Economies*, 2, 413–16.

Linneman, P.D. and Megbolugbe, I.F., 1994, 'Privatization and housing policy', *Urban Studies*, 31(4/5), 835–51.

Lloyd, J., 1994, 'Russia in deep crisis as output plunges by 25%', *Financial Times*, 9 May.

Lovenduski, J. and Woodall, J., 1987, *Politics and society in Eastern Europe*, London, Macmillan.

Lowry, I., 1992, *Real estate tenure and taxation in the Russian Federation*, Washington DC, Urban Institute.

Ludwig, M., 1992, 'Ethnische Vielfalt und Minderheitenschutz in Osteuropa', *FAZ*, 11(3), 7.

McAuley, M., 1992, *Soviet politics 1917–1991*, Oxford, Oxford University Press.

McCarthy, J.D. and Zald, M.N., 1977, 'Resource mobilization and social movements: a partial theory', *American Journal of Sociology*, 82(4), 1212–39.

McGregor, J., 1993, 'How electoral laws shape the Eastern Europeans' parliaments', *RFE/RL Research Report*, no. 4, 11–18.

Maclennan, D., 1993, 'Decentralization and residential choices in European cities: the roles of the state and market', in A.A. Summers, P.C. Cheshire and L. Senn (eds), *Urban change in the United States and Western Europe*, Washington DC, Urban Institute Press, 528–51.

MacPherson, C.B., 1962, *The political theory of possessive individualism*, Oxford, Oxford University Press.

MacPherson, C.B., 1978, *Property: mainstream and critical positions*, Toronto, University of Toronto Press.

McQuaid, D., 1993, 'Poland: the parliamentary elections: a postmortem', *Report on Eastern Europe*, 8 November, 15–21.

Maggs, P.B., 1990, 'Constitutional implications of changes in property rights in the USSR', *Cornell International Law Journal*, 23, 363–75.

Mainwaring, S. and Viola, E., 1984, 'New social movements, political culture and democracy: Brazil and Argentina in the 1980s', *Telos*, 61, 17–52.

Malpezzi, S. and Mayo, S.K., 1987, 'User cost and housing tenure in developing countries', *Journal of Development Economics*, 25, 197–220.

Mandic, S. and Stanovick, T., forthcoming, 'Slovenia: fast privatization of the stock, slow reform of housing policy', in R. Struyk (ed.), *Economic restructuring in the former Soviet bloc: evidence from the housing sector*, Washington DC, Urban Institute Press.

Marcuse, H., 1958, *Soviet Marxism: a critical analysis*, New York, Columbia University Press.

Marcuse, P., 1990, 'Reformvorschläge zur Wohnungspolitik in der DDR', MS.

—— 1991, *Missing Marx: a personal and political journal of a year in East Germany, 1989–1990*, New York, Monthly Review Press.

—— 1992, 'Property rights, housing, and changing societal systems', mimeo, paper presented at MIT Conference on Property Rights, Spring.

—— 1994a, 'Privatization, tenure, and property rights: towards clarity in concepts', in B. Danermark and I. Elander (eds), *Social rented housing in Europe: policy, tenure and design*, Delft, Delft University Press, 21–36.

—— 1994b, 'Marcuse on real existing socialism: a hindsight look at *Soviet Marxism*', in J. Bokina and T.J. Lukes, *Marcuse: from the New Left to the next Left*, Laurence, KA, University Press of Kansas, 57–72.

Marcuse, P. and Schumann, W., 1992, 'Housing in the colors of the GDR', in B. Turner, J. Hegedus and I. Tosics (eds), *The reform of housing in*

Bibliography 329

Eastern Europe and the Soviet Union, London and New York, Routledge, 74–144.

Marcuse, P. and Staufenbiel, F. (eds), 1991, *Wohnen und Stadtpolitik, im Umbruch: Perspektiven der Stadterneuerung nach 40 Jahre DDR*, Berlin, Akademie Verlag.

Marx, K., 1859/1968, 'Preface to *A contribution to the critique of political economy*', in K. Marx and F. Engels, *Selected works*, London, Lawrence and Wishart, 181–5.

—— 1875/1968, 'Critique of the Gotha Programme', in K. Marx and F. Engels, *Selected works*, London, Lawrence and Wishart, 315–35.

Marx, K. and Engels, F., 1848/1962, *Manifesto of the Communist Party*, in *Selected Works in Two Volumes*, Moscow, Foreign Languages Publishing House, vol. 1, 98–137.

Mateju, P., Vecernik, J. and Jerabek, H., 1979, 'Social structure, spatial structure and problems of urban research: the example of Prague', *International Journal of Urban and Regional Research*, 3(2), 181–200.

Matthews, M., 1979, 'Social dimensions in Soviet urban housing', in R.A. French and F.E.I. Hamilton (eds), *The socialist city: spatial structure and urban policy*, Chichester, John Wiley, 105–18.

Mayo, S.K., 1991, 'Housing policy and housing research: the view from the World Bank', *Housing Finance International*, December.

Megbolugbe, I.F. and Linneman, P.D., 1993, 'Home ownership', *Urban Studies*, 30(4/5), 659–82.

Mizsei, K., 1993, *Bankruptcy in the post-communist economies of East Central Europe*, Boulder CO, Westview.

Morton, H.W. and Stuart, R.C. (eds), 1984, *The contemporary Soviet city*, London, Macmillan.

Moscow News, 1992, 'Prices out of control after January 1992', *Moscow News*, 1, 5–12 January.

Moscow Times, 1994, 'Investment here more risky', *Moscow Times*, 23 March.

Murray, P. and Szelenyi, I., 1984, 'The city in the transition to socialism', *International Journal of Urban and Regional Research*, 8(10), 90–107.

Musil, J., 1968, 'The development of Prague's ecological structure', in R.E. Pahl (ed.), *Readings in urban sociology*, Oxford, Pergamon Press, 232–59.

—— 1980, *Urbanisation in socialist countries*, New York, M.E. Sharpe.

—— 1987, 'Housing policy and the sociospatial structure of cities in a socialist country: the example of Prague', *International Journal of Urban and Regional Research*, 11(10), 27–37.

Muziol-Weclawosicz, A., forthcoming, 'Polish housing in transition: 1991–1994', in R. Struyk (ed.), *Economic restructuring in the former Soviet bloc: evidence from the housing sector*, Washington DC, Urban Institute Press.

Neckel, S., 1992, 'Das lokale Staatsorgan: Kommunale Herrschaft im Staatssozialismus der DDR', *Zeitschrift für Soziologie*, 21(4), 252–86.

North, D.C., 1990, *Institutions, institutional change and economic performance*, Cambridge, Cambridge University Press.

Offe, C., 1992, 'Ethnic politics in East European transitions', mimeo.

Oltay, E., 1992, 'Hungary Csurka launches "National Movement"', *RFL/RL Research Report*, 13, 25–31.

Olzak, S. and Nagel, J. (eds), 1986, *Competitive ethnic relations*, Orlando, Academic Press.

OMRI, 1995, 'Oil deliveries from Russia to Czech Republic interrupted', *Daily Digest*, 7, 10 January.

Orbant, S. and Sinochkin, D., 1992, 'Zemlyu vse chashche menyayut na kvartiry', *Kommersant*, 9 December.

Osakwe, C., 1991, 'The host country perspective on foreign investments in the Soviet Union: law and policy', *Vanderbilt Journal of Transnational Law*, 24(2), 208–33.

Pahl, R.E., 1977a, 'Collective consumption and the state in capitalist and state socialist countries', in R. Scase (ed.), *Industrial society – class, cleavage and control*, London, Allen & Unwin.

—— 1977b, 'Managers, technical experts and the state', in M. Harloe (ed.), *Captive cities*, Chichester, John Wiley, 49–60.

Park, R.E., 1928, 'Human migration and the marginal man', *American Journal of Sociology*, 33, 881–93.

Pashukanis, E.B., 1927/1978, *Law and Marxism: a general theory* (ed. C. Arthur), London, Ink Links.

Patterson, P.L. (ed.), 1993, *Capitalist goals, socialist past: the rise of the private sector in command economies*, Boulder CO, Westview.

Pensley, D.S., 1995, 'City planning and state policy in the GDR: the example of Neubaugebiet Hellersdorf', *International Journal of Urban and Regional Research*, 19(4), 547–73.

Persanyi, M., 1993, 'Red pollution, green evolution, revolution in Hungary', in B. Jancar-Webster (ed.), *Environmental action in Eastern Europe*, Armonk, NY, M.E. Sharpe.

Persanyi, M. and Lanyi, G., 1991, 'Waste import at the turn of the epoch: how problems are tackled in Hungary', in T. Deelstra and O. Yanitsky (eds), *Cities of Europe: the public's role in shaping the urban environment*, Moscow, Mezhdunarodnye Otnoshenia.

Pickvance, C.G., 1985, 'The rise and fall of urban movements and the role of comparative analysis', *Society and Space*, 3, 31–53.

—— 1986, 'Comparative urban analysis and assumptions about causality', *International Journal of Urban and Regional Research*, 10(2), 162–84.

—— 1994, 'Housing privatization and housing protest in the transition from state socialism: a comparative study of Budapest and Moscow', *International Journal of Urban and Regional Research*, 18, 433–45.

—— 1995a, 'Social movements in the transition from state socialism: convergence or divergence?', in L. Maheu (ed.), *Social movements and social classes: the future of collective action*, Newbury Park, Sage.

—— 1995b, 'Where have urban movements gone?', in C. Hadjimichalis and D. Sadler (eds), *Europe at the margins: new mosaics of inequality*, London, John Wiley.

Pokshisevsky, V.V. and Lappo, G.M. (eds), 1976, *Problemy urbanizatsii i rasseleniya*, Moscow, Mysl.

Powell, W.W., 1991, 'Expanding the scope of institutional analysis', in W.W. Powell and P.J. DiMaggio (eds), *The new institutionalism in organisa-*

tional analysis, Chicago and London, University of Chicago Press, 183–203.

Putnam, R.D., 1993, *Making democracy work: civic traditions in modern Italy*, Princeton NJ, Princeton University Press.

Ragin, C.C., 1989, *The comparative method*, Berkeley CA, University of California Press.

Ranki, G., 1983, *Economy and foreign policy: the struggle of the Great Powers for economic hegemony in the Danube Valley*, Boulder CO, East European Monographs.

Regulska, J., 1987, 'Urban development under socialism: the Polish experience', *Urban Geography*, 8, 321–39.

Reisch, A.A., 1992, 'Meciar and Slovakia's Hungarian minority', *RFE/RL Research Report*, 43, 13–20.

Renaud, B., 1990, 'Overcoming the housing crisis', *Transition*, 1(7), 11–12.

—— 1991, *Housing reform in socialist economies*, discussion paper no. 125, Washington DC, World Bank.

—— 1992, 'The housing system of the former Soviet Union: why do the Soviets need housing markets?', *Housing Policy Debate*, 3(3), 877–99.

Richardson, H.W., 1973, *The economics of urban size*, Lexington MA, Saxon House.

Roberts, B., 1978, *Cities of peasants*, London, Edward Arnold.

Rogovin, V., 1986, 'Sotsial'naya spravedlivost' i sotsialisticheskoe raspredelenie zhiznennkh blag', *Voprosy filosofii*, 9, September.

Rokkan, S., 1970, 'Methods and models in comparative study of nation-building', in S. Rokkan, *Citizens, elections, parties*, Oslo, Universitetforlaget, 46–71.

Ronnas, P., 1984, *Urbanisation in Romania*, Stockholm, EFI.

Rootes, C.A., 1992, 'Political opportunity structures, political competition and the development of social movements', paper to the First European Conference on Social Movements, Berlin.

Ruble, B.A., 1990, *Leningrad: shaping a Soviet city*, Berkeley CA, University of California Press.

Rugg, D.S., 1972, *Spatial foundations of urbanism*, Dubuque, IA, Wm C. Brown.

Rukavishnikov, V.O., 1978, 'Ethnosocial aspects of population distribution in cities of Tartaria', *Soviet Sociology*, 8, 59–79.

Sanger, J., 1992, 'Preliminary assessment of laws and institutions for private real estate markets in Kazakhstan', prepared for the Agency for International Development by the International City/County Managers Association, Washington DC.

—— 1993, 'Report of the short-term legal advisor to the republic of Kazakhstan', prepared for the Agency for International Development by the International City/County Managers Association, Washington DC.

Savvateeva, I., 1994, 'Zemel'nyi kodeks: Sovetskie feodaly toropyatsya upravit'sya s privatizatsiei dokhodov', *Izvestiya*, 3 June.

Sawicki, S., 1977, *Soviet land and housing law*, New York, Praeger.

Sazunov, B.A., 1991, 'Nouveaux concepts pour la gestion urbaine à Moscou', *Les Annales de la Recherche Urbaine*, 51, 16–27.

Schlesinger, R., 1945, *Soviet legal theory*, London, Kegan Paul, Trench, Trubner.

Schneider, R.C., Jr, 1990, 'Developments in Soviet property law', *Fordham International Law Journal*, 13(4), 446–80.

Scholz, C., 1993, *Stadtentwicklung im Umbruch. Eine Bestandsaufnahme der spezifischen Entwicklungsbedingungen ostdeutscher Städte und Regionen*, Materalien 5/93, Cologne, Deutsches Institut für Urbanistik.

Senghaas, D., 1992, 'Vom Nutzen und Elend der Nationalismen im Leben der Völker', *ApuZG*, B31/32, 23–32.

Seton-Watson, H., 1967, *The Russian Empire, 1801–1917*, Oxford, Clarendon Press.

Shomina, E.S., 1996, 'Housing movements in Russia', in K. Láng-Pickvance, N. Manning, and C.G. Pickvance (eds), *Housing and environmental movements: grassroots experience in Hungary, Estonia and Russia*, Aldershot, Avebury Press.

Shvarts, E.A. and Prochozova, I., 1993, 'Soviet Greens: who are they?', in B. Jancar-Webster (ed.), *Environment Action in Eastern Europe*, Armonk NY, M.E. Sharpe.

Siderov, D.A., 1992, 'Variations in the perceived level of prestige of residential areas in the former USSR', *Urban Geography*, 13, 355–73.

Sik, E., 1994, 'From the multicoloured to the black and white economy: the Hungarian second economy and transformation', *International Journal of Urban and Regional Research*, 18(1), 46–70.

Sillince, J.A.A., 1985, 'The housing market of the Budapest urban region 1949–1983', *Urban Studies*, 22, 141–9

Simic, A., 1973, *The peasant urbanites: a study in rural-urban mobility in Serbia*, New York, Seminar Press.

Simiénska, R., 1993, 'Zaufina Polaków do róznych narodów w okresie przemiam politycznych I ekonomicznych', in A. Jasínska-Kania (ed.), *Bliscy i dalecy*, Warschau, Institut socjolgii, 201–18.

Simmel, G., 1964, 'The metropolis and mental life', in K. Wolff (ed.), *The sociology of Georg Simmel*, New York, Free Press, 409–24.

Sitinkov, V., 1992, 'Kolorton' postroit zakrityi gorodok dlya elity', *Kommersant*, 42.

Smith, D.M., 1987, *Geography, inequality and society*, Cambridge, Cambridge University Press.

—— 1989, *Urban inequality under socialism: case studies from Eastern Europe and the Soviet Union*, Cambridge, Cambridge University Press.

Smith, N. and Palen, J.J., 1984, 'A class analysis of gentrification', in J.J. Palen and B. London (eds), *Gentrification, displacement and neighborhood revitalization*, Albany NY, State University of New York Press, 43–64.

Sovani, N.V., 1964, 'The analysis of overurbanization', *Economic Development and Cultural Change*, 12(2), 113–22.

Stark, D., 1989, 'Coexisting organisational forms in Hungary's emerging mixed economy', in V. Nee and D. Stark (eds), *Remaking the institutions of state socialism: China and Eastern Europe*, Stanford, Stanford University Press, 137–68.

—— 1990, 'Privatization in Hungary: from plan to market or from plan to clan?', *East European Politics and Societies*, 4(3), 351–92.
—— 1992a, 'The great transformation? Social change in Eastern Europe', *Contemporary Sociology*, 21, 299–304.
—— 1992b, 'Path dependence and privatization strategies in East Central Europe', *East European Politics and Societies*, 6(1), 17–54
—— 1996, 'Recombinant property in East European capitalism: organisational innovation in Hungary', in D. Stark and G. Grabher (eds), *Legacies, linkages and localities*, Oxford, Oxford University Press.
Stephan, P.B., 1991, 'Perestroyka and property: the law of ownership in the post-socialist Soviet Union', *American Journal of Comparative Law*, 39(1), 35–65.
Stevens, J., 1980, 'The public trust: a sovereign's ancient prerogative becomes the people's environmental right', *UC Davis Law Review*, 14, 195–232.
Struyk, R., 1992, 'Housing policy in Moscow: where to go from here', mimeo, remarks to the Government of Moscow, 19 May.
—— 1994, *Transition in the Russian Housing Sector: 1991–1994*, Washington DC, Urban Institute.
—— (ed.), forthcoming, *Economic restructuring in the former Soviet bloc: evidence from the housing sector*, Washington DC, Urban Institute Press.
Struyk, R. and Kosareva, N.B., 1993, 'The Russian housing market in transition', mimeo, Moscow, Urban Institute.
—— 1994, *Transition in the Russian housing sector: 1991–1994*, Moscow, Urban Institute Technical Cooperation Project Office.
—— forthcoming, 'Privatization', in Wm van Vliet (ed.), *The encyclopedia of housing.*
Struyk, R. and Romanik, C., 1995, 'Residential mobility in selected Russian cities: an assessment of survey results', *Post-Soviet Geography*, 36(1), 58–66.
Struyk, R., Mark, K. and Telgarsky, J., 1991, 'Private management for Eastern Europe's state rental housing', *Journal of Housing Economics*, 1(1), 90–109.
Sutela, P., 1994, 'Insider privatization in Russia – speculations on systemic change', *Europe–Asia Studies*, 46, 417–35.
Swain, G. and Swain, N., 1993, *Eastern Europe since 1945*, London, Macmillan.
Sweezy, P., 1992, 'Base and superstructure revisited', *Monthly Review*, June, 56–61
Szakadat, L., 1993 'Property rights in a socialist economy: the case of Hungary', in J.S. Earle, R. Frydman and A. Rapaczynski (eds), *Privatization in the transition to a market economy: studies of preconditions and policies in Eastern Europe*, London, Pinter.
Szelenyi, I., 1983, *Urban inequalities under state socialism*, Oxford, Oxford University Press.
—— 1987, 'Housing inequalities and occupational segregation in state socialist cities: commentary on the special issue of IJURR on East European cities', *International Journal of Urban and Regional Research*, 11(1), 1–8.
—— 1988, *Socialist entrepreneurs*, Madison, University of Wisconsin Press.
Szelényi, I. and Konrád, G., 1969, *Az új lakótelepek szociológiai problémái*, Budapest, Akadémiai Kiadó.

Szirmai, V., 1993, 'The structural mechanisms of the organisation of ecologi-cal-social movements in Hungary', in A. Vari and P. Tamas (eds), *Environment and democratic transition*, Dordrecht, Kluwer.

—— 1996, 'Environmental movements in Hungary', in K. Láng-Pickvance, N. Manning and C.G. Pickvance (eds), *Housing and environmental movements: grassroots experience in Hungary, Estonia and Russia*, Aldershot, Avebury Press.

Teague, E., 1994, 'Russia's local elections begin', *RFE/RL Research Report*, 3(7), 18 February.

Telgarsky, J.P. and Struyk, R., 1990, *Toward a market-oriented housing sector in Eastern Europe: developments in Bulgaria, Czechoslovakia, Hungary, Poland, Romania, and Yugoslavia*, Urban Institute Report 90–10, Washington DC, Urban Institute.

Timberlake, M. and Kantor, J., 1983, 'Economic dependence, over-urbanization and economic growth – a study of less developed countries', *Sociological Quarterly*, 24(4), 489–507.

Times-Mirror Center for the People and Press, 1991, 'The pulse of Europe: a survey of political and social values and attitudes', available from Times-Mirror Center, Washington DC.

Tinbergen, J., 1961, 'Do communist and free economies show a converging pattern?', *Soviet Studies*, XII (4).

Tolokonnikov, A. et al., 1994, 'Stroitel'nyi bum neizbezhen. Marketing stroitel'nykh materialov', *Delovoi Mir*, 21–7 March.

Tönnies, F., 1887/1974, *Community and association*, London, Routledge and Kegan Paul.

Topfstedt, T., 1988, *Städtebau in der DDR 1955–1971*, Leipzig, VEB E.A. Seeman Verlag.

Touraine, A., 1981, *The voice and the eye*, Cambridge, Cambridge University Press.

'Transforming the Polish economy', 1994, vol. 2, Warsaw, WERI/CEG.

Trotsky, L., 1967/1932–3, *The history of the Russian Revolution*, vol. 1, London, Sphere Books.

Tsenkova, S., 1994, 'Economic and social efficiency of Bulgarian housing provision system', mimeo, paper prepared for European Network for Housing Research, Karlslunde Strand, Denmark, 16 May.

Turner, B. and Victorin, A., forthcoming, in R. Struyk (ed.), *Economic restructuring in the former Soviet bloc: evidence from the housing sector*, Washington DC, Urban Institute Press.

Turner, B., Hegedüs, J. and Tosics, I. (eds), 1992, *The reform of housing in Eastern Europe and the Soviet Union*, London and New York, Routledge.

Turner, J.W., 1941, 'Some reflections on ownership in English law', *Canadian Bar Review*, XIX, 342–52.

Vaksberg, A., 1991, *The Soviet Mafia*, London, Weidenfeld and Nicolson.

Van Atta, D., 1993, *The 'farmer threat': the political economy of agrarian reform in post-Soviet Russia*, Boulder CO, Westview.

Van den Berg, et al., 1982, *Urban Europe. Vol. 1: a study of growth and decline*, Oxford, Pergamon Press.

Verheyen, D. and Soe, C., 1993, *The Germans and their neighbours*, Oxford, Westview.

Vinokur, A. and Ofer, G., 1987, 'Inequality of earnings: household income and wealth in the Soviet Union in the 1970s', in J. Millar (ed.), *Politics, work and daily life in the USSR: a survey of former soviet citizens*, Cambridge, Cambridge University Press.

Waller, M., 1989, 'The ecology issue in Eastern Europe: protest and movements', *Journal of Communist Studies*, 5, 303–28.

Waller, M. and Millard, F., 1992 'Environmental politics in Eastern Europe', *Environmental Politics*, 1, 159–85.

Wallich, C., 1994, *Russia and the challenge of fiscal federalism*, Washington DC, World Bank.

Wardwell, J.M., 1980, 'Toward a theory of urban–rural migration in the developed world', in D.L. Brown and J.M. Wardwell (eds), *New directions in urban–rural migrations*, New York, Academic Press, 71–114.

Weclawowicz, G., 1979, 'The structure of socio-economic space of Warsaw 1931 and 1970: a study in factorial ecology', in R.A. French and F.E.I. Hamilton (eds), *The socialist city: spatial structure and urban policy*, Chichester, John Wiley, 387–423.

—— 1981, 'Towards a theory of intra-urban structures of Polish cities', *Geographia Polonica*, 44, 179–200.

—— 1991, *The socio-spatial differentiation in urban region of Warsaw*, Warsaw, Institute of Geography and Spatial Organisation, PAN.

—— 1992, 'The socio-spatial structure of the socialist cities of East-Central Europe', in F. Lando (ed.), *Urban and rural geography*, Venice, Cafoscarina, 129–40.

Werner, F., 1981, *Stadt, Städtebau, Architektur in der DDR: Aspekte der Stadtgeographie, Stadtplanung und Forschungspolitik*, Erlangen, Geograpische Hefte.

Whitehead, C., 1993, 'Privatizing housing: an assessment of the UK experience', *Housing Policy Debate*, 4(1), 101–39.

Wilson, F.D., 1983, *Contemporary patterns of urbanization*, CDE Working Papers 84-2, Madison, University of Wisconsin Center for Demography and Ecology.

Wirth, L., 1938, 'Urbanism as a way of life', *American Journal of Sociology*, XLIV(1), 1–24.

World Bank, 1991, *Housing Policy Reform in Hungary*, report no. 9031–HU, Washington DC, World Bank.

Yanitsky, O., 1993, *Russian environmentalism: leading figures, facts, opinions*, Mezhdunarodnyje Otnoshenija, Moscow.

Yanowitch, M., 1989, *A voice of reform: essays by Tat'iana Zaslavskaya*, London, M.E. Sharpe.

Zaslavskaya, T., 1983, 'The Novosibirsk Report', tr. T. Cherfas, *Survey: a Journal of East and West Studies*, 28(1), 1984; reprinted in M. Yanowitch, *A voice of reform: essays by Tat'iana Zaslavskaya*, London, M.E. Sharpe (1989), 158–183.

—— 1993, 'Vperegonki so vremenem', *Obshchestvennye nauki i sovremennost'*, 3.

Index

Abalkin, L., 183
administrative-command economy, defined, 37–8
administrative-command economy, reform and breakdown, 38–41
affirmative action, 282–4
Albania, 100, 175, 275, 277, 284, 285
Alma-Ata, 94–5
Almaty, *see* Alma-Ata
amoral familism, 25
amoral nationalism, 25
Andrusz, G., 11–12, 27, 83, 186
anti-Semitism, 273, 279
Arbat (Moscow), 80, 250
Armenia, 51, 52, 194, 196–7, 201, 204, 275
Austro-Hungarian Empire, *see* Habsburg Empire
Azerbaijan, 51, 52

Baltic States, 52, 171, 270, 274–5
Bater, J., 84
bazaar economy, 27, 66, 272
Belarus, 50, 51, 53, 274–5, 279
Belgrade, 117
Benácek, V., 8
Berlin, 19–22, 217, 218, 219, 226
    see also East Berlin; West Berlin
black economy, 12
Bosnia, 277
Bourdieu, P., 28
Brezhnev, L., 39, 270
Brzezinski, Z., 317
Bucharest, 287
Budapest, 23, 24, 62, 72, 173, 198, 199, 208,

248, 251–6, 257, 258, 259, 261–4, 266, 287, 300, 301, 305, 306, 312, 313, 314, 317
    Green Future, 254–6, 262–3, 267
    Metallochemia plant, 254–5
    socio-economic differentiation, 89–92
    Tenants Association, 252–4, 262, 267
Bulgaria, 35, 38, 41, 47, 54, 55, 100, 128, 131, 149, 175, 179, 194, 196–7, 201, 205, 211, 278, 279, 282, 284
Burawoy, M., 8, 28, 309
Burgess, E., 293

Caucasus, 51, 273, 275
Central Asia, 277
central planning, 21
    breakdown, 43
Chechnya, 51, 281
Chicago, 293
Ciechocinska, M., 87
citizen organizations, 234–6
    under state socialism, 235–6
    see also urban social movements
citizenship, 10, 25, 48–50, 285
civil society, 25, 269, 277
class differentiation, 273
class restructuring, 56–9
class structure of transition societies, 7–8, 9–10, 12, 308
class-based stratification, 27
collectivization of agriculture, 128
Comecon (CMEA), 38, 39, 279, 311
Commonwealth of Independent States (CIS), 53, 55, 62, 276
communist party, 50–1, 54, 146, 236–7, 239,

Made in the USA
Lexington, KY
12 February 2010